Sir Basil Liddell Hart
Life, Thought, Legacy

Bruce Oliver Newsome, Ph.D.

PERSEUBLISHING

Sir Basil Liddell Hart: Life, Thought, Legacy
by Bruce Oliver Newsome, Ph.D.

https://www.BruceNewsome.com

Sign up online for news, special offers, bonus chapters, photographs, and videos.

Published by: Perseublishing,
PO Box 181802, Coronado, California 92178, United States of America

Copyright © 2025 Bruce Oliver Newsome, Ph.D

All rights reserved. No part of this publication may be reproduced or stored in a retrieval system or transmitted, in any form or by any means, electronic, mechanical, photocopying, recording or otherwise, without prior permission in writing from the author.

HIS027090	HISTORY / Military / World War I
HIS027100	HISTORY / Military / World War II
HIS027240	HISTORY / Military / Vehicles
NHWR5	First World War
NHWR7	Second World War
NHWL	Modern warfare
JWMV	Military vehicles

ISBN: 978-1-951171-23-0

Every reasonable effort has been made to supply complete and correct credits; if there are errors or omissions, please contact the publisher or author so that corrections can be addressed in any subsequent edition.

Acknowledgements

The author wishes to thank:

- Emma De Angelis, for permission to quote from "The RUSI Journal"
- Faber & Faber, for permission to quote from "The Real War, 1914-1918"
- David Fletcher, Historian, The Tank Museum
- Rachael Gardner: Senior Archivist, University of Bristol Library
- Andrew Hart, patron
- Gemma Hollman, Senior Archives Assistant, Libraries & Collections, Kings College London, for permission to quote from Liddell Hart's papers
- Jonathan Holt, Archives Assistant, The Tank Museum
- Imperial War Museum Collections
- King's Own Yorkshire Light Infantry Regimental Museum, Doncaster, UK
- Christian Lea, Manchester University Press, for permission to quote from "Men, Ideas and Tanks" by J.Paul Harris
- Bryn Loyd, Archives Assistant, The Tank Museum
- Scott Meyer, patron
- Midland County, Texas, libraries
- Michael Morris, Cornell University Press, for permission to quote from "Liddell Hart and the Weight of History" by John J. Mearsheimer
- The National Archives, Kew, UK
- Orion Publishing Group, for permission to quote from "Alchemist of War" by Alex Danchev
- Michelle Pfalzgraf, Librarian, University of Texas Permian Basin
- Sheldon Rogers, Archives Assistant, The Tank Museum
- Rutgers University, Special Collections, New Brunswick, New Jersey
- Oliver Snaith, Archives Assistant, King's College London
- Stanford University, Special Collections
- Katie Thompson, Archives Assistant, The Tank Museum
- University of St. Andrews archive
- Marjolijn Verbrugge, Archive and Supporting Collections Manager, Tank Museum, for permission to quote from the archives
- David Willey, Curator, Tank Museum

Contents

Acknowledgements   2
Contents   3
Illustrations   4
Abbreviations   5

Introduction   7

Chapter 1: Prodigy   15
Chapter 2: Family Man   21
Chapter 3: Intellectual   31
Chapter 4: War Hero   47
Chapter 5: Great War Historian   57
Chapter 6: Historian   73
Chapter 7: Doctrinist   79
Chapter 8: Strategist   87
Chapter 9: Journalist   97
Chapter 10: Army Insider and Outsider   105
Chapter 11: Political Sage   123
Chapter 12: Appeaser   143
Chapter 13: War Official   157
Chapter 14: Peacemaker   171
Chapter 15: Low-Cost Warrior   185
Chapter 16: Germany's Prophet, 1940s-1950s   195
Chapter 17: America's Adopted Hero, 1950s   201
Chapter 18: Israel's Inspiration, 1940s-1960s   207
Chapter 19: Academic, 1950s-1960s   215
Chapter 20: Final Publications   223
Chapter 21: Biographies   229

References   238
Index   247
About the author   256

Illustrations

BHLH poses with a display of newspaper cuttings from the Great War, at the Tank Museum, Bovington, Dorset, on 20 November 1951 (RACTM).	Front cover
BHLH with his father, mother, and brother, circa 1897...	14
Basil and Jessie, and Adrian and Jessie, in 1937...	20
BHLH in mid-1917...	56
BHLH at the RTR's celebration of Cambrai Day, 1951...	72
General Siegfried Westphal and BHLH, 1956...	86
BHLH and Field-Marshal Sir Bernard Montgomery, 1958...	86
BHLH, Leslie Hore Belisha, and Major Sir Sydney Markham, 1950...	96
BHLH and David Lloyd George, 1934...	142
BHLH and David Lloyd George, 1940...	156
Field-Marshal Sir Claude Auchinleck and BHLH, 1951...	170
Field-Marshal Heinz Guderian and BHLH, 1950...	200
Manfred Rommel, General Hans Speidel, and BHLH, 1950...	200
BHLH's portrait, signed and gifted to John Wheldon, 1967...	206
Peter Paret and BHLH in the back yard of BHLH's gratis home at 37 Parkside Place, Davis, California, about 700 yards from the University of California campus, on 1 November 1965, when he celebrated his 70th birthday (LH 13/104/18).	Back cover

Abbreviations

AA	Anti-Aircraft
AFV	armoured fighting vehicle
AG	Adjutant General
AJLH	Adrian John Liddell Hart
BEF	British Expeditionary Force
BHLH	Basil Henry Liddell Hart
BUF	British Union of Fascists
c.	circa
C-in-C	Commander in Chief
co.	company
CBE	Commander of the Order of the British Empire
CIA	Central Intelligence Agency
CIGS	Chief of the Imperial General Staff
DCIGS	Deputy Chief of the Imperial General Staff
DDM	Design Department Mechanization, Superintendent of Design
DGFV	Director-General Fighting Vehicles
DME	Director(ate) of Mechanical Engineering
DMI	Director(ate) of Military Intelligence
DMO	Director(ate) of Military Operations
DMO&I	Director(ate) of Military Operations and Intelligence
DMT	Director(ate) of Military Training
DRAC	Director(ate) Royal Armoured Corps
DSD	Director(ate) of Staff Duties
DT	The Daily Telegraph
FSR	Field Service Regulations
GHQ	General Headquarters (usually regional echelon)
GSO	General Staff Officer
HE	high-explosive
HMSO	His (or Her) Majesty's Stationery Office
hp	horse-power
HQ	headquarters
in.	inch
IRTC	Inspector Royal Tank Corps
IWM	Imperial War Museum, London
KLH	Kathleen Liddell Hart
km	kilometers
kmh or kph	kilometers per hour
LG	David Lloyd George
LH	Liddell Hart; Liddell Hart papers at LHCMA
LHCMA	Liddell Hart Centre for Military Archives
MCS	Military College of Science
MEC	Middle East Command
MI5	Military Intelligence Section 5; Security Service
MI6	Military Intelligence Section 6; Secret Intelligence Service
mm	millimetres
MOR	military operations research
MP	Member of Parliament
mph	miles per hour
MS	manuscript

Panzer	*Panzerkampfwagen* (armoured fighting vehicle)
RAC	Royal Armoured Corps
RACTM	Royal Armoured Corps Tank Museum, Bovington, Dorset
RAF	Royal Air Force
RAOC	Royal Army Ordnance Corps
RASC	Royal Army Service Corps
RE	Royal Engineers
RN	Royal Navy
RNAS	Royal Naval Air Service
RNVR	Royal Navy Volunteer Reserve
RTC	Royal Tank Corps
RTR	Royal Tank Regiment
RUSI	Royal United Service Institution (now: Royal United Services Institute for Defence and Security Studies)
TT	The Times
UK	United Kingdom
UKNA	The National Archives, United Kingdom
US(A)	United States (of America)
USSR	Union of Soviet Socialist Republics
VCIGS	Vice Chief of the Imperial General Staff
WD	War Department
WO	War Office

Introduction

Nobody had more influence on Anglophone military thought over the last 100 years than Basil Liddell Hart (1895-1970). He was born in the reign of Victoria, came of age in the year before the Great War, and wrote doctrine from the year after. In 1925 (when he was still 29 years of age), the rising Chief of the Imperial General Staff (CIGS), desperate for good press, encouraged *The Daily Telegraph* to hire him as military correspondent. From that year, he published journalistic reports every few days, magazine articles every few months, and about one book per year, for a total of at least 35 books.[*] He claimed to have been published in 42 countries and 31 languages.[†]

He was yet more prolific as a letter-writer. His own archive contains almost 1,000 correspondents. He garnered inside information, which raised the value of his journalism and thence the books based on his journalism. By the 1930s, he directly advised ministers and flag officers.

> I think I can claim to have become, in the interval, the best known military writer in the world (to Fred Lawson, c. 7 June 1932, LH 3/97).

> He is just about the most brilliant anatomist of war (Poore 1934).

> Far better known to the public at large are the military works of Captain Liddell Hart, who, though not a professional soldier, has…gained a popular reputation as a critic of military affairs (Beadon 1936: 747).

> [N]one can seriously question his claim to be treated with great respect as the towering military intellectual of the inter-war years (James 1970: 56).

> Liddell Hart was probably the world's best known military commentator and pundit in the 1930s (Bond 1978: 421).

> During the 1930s the defence debate in Britain was dominated by Captain Basil Liddell Hart (O'Neill 1990: 101).

> As military correspondent for Daily Telegraph he was perhaps the best-known commentator in the world on military affairs (Citino 2002: 186).

> Liddell Hart [was] the most influential public commentator on defence matters in inter-war Britain (Allport 2020: 144).

---

[*] The count is confused by other editions, some of different titles. As of 1952, Liddell Hart claimed "some 30 books" (1952: 30). His final book was published with a list of 31 books by the same author (including itself and other editions and volumes) and three edited volumes, for a total of 34 unique books, plus two chapters in other edited volumes (1970: 767-768). One edited volume was published posthumously, by his son. Brian Bond (1977: 277-278) listed 31 "principal" published books, not counting other editions, plus four edited books, for a total of 35 unique books. Reid (1987: 1; 1998: 2, 182) reported 36 published books. Alex Danchev (1998: 329-330) lists 42 editions.

[†] The claim is dated "up to 1962" (Wheldon 1968: 39).

Most of his policies, prescriptions, and predictions seemed discredited by the Second World War. However, during the 1950s, he popularized himself as prodigy, family man, intellectual, war hero, exposer of hard truths about the Great War, rigorous historian, author of British doctrine, strategist, fearless journalist, Army insider and outside critic, political sage, opponent of appeasement, secret guru to Britain's government during the Second World War, misunderstood proponent of negotiated peace, maligned proponent of a low-cost war, inventor of Blitzkrieg, America's adopted hero, Israel's inspiration, academic, writer, and mentor to a new generation of historians. In 1965, his memoirs cemented the narrative. In 1966, he was knighted by the Queen and photographed for the National Portrait Gallery.

> Written off as a pacifist crank or a false prophet by every respectable British general, admiral, and air marshal, he obstinately demands to be taken seriously as a military theorist (Crossman 1958: 223).

> [H]istory and the testimony of his more successful pupils offer convincing proof of his influence (Luvaas 1964: 376).

> It is beyond doubt that Liddell Hart's influence has been immense (Beaufre 1965: 141).

> Where Liddell Hart stands high above all other military writers is that not only is he an historian, able to analyse and comment, but he is also a theorist (Montgomery 1968: 20).

When he died in 1970, he left his legacy to a second wife, a son, and dozens of direct mentees and disciples, who would memorialize, biograph, and defend him for decades.

> In the Himalayan range of the great thinkers about warfare he was one of the last and undoubtedly one of the pre-eminent peaks (Lewin 1971:79)

> Liddell Hart was…one of the most profound, original, and influential military thinkers of modern history (Luvaas 1970: 1573).

> [T]he depth and intensity which he brought to it over 50 years have transformed the nature of military thought itself (Howard 1970b: 37; 1984: 199).

> For 50 years, Captain Sir Basil Liddell Hart cut a broad path through the field of military literature (Larson 1980: 70).

> [He was] for almost half a century the most important writer on strategy and military matters in the English-speaking world…When he died in 1970, Sir Basil Liddell Hart was the most famous and widely admired military historian and theorist in the world, and he probably remains so today (Mearsheimer 1988: ix, 1).

> Liddell Hart remains a leading figure in twentieth century military thought (Swain 1990: 35).

> His language and his learnings saturate later thought, often unwittingly... [He is] the most influential military writer of the modern age (Danchev 1998a: 5; 1999a: 29).

> Liddell Hart [is] one of the preeminent military thinkers of the twentieth century (Reid 1999: 66).

> [He was] once considered the world's most distinguished military historian and theorist (Unterseher 2023: 13).

He opined on everything from politics to femininity. Even where we criticize him, we cannot ignore him.

> He made so many prophecies that some were bound to be wrong. What he did succeed in was wrenching military thought from its rigid mould and forcing soldier and academic strategist alike into looking at the whole field of warfare with fresh eyes. We must still study Liddell Hart, for even to disagree with him is to learn (Bidwell 1973: 214).

> [A]s a general stimulant to thought (or, as [Archibald] Wavell put it, a "mental irritant") Liddell Hart's books, articles, letters, and discussions give marvellous value (Bond 1977: 59).

> To the extent he continues to make soldiers and politicians more circumspect about their business, he continues to be an important guide (Swain 1990: 47).

> Liddell Hart...may not have been quite the original thinker he spent much of his life claiming to be, but he was an important gatherer of original ideas, and had the gift of expressing what he had harvested in clear and fluent prose (Baynes 1995: 238).

> He presented intriguing and often prescient perspectives for analysis and deliberation[,] and, whilst frequently tendentious, biased[,] and intemperate, served to highlight critical issues (Lord 1997: 62).

> [N]o serious student of war can afford to ignore his teaching...Whatever his shortcomings and failures, Liddell Hart's place in the pantheon of great military thinkers remains secure (Howard 1999: ix).

Previous memorialists and biographers relied on what Liddell Hart said or wrote late in life – about what he had said or written early in life (Howard 1970a; 1970b; Luvaas 1964; 1970; Bond 1977; Reid 1998; Danchev 1998). They themselves were never satisfied, but their consensus survived John Mearsheimer's revisionism (1988). They colluded in various counter-revisionist works and authorized biographies. More than a quarter century has passed since the last authorized biography, and 55 years since the subject's death.

Since then, new archives of correspondence have been opened. My biography is the first to cite those archives. It gives a fresh and objective insight into Liddell

Hart's life, thought, and legacy. Major parts of his life have not been biographed before (such as his influence on academia). Other parts have been covered up (such as his sympathies for fascism). The final part of his life has been dominated by reinvention, to the neglect of embarrassments (such as appeasement and defeatism). While academics celebrate his liberalism, they cover up his sympathy for fascism. While mentees highlight his tolerance, they ignore his viciousness. While disciples celebrate his reforms of the Army, they neglect sycophantic promotions. While he and they quote his urgings for mechanization, they skip over his vague and mistaken specifications of the machines. While they champion his progress towards anti-aircraft defence, they minimize his regression to static defences. While his fabrication of Blitzkrieg has been exposed, his confidence in hit-and-run raids by light tanks has not. While disciples champion his worthy searches for "indirect approaches," they skip over his unstable agendas, analogies, and abstractions. While they highlight his concern for lower casualties, they neglect his expectations and prescriptions for a long, indecisive war. While his urgings for negotiated peace have been retold, his invention of peace-feelers has not. This book reveals a more nuanced person and legacy than previously presented. Only honest admission of the nuances enables us to take his positive contributions without the negative.

The chapters review Basil Liddell Hart in terms of his own self-images. From the start, he saw himself as a prodigy. The first chapter describes his unusual childhood, physiognomy, and psychology.

Second, he saw himself as a family man, with a quick first wife (Jessie), a troubled son (Adrian), a long-term mistress and eventual second wife (Kathleen), and two step-daughters.

Third, he presented himself as an intellectual. The third chapter compares his self-images and performances as a scholar, genius, scientist, truth-seeker, arguer, lecturer, correspondent, tolerator, theorist, logician, and operations researcher.

Liddell Hart was a war hero who nonetheless exaggerated his heroism. As explained in the fourth chapter, before he joined the Army, Liddell Hart was an anti-militarist and a failing undergraduate of history. Upon war, he pivoyed to militarism. However, he remained socially isolated and psychologically fragile. His operational experiences were short and inglorious, to which he attached fictional commands and injuries. He spent the rest of his service in minor training roles.

From war hero, he morphed into historian. The fifth chapter traces his evolution as a historian of the Great War – at first a sycophant, eventually a critic. His targets were Douglas Haig (the final commander of the British Expeditionary Force in which he had served), professional soldiers in general, and official historians. His own histories went to four editions, almost to the eve of the Second World War. Afterwards, he influenced a narrow but popular caricature of the First World War.

Even before forming his views on the Great War, Liddell Hart sought to become an academic historian, but, as the sixth chapter shows, his academic training was incomplete. He harvested private information, but was otherwise inattentive to sourcing and methodology. Like the stereotypical applicatory historian (without realizing the stereotype), he memorialized some commanders and strategies – and demonized others, to the neglect of logistics, acquisitions, economics, technologies, and tactics.

In Chapter 7, I explain how he leveraged his wartime training into peacetime doctrine, and thence co-authorship of the *Infantry Training* manual. Disappointed with official rejection, he both denigrated all official manuals and misrepresented himself as sole-author.

Chapter 8 analyzes his self-appointed role as "strategist." His strategies are often insightful. He certainly focused attention on the highest level of strategy. However, his high-mindedness about the semantics and approaches belies confused definitions, conflated levels of analysis, and unstable agendas, such as his keenness for quick decisive wars at one time or long indecisive wars at another. His strategies were further corrupted by over-reliance on analogies – not as means for communication, as he excused them, but as premises for theories. He preferred abstractions over study of technologies and techniques. His abstractions could be mindful, such as "indirect approach," but also naive and agenda-driven, such as his offering of unilateral "good manners" and disarmament as stable and ethical alternatives to mutual nuclear deterrence.

Disappointed with his military career, he shifted to journalism (the subject of Chapter 9), first as a freelance sports reporter, soon as a temporary military correspondent for *The Morning Post*. From there, he earned a permanent position at *The Daily Telegraph*, an incongruously prestigious and indulgent position for such a young and inexperienced correspondent, but one enabled by the War Department itself, which mistakenly forecast that he would improve the Army's public image. Instead, he lobbied for policies of personal appeal, such as isolationism, and against targets of personal prejudice, such as senior officers. His ageism and progressivism were fashionable. He jumped ship to *The Times*, the newspaper closest to government, and thence enjoyed his most direct and consistent influence on government.

Chapter 10 reveals his posturing as both an Army insider and an outside critic. He presented himself as both a commander by practical experience and a commander by historical study, both the Generals' pet and an anti-professional, both a recovering convalescent and an involuntary invalid, both propagandist and leaker, both a forced retiree and a "Great Captain."

With influence through mass media, private correspondence, and official advice, he developed himself as a political sage, as told in Chapter 11. He and his disciples portrayed him as liberal. Indeed, he favoured David Lloyd George, the erstwhile prime minister. Liddell Hart rejected Lloyd George's rivals for the Liberal caucus (most notably John Simon), but enjoyed his greatest policy influence on the other surviving Liberal in the last peacetime cabinet – Leslie Hore Belisha. His influence was regrettable by 1938, following a purge of the General Staff, and recriminations from even the beneficiaries. In the same year, Liddell Hart joined a multi-partisan discussion group ("Focus"), founded by Winston Churchill (a defected Liberal). He briefly pushed his own Movement for Freedom. Yet his liberalism was always fuzzy, and tended to break down when policies were detailed or administrations changed. His liberalism during the Second World War was policy-driven: for instance, he was against conscription, but prioritized peace at the expense of liberalism. He had always compared democracy to mob rule. He admired Italian fascism. He agreed with the policies although not the paramilitarism of British fascism. He portrayed Nazis as victims. He ended his political life where it had begun and always belonged – with progressive socialists.

His historicizing, strategizing, journalism, propagandizing, critiquing, and politicking mesmerized some military and political principals. From 1935 to 1939, he was effectively a paid special adviser to three successive War Secretaries. In the same period, his books and private papers influenced prime ministers. Chapter 12 reveals his influence on Britain's appeasement of Germany's reoccupation of the Rhineland, Italy's invasion of Abyssinia, Germany's and Italy's (and the USSR's) intervention in Spain, and Germany's claims to Austria, Czechoslovakia, and Poland.

He suffered at least two breakdowns in the months before the Second World War. He was jobless when it began. Yet he sought to return to official influence, as Chapter 13 tells. He targeted Lloyd George, Belisha, Churchill, Lord Beaverbrook, James Grigg (Churchill's final wartime War Secretary), and the soldiers he had promoted in 1937. He was never officially employed, although he received privileged information, and later would suggest he was regularly employed on secret work.

Chapter 14 reveals his efforts to persuade Britain to make peace. In Spring 1939, he had argued pre-emptively for quitting. He argued for quitting when war broke out in the Autumn. He argued for negotiations. He pondered emigration. He opposed Western plans to intervene in Scandinavia, and thence blamed the West for provoking Germany's intervention in Scandinavia. He promised that Germany would not invade Western Europe, and thence blamed the West for provoking Germany there too. He urged Britain to quit unilaterally or lose the war. With some merit, he warned that alliances would lead to dependency. He pondered emigration again in 1941. He argued for unilateral negotiated peace even after Germany and its allies had invaded the Soviet Union. In 1942, he invented a missed opportunity to agree peace with German agents in Sweden. He opposed the policy of unconditional surrender in 1943, with some merit but also self-interest. He invented a missed opportunity to agree peace with German agents in Stalingrad in 1943. Despite Allied advances everywhere from 1943, he still urged negotiations for peace without regime change or accountability. He remained an apologist for Nazism and a critic of the West for provoking war and refusing peace.

Liddell Hart expected the Second World War to be long and indecisive, in hope that it would be less costly than the First, as Chapter 15 explains. In the 1920s, he had realized that mechanization enables quicker invasions. In the 1930s, he decided that machines are better at carrying defenders than invaders. He proscribed offensives, as the quickest way to bleed Britain's economic advantages, but allowed for raids by light tanks and heavy bombers. By the Second World War, he no longer believed that aerial bombing is the exception to defence-dominance, or that it is ethical. He wanted a largely economic war, executed by blockade and sanctions, from which Britain would emerge best, given its maritime trade and economic depth. He hoped that a largely non-kinetic economic warfare would add to the moral pressure on the aggressors. He expected defensive stalemate. Thence, he expected political revolution in the homelands of aggressors.

Most of his expectations and prescriptions were discredited by events. His reinvention did not go as planned, although it succeeded eventually, as explained in Chapter 16. By 1944, he was still reframing his military views, but also intent on a new career as philosopher of femininity. He sought to revive his journalism. He applied for academic jobs. His failures added to his Anglophobia. Finally, and most consequentially, he falsified the pre-war record to portray himself as influenceless in Britain, influential in Germany, and thus the inventor of Blitzkrieg.

His reinvention gathered steam in America, where he had remotely cultivated correspondents since the early 1920s. Chapter 17 tells how he leveraged his interviews with German prisoners of war to persuade Americans that his pre-war confidence in defence-dominance was actually confidence in mechanized offensives. He undertook a speaking tour of American military institutions, with the help of his long-time pen-pal Robert Icks. Icks introduced him to Theodore Ropp, who, in turn, introduced him, more consequentially to Jay Luvaas, who was first to hagiograph him. He tried to persuade Douglas MacArthur that the General's strategy during the Korean War was inspired by his pre-war writings. Still dissatisfied at home and abroad, he once again considered emigration.

From America, Liddell Hart found his next most receptive nationality in Israel, the subject of Chapter 18. He pretended that he had influenced the Zionists who visited from Palestine in the 1930s. He was delighted to allude to his influence on Israel's War for Independence in 1948. He fished for credit for Israel's victory in the war of 1956. He toured Israel in 1960. He sought evidence for his influence on Israel's victory in the Six Day War of 1967. Even after his death, disciples imagined his influence on the Yom Kippur War of 1973.

Amidst this belated kudos, Liddell Hart again sought an academic career. Chapter 19 starts in the 1950s, when Michael Howard's insecure request for advice on building a one-man program in military history contributed to the success of what would become the War Studies program at Kings College London and, eventually, most pf Britain's military schools. Liddell Hart again applied for the Chichele Professorship of Military History at Oxford, but settled for honorary degrees and a visiting professorship in California, only to drop out within months.

Chapter 20 explains how Liddell Hart's final publications cemented his reinvention. He was abandoned by his pre-war publishers, but was lucky to be approached by younger publishers. While Liddell Hart strung Hamish Hamilton along, he committed most of his post-war books to Cassell. In 1965, he released his *Memoirs*, which claim responsibility for everything creditable but irresponsibility for everything debatable. Simultaneously, he and Howard edited a *Festschrift*, most of whose contributors were mentees who retold what Liddell Hart had told them. He was invited to contribute to the *New Cambridge Modern History*, four decades after he had failed to influence the old. He finished his *History of the Second World War*, decades after he had contracted for it with Cassell, without the normal editorial oversight or fact-checking. He died just before publication in 1970.

Subsequently, as revealed in Chapter 21, his son, mentees, and their students competed to memorialize or biograph him, but their self-selection and selection biases, and their concessions to his widow, inevitably corrupted the process and the products. Although none of their products satisfied, they rationalized a consensus that has viciously suppressed revisionism.

Now, more than a century after Basil Liddell Hart started publishing, the reader needs a comprehensive and honest guide to his life, thought, and legacy – including his insights and errors, truths and lies, achievements and omissions, virtues and vices, so that we can advance the good without the bad.

Basil, aged about 2 years, is restless on the knee of his father (Bramley Hart), in front of his mother (Clara Hart neé Liddell), and above his brother (Ernest Hart), on Bishop Rock (the westernmost land of the Isles of Scilly and England), in 1897 (LH 13/104/1).

1
Prodigy

Liddell Hart was raised and presented himself as a rare prodigy. His childhood, physiognomy, and psychology were certainly unusual, as told in sections below.

Childhood

Basil Henry Liddell Hart was born on 31 October 1895 to a clergyman and a well-dowried housewife. He admired his mother most, for her family's entrepreneurship in railways.

> [R]ecent[ly]...I came upon a volume of cuttings, yellow with age, which related to speeches delivered and papers written by my great-grandfather a century ago. He was a pioneer of railways and instrumental in starting the first railway in the West of England. It was amusing to find that his arguments on behalf of railways had been very similar to my own in regard to military mechanization (1935a: 297).

His maternal grandfather retired from the London & South-Western Railway as Assistant General Manager. The benefit that Liddell Hart recalled most was free first-class travel, at home and abroad, until the Great War (1965: I, 3).

Henry was his maternal grandfather's first name. Henry was also his father's first name, except his father preferred to be known by his second name (Bramley). His birth was registered with Basil as first name (for no recorded reason), Henry as second name, and his mother's maiden name as third name – the latter on her father's insistence, according to Basil's own story. By the end of the Great War, aged 23, he signed off as Liddell Hart, BHLH, LH, or L-H, as if his mother's maiden name were part of his family name. His first military articles were published with attribution to "Captain B.H.L. Hart" (1919a; 1919b), "Captain B.H. Liddell Hart" (1920a),* "B.H. Liddell Hart" (1920b), "B.H. Liddell-Hart" (1920c), and "Captain B.H. Liddell Hart" (1921a). He settled on the latter.

Given one brother, seven years older and in school, and no other siblings, Basil practically grew up as an only child. They resided in Paris (where his father ministered a church), remote from other family, for six years. His first "autobiography" admits that mother "rather spoilt me as regards hardening me. In fact she made me altogether too soft" (LH 7/1920/38). Clara relied on a nurse. His resentment hardened in 1937, when his father died. He published only one comment on her.

> She had a keenness of observation and a tactless honesty in pointing out faults, that was apt to make her uncomfortable company – all the more because she was usually right in spotting what was wrong. It was only by degrees, and in retrospective reflection, that one came to appreciate the value of her precision, thoroughness, and indomitable persistence (1965: I, 5).

---

* This article ends with the signature "B.H.L. Hart."

While Liddell Hart resented his mother's aggression, he resented his father's passivity.

> Sometimes it seemed to me that he lacked critical sense, and was too inclined to turn a blind eye to palpable faults, but it was often evident that he had a knack for making people behave better by assuming that they were on the way to become better (1965: I, 5).

He certainly resented his father's inferior socioeconomic standing. Bramley was descended from farmers, and happy as a Methodist minister. Their correspondence was infrequent. In Summer 1932, they started to align, after his brother's death, and his father's suggestion that he should turn his literary skills to Christianity. He replies vaguely that he dreams of developing his "philosophy" into "divine truth." In 1934, following speculation from admirers that he might be descended from Joan Hart – William Shakespeare's sister, he belatedly asked his father, via a stilting and unloving letter, to "tell me anything you know about your family origins." He did not preserve a reply, which suggests that his father disabused him (father to son, no date, son to father, 27 July 1932, son to father, 8 October 1934, LH 8/356 and 9/10/4).

His father's death in 1937, aged 77 years, provoked more sympathy. His nervous breakdowns in 1939, and subsequent estrangement from his only child, accelerated the trend. In memoirs (28 years after his father's death, 11 years after his mother's death), he misrepresents descendancy from Joan Hart as a family "tradition," writes about his father before his mother, and reverses the order in which he grew to appreciate one over the other. Here, he appreciates his father's "tolerance," religious "service," and "humour" (in that order), and describes his father's "sympathy" as "comforting…healing, invigorating, and creative" (1965: I, 5).

Physiognomy

Liddell Hart's cloistered upbringing, hypochondria, and weakness curbed his physical education. He liked to watch and report on team sports, but found participation nerve-wracking and usually unrewarding. Aged 13 years, he failed the physical test for naval school. At a new school (St. Paul's), he claimed a brief period of prowess in soccer and cricket, but blamed his teachers for misusing his talent. He blamed short-sightedness for his abandonment of team sports, although, with spectacles, tennis became his favourite sport to watch and play ("Notes for an Autobiography," LH 7/1920/38).

His favourite games were croquet and chess,* which he played with more vigour than skill or fairness. In March 1942 (a year after the publication of *The Strategy of Indirect Approach*), the novelist Arthur Ransome confided to a friend:

> I won all three [chess] games really because Liddell Hart do[es]n't practice what he preaches, and is prone to make a direct and premature attack of the exact kind that his book deprecates (Arthur Ransome to Charles Renold, 12 March 1942, in Brogan 1997: 291).

In the 1950s, a mentee saw him surreptitiously keeping a croquet ball in bounds

---

* In memoirs, Liddell Hart (1965: I, 77) lists chess as his second remaining recreation, after croquet.

with his feet. "The Captain never liked to lose at anything – he was a fierce competitor" (Luvaas 1990: 18).

Physical incapacity was at odds with noticeablity. Liddell Hart grew abnormally narrow and tall (6 feet 4 inches; 1.92 meters), which he accentuated with girdles, waistcoats, and tightly-tailored jackets. He favoured expensive double-breasted suits in the city, tweed jackets and knickerbockers in the country, homburg hats in both city and country, colourful waistcoats in the evening, round spectacles, gold tie clips, collar studs, cufflinks, a pipe for gesticulating (but not smoking), and big touring cars. The novelist Bernard Newman (1897-1968) met him in 1931.

> He...looked far more like the cartoonist's idea of a learned professor than a military man at all. Tall and exceedingly thin, the only distinguishing feature about him was the great, broad forehead which crowned an exceptionally small face...

> I took to this man at once. It was obvious that his cranial make-up did not belie the truth, for he seemed to me to be literally bulging with brain (Newman 1935: 113-115).

Margaret Storm Jameson (1891-1986) met him in 1937.

> Lean and tall, he has a head by [Francisco] Goya, tempered by an air of amusement and kindness (1969: II, 93).

US Army General George S. Patton (1885-1945), who received him in March 1944, wrote of "a funny looking man, tall and skinney" (Blumenson 1996: 426).

In 1917, maidens in Stroud, Gloucestershire, had nicknamed him "the camel." Jameson fictionalized him as "Heron," and alluded to his flamboyance.

> [H]e had strolled – like an actor who has been told: Stroll, don't walk – to the door: he stood there, hand on his hip, head flung back, and examined the airfield through half-closed eyes. Turning, he caught the young man's eye on him, and sauntered back into the middle of the room: he had a remarkable face, Kent now saw, crumpled as though he slept on it, with delicate features and thick fair hair, of an unmilitary length. He was tall...A flush spread over [his] protrusive forehead (1949: 22-23, 79).

An overbite fulfilled the stereotypical upper-class English "chinless wonder." A similarly tall chinless wonder was asked to parody Liddell Hart in the British Army Staff College's pantomime before Christmas 1932: "a great deal of energy and thought entered into this exercise, and I remember on one such occasion that, largely because of my height, I was cast in an impersonation of him under the inelegant sobriquet of 'Diddle Dart'" (Strong 1968: 18). The script made its way to Liddell Hart, who reproduced part in his memoirs, as if the satire of his ego ("the greatest captain of them all") and anti-militarism ("staff-itis is contagious") are compliments. The cast sings: "Tho' our tactics are old-fashioned, and strategy is dud / He will argue with a pen impassioned, make our problems clear as mud" (1965: I, 234).

Psychology

Liddell Hart was indulged by mother, nannies, and tutors, as he fairly admitted.

He was eight years old before he was schooled. He would not see out the conventional five years in any school. Aged 11, he moved from his first school (Edgeborough, Surrey, south-east of London) to another (Willington, near Putney, within the County of London). His first, private autobiography blames a tempestuous headmaster, although other writings show he was bullied and frequently home. His ageism probably started here (LH 7/1920/38).

After failing to win entry into naval school, he moved to St. Paul's, in central London, at the conventional age of 13 for a private secondary school. He suggested to his closest mentees, Jay Luvaas (1964: 377) and Brian Bond (1977: 7), that one schoolmaster (Reverend Horace Elam) taught him to question orthodoxy. However, Elam was not good for his psychology or his education. He needed extracurricular tuition and parental help to get into university, in 1913.

Liddell Hart was confident in his genes and genius, but not society. He claimed to be friendly with everyone, but was comfortable with no-one. Nobody characterized him as an intimate friend. Yet he could be unusually self-aware. At the start of his second term at university, he wrote a private self-assessment:

> Logical, self-love,* too [much] egotism, affectionate but not demonstrative, large brain-power, tactful and diplomatic, conventional, certain am[oun]t of individuality of thought, rather too methodical or even fussy, inclined to be philosophical not practical, head and heart fairly evenly balanced, too much love of detail, may fail to grasp whole.

> No insanity, no suicide, no ermine, fairly long-lived, work out own destiny, fortunate and successful, know what I want, not influenced by other people, simple life, not travel mind[ed], extremely jealous in affections concerning Mary [unidentified], opposite in tastes and temperament, not flirtatious by nature, health good, cultivate will, art and poetry not great influences but may incline towards them, not nervy, but sensitive, well-balanced mentally, slightly indolent (January 1914, LH 7/1913/13).

He over-estimates his psychological stability. During the Great War, he broke down soon after arriving on the front in 1915, and on every subsequent stay on the front (at least four times in total), until he was invalided home for good in 1916 (on which more in Chapter 4). In December 1920, he wrote another self-assessment.

> Highly strung and sensitive, though I have learnt by experience to conceal it. Not physically brave. Hate to take blind risks and jumpy, but perfectly all right as soon as I have had a moment to seize control of my nerves. As my nerves are usually on edge, I have learnt the art of always being ready to control them, and successfully so far. Yet in the sudden emergencies which have befallen me – mostly in motoring – I have usually kept my head and instantly done the right thing, which has earned me a reputation for coolness (LH 7/1920/32).

By then, he was vicious towards elders, conservatives, professional soldiers, and sceptics. Criticism of his first public talks and articles encouraged him to give up public speaking from 1921 until 1932, although he liked private audiences with

---

* This term is written and struck out by the same hand.

admirers and influencees. His memoirs hint at sycophancy, where he lists "the few" displaying "generosity in acknowledging help." They are: Ivor Maxse (the General who gave him his first breaks in doctrinal writing, military journalism, and public speaking in 1920); David Campbell (who took the lead in granting and protecting privileged access to the War Office in 1926); Liberal premier David Lloyd George (whom he contacted in 1922); and Liberal minister Leslie Hore Belisha (whom he met in 1937) (1965: II, 225). Yet even these relationships collapsed. In each case he proved too ambitious, pushy, and guiltless. Storm Jameson's (1949: 32) fictionalized version is "a born snob, he would have thrown away all his exalted friendships if that would have helped him to write a great book."

He over-compensated for intimacy issues with energetic correspondence, self-publicizing, and politicking. In many ways, he fulfilled the roles of tortured artist and celebrity. His prescription for younger soldiers is surely a wish for himself:

> For the boy who develops late, a little guidance in the art of leadership might often suffice to bring out his capacity while still a cadet, and so preserve for the benefit of the Service many a career of great possibilities which at present comes to an untimely end. The rudiments of psychology should, it is therefore suggested, form part of the curriculum of the military cadet, together with a more advanced course for the young officer at the Junior Commanders' School (1924c: 47).

Liddell Hart repeatedly claimed insight into "psychology," and prescribed study of psychology to his peers (1932c: 108; 1935a: 93). Yet no evidence appears in his archive or citations for any reading of psychology. His psychological assumptions are often naïve. For instance, he expects morale to rise when "only a few men drop" from indirect artillery fire during a pedestrian assault (1922c: 719). This assumption contradicts his own wartime breakdowns under minor indirect fire.

His psychology remained tumultuous, even at the height of his professional and official influence in 1937. Storm Jameson's (1949: 22-23, 78) fictionalized version "did not raise his voice. His nerves betrayed themselves by a twitching muscle in his cheek, below the eye…His nervous smile pulled [his] mouth out of shape."

He admitted at least two breakdowns in 1939. Probably he suffered more during the Second World War. His reinvention leveraged breathtaking dishonesty and sophistry. He was publicly successful, but privately edgy, even with family. From 1954, Michael Howard (1970b: 42; 1984: 206) observed his "almost pathetic need for praise and appreciation, treasuring every scrap of evidence of his influence and every tribute to his abilities in a way that surprised his disciples, who took them for granted, and occasionally exasperated his dearest friends." After organizing his archives, Bond (1977: 31) realized that "his craving for praise and recognition of his 'greatness' is a constant trait in his character and not something he developed later as a reaction to the temporary eclipse of his reputation during the Second World War." Another biographer judged that "Liddell Hart wrote to be fed and to be famous. But he also wrote to be right, and to demonstrate his rightness to others: to make a difference" (Danchev 1998b: 33; 1999a: 32; 1999b: 314). A historian realized "a shameless self-publicist who rarely missed an opportunity to hawk his own intellectual brand" (Allport 2020: 144).

Basil and Jessie at Ascot racecourse, 17 June 1937, and Adrian and Jessie at a cricket match between Harrow and Eton (Adrian's school) on 9 July. Jessie wears the same costume in each photograph. In June 1935, the *News Chronicle* **had headlined a photograph of her in a similar Victorian costume, of ostrich feathers, lace, crinoline, and velvet, as: "This might be 1860 – but it's 1935!" (LH 13/104/4).**

2

Family Man

Liddell Hart's private life was stormy, particularly with women. His self-assessment of January 1914 admits he is "extremely jealous in affections concerning Mary," who appears in no other document. In November, he wrote: "My belief in the necessary inferiority of women is more pronounced than ever" (LH 7/1913/13; LH 7/1914/10). Through a first marriage, one prodigal son, a mistress who belatedly became his second wife, two unwilling step-daughters, and at least one proxy son, his private life remained strained and disappointing.

Jessie

In December 1917, Liddell Hart was in the final month of his adjutancy of the Gloucestershire Volunteers. He proposed to the daughter of his assistant – a wealthy stock-broker and part-time soldier, too old for frontline service. Jessie Stone (1895-1976) was about a year older than average for British women at marriage, so perhaps was in a hurry. Certainly Liddell Hart was in a hurry (even though the average age for men was a couple years older). His memoirs portray her as a professional aide: "after a brief honeymoon [April 1918] we took a furnished house in Jesus Lane as our first home. Marriage was a stimulus and also an aid in settling down to work on the development of my military ideas" (1965: I, 31).

Although Jessie was slightly older and much wealthier, he called her "kid" or "kiddie." Two years later, he wrote an assessment.

> The most lovable and adorable child of nature. Might be summed up thus according to the verse: "When she was good, she was very good and when she was bad she was horrid." Utterly fascinating when she likes, a most capable manager and hostess, and always behaves with people in a way that makes me proud of her, and a social asset by her great knack of making friends.
>
> A very quick and violent temper and distinctly a jealous disposition. Apt to nag terribly when once started, but equally quick to change her mood and be too sweet not to be forgiven. Inclined to be suspicious and very curious, but again extremely kind-hearted and tender towards any trouble. Often provokes almost beyond endurance, but when she is good she is so utterly adorable that that one loves her more and more in spite of it all. Life with her is like an April shower[:] sunshine, a downpour[,] and then sunshine again. Certainly never monotonous! The dear kid! (7/1920/32).

Subsequently, he wrote about her rarely, usually only in criticism. He expected her to entertain his acquaintances, but rarely took her to them. One inconsistency was a weekend at a seaside resort with T.E. Lawrence (Lawrence of Arabia).

Jessie happened to indulge in one of her rhapsodies about policemen –

T.E. said she would have a less idyllic view of them if she belonged to the poorer classes and saw them from that angle (note, 12 May 1929, in 1938g: 26).

Lawrence felt bad for her.

I only fear that we chattered too constantly and bored Mrs. Liddell-Hart. She hasn't had the vexations of serving under [General Sir Louis] Bols or [General Sir] Archie Murray, or the pleasure of [Marshal of the Royal Air Force Hugh] Trenchard: and so couldn't properly follow our short-hand remarks. Please apologise for me, if she feels she had an overdose of tactics! (Lawrenc to LH, 17 May 1929, in 1938g: 27).

Jessie found her husband secretive and controlling. He certainly controlled her finances and clothing, and treated her more as a prop than a partner, although she delighted in fashionable clothing and public appearances. His eroticism centered on Victorian clothing, as indicated by the following analogy to Lawrence: "like the mystery of a woman who dons a gauzy veil, who exposes her legs while wearing a high-necked dress, who wears a crinoline while exposing her bosom" (1965: I, 356).

In the second half of the 1920s, as his income and her expenses rocketed, the marriage degenerated into an open marriage. In 1934, he told a gynaecologist that his sexual "connection" with Jessie had ended "years" earlier. The reason for their consultation was her "hysteria." They were then in dispute over a particularly drunken and invasive lover, until they trilaterally agreed to "ration" the man's time in their home (note, 31 July 1934, LH 11/1934/1). Nevertheless, husband and wife would not give up cohabitation for years more.

Jameson met Jessie in 1937. Jameson's fictionalized version is "exhausted" but "elegant" (1949: 19).

[Her husband] fell in love with a girl who was the daughter of a village doctor, with no money at all, and married her. And was very soon unfaithful to her, but with great reserve…

"If I came in and told you I'd murdered someone, you'd say it was your fault…You're the only person I love. Except myself, of course," he added bitterly.

"Yes," she said, "I think you love me" (1949: 32, 102).

His memoirs date the last of Jessie's "successive eruptions" to August 1938, which is his longest public reference to her.

We had shared both happy and difficult times together and I shall always be deeply grateful for the stimulus she provided. In many respects the quintessence of femininity, and volcanic in temperament, she combined great attractiveness with an impulsive generosity that was manifested in many spontaneous acts of kindness, especially towards servants and friends too poor to repay her (1965: II, 187).

Around Jessie's death (in 1976), their son summarized their competing perceptions, of which he favoured his mother's.

> According to one view, my father was a rather simple and essentially normal young man who, after the harrowing experiences of the First World War and without too much thought, had been lured into marriage at an early age. Then, after he had been invalided out of the Army as a result of his wartime disabilities, he had immersed himself in his work and by his own efforts rapidly moved into a world to which his wife had been unable or unwilling to adapt herself – and to help him. Despite his devotion, she had become involved with other men[,] and this, coupled with temper and extravagance, had led to the breakdown – from which he had been rescued, to live happily – and creatively – ever afterwards.
>
> According to the other view, my father was a very neurotic and demanding young man from a spoilt and sheltered home who had been introduced to his innocent young wife by a sex pervert in her home town where she was then doing some kind of war job. He continued the transvestite* practices with which he was already engaging and required a submission, involving a degree of physical sadism as well as violent outburst of temper; with this she long continued to put up, while helping him in his early struggles for success. Other men had been introduced by my father himself into this set-up and then my father, bored by his wife's companionship, had been enticed away, leaving her to live unhappily ever afterwards (and himself discredited) ("Father's Life," LHCMA AJLH/13).

Adrian

After four years of marriage, and two miscarriages (latterly of twins), Jessie gave birth to Adrian John Liddell Hart on 24 August 1922. Adrian's only appearance in his father's memoirs is as a birth (1965: I, 63).

As godfather, Basil chose a man he had not contacted until 1920, a man he did not meet until 1922, an atheist without children of his own, but a man most beneficial intellectually and professionally in those years. Colonel JFC Fuller was already internationally known as the Tank Corps' operations officer (1916-1918), its representative (SD7) on the General Staff (1918-1919), and its historian (1920). He was then in charge of the General Staff department for doctrine and training (SD4), prior to starting as Chief Instructor at the Staff College (1923-1926). Liddell Hart chose Fuller's first name (John) as his son's second name.

Adrian's memoir does not mention Fuller, and refers to his father infrequently, usually negatively.

> My father remained for some years an aloof, awe-inspiring figure entrenched in his book-lined study and occasionally given to teasing. My gay and much-admired mother was frequently in company. We moved house several times and my parents were often travelling, sending me exotic presents from abroad which I fancied – Evzone tin-soldiers, an Italian military cap [in 1928]. As I grew older, I spent more time in hotels, and I heard the rustle of my mother's taffeta dresses, which she wore in

---

* Only the wearing of corsets is specified elsewhere.

> the high-waisted Victorian fashion to please my father, as she came to kiss me good night in the unfamiliar bedrooms where I always had to peer under the bed and into the wardrobe to reassure myself that there were no "ghosties and ghoulies and things who go bump in the night." The main role was filled by a small, wrinkled woman [nanny] who was already old to take charge of a small child...
>
> I shared many of the interests and views of my father, but the relationship between an only son and a well-known father, however sympathetic, tends to create tensions, if only in reaction against the misconceptions which other people are liable to hold at times...
>
> I had become conscious in early childhood of my essential isolation (1953: 15, 29, 30).

Jameson met Adrian when he was about 15 years old. The fictionalized version "had dark sorrowful eyes in a white face...The child's smile altered his face instantly, to a lively mischief...[V]ery old people sit with the same quietness...For a young child he cries too quietly...As soon as he began to talk, his face lost the air of sadness it had in repose" (1949: 19, 25, 84, 88, 95).

> [The father] loved his son, and was proud of his intelligence and his looks, but to spend any time with a child bored him terribly; he did not know what to talk about with children. "He's too self-possessed for his age. I don't even know whether he likes me" (1949: 33).

Like the father, Adrian was an only child, focused on his mother, bullied at boarding school, contrary, and often home in term time. Unlike his father, he did not rush to join a university, a war, or the Army. In early 1939, his father was still mediating with his teachers (at Eton), and arranging for his study of history at Cambridge.

> I have no particular feeling as between Oxford and Cambridge, although I am inclined to think that the Cambridge History School might be a better mental discipline and a corrective to his tendency to diffuseness and abstractness of ideas. If he should go to Cambridge, then your suggestion of King's [College, where Basil had based himself in 1918] appeals strongly to me. My own college was Corpus [Christi] – the Master was anxious for him to go there – but I feel that the atmosphere is rather too Tory and Anglo-Catholic to be congenial for Adrian (to Thomas Lyon 10 March 1939, LHCMA KLH).

Adrian chose an extra term at Eton, until December 1939. Then he chose to study at King's, which would not start until October 1940. In the meantime, he worked as a researcher in educational reform for an institute in London. Once France was invaded, he moved to an artists' retreat, school, and pacifist institute in faraway Devon, as arranged by his father's friends, who owned the estate (Dartington Hall). Later in the year, Adrian joined the Home Guard.

At Cambridge, he focused on English literature, under George "Dadie" Rylands (1902-1999). By November, he started a sexual relationship with John Lehmann

(1907-1987), founder of *New Writing* magazine and Lehmann's publishing house. Lehmann had left London (except for one night a week), for a room at King's College, arranged by Rylands, to escape German bombing and to be closer to academic and literary friends. Lehmann's autobiography mentions Adrian only as an introducer to Demetrios Capetanakis (1912-1944), a Greek writer, who was 10 years older than Adrian and already in a post-doctoral position.

> I had not long been established in my little room in St. Edward's Passage long, before I began to collect a small group of young men interested in writing, who would come and talk over drinks before dinner during my weekly sojourn. One of these, Adrian Liddell Hart, a freshman from Eton and son of the distinguished military historian, I had met in the rooms of George Rylands, whose pupil he was; and one evening he appeared at my door in his sky-blue polo jersey with Demetrios in tow. He introduced him as a fellow-pupil of Dadie's, a fabulous connoisseur of modern literature, and a fan of New Writing (Lehmann 1960: 119-120).

Lehmann realized Adrian's instability in the same month they met. Adrian introduced Lehmann to his father, early in 1941, before eloping for military service. As Adrian later admitted, he treated Lehmann with indifference. Lehmann wondered whether his own role was masochistic. In any case, Lehmann was not compatible: he was polygamous and 15 years older. Adrian wished to escape Lehmann, his father, and Cambridge. Additionally, his lack of military service genuinely rankled (Lehmann to AJLH, 16 November 1940, LHCMA AJLH/5; Lehmann 1960: 119-120; Wright 1998: 119-135).

Adrian did not choose the Army. When Adrian was 12 years old, his father had warned that the Army involves "sealing up part of the mind." When he was 13, his father said that "for all its good points it is no place for a thinking man" (notes, LH 11/1934/7 and 11/1935/37). Adrian accompanied his father to Army manoeuvres from August to September of each year, but did not enjoy them.

> The exercises were often confusing; the battles sometimes seemed to go on a long time, especially when it rained, as it often did. On one occasion [April 1938] I found myself on the battlefield of Waterloo...[alongside] King Leopold of the Belgians who was watching his army manoeuvre from the top of the convenient Victory Monument. Such are the revolutions of fortune that I fell into a manure heap at the farm of La Haye Sainte on the same day (Liddell Hart and Liddell Hart 1976: 2).*

Adrian's retrospective explanations for rejecting the Army are: fear of horses, after a stray bolted past him; lack of mechanical aptitude; and horror at disabled veterans. Additionally, he admits that he "lacked an instinctive coordination, a certain suppleness" (at least in comparison to fellow recruits to the French Foreign Legion, in 1951). Further, he admits an anti-authoritarian "pattern" (to which he reverted in the Legion): "I had challenged the authorities; then threatened them with my withdrawal" (1953: 18-22, 64, 99).

In 1941, Adrian was commissioned into the Royal Navy Volunteer Reserve. His

---

* His father recalled the visit, the monument, and Adrian and Leopold in conversation, but not his son's disinterest or embarrassment (note, April 1938, LH 11/1938/47-51; 1965: II, 205).

initial service was on surface ships, escorting convoys in the Atlantic and (by 1942) the Arctic.

> Another year and I was playing other war games. By this time I was aware that such games were different when played out on a small ship's deck in a freezing ocean, into which one might at any moment be blown (Liddell Hart and Liddell Hart 1976: 3).

In late 1942, he volunteered for Combined Operations, after hearing a talk by its commander, Admiral Louis Mountbatten. He was tasked with receiving the first Tank Landing Ship in New York. He begged to be relieved, so in mid-1943 was transferred to shore duty in Algeria, administering Landing Ships before the invasion of Italy. After bathing in the sea, he somehow fell onto rocks. He spent months with his neck in a plaster cast. In 1944, he worked in the Admiralty in London, until he was passed fit for service at sea, when he was posted to an anti-submarine trawler in home waters.

He earned a desk-job in Iceland, effective January 1945. On his last day of leave in London, he visited his mother, who was managing a Canadian servicemen's club. She brought the on-off lover whose "ration" of time she had negotiated back in 1934.

> Dined with Bill and M[other] at Prunier's. Bill the same as ever, yet strange that he sticks down at Richmond and is so out of touch with the beau monde. M behaved very badly, with long, dreary stories about her Canadians, ridiculous patriotic gibberish, and sarcastic remarks to me, besides behaving like a tart with a drunken American in the Dorchester Bar. How I could strangle her at these times. I really feel she resents I'm not fighting, and even dying at the front. Looking over-dressed too. I feel guilty for being so disloyal (diary, 6 January 1945, LHCMA AJLH/5).

The next day he realized she was lonely, but happy to see him go: "M in a good mood this evening whilst I'm packing, and I feel very affectionate towards her, and sad for her loneliness."

He served as Flag Lieutenant to the Admiral Commanding Iceland until May, when he returned to Britain to stand in the general election. His autobiography puts this event in the passive tense: "I found myself the successor of Edgar Wallace as the Liberal candidate for Blackpool South" (1953: 25). He was soundly defeated in July (although he had to wait until August before the results were confirmed).

His next years are bewildering: his own account is short and flippant. Nevertheless, his pattern of privileged opportunities, loneliness, accidents, unreliability, and transience is clear. He won special release from the Navy, joined the staff of the United Nations in New York, and was chosen as Secretary to the new Atomic Energy Commission, but quit within months.

> I took the train to New Orleans where I lived for a short time in the Vieux Quartier. After a head-on car smash in which I miraculously escaped with my life, I turned up in San Francisco. There I earned money by cleaning shops and factory buildings until I got a lift back to Milwaukee with a sailor. Divided between the pioneering enthusiasm of the American way of life and its standardized banality in many respects, I eventually

returned to Europe (1953: 25-26).

From 1947, he worked for the Allied Control Council in Berlin, but that dissolved in 1949. He worked at the Outward Bound Sea School in Wales. "But it was too simple for a career." He went to Yorkshire as a reporter for Westminster Press Newspapers, but viewed Northern England harshly, and realized harsh truths about himself.

> Through this depression I worked on a novel of Berlin without satisfaction...
>
> I found it hard to be entirely sincere in any situation. I felt a sense of the ludicrous, a sense of history – and, in the end, despite indiscretion and impulsiveness, a sixth sense of the moment for compromise, for disengagement. I wanted to be on the frontier and in the centre; to be accepted and yet to remain an exception...I had come to realize in the months that followed my return from Berlin that I did not perpetually wait in the ante-chamber of achievement (1953: 29-30).

He transferred to the House of Commons as a Lobby Correspondent. While Parliament was in recess, he acted as a Defence Correspondent. His next election defeat came in February 1950.

A year later, he joined the French Foreign Legion. He found it less salacious and harsh than expected. Adrian admits in memoirs that his real name (despite the *nom de guerre* Peter Brand) provoked suspicions of short-termism, political intervention, and public memoirs. His father wrote to French officials, and eventually the French commander in Indochina (Jean de Lattre de Tassigny, 1889-1952), to seek his release (although none of their memoirs admits this). His father managed to get a letter to Adrian, which is revealing about both men.

> Like you, I have a sense of non-attachment, except emotionally to individuals, but find that state more agreeable than you seem to have done. For my own part I have found that a deep fondness for new people, and a liking for most people, suffices to counteract the chilliness that might otherwise come from the mental detachment that I have, and prefer. Like you, too, I have long had the desire to "cut loose from communications," applying [General William T.] Sherman's maxim in one's individual sphere – as Lawrence did. The desire grew as one came to realise the futility of most of one's activities and accomplishments. But although I managed to fulfil it in some degree, the attempt was limited partly by material complications and human ties, and partly by happier circumstances than yours. But my unfulfilled desire helps me to understand and sympathize more fully with what you have done. Nevertheless I hope – particularly because of what you mean to me, as well as your potentialities – that yours will prove another case to illustrate Toynbee's definition of the principle of "withdrawal-and-return" (17 March 1951, LHCMA KLH).

Adrian spent around three months* being interviewed in Marseilles and Sidi bei

---

* His account is largely undated. The Foreign Legion will not release his records.

Abbes, Algeria. He was indulged by commanders, with invitations and offers, such as easy service in the boat arm. Once he was permitted into basic training, he found it had been reduced from 9 months to 6 weeks (1953: 102-104). By his own account, basic training "was a mélange like everything else in the Legion."

> On most days we marched in open order to the fringes of a small wooded valley half a mile from the barracks. We were supposed to look as though we were looking for Viet-Minh. "You always look like a tourist observing the sights," remarked Klaus (1953: 61).

After basic training, his cohort enshipped for Indochina, while he was visiting the Legion's commander. He sailed on 14 July 1951. He chose the amphibious arm, operating in the Mekong Delta. Training and discipline were lax. Legionnaires operated weapons and vehicles without training, drank alcohol on operations, dined on stolen livestock, pocketed private property, occupied villages, burnt homes, and opened fire without positively identifying any enemy. He never saw or fired upon any enemy. A tour or deployment was supposed to last 18 months, but he was taken off operations within weeks to months, after arguing with immediate superiors and rebuffing new offers from their superiors. He was shipped back to Algeria in December 1951. He was demobilized in Marseilles in January 1952, after 11 months in the Legion. "That I should feel a sense of injustice was partly, no doubt, a matter of temperament" (1953: 172). The following passage is his least evasive.

> My nationality and antecedents, the [e]specially "free" circumstances in which I had joined the Legion, the repeated choices which I had been given, the goodwill and high expectations which had been shown, only underlined my failure from the point of view of the authorities to serve with honour and fidelity…I assumed, ambitiously and vainly, that the French would see some practical military advantages in my varied experience or even some special propaganda benefits in my circumstances (1953: 171).

Adrian's memoir was poorly received. It is a frustrating jumble of allusions, suggestions, observations, and admissions, without his father's talent for spin. Both father and son are tragic heroes, except the father reinvented himself. Adrian returned to pattern. By the 1960s, the father was telling people that Brian Bond (2018: 110) – a neighbour and budding undergraduate of history – was more like a son. After the father's death in 1970, Adrian returned to public notice only when he commented on his father. He died in 1991, at a younger age than his father.

Kathleen

Basil became involved with Kathleen Nelson (1902-2001) sometime after April 1934, when her father (Alan Sullivan) sought his help to publish an anti-war novel. His memoirs claim that he met her "several years" after he met her father. Surviving correspondence suggests he met Kathleen in 1936, when her first husband – a pioneering surgeon – died from an infection. She always claimed she did not break up his first marriage, but they were certainly intimate by the time he left Jessie for the last time in August 1938. Jessie complained to Adrian that he had "been enticed away" ("Father's Life," LHCMA AJLH/13).

He reminded Kathleen of her father (a profligate, attentive, tall, pipe-smoker), except his attentiveness was conflicted. He kept a house in the country for Jessie, and a flat in London for himself and his lovers. He likely would have returned to Jessie in September 1938, except that Germany's threats against Czechoslovakia, and his paranoia about German bombing, encouraged him and Kathleen to search for a furnished home near his family home. On the second day, they quarrelled about her need for security, and his willingness to give Jessie another chance.

> Left miserable – looked for Basil and found he had gone out in the car. He came back about 7:00 looking more tired and strained, we had more discussion – slightly easier – and again after dinner in his room until midnight. He said he had been unable to work after our "quarrel." We discussed Jessie and his conscience about her plea to have one more chance. I agreed that a compromise of my coming to the flat as secretary if she behaved sensibly might work. The telephone rang constantly – Jessie several times about taking Adrian away from Eton. Went to bed with a heavy heart (Kathleen's diary, 25 September 1938, LHCMA KLH).

They spent the next week in London, walking and talking after work hours. By the end of Thursday, he heard of the international settlement in Munich, and she noted "a feeling of relief and slackening of tension." A month later, he wrote to her as "my first love, of my lifetime, in the full-grown sense." However, he did not commit to a shared home until after his breakdown on 17 June 1939. A doctor persuaded her that she would be necessary to his recovery. They rented a home in South Devon, although by July he was travelling to London again. Robert Graves met her in December: "her presence was so immediately good in its exhalation. I think that your luck has obviously changed" (BHLH to Kathleen, 23 October 1939, LHCMA KLH; Graves to BHLH, 15 December 1939, LH 1/327; Danchev 1998a: 205-209). Yet he would not marry her until 1942. His memoirs portray a partner in crime:

> My second marriage brought me a most lovely companionship with a helpmate in my work whose grace and charm endear her to everyone who comes to know here. It has been my good fortune to spend many years in closest company with a woman who combines a radiant spirit with a critical mind (1965: II, 187).

> Above all, I wish to express once again how much I owe to my wife, Kathleen, for her many helpful suggestions and criticisms, and for the way she has looked after a mass of documentary files, as well as in more other ways than she will ever realise (1965: I, i).

Since 1931, Liddell Hart had categorized most wives as "handicaps" (including Sonia Fuller), the next largest proportion as "doubtful," the smallest proportion as "assets," without coding either Jessie or Kathleen. From 1959, Liddell Hart often told Brian Bond that most wives are handicaps, but Bond judged Kathleen an asset. At group lunches, "Kathleen attempted to interrupt Basil's flow of talk to ensure that everyone had a chance to speak." Richard Ogorkiewicz "kept in touch for a number of years [after Basil's death] with his charming wife, Kathleen, who loyally supported him in his activities and zealously guarded his reputation" (note, LH 11/1931/26; Bond 2018: 22, 24; Ogorkiewicz 2021: 21).

Step-Daughters

Liddell Hart gained two step-daughters (Jennifer and Judith Nelson), although they did not travel as a foursome until that panicky drive to the country on 23 September 1938.

> The children delighted with the prospect of a weekend at a hotel...Very expensive and comfortable, really spacious grounds, swimming pool and all the amenities for the Js, who were highly impressed by their "first hotel"...
>
> Sunday a rain [storm] and an atmosphere tense and threatening. Basil worked on an article for The Atlantic. Had a serious conversation before lunch. Afterwards went for a walk in the gardens discussing plans. I made several suggestions about the children and seeing them to safety, quite sure in my heart that I wanted to be with Basil in any emergency provided that the Js were well looked after – surprised and hurt by his attitude – though it was admittedly "rational." Felt horribly the pull of Basil and of the Js – so like the old conflict that occurred so often with [first husband] Tim (Kathleen's diary, 23 and 25 September 1938, KLH).

The Js enjoyed the high-living but resented the suitor. They nicknamed him "Tiny" or "Ty." They made up a verse: "Liddell Hart is very tall / And his head is very small / And he has no brains at all." They lived mostly with relatives. From 1940 to 1944, they went to Canada (where Kathleen had been born). They returned, as teenagers, when their new step-father tried his latest theories of feminine dress and manners. Kathleen conceded to him the parenting.

> You would be delighted if you could see how well the Js have settled down and how helpful they are in the house, learning to cook and how to make jam and bottle fruit. We have an impressive schedule for each day with our various jobs, and also certain rules that have to be obeyed. Basil is quite perfect with them and has taken enormous pains to establish the right relationship. In fact he has spent so much time with them that his work has been somewhat neglected, but he felt the importance of starting off in the right way. He is very keen that they should grow up to take their place as the daughters of the house. Their short and baggy sweaters have to be kept for the fells and climbing. Anna [their aunt] has sent them home with lots of pretty clothes so they are extremely well off in that way. I see now the folly of my weakness and inability to exact discipline and the dire consequences, so am grateful and thankful for Basil's wise help and understanding (to her parents, 13 July 1944, KLH).

From stockings and pretty clothes, he moved on to corsets, and thence to measuring their waists. They rebelled. He drew up written contracts, which the girls refused to sign. He threatened to leave. Kathleen was torn. Her brothers sided with the girls. He lectured them on the health benefits of corsets, and the social benefits of manners. The correspondence continued into at least 1948. The Js soon made families of their own. They left no public comment, and barely cooperated with their mother's choice of biographer (Danchev 1998a: 206, 215-217).

3
Intellectual

From early age, Liddell Hart saw himself as intellectual. This chapter compares his self-images and performance as a scholar, genius, scientist, truth-seeker, arguer, lecturer, correspondent, tolerator, theorist, logician, and operations researcher.

Scholar

Liddell Hart was expensively educated, but infrequently, due to nervous and physical complaints. He was aged nearly 6 years before he moved from France to England, and nearly 8 when he started school. He was frequently home in term-time, due to ill-health and bullying. At home, he spent his time reading historical fiction and history. He focused on Christianity (after his father) and railways (after his mother's father and grandfather). In his mid-teens, he found some stability at St. Paul's in London. Here, his writings shift to sports, aviation, and historical fiction. He excelled in history, scripture, geography, and French, but struggled in classics, sciences, and mathematics. Belated crunching and extra tuition got him accepted for higher education (LH 7/1920/38; Bond 1977: 7, 13-14).

In September 1913, a month before his 18th birthday, he started the undergraduate History Tripos at Cambridge University. He barely completed the first year. He might not have returned for the second year, except that he needed to join the Officer Training Corps before he could be commissioned into the Army. On 28 November 1914, days before leaving the University, he repudiated scholarship.

> 1. I believe (i) in the supremacy of the aristocracy of race (and birth) (ii) in the supremacy of the individual; [and]
>
> 2. in compulsory military service because it is the only possible life for a man and brings out all the finest qualities of manhood.
>
> 3. I have acquired rather a contempt for mere thinkers and men of books who have not come to a full realization of what true manhood means. Military service if intelligently conducted develops and requires the finest mental, moral, and physical qualities,
>
> 4. I exalt the great general into the highest position in the roll of great men and consider it requires higher mental qualities than any other line of life (LH 7/1914/10).

His repudiation of scholarship was somewhat convenient. He never sought further education. He did not work hard in the methodical or rigorous senses, although he energetically corresponded and archived, and was productive with the pen. Routinely, he was over-committed. For instance, in 1930, when still a full-time journalist, he contracted to write four biographies at once, of which he completed only one.

Genius

Liddell Hart saw himself as a genius from an early age. Indeed, he viewed genius as genetic and youthful (even after he reached seniority). Aged 27 years, he wrote that "genius" or "intellect ripens early…by the time he is 25 or 30" (1923a: 324). Later, he offered the adage (he misdescribed it as a definition) that "genius" is "an infinite capacity for taking pains" (1938e: 109), although he was really taking pains quantitatively rather than qualitatively.

Liddell Hart preferred the intimacy of artists, poets, novelists, and fashion designers, who admired his style, but knew little of his subjects. Aged 39 years, he received a novelist's praise of his "genius."

> I'm certainly not conscious of any "genius" – merely of a moderately smooth-working mind, and a desire to see things clearly. If I have any special power it seems to be that of registering facts that I observe and relating them to each other – my mind works like a cash-register of mental values (to F. Britten Austin, 21 March 1936, LH 11/1936/9).

Revealingly, for his definitive "philosophy of war," the only proof-readers were (in order) the poet Robert Graves (1895-1985), the novelist John Brophy (1899-1965), the failed British soldier and future Irish nationalist Eric Dorman-Smith (1895-1969), the biographer and hill-walker Katherine Chorley (1897-1986),* an obscure friend (G.R. Atkinson), and an indiscrete and partisan (Liberal) civil servant (Sir Archibald Rowlands, 1892-1953). The preface offers Liddell Hart's most specific description of his own intellectual approach.

> When thinking into problems I have tended to proceed on the operational method of advancing to a point; immediate consolidation of the ground gained; flankward extension of the penetration to link it up with those made on other sectors; further advance in depth from this broadened springboard. It was in the course of pursuing this consecutive process that my thought, starting with a local penetration into minor tactics, came to be successively extended through the sphere of combined tactics, strategy, combined strategy, and policy, to the philosophy of war (1944a: 7).

This approach overlaps his imperative to counter "orthodoxy." He once asserted that "originality is generally regarded as a sign of genius" (1959b: 20-21).

Jay Luvaas (1964: 384) admired Liddell Hart's "uncanny ability of being able to grasp the essentials of any new development and present the issues to the reading public with clarity and imagination." Brian Bond (1977: 274) admired the breadth and cross-fertilization of Liddell Hart's work, "but possibly he would have done better at some of them, as a historian especially, had he not spread his interests so widely." Alex Danchev read less than Bond before concluding: "His thinking was marvellously clear, with nothing and no one to guide him" (1998: 255). Michael Howard (1999: vii) reprinted his "thoughts on war" with the self-interested claim that Liddell Hart's "intelligence was as precise and penetrating as a laser-beam, shedding a bright and novel light on all that it touched."

---

* Katherine Chorley (neé Hopkinson) had corresponded with Kathleen Liddell Hart since 1931. In 1943, Katherine published her only military subject: *Armies and the Art of Revolution*.

Scientist

Liddell Hart routinely posed as a scientist, but never pursued any scientific training, either disciplinary or methodological. Practically, a scientist is differentiated by at least replicability (Newsome 2016: 6). Liddell Hart rarely defines anything, declares sources, describes methods, or proves anything, so is rarely replicable.

He was born in the waning years of the Victorian age, to a clergyman and a housewife, who encouraged his arts. At that time, some schools allowed pupils to choose "the Classical side" (arts) over "the modern side" (sciences). He stayed on the Classical side until his final school, where he was a dunce at science.

He studied only history at Cambridge. In January 1914, he concluded that "art and poetry [are] not great influences but [I] may incline towards them." He did not then claim any scientific skills or interests (LH 7/1913/13). His formal tutor was Geoffrey G. Butler, later better known as the Conservative Member of Parliament for Cambridge University (1923 to 1929), i.e., in opposition to Liddell Hart's liberalism and progressivism (see Chapter 11). Liddell Hart's scientific pretensions likely were influenced by Professor John Bagnell Bury (1861-1927). In 1902, Bury had been appointed Regius Professor of Modern History, despite specializing in Byzantine history. In his inaugural address, in January 1903, Bury (1930: 9) miscategorized history as "science," just because history is (supposed to be) factual.

Upon the Great War, Liddell Hart took up soldiering as a practical art. He chose the infantry over any "trade" or service branch, where he would have learned some applied sciences. After the war, he described himself as "idealistic and romantic, but practical; [a]rtistic, but [with] no idea of art or music" (LH 7/1920/32).

In 1919, he switched to education and doctrine (see Chapter 7). He induces doctrine from history, but mischaracterizes it as science. He promises "a simple and scientific tactical [family] tree, which will clearly convey to the military student the essential principles and their broad application to the phases of war," and from which "we can deduce the essential principles." In fact, the "tree" is hung with convenient assumptions and analogies, which he misdescribes as "truth." From these unsound premises, he deduces what he misdescribes as "a complex system of watertight compartments for each tactical action [that] appears truly scientific" (1921a: 16; 1921c: 218). His semantics, at least, were corrected by Colonel Lionel Bond (Royal Engineer, graduate of the Staff College, current instructor at the Indian Army's Senior Officers School).

> Careless in his use of analogy, he is, it is to be feared, equally careless in his use of terms. Science has but one method of procedure, and that is invariable. It aims first, with a just and open mind, at the collection and correct observation of facts – of phenomena. It proceeds then to classify these phenomena into groups or series. Finally it endeavours to find a formula which shall explain all these facts, which shall be universally true for all the observed phenomena. Produce one instance where the formula fails and there is no science. A science must be universal or it cannot exist. Yet Captain Hart's system, as we have already shown, owes nothing, as far as we have been allowed to see, to the patient collection and examination of actual phenomena. On the contrary, it appears to be the result of pure theory unconnected with experience (Bond 1922: 158-159).

Liddell Hart's rebuttal misrepresents science as anything generalizable:

> To give one or two isolated experiences of my own or of others might be interesting, but from the point of view of serious scientific investigations affords no practical test.
>
> Colonel Bond is so anxious to find any stick to beat me with that, whilst in one place he calls for my personal experiences, in another he, rightly, points out that any science of tactics must be founded not on individual, or even on multitudinous personal experiences of any one time, but on universal experience as contained in history (1922e: 298-299).

He defines science with remote synonyms: analysis, reason, and sense-making.

> Thomas Huxley's definition is perhaps even better, that science is "organized common-sense...the rarest of all the senses" (!) (1922e: 298-302).

He used the semantic frame "science" just as he uses "theory," "logic," and "truth" – to intimidate. His disputes with Fuller are characteristic. Fuller genuinely studied the sciences, although he too over-reached in his claims to be scientific. Fuller tended to withdraw from confrontation, but nevertheless publicly separated from Liddell Hart's (1921a: 2) "simple and scientific tactical [family] tree."

> It may be possible to establish such a science, personally I do not consider it feasible, for though I believe in a science of war, I consider that tactics are the application of this science to the ever-changing conditions of active operations (Fuller 1923b: 61).

Liddell Hart used the semantic frame "science" to mean also the process of research, the development of technology, and even progress in general. For instance, in writing about the future of warfare, Liddell Hart emphasizes "scientific discovery" and "scientific invention," but synonymizes progress.

> Scientific invention, on the other hand, is concerned with the evolutionary development of the powers and properties which are already known to us (1924a: 90).

He goes on to promise "a scientific means of test," "a compass or test-tube for military thought," and "a means of test for military truth," but does not define, specify, or operationalize any of these things (1924a: 91).

Increasingly, he uses "science" interchangeably with "truth" (1925: 16; 1926: 34, 129). He idealizes objectivity and "the solitary research of some individual, whose mind is able to investigate unfettered by the mental grooves characteristic of all types of corporate institution" (1927b: 183). "Most people" are not objective, he claims, epitomized by soldiers (1932c: 8; 1932d: 595; 1933c: 146, 171; 182; 1935a: 300; 1938e: 272; 1939a: 127; 1939b: 10).* He complains that the "uncertainty of war" is "aggravated by its unscientific study." Hypocritically, he adds that "war is a science which depends on art for its application," without defining either science or art (1932c: 99; 1935a: 84). In April 1935, he wrote the following note, which he

---

* "Scientific" is his strongest compliment. For instance, Gustavus Adolphus (1594-1632) "stands out among the Great Captains as a scientific army organizer" (1935a: 268).

eventually slipped into neglected publications.

> Those who have progressed furthest in exploration of war realize that its scientific study has barely begun. They will also be the least inclined to venture upon detailed predictions. Confident prophecy is best left to Generals, who as a class have a traditional fondness for it, and as prophets have no reputation to lose. We have only to recall some of their prophecies that stand on record.
>
> There is doubtless a science of war: but we are a long way from discovering it. Apart from the mere technique of utilizing weapons, what passes for "military science" is hardly more than the interpretation of conventions nurtured by tradition and warped by sentiment, patriotic and professional (LH 11/1935/73; 1937b: 277; 1944a: 24).

In an American magazine, he reviewed a book on "future warfare" with the caveat that the subject "requires examination by scientific students of war" (1936b: 687). Two US Army officers objected.

> It is, however, a far cry from the admittedly great changes in methods, in the application of principles, which new weapons now as ever in the past have occasioned, to the contentions of the new "scientific school" of military writers which has sprung up since the war – the school which we have mentioned above in connection with the power of the defensive. This school emphasizes above all else the importance of weapons, of means of transportation and communication, of what they call "scientific warfare." They even write of a "New Science of War." As we have already stated, there is no such thing as a science of war…It is this moral element, the human element, the man who is the foundation of all armies, that those ignore who speak of weapons of material things as having created a new "science of war" (Dupuy and Eliot 1937: 37, 40).

Liddell Hart doubled down. He pretended that his current book on current armies is the first "scientific" study.

> Those who have studied war the most cannot avoid becoming acutely conscious that the exploration of war as a scientific subject has scarcely been begun (1937b: 169, 200).

A recipient of a gratis copy was unconvinced: "his own examination of problems is not really scientific, but is swayed too much by his catchwords" (Ridley Pakenham-Walsh, diary, 26 March 1937, LHCMA Pakenham-Walsh).

By January 1939, Liddell Hart was challenged by the gap between real trends and his expectations (see Chapters 12 to 15). Liddell Hart pretended that popular realization of real trends is "wishful thinking," "the desire to suit our conclusions to our interests," or "the habit – on all sides – of saying something less, or something more, than we know to be true." He claims to have spent "the post-war era… studying war scientifically…in the spirit, and with the method, of the scientist – whose predominant interest is to discover the truth" (1939b: 9-11).

Discredited by the course of the Second World War, he shot back that "any scientific student of war is labelled a 'pessimist'" (1940c: 182). He offered "the scientific attitude of compete detachment from any preferences" (1940d: 222). He falsely claimed to have predicted the fall of Poland thanks to "the scientific method in studying the evidence" (1941a: 190). He described himself as one of the "serious students of war" – "a military scientist," "applying the scientific method to the study of war" (1942a: 9-10). Even after Britain's victory, he claimed that British military training is "unscientific," and requires a "military elite," a "corps of scientists," to guide everybody else (1946b: 91).

Liddell Hart persuaded Luvaas (1964: 395) that "history serves also as a scientific basis for theory," but they seem to be mistaking inductions for science. Adrian (1972: 2) recalled his father as "scientific in his approach to causes," but also seems to mistake inductions for science. John Mearsheimer, a Professor of Political Science, but methodologically a historian, described Liddell Hart as a "social scientist," just because he made "generalizations" (1988: 10), but "generalizations" are not sufficient to make a scientist.

Michael Howard (1999: vi) quoted Liddell Hart's claim to "a purely scientific spirit" as evidence for "a supreme rationalist, a child of the Enlightenment who would have been more at home in the age of Newton and of Voltaire." Similarly, Brian Holden Reid (1998: 6) declared that "Fuller and Liddell Hart believed first and foremost in the power of reason." However, believing is not the same as achieving. Brian Bond (1977: 56, 112), to his credit, admitted that "Liddell Hart's approach to history was intuitive and eclectic rather than, as he liked to believe, 'scientific.'" Danchev (1998b: 33; 1999a: 31) admitted that he should "not be seen as a scholar or a scientist," but rather an "artist."

Retired Brigadier Shelford Bidwell (1973: 212) characterized Liddell Hart's and Fuller's "sciences of war" as "anti-science."

> The feeling grows after patient study of the great masters – of Clausewitz, Liddell Hart, Sun Tzu, Mao, and Fuller – that they are all saying the same thing over and over again in different words, and that much of it is obvious…This is why professional soldiers have a rooted objection to theorists and to theories concerning the successful prosecution of war. They are also shy of the word "science." When soldiers talk about "science" they really mean weapon technology. They do not consider that warfare has any controlling laws in the sense that natural phenomena are controlled by laws or that phenomena recur according to pattern (Bidwell 1973: 2-3).

In itself, not being a scientist is no dishonour, but claiming to be a scientist while ignoring the scientific process is at best inaccurate.

Truth-Seeker

Liddell Hart explicitly sought "truth," but also was governed by certain biases, prejudices, and vanities. His rebuttal of Colonel Bond sets the pattern of a lifetime.

> The object of all of us, I hope, is to get at the truth which lies hidden behind the mass of facts and theories. Unprovoked violence is scarcely a helpful method of criticism…I had hoped for some really helpful criticism which would take us a further measure towards the common goal of all students of war – truth (1922e: 297).

This illustrates several mischaracterizations: written criticism as "violent attack," personal observations as facts, and facts as masks of truths. Facts are truths. He seems to be conflating data, which are not necessarily facts (Newsome 2016: 259).

His observations are unstable, as best illustrated by his sycophancy towards the principals of the Great War, until the late 1920s (see Chapter 5), his confidence in offensives, until 1930 (see Chapters 7 and 8), and his enthusiasm for international legalism, until 1931, when he invented a unilateral "British way in warfare." He rationalized his U-turn as conflict between truth and influence.

> The men who have influenced thought by their words, especially their written words, are engraved more deeply in history and remembered better in proportion to their numbers than the host of conquerors and kings, of statesmen and commercial magnates (note, 7 June 1932, LHCMA AJLH 4).

Liddell Hart's prioritization of influence contrasts with Fuller's confidence in truth without influence.

> I have never attempted to make an appeal to the people in order to gain a following. It amuses me to state what I believe to be true, but whether my audience understands or not I do not much care, because truth in the end wins through (Fuller to LH, 27 March 1923, LH 1/302).

Unlike Fuller, the men Liddell Hart admired most were exquisitely self-serving influencers. He corresponded for years with Lloyd George and Lawrence, in hope of biographing them, before they agreed to meet. Lloyd George waited until September 1932, when Lloyd George wanted help with his memoirs. Lawrence waited until December 1933, when Liddell Hart spent hours trying to disentangle the contradictions and evasions in Lawrence's correspondence. As they exited their lunch venue, Liddell Hart stressed his "desire to get at the root of things," but Lawrence pointed to a match-seller and said, "If you let the passion for truth grow upon you like this, you'll finish by selling matches in the Strand" (1938g: 202).

After publishing his biography of Lawrence, a second edition of his history of the Great War, and more controversial opinions about the Army's annual manoeuvres, Liddell Hart rationalized himself as a misunderstood peace-maker.

> To me, it seems that the best hope of curtailing war lies in promoting the search for objective truth – the truth about war in all its aspects. Most important of all is a scientific study of its causes – some day, I hope, we shall provide the means of undertaking a research that has hardly begun (note, November 1934, LH 11/1934/53; 1944a: 38).

A month later, during a dispute with his employer about compensation, he rationalized himself as a tortured prophet.

> The thought of the part that the "prophets" had played in human history suggests that there may be an ultimate practical value in proclaiming unreservedly the truth that one sees…But at least he avoids the more common fault of leaders, that of sacrificing truth to expediency without ultimate advantage to the truth (note, 20 December 1934, LH 11/1934/32; 1954a: 19; 1967: 19-20).

In 1936, disappointed with the unreceptiveness of a new CIGS (Cyril Deverell), he again painted himself as a maverick truth-seeker.

> Yet I am not a natural critic – only a faculty of seeing things clearly and a compulsion to state honestly what I see. Indeed, I have constantly to reproach myself for not stating them more honestly. This glance back helps me to realize the prizes that were open if only I could have been a little more "tactful" – a euphemism for dishonesty (note, 28 July 1936, LH 11/1936/16).

In the next month, he complains that "people assume that no training is needed in the pursuit of truth." At best, his "training" is self-disciplined objectivity: "to detach his *thinking* [original emphasis] from every desire and interest, from every sympathy and antipathy." He developed this claim into the conclusion to a book, which contrasts his "honesty" with elite "expediency" – which he blames for bad "policy" (1938e: 370, 363; 1944a: 105). Ultimately, his "honesty" is (ironically) subjective: "Truth may be hard to attain, as we all know; but the best chance of approaching it lies in consistent care to avoid untruth" (1939b: 11).

Adrian admitted that his father "felt strongly about personal friendships and loyalties, transcending other loyalties, and this led him on occasions to disregard interests – and facts" (letter, 18 August 1988, Crawford 1998: 72, 213). Bond (1977: 3, 38, 84) observed that he "was a tireless advocate of independent judgment in the pursuit of truth," but his "obsession with the Army's hostility to 'the truth' was lacking in proportion," and his "conception of truth was to some extent limited and subjective."* O'Neill (1990: 109) admitted similar, but blamed over-work and isolation. Danchev admitted "his best ideas were other people's, made matchlessly his own" (1998b: 33; 1999a: 31), and his "hypotheses ruled his proofs" (1999b: 332).

Arguer

Aged 25 years, Liddell Hart already saw himself as a great arguer.

> Very good in argument, always being quick to seize the weak points in my opponents' case and turn them to success. Normally lazy, but when the mood or the need comes ready to use up my last ounce. Model my life in all matters on the two tactical principles of Economy of Force and Security. Inclined to be selfish and think of myself first, and yet often going to the other extreme. A peaceful and philosophic temperament, but when really roused, become almost blind with rage, though I never completely let myself get out of hand. Generally thinking ahead of the immediate present. Always write on any subject, particularly military, with one eye on the historian of the future.†

> One thing I can put on record, and that is that in all my meetings and

---

* Later, Bond (1998: 427) admitted that although "Liddell Hart laid great stress on the need for dispassionate analysis yet his own vision was coloured by nostalgic wishful thinking."
† In 1929, he appended a note claiming that he had "meant enabling an historian to trace the process of thought." However, this same note doubles down: "I had become conscious that my ideas were likely to have an important effect in shaping future events."

arguments with the pick of our Regular soldier brains, I have been able to out-argue and out-think them, fine as they were, and have been conscious that mentally my brain was both deeper, clearer, and more agile than those I have encountered (December 1920, LH 7/1920/32).

By 1928, he abandoned "modesty – which I despise as a hindrance to truth." This was convenient to a dispute with Fuller about influence and credit.

You seem to be lacking in receptiveness, and often as unwilling to recognise other points of view as are your opponents (to Fuller, 11 March 1928, LH 1/302/128).

In person, he could seem either intimidating or maddening – depending, mostly, on the other's disposition. Storm Jameson was favourably disposed, given shared interests in disarmament.

My one rational human being…I believe he respects the rights even of fools. Certainly he only recognizes two sins – cruelty and intellectual dishonesty. One of his most disconcerting traits is the mental flexibility which allows him to think an opponent's thoughts for him (1969: II, 93).

Stylistically, he could be pleasing and enlightening, but also evasive and superficial. Sometimes he engaged in outright Sophistry: he used suggestion, shifty terms, reinterpretations, flattery, diversion, high-mindedness, intimidation, and name-drops to disarm sceptics. He plagiarized, joined the consensus after events as if he had known all along, tilted at supposed orthodoxy and conservatism, and promoted himself as the inspired solution. Simultaneously, he kept his prescriptions so vague that he could never be wrong – except by degree. He would reinterpret what he had written, and characterize criticism as misinterpretation. He became the master of misleading framings, such as a paper entitled "The Need for a New Technique of War" – actually an urging to negotiate peace, days after the outbreak of the Second World War (8 September 1939, LH 1939/100).

From 1954, Michael Howard (2006: 155) observed that Liddell Hart was "at once a monster of egocentricity and one of the kindest people I have ever met." In the 1960s, Robert O'Neill (1990: 112) observed his "vanity." John P. Campbell (2000: 458) observed that he "took himself very seriously indeed and was unusually resistant to criticism." Brian Bond (1977: 228) observed that he "was rather naively vulnerable to flattery." "[U]nashamedly egocentric, he liked to win a point and make converts to his way of thinking, but he would accept failure philosophically[,] provided the usual courtesies were maintained" (1977: 7). He "relished intellectual discussion and controversy," and "liked people to stand up to him in argument" (1977: 3), but "few were spared from his scathing sarcasm" (2015: 32). Bond's student Alex Danchev (1998b: 33), confirmed his "monumental egocentricity," while Howard's student Azar Gat (2000: 1) confirmed he was "egocentric and vain."

Lecturer

Liddell Hart preferred lonely writing to real-world exposure. With Maxse's protection, he "lectured" to the Royal United Service Institution and the School of Military Engineering from 1920 to 1921. Maxse did not allow questions at the time, but rebuttals arrived by letter. Liddell Hart preferred written counter-rebuttals, until 1931, when he lectured on his "British Way in Warfare" to military audiences, at the invitation of sympathetic commanders. However, he developed subsequent editions without public speaking. Alarmed by the war scare of September 1938, he undertook a rash of public lectures, against Britain's rearmament and alliances, until a breakdown in June 1939. His next speaking tour was in America in 1952. His second foreign speaking tour was in Israel in 1960. In 1965, he agreed to lecture to the University of California Davis, but quit between the quarter in which he wrote the lectures and the quarter in which he was to start delivering (see Chapter 19).

As a public speaker, he read from a script. He became most nervous when asked questions. With his left hand, he wielded a pipe that he did not smoke but repeatedly lit with his right hand. Margaret Storm Jameson (1969: II, 94) was in the audience in 1938: "One has to listen with desperate attention to hear what he says in his low rapid voice." In 1960, he started his lecture to the Israeli Staff College by sitting in stunned silence, until an officer with experience of the same situation in England brought whiskey, disguised in a tea cup. Refilled several times, Liddell Hart spoke for an hour, but not eloquently (Unterseher 2023: 85-86).

> A gold watch chain decorates his waistcoat, a pipe never moves from his mouth, and he speaks – but that's a story in itself – he swallows every word, skips half a sentence and finally – repeats himself...The story is told that somebody once suggested to a Defence Minister in one of the western states that he invite Liddell Hart as a military adviser. "In the atomic age, that's impossible," the Minister answered. "By the time I've understood what he's advising me to do, we'll already have lost the war" (newspaper cutting, March 1960, LH 13/80).

Correspondent

Liddell Hart preferred to communicate privately by letter. Letters, in fact, were the means by which he received most of his primary sources, including leaked official documents. His own archive preserves nearly 1,000 correspondents.

Brian Bond (1977: 3) reports his letters as "cool, dispassionate – almost clinical," but Mearsheimer (1988: 59) found "a formidable intellect and a skilful debater," an energetic, indiscreet "gossip" (who accused others of "gossip"), and a dishonest self-advocate. Brian Holden Reid (1998: 150) characterized Mearsheimer's finding as a "polemic" and a misrepresentation, but admits Liddell Hart's self-interested correspondence with Robert Graves, for instance. Azar Gat (2000: 1) confirmed that Liddell Hart "misleadingly presented" himself in letters and notes-to-self.

Tolerator

Tolerance is the acceptance of something to which one is subjected. Liddell Hart saw himself as tolerant. His mentees validated his tolerance. However, as we have seen, he could be vicious in disputes, and was prejudiced against women, seniors, professional soldiers, conservatives, and Britons in general (at least in comparison with the French).

In January 1914, he described himself as "tactful and diplomatic." However, his list ends: "slightly indolent." By November, he embraced "the supremacy of the aristocracy of race (and birth)," and "acquired rather a contempt" for scholars,

Germans, and women (LH 7/1913/13; LH 7/1914/10). In December 1920, in his first of year of influence on doctrine (see Chapter 7), he described himself as

> Original in ideas, with no prejudices of any kind. Very sympathetic and keen to understand other people's point of view – to which I owe my ability to handle men. Very generous, in fact foolishly so...Extremely broad minded (7/1920/32).

Yet, within a year he mischaracterized Colonel Bond's argument as *ad hominem*, before launching a vicious *ad hominem* attack (1922e: 297). Later in the same year, he mischaracterized his critics as old, conservative, military, and British. From there, he realized prejudices against fellow journalists and commoners (1923a: 320). His prejudice against journalists was tempered by promotion to full-time journalism, in 1925. His prejudice against commoners was in tension with his prejudices against military and conservative elites. His prejudices were acute by 1930, but not credible: years earlier, he had been published by national newspapers and presses, advised international lawyers, Generals, and ministers, and reached middle age.

Adrian learned the hypocrisy in 1930, when bullied at his first boarding school, for a slight cockney accent (derived from his governess).

> My first humiliation was particularly unfortunate as my parents, largely tolerant in my upbringing, were soon concerned to repress any incipient symptoms of class-consciousness or snobbishness. Class, indeed, came to have a similar connotation to sex and I had to be careful to avoid certain phrases or references before I realized their significance (1953: 16-17).

From 1937, Storm Jameson (1969: II. 93) found that he "is governed, or governs himself, by an extreme distaste for the human vices of intolerance and prejudice." Adrian fairly recalled his father as "a humane man who believed that human beings, in possession of the facts and undistorted by prejudice, could work out fair solutions for their common problems, based on moderation" (1972: 3).*

Bond (1977: 3, 9, 275) described Liddell Hart's "philosophy of life" as "humanitarian idealism," "embracing the precepts of willingness to compromise, to limit effort in proportion to the goal, and to practice restraint, moderation[,] and tolerance." Adrian had described his father's beliefs rather than practices, but Bond ignored the difference. He recalled Liddell Hart as "remarkably tolerant towards divergent views irrespective of the age or status of the person." "[H]is correspondence files prove that he rarely broke off a relationship out of pique, impatience or intolerance." Yet Bond contradicts himself. "It is curious that Liddell Hart's humanitarian feelings were seldom explicitly expressed in his writings."

Mearsheimer (1988: 156) found "no instance I know of in his massive files where he speaks disparagingly of anyone because of religion, race, or ethnic background. He was in that regard a tolerant and decent man." However, he "had very traditional views about women," and held Britain to higher standards than Germany during the Second World War. Danchev (1998a: 66) described Liddell Hart as "generally unprejudiced, and usually magnanimous," except towards elders, senior

---

* Adrian appears to paraphrase how his father (1965: I, 4-5) described his grandfather, whose qualities begin with "tolerance" and "freedom from prejudice," and end with "a knack of making people behave better by assuming that they were on the way to become better."

officers, women, and Britons as a whole.

However, Reid (1998: 173) admitted that "Liddell Hart could also be arrogant and offensive." John Terraine pointed out "a reverse side: a vindictive malice with which he pursued selected targets, especially when his deep vanity was touched. As one who incurred this malice [for rebutting his presentation of the Great War], I merely record that he could be kind, and set it to his credit" ("Liddell Hart: A Reassessment," The Daily Telegraph, 25 August 1977, in Bond 2018: 125).

Theorist

Liddell Hart often claimed theoretical reasons for his conclusions and recommendations, but he did not use the semantic frame correctly. A theory is an argument used to explain facts (Newsome 2016: 203-204). Liddell Hart used "theory" interchangeably with "strategy," "doctrine," "thought," and "philosophy."*

His arguments to explain facts are broad and deep, but also over-reduced and -generalized. Reductionism usefully makes issues or concepts more manageable, but should not be an end in itself. Rather, it should be a step towards communicating or analysing the subject's true complexity. Otherwise, reductionism ends in fallacies, such as incrementalism. While working as an Army trainer and educator, he used reductionism properly as a means to an end. In December 1920, he wrote of "a very clear analyzing brain, not very retentive or persistent, but fond of getting down to the root of everything and then crystallizing and simplifying it into a clear framework" ("Some personal impressions," LH 7/1920/32). By the 1930s, his reductionism was undisciplined and agenda-driven, such as his reduction of Britain's interests to avoidance of war (see Chapters 12 to 14).

He tended to over-generalization too. Generalization is the process of taking lessons from one case for a population of cases. This is justifiable if the case is representative of the population (Newsome 2016: 174), but he reflected a preferred case on to a population. Worse, he generalized from personal experience. For instance, when he first wrote to Fuller, he claimed "that we are only two, so far as I am aware, who have taken the obvious and simple, and therefore the truest line of deduction, that of working upwards from personal combat with the naked hands" (to Fuller, 14 June 1920, LH 1/302). Within months, he concluded a lecture similarly:

> Thus we see that by working out our principles of tactics upwards from the elementary, instead of downwards from the complexities of large operations, we can simplify infantry tactics to a flexible framework of clear principles which are applicable to all forms of action (1921a: 20; 1921c: 223).

Over-generalization is appealing in politics, where it is used to justify minority interests and choices as if majoritarian. Samuel Hoare, a high-flying politician (whom Liddell Hart contacted in 1925), recalled his "un-English gift of generalization." Mearsheimer (1988: 10) concluded that his theories were "generalizations."

---

* For an early instance, see his casual conflation of "Napoleonic theory," "doctrine," "military thought," and "military mind," from the Napoleonic Wars through the Great War (1925: 4-14). Brian Bond (1977: 59) perpetuated Liddell Hart's mischaracterization of his theories and histories as "philosophy."

Bidwell (1970: 61-63) more accurately categorized them as abstractions.

> We can see Liddell Hart as a thinker in the tradition of [Charles] Darwin, T.H. Huxley, [Karl] Marx[,] or [Sigmund] Freud. He resembles the last two more closely because, like theirs, his theories are abstract, often arrived at intuitively and based on a highly individual reading of history (1973: 214).

Brian Bond admitted the abstractions, aggregations, and self-plagiarisms.

> This habit of endless overlaying and repetition (of "interweaving" as he euphemistically called it) was probably in part necessary to earn a living, but it often irritated his reviewers (1977: 53).

Two of Bond's students agreed:

> Liddell Hart's books were very often rehabilitations, not to say recyclings, rounded up and hitched loosely to the wagon of a highly developed idea... His oeuvre is not so much an oeuvre as an aggregation, and very often (too often) a repetition (Danchev 1998a: 78, 253).
>
> Fundamentally, Liddell Hart, like Jomini, had only one idea and spent his entire life, repeating, reformulating, and inflating it (Reid 1999: 70).

Logician

Liddell Hart and disciples made high-minded claims about "logic" that they never defined (for instance; Luvaas 1964: 395; 1990: 18). Logic is an argument whose propositions guarantee a conclusion. He used only one term associated with logic – "deduction," but he (like the fictional Sherlock Holmes) used it to mean "implication" or "inference," rather than a proposition guaranteed from its premises. At best, what he called "deductions" might be "inductions" (propositions derived from observations). Some arguments are internally contradictory (his propositions contradict each other). Some are circular (he offers premises as conclusions, or offers the same observations as both inductions and evidence). Relatedly, he mischaracterized historical inference as "pure reasoning"* (January 1914, LH 7/1913/13; 1932c: 201; 1935a: 175; Newsome 2016: Chapter 7).

When critics pointed out his formal fallacies, he would claim their formal fallacies, and commit informal fallacies – especially *argumentum ad hominem*.

> Colonel Bond's criticisms were so violent in tone that he could scarcely have complained if I had counter-attacked in similar style. Let me however suggest in conclusion, that it is always a pity when any searcher after truth quits the path of dispassionate and logical constructive argument in order to abuse a fellow searcher (1922e: 308).

He was first exposed to the principles of logic in 1923, when Fuller sent drafts of what was eventually published as *The Foundations of the Science of War*, although

---

* Thus, Luvaas (1964: 395) misreported the "man-in-the-dark" and "expanding torrent" doctrines as "formulated...by...inductive reasoning." In fact they are deduced from analogies.

Fuller was not a reliable logician. Liddell Hart did not refer to logic in his many comments on the drafts, or when reviewing the publication in 1926. Nevertheless, two years later, during an unrelated dispute, he accused Fuller of inferior logic.

> I have come to the conclusion that your conceptions owe less to logical processes than to inspiration, and that you are apt to use the former in a subsequent stage to explain the latter...I find confirmation...in your own imperviousness to argument (to Fuller, 11 March 1928, LH 1/302/128).

He deployed the same hypocrisy against soldiers and politicians. Take his report on a Parliamentary debate about "air control" in 1930.

> Instead of logical argument there was too evidently an unyielding determination to maintain sectional service interests without regard to the general interests of the country (1932c: 139; 1935a: 125).

He deployed the accusation most viciously against critics. Take his reaction to criticism of his unsound proposal to replace cavalry horses with tankettes.

> It is characteristic of human nature to shrink from pitiless logic, and characteristic also to cling to an old friend which may have an occasional value for an exceptional purpose (1932c: 226; 1935a: 200).

Yet when convenient, he criticized others for relying on logic. His most spectacular home goal is to criticize Carl von Clausewitz for being "carried away by his passion for pure logic." He did not realize that Clausewitz used the dialectic (which is non-logical) to synthesize a concept from two opposing concepts. For instance, Clausewitz conceptualized "absolute war" in opposition to "friction" and other things, but Liddell Hart misinterpreted "absolute war" as Clausewitz's ideal (1925: 12). Liddell Hart himself used the dialectic, without apparently realizing he was doing so (1952: 5; 1954a: 354).

Operations Researcher

Liddell Hart often used mathematics fallaciously. For instance, he estimated the future lives lost to bombing by multiplying the lives lost to bombing in the Great War by the proportionate growth in the number of aircraft, without accounting for defences (1925: 39, 42, 82-83; 1932c: 140-146). He even used the words incorrectly, such as his use of the semantic frame "infinite" as a superlative, as in: "the infinite value of surprise" (1930b: 390);* and "an infinitesimal fraction" (1950: 94).

Bad mathematics aside, he did not engage mathematical military analysis. Nevertheless, in 1960 he claimed credit for "operations research." Operations research (or "operational research") has no consistent definition. Today, military operations research (MOR) is characterized as mathematical, analytical, or practical (although a characterization does not make a definition). A definition from the intelligence community is: "a method of objectively comparing alternative means of achieving a goal, or alternative means of solving a problem, and selecting an optimum choice" (Clark 2020: 268). Militaries have always attempted this. Although their methods

---

* This is contradicted in the same book by his statement that German offensive "success was almost in mathematical ratio to their degree of surprise" (1930b: 415).

vary, their roots are statistical. British and US military services formed statistical sections in the 1800s. These sections administered acquisitions and supplies. Soon they were assessing requirements and operations. The British Army's General Staff formed a Directorate of Military Intelligence (DMI) in 1888, formed a Directorate of Military Operations (DMO) in 1904, and grouped them as a Directorate of Military Operations & Intelligence (DMO&I) in 1922. Also in 1904, the General Staff formed a Directorate of Staff Duties (DSD), initially to administer the Staff. Soon DSD researched force structure and employment. DSD directed training too, from 1907 until 1927, when the Directorate of Military Training was re-established.

Liddell Hart never understood what these departments did, partly because, by the time he dealt with the War Office, in the 1920s, he had already dismissed it as incompetent and conservative. In 1924, he proposed a "tactical research department," even though DSD already fulfilled tactical research. In 1960, he spun his proposal of 1924 as an "operational research department." He claimed to be "one of the early advocates of what is called operational research – the application of the scientific method of inquiry to the study of warfare." Later in 1960, he told an interviewer that his friend Frederick "Tim" Pile was the source of this claim. Five years later, the claim was published under Pile's name, in a book partly edited by Liddell Hart. In this narrative, Liddell Hart proposes an operational research department in 1924, the incoming CIGS (George Milne) agrees in 1925, but the War Department cannot fund it when Milne takes over the General Staff in 1926. At least one correspondent took this narrative "with a grain of historical salt" (1924c: 49; 1960a: 252; Walters 1961: 22; Pile 1965: 173, 176-177; Higham 1966: 86).

In the 1930s, Liddell Hart proposed to abolish the military academies (in favour of civilian universities) and to establish a "research department of the General Staff." In May 1937, the Minister for Co-ordination of Defence (Thomas Inskip) asked for a paper on restructuring the Army. Liddell Hart responded that civilian universities and a research department of the General Staff would produce civilian graduates and military officers able to "analyse scientifically."

> They ought to be given time to think them out, to explore the data, to collect the data by going [a]round the Army to consult people instead of merely relying on War Office files, and to work out the conclusions unhampered by time restrictions. The way that decisions are reached on questions of organization, tactics, etc., from inadequate knowledge, is farcically unscientific ("Measures to Improve the Officers' Situation in the Army," 31 May 1937, LH 11/1937/67).

His alternative is data-driven, but otherwise does not fulfill operations research.

In August, the new Defence Secretary (Leslie Hore Belisha) asked for more papers on these proposals. In September, Liddell Hart suggested a "Directorate of Military Research or Military Studies." His suggestion sounds like DSD, although his proposals are as vague in 1937 as in 1924. In November, he proposed to replace DSD with a "Directorate of Military Research (examination of experience, forecast of future trends[,] and suggestion of experiments)." Simultaneously, he colluded in a purge of the General Staff. The beneficiaries were not so ambitious: the DCIGS (Ronald Adam) added to DMI a section to research future trends, with just two officers. In memoirs, and in hearsay to disciples, Liddell Hart misrepresents the section as an "operational research department," and takes the credit (note, 17 August 1937, and letter, 24 November 1937, LH 11/1937/67; 1939b: 343, 348; 1965: II, 12, 61, 83; Luvaas 1964: 411; Pile 1965: 178).

In late 1938, John Desmond Bernal (1901-1971), Professor of Physics at Birkbeck College, University of London, shared a paper entitled "Science and National Defence." The paper concerns hard and applied sciences, as Liddell Hart acknowledges by reply. However, in 1960 he archived it in a file labelled "operational research." In memoirs, he mischaracterizes his reply as "extending such research to the operational field," and claims that this reply stimulated operational research in the Air Ministry and the War Department during the Second World War (LH 15/5/191; 1965: II, 105-109, 185-186).

In fact, the momentum started before 1938. One mover was a second Professor of Physics, Patrick M.S. Blackett. Another was a chemist, Sir Henry Tizard. In 1935, Tizard had invited Blackett to join the Aeronautical Research Committee. Its focus was research towards anti-aircraft capabilities, given requirements drawn up by the Committee for the Scientific Survey of Air Defence (which Tizard had chaired since 1933). The best-known product is radar. In September 1939, Tizard helped to set up two Royal Air Force Operational Research Sections, at Coastal Command and Fighter Command respectively. In August 1940, Blackett set up the first Army Operational Research Section, at Anti-Aircraft Command. The Section was not as novel as Liddell Hart would portray it in 1960: it recruited from the War Department's Air Defence Experimental Establishment, whose antecedents date back to 1917. The second and third sections were formed in June 1942 (for the armoured and artillery arms respectively), the eighth by February 1943, when they were placed under an Army Operational Research Group. By 1944, six new sections were attached to operational commands overseas (Swann 1945; McCloskey 1987).

In memoirs, however, Liddell Hart claims that he had given Blackett the idea verbally – in 1942! In this story, he proposes operational research to Archibald Rowlands (then the top civil servant in the Ministry of Aircraft Production), who urges his friend, the new War Secretary (James Grigg), to stand up an operations research department under Liddell Hart and Tizard, in February. In fact, Liddell Hart's archive proves that he and Rowlands did not discuss a new department until March, and this was specified as "scientific," not operational. In April, Rowlands revealed that senior soldiers and (thence) Grigg had blocked Liddell Hart's involvement. His archives provide no evidence that he communicated with Blackett until 1946. Nevertheless, his memoirs claim that within the same week he told the proposal to both Rowlands and Blackett. His memoirs do not admit that Blackett was then working for the Air Ministry. Later in 1942, Blackett joined the Admiralty as Director of Operational Research. Presumably, Liddell Hart misinterpreted or misrepresented Blackett's start at the Admiralty as the start of MOR too (notes, 18 March and 30 April 1942, LH 11/1942/14 and /30; 1965: I, 200; 1965: II, 185-186).

4
War hero

Liddell Hart was a self-described anti-militarist when he came of age. The outbreak of the Great War, and his near failure as an undergraduate of history, turned him into a militarist. Yet, as a regimental officer, he remained an outsider. This contributed to psychological fragility. Each rotation to the trenches ended in medical treatment, for which he gave inconsistent explanations. He was kept out of the first day of the offensive on the Somme, but often implied otherwise. He was evacuated from the next attack. He spent the rest of the war in England. From 1917 to 1918, he went through five billets in 12 months, before finding his calling as a drill master.

Anti-Militarist

Before the Great War, Liddell Hart was opposed to Britain's military. For one thing, he was Francophilic. He had been born in Paris, spent his happiest years there, and identified with its aesthete, philosophical culture more than Britain's muscular Christianity. A second explanation is his physical fragility, a third his psychological fragility. A boy of his class and generation would typically enrol in the local Boy Scouts, drill with his school's cadet corps, and play military games. No evidence appears in his records or memoirs for any of these. Aged 13 years, he failed the physical test for naval school. He took more interest in sports that year, but did not stick to any ("Notes for an Autobiography," LH 7/1920/38). Nevertheless, his memoirs claim that his interest in sports was actually a "tactical" interest (1965: I, 7-8). He persuaded Robin Higham (1966: 82) he was familiar with "tactics" before joining the army, having "played at military games as a youth." He persuaded Brian Bond (1977: 12) of "a precocious tactical interest in boyhood games."

Liddell Hart joined Cambridge University in October 1913. He ignored the Officer Training Corps, which then boasted hundreds of cadets. Trinity College Cambridge was distinguished by a Lectureship in Military Science (benefacted since 1912 by an alumnus – Sir Lees Knowles, 1857-1928). In its early years, serving soldiers were invited to deliver the annual lectures. Liddell Hart recorded no interest. His letters reveal that he resented sportsmen and intellectual inferiors, and preferred the company of Methodists and swots, but felt overwhelmed by work. More than 50 years later, when surveyed on "What I owe to Cambridge," he started with his tastes for food and wine (10 September 1965, LH 2W/181/1). Nevertheless, he persuaded Luvaas (1964: 377) that "he began seriously to study military history and tactics," and Brian Bond (1977: 14) that he was busy "studying military history and working out tactical problems," and "writing to magazines and newspapers about aeroplanes and sport."

Militarist

Once Britain definitely joined the war, Liddell Hart suddenly embraced militarism, to escape from a degree program that he might fail. He passed the Army's physical tests with the collusion of his examiners, particularly the test of eyesight. (He already wore spectacles, and wore spectacles in the field.) He refused the officer training course at Sandhurst (by then reduced to just three months) and petitioned for an immediate temporary commission. Since this could be achieved only though his university, he joined its Officer Training Corps in October, while worrying that the war would end before he could get to France.

His parents worried that he would fail physically. He reassured his mother that he was enjoying the training. He paraphrased a tutor's (Will Spens') remark that the Army "would be the making of us [six tutees] both physically and in character." In the next month, he repudiated his pre-war self as "a socialist, a pacifist, an anti-conscriptionist." Now, "[I[believe" in "compulsory military service" as a means towards "developing true manhood" (to his mother, October 1914, LH 7/1914/4; self-assessment, November, LH 7/1914/10).

He was gazetted on 7 December 1914, as a second-lieutenant in the King's Own Yorkshire Light Infantry. He spent the rest of the month in the regiment's short course for new infantry officers, and subsequent months in an administrative unit.

Outsider

Liddell Hart's war service remains foggy. He passed through many units, all of which were disbanded before the end of 1918, without complete war diaries. He saved few notes and records. His recollections are infrequent, vague, and contradictory. He did not make friends. His comrades and units did not record anything remarkable about him. He miscategorized them as peacetime professionals ("regulars"), even though most were wartime volunteers, like him.

> It is widely recognized that one of the greatest sources of friction in our armies during the Great War was the "superior" attitude of the regular soldier to his Territorial and New Army brethren.
>
> This air of superiority, based not so much on the former's consciousness of being better equipped with professional knowledge, but rather on the implied assumption that by virtue of being a Regular he must in consequence know more of war, gave rise to constant irritation (1923a: 318).

He blamed the regimental system too.

> The exceptional professional soldier…realizes that the advantage he may have from personal acquaintance with the difficulties and "friction" of military operations and movements and with the psychology of the time-serving soldiers of his particular Army is counterbalanced by the more independent mind of the civilian student of war, unfettered by years of military routine and the inevitable narrowing influence of a lifetime spent in the circumscribed sphere of army [life] and, worse still, of regimental life (1923a: 319).

He attended the first regimental reunion in 1928, but eschewed further reunions until 1946. He attended most energetically in the 1960s, coincident with the revived fashionability of his critique (see Chapter 5). The regiment was amalgamated in 1968. The regimental museum has no record of any correspondence or visit.

Psychological Fragility

By November 1914, soldiers in France were using the term "shell shock" as a euphemism for a spectrum of symptoms and conditions: psychological (such as nervousness), social (such as self-isolation), cognitive (such as indecisiveness), and physical (such as tremors). Today, the preferred terms include stress, trauma, post-traumatic stress disorder, and (given physical causes) traumatic brain injury.

"Shell shock" evokes a psychological response to exploding shells, although explosions are not necessary to the symptoms and conditions above. Liddell Hart's self-assessment of November 1914 reveals foreboding about explosions.

> I certainly believe that absolute peace is detrimental to true manhood, but 20th Century war is too frightful. If you could have war without its explosive horrors it would be a good thing (LH 7/1914/10).

Almost a year later, his rotation in the frontline confirmed his worst stressor. "During this first visit to France I found that I did not mind bullets at all, but disliked shells exceedingly" (autobiography, 1920, LH 7/1920/38).

Normally, soldiers help each other to manage stress, particularly given cohesion (the group's stick-togetherness). Such cohesion can develop early in the group's lifecycle, particularly given group challenges, such as collective training (Newsome 2003a; 2003b; 2007: chapter 4). However, Liddell Hart was alienated, did not record any training, did not stay long in any unit, was kept in reserve before operations, and rotated between hospitals and units during operations.

His service in France lasted ten months, during which he transferred between four units of his regiment. These units reserved him before each of three operations. He was sent into the front line four times,* and evacuated within days each time – finally in July 1916. One retrospective account, never quoted before now, realizes the theory of cohesion as stress-management, particularly what was later termed "vertical cohesion," although he never used the semantic frame. Here he refers to the "little compact group," formed in "training and recreation," under a known and respected leader. He gives the causes of breakdown as (in order) poor leadership, isolation, darkness, and gas shells.

> Infantry, led well, will forget self, will risk the sacrifice of their own lives by advancing to close with the enemy, but only so long as they feel that other troops are coming on to back them up. Men who are assigned to fill the van of an attack will only sacrifice themselves readily if they feel that their efforts will not be in vain. It is again the idea of isolation which undermines moral[e]...
>
> Fear is always worse when man is isolated; it is least prominent when following an example. This consideration points to the true cellule of

---

* One of Liddell Hart's self-biographies counts "two periods of service on the Western Front." Prior biographers count three rotations to the front, but are actually counting major battles or campaigns. They were likely anchored in Liddell Hart's own "last letter if killed on duty," in which he foresees going to the front for the third time. In fact, he rotated to the frontline twice in the third campaign: 1 to 3 July; and 16 to 19 July (last letter, 27 May 1916, LH 7/1916/8; Howard 1965: 373; Bond 1977: 17; Danchev 1998a: 47).

combat on which infantry tactics should be built up. The little compact group, formed of men who have long shared their training and recreation, following the leader it knows and who has trained it, is the ideal formation for battle…

The quality of personal example, which overcomes fear, is only felt by a handful of men, few enough to leef [leave?] the direct influence of their leader (1922c: 713, 718).

In a concurrent publication, he alludes to personal experience of shell shock.

There are two principal ways in which the control of the nerves can be upset: by the gradual and cumulative effect of a constant strain or by a sudden shock. A combination of these effects is the normal means. The anxiety and uncertainty of waiting for an enemy blow, the effect of shell fire by the ghastly sights it produces as equally by its concussive effect, the lack of invigorating sleep – all these causes combine to wear thin the will to resist (1922b: 459).

In a note to self, he admits he was "not physically brave" (December 1920, LH 7/1920/32). In reply to a fellow veteran of the fighting in France, he admits "panic."

[W]e also know, if we are honest with ourselves, that men were not always like they are pictured in heroic poems; that it is hard to keep up morale when men are tired, hungry[,] and sick; that it is worst of all when they cannot ease the strain by having someone to fight against; and that there are more than a few occasions when even "the men of England" suffered from panic like normal human beings, especially when suffering from shock and surprise and shaken by some intangible danger (to Lord Castlerosse, 23 April 1935, LH 13/31).

He was writing this in 1935, when his psychology was disturbed by accelerating international, familial, and professional troubles. Two years later, he admitted that "I know myself well enough to be quite aware that I am rather below, than above, the average in physical courage" (to General Edmund Ironside, 25 March 1937, LH 1/401). In the next year, he published another allusion to personal breakdown.

For the soldier who has had experience of war knows that the reality is so utterly different from the customary account that he may well shrink from being a pioneer in bridging the gap. He knows so well the strain on, and the frailty of, human nature, his own included, that he is inclined towards charity (1938e: 213-214).

His sensitivity to explosions is unenviable. Other soldiers could envy his luck to avoid direct fire. His luck or insensitivity encouraged his dismissal of "close quarter fights" as the stories of "imaginative soldiers." He imagined that "the real fighting soldier soon found that two sides did not cross bayonets in mortal conflict," because the "weaker broke and fled" (1925: 30).

Trenches, 1915

Liddell Hart's first year of war was peaceful and mostly spent in England. He should have enjoyed it, except that it fell within his forecast of either quick victory or slow disaster.

> If the war ends by Easter it will be a great thing for the virility and manhood of Europe. If it continues until Xmas 1915 it will be a disaster (November 1914, LH 7/1914/10).

A quick victory would have prevented his deployment to France, yet he did not seek to get to France as quickly as he sought a commission. He kept few official records for the year, so we know only that he was with an administrative unit. Years later, he would claim to have been offered "a staff job, which would have carried promotion." This is far-fetched. A peacetime officer would undertake a regimental rotation overseas, a regimental recommendation, some study, a test, and a promotion to Captain rank before his first staff job. The process took years, even in wartime (except within the units formed from conscripts in 1916). Liddell Hart would have needed two promotions within less than nine months of non-operational service. He claimed he "refused the offer…in order to seize the first chance of going out to France." This too is far-fetched. Officers could request to replace casualties in units already in France, even in other regiments ("Reflection," 23 April 1939, LH 11/1939/46).

Liddell Hart was deployed to the frontline in September 1915, more than a year after he had volunteered for the Army. He joined a quiet sector, along the River Ancre in Picardy. Within days, he wrote to reassure his parents. "So far I am thoroughly enjoying the experience and though one has to rough it far more than in England it reminds one most of a great picnic" (29 September 1915, LH 7/1915/27). His first history of the Great War confirms the ease.

> I can vouch for the fact that in the first months after the British had taken over this front it was possible for battalions to drill undisturbed on fields in full view of the German lines (1930b: 232).

Despite this ideal introduction to trench warfare, his first rotation ended after three weeks, with a two-week stay in hospital. A notebook, dated a year later, recalls "intestinal poisoning due to gas shell." A draft "autobiography" embellishes: "the only apparent cause was that the previous day in search of adventure near our trenches I had got into contact with the gases of an exploding shell" (LH 7/1916/2). This is the least likely of his explanations. The Germans had started firing gas shells in France in May, as preludes to offensives, on other fronts. Supplies remained low, and were not distributed to defensive sectors. Indeed, the notebook adds food poisoning as a cause. His memoirs add an unspecified "fever" (and postpone the exploding gas shell to July 1916, during his fourth and final rotation into the front).

> I was stricken by a sudden fever and carried off to hospital at Corbie. Next day I felt better and asked permission to go back to the battalion – which merely had the effect of convincing the staff that I must be really ill, so that despite my protests I was despatched, still on a stretcher, to the base hospital at Rouen. Here the same thing happened, and I had difficulty in persuading the doctors not to put me on a hospital-ship for home (1965: I, 14).

Liddell Hart persuaded Brian Bond (1977: 16; 2015: 30) of the above, but

Danchev (1998a: 48) admitted "several" accounts, and suggested that the fever was at least partly psycho-somatic.

Eager for action, or over-compensation, Liddell Hart requested transfer to a battalion already allocated to the Allied offensive around Ypres. He reached it in mid-November. His first duty was to lead a party of men carrying supplies through communication trenches to the forward defensive line, overnight. When the battalion shifted sector, he was sent, after dark, with a scratch platoon, into the second line. After dark the next day, they were withdrawn. He was carried away by stretcher. In a retrospective diary, he wrote of a shell fragment falling into a dugout "within a few inches of me." He wrote to his parents that "only dirt hit me. The shock however shook me up a good bit and burst blood vessels in my nose, causing frequent nose-bleeding for 24 hours." In memoirs, "dirt" becomes "sandbags"; the near-miss from a fragment becomes a hit from sandbags; and shock to the nose becomes concussion to the brain.

> Although feeling very groggy, with bouts of nose-bleeding and vomiting, I went up to the forward trenches again with the company on the following night, but became worse and was carried back when darkness came again, the next day. I remember enough to recall that lying helpless on a stretcher under fire was far more frightening than when mobile on one's feet and able to take cover (1965: I, 15-16).

He persuaded Bond (1977: 16; 2015: 30) that "he was concussed by a shell exploding above the doorway of a shallow dugout in which he was sheltering." However, neither a nosebleed nor a concussion is sufficient to explain why he convalesced in England for more than three months. Danchev (1997: 73; 1998a: 50-51) concluded, given conversations with his second wife, that likely he had broken down psychologically, while feeling lonely and exposed in the dark.

Somme, 1916

After three months of convalescence, he was posted to his regiment's training battalion, still in England, in February 1916. In June, he was posted to yet another battalion of his regiment, this time in France, with promotion to Lieutenant (backdated to April 1915) and to second-in-command of a company. (The company was short of officers. Normally, its second-in-command should rank Captain.) The unit reserved him at the battalion's rear HQ, while the companies attacked on the first day of what became known as the Battle of the Somme (1 July). In later years, he commented on that day more than any other, sometimes as if to suggest presence.

> From my own experience I have discovered that "the men" are capable of more intelligent action than their leaders often give them credit for. On the Somme, in 1916, when the serried waves imposed by authority broke down under machine-gun fire, the men often coalesced into natural groups and settled German machine-gun nets by manoeuvre (1922e: 300).

The biography that accompanied his first tour of America states that "he participated in the fierce fighting of the battle of the Somme" (1956b: 2). He persuaded two American historians that he had "served much of the First World War in the front-line trenches with the King's Own Yorkshire Light Infantry," until "severely wounded" (Icks 1952: 25; Higham 1966: 46). By contrast, his memoirs admit to feeling "lucky" to "being out of the initial assault" (1965: I, 23).

In the afternoon, he was one of five reserve officers sent from rear unit HQs to Brigade HQ. That night, Brigade HQ sent them forward to a battalion whose commander and company commanders had been killed. The most senior, oldest, and experienced subaltern (Lance Spicer) took command. At some point, Liddell Hart decided that Spicer was not within his rights. In 1931, he told the novelist Bernard Newman that he had commanded a battalion.* In the 1960s, he persuaded Luvaas (1965: 377) and Bond (1977: 17) of the same. His memoirs slyly transfer this claim to a "neighbouring battalion [that] had no officers left" (1965: I, 22). Danchev (1997: 77-78; 1998a: 56) found contradictory evidence. Subsequently, Bond (2015: 30) realized that at most Liddell Hart took "command of the company."

The brigade was relieved on 3 July. The next day, he boasted in a letter to his parents that he had grown from a civilian who could not stand blood to a soldier who could bear mangled limbs. In later letters to his parents, in other correspondence, and in memoirs, he claims to have been hit three times in two days by shell splinters, causing only a bruise, a torn sleeve, and a dented helmet (4 July 1916, LH 7/1916/11; 1965: I, 23; Bond 1977: 17; Danchev 1997: 79; 1998a: 57).

In the early hours of 14 July, his battalion was part of a new attack, except his company was in brigade reserve. Later, he compared the battlefields of 1 July and 14 July, as if he himself had observed both assaults.

> It is one of my own memories that in the former case the khaki-clad corpses which were strewn over the ground far outnumbered those in field grey, whereas on the battlefield of July 14th the German dead appeared to exceed our own (1939b: 406; 1960a: 203).

In fact, he was sent forward after dawn on 16 July. His memoirs clarify:

> This time, grey-clad corpses outnumbered khaki ones on the battlefield. That sight, and contrast, deeply influenced my future military thinking (1965: I, 24, 216).†

His part of the company was sent to occupy a captured trench, which a separate battalion had failed to find. During the night of 17-18 July, the battalion arrived, yet he was evacuated for the fourth time. In that month, he wrote no explanation. Yet by August he was energetically exploring his regimental options. He preserved no medical records until September, when the diagnosis is 50 percent disabled due to "exposure to toxic gas." Like his fever, concussion, and splinter wounds, his "exposure to toxic gas" is self-reported and contradicted by other accounts. Later in September, he drafted some "impressions" for publication.‡ From the start, his account is misleading. He identifies himself as "a company commander who saw three and a half weeks of…the great British offensive on the Somme." In fact, he was the company's deputy commander, and commanded only a part, only on 16 July, after the commander and staff were sent elsewhere. His first-person account

---
* Newman's novel (1935: 115) places the event in 1915.
† See also: 1960a: 203; 1965: I, 216. In fact, he was never in "sight" of any night attacks, and was sceptical of their viability (1921e: 70), until 1931 (1933b: 62; 1944a:284; 1954b; 1960a: 205).
‡ He sought to publish, until, in January 1917, the War Office refused permission.

53

ends with the plops and pops of gas shells (they plop to the ground and pop open, rather than explode). This account does not specify any effects on himself, although the gas "killed a lot of our gunners and others. My personal interest in the offensive ceased from now on." He spends the next 87 pages analysing war-making from the top, of which he had no direct knowledge. The manuscript ends with dissonance about war-making at the bottom.

> War, at least modern war, as waged on the Western Front, is horrible and ghastly beyond all imagination of the civilian. Nevertheless it has an awe-inspiring grandeur of its own, and it ennobles and brings out the highest in a man's character such as no other thing could. Could one but remove the horrible suffering and mutilation it would be the finest purifier of nations every known. Even as it is, it is the finest forge of character and manliness ever invented, when taken in small doses. The unfortunate thing is, that war has become an over-dose. Still, with all its faults and horrors, it is above all a man's life, in the fullest and deepest sense of the term ("Impressions of the Great British Offensive on the Somme," 1916: 1, 6, 93, LH 7/1916/22).

In 1920, he drafted an autobiography, which reports that between midnight and dawn, 18 July, "I had developed bronchitis and my heart was dilated" (LH 7/1920/38). Heart damage became his most frequent explanation for the end of his combatant service in 1916 – and non-combatant service in 1927. However, as we shall see in Chapter 10, he accelerated the end of his Army career by leaking official information and criticizing his chiefs. Bronchitis, heart dilation, and gas exposure were often recorded by sympathetic doctors to evade the shame of psychological breakdown. Soldiers diagnosed "shell shock," but doctors recorded "soldier's heart." Liddell Hart himself was the main source of his symptoms. After the war, his most frequent self-reported symptom is heart palpitation; before the war, it was nervousness. Palpitation is symptomatic of both nervousness and post-traumatic stress disorder. Palpitation is consistent with exposure to toxic gas, but also almost any disorder, including stomach gas ("heart burn"). From 1921, he recorded several "heart attacks" and "collapses," but always describes the cause as fatigue, and the solution as rest, which again suggests that the cause was psychological. Perhaps his only heart attack was the one that would kill him at the age of 74 years (three years older than British life expectancy at the time).

In April 1939, after months of lonely campaigning against policies that he considered to be warmongering, he wrote a new private account of his breakdown of 1916, before admitting that his injury was largely psychological.

> [I]n the Somme offensive I remained in the front line two days, until we were relieved, after having had an adequate excuse for going back – in a puncture which at any rate was not so slight as the wound which my second in command got and for which I sent him back. It is a fact that my service at the front was only ended by gassing (from a surprise burst of the new phosgene gas-shells onto the track through Mametz Wood) sufficiently serious for me to receive the maximum wound award, and that the effects I suffered were largely due to the efforts made in warning my other platoons when I should have let myself be carried down.

> All that sounds quite noble. But it is not all the facts – as I am aware of them. It does not record the extent to which they were due to a fear of being afraid, nor the extent to which I yielded to fear ("Reflection," 23 April 1939, LH 11/1939/46).

His memoirs mix his note of April 1939 with "Impressions" of September 1916.

> The enemy's harassing fire was all the more unpleasant here because the shells often hit the branches of trees and exploded with a shower of descending splinters. On the way I had got a puncture in my right hand, but after having it bandaged had carried on, as only one other officer was left, and he was too inexperienced to take over. When two companies of another battalion eventually came up to relieve us, my company was withdrawn, and moved back to rejoin our own battalion. As we were passing through Mametz Wood in the dark we heard a lot of shells hitting the ground around us, but only with a faint "plop"…I was coughing violently but stayed on the spot to warn and direct the platoons that were following, and then hurried on to catch the leading platoon at the rallying point, and lead them all back to the battalion bivouac. When morning came I went to the nearest field ambulance to get my earlier wound freshly dressed – feeling rather bad but still unaware how bad. There they insisted on examining my chest, and immediately put me on a stretcher (1965: I, 25-26).

Liddell Hart told Jay Luvaas (1964: 377) of gas shells, but no incapacitation, until he "became a stretcher case when he reported to a dressing station next morning to have a hand wound looked after." Brian Bond (1977: 5,9,16-17) heard that "he was badly gassed and 'knocked out' as his company was going out of the line." An American admirer heard that Liddell Hart "nearly died of the ugly effects of its use and suffered its ill-effects for the rest of his years" (Stearns 1972: 14). However, Danchev (1997; 82; 1998a: 61, 67) judged that "Liddell Hart, already shocked, was shelled, panicked, and gassed, probably in that order, in a dark wood," and broke down. Subsequently, Bond (2015: 30-31) conceded Danchev's interpretation.

Trainer, 1917-1918

Liddell Hart's second convalescence lasted six months. At the end of January 1917, he was posted to the regiment's training unit. Within a month, he separated from his regiment for good, to assist the Director of Infantry Records. His excuse in memoirs is that he was passed for only "light duty in an office," but he was already performing such duty for the training unit. Weeks later, he transferred to an Australian squadron of the Royal Flying Corps, to serve as its adjutant (administrator), with the temporary rank of Captain. His only published explanation is that he "received the offer." In April, he was replaced by an Australian. He joined a part-time battalion of the Gloucestershire Regiment, again serving as adjutant. He asked to leave in August, after falling out with its commander. By his own account, the commander drunkenly issued the codeword for enemy invasion, and called out the men on parade, whom Liddell Hart dismissed. However, Liddell Hart did not leave the unit for months. He archived notes for his farewell address in November, but nothing from his final departure in December, when he hastily proposed to his deputy's daughter. Years later, he claimed that the men gave him, as a parting gift, a cigarette case inscribed to the effect that they would follow him "to hell." He cited the gift as proof "that the ability of winning men's confidence in one's leadership does not depend on being physically brave." However, he did not preserve any cigarette case. In memoirs, the cigarette case becomes a Wartime Record of Service, in which the commander writes that "at numerous times the men have said that they would follow Captain Hart to the very depths of Hell." "It was a surprise because I had never felt that I possessed the obvious characteristics and magnetism of leadership" (to Ironside, 25 March 1937, LH 1/401; 1960a: 70; 1965: I, 27-33).

In January 1918, he started his fifth billet in 12 months. He joined the home battalion of the Cambridgeshire Regiment, as adjutant, except he slept, dined, and socialized at a college of the University, and trained its Officer Training Corps. He leveraged this into a new venture as doctrinist, as described in Chapter 7.

Liddell Hart in mid-1917, wearing the three pips of a Captain on his sleeves and the badge of the King's Own Yorkshire Light Infantry on his collars (LH 13/104/1).

5

Great War Historian

Before Liddell Hart reinvented himself as a doctrinist, he rediscovered himself as a historian. Initially, he praised the BEF's commander-in-chief (Field-Marshal Douglas Haig), although more than a decade later he would blame Haig most for wartime disappointments. He had already condemned professional soldiers as a class. During the 1920s, he both influenced and consumed the official histories, before turning against the lead historian. He published four histories of the Great War from 1930 to 1938, which relied upon, and confirmed, some parts of the official histories, but increasingly indulged popular prejudices. During the Second World War, he admitted that the First grounded his thinking, yet he also U-turned on some of its lessons. Later, his reinvention as neglected prophet included retrenchment of popular cultural clichés about conservative and stupid seniors carelessly sending most of his peers to death.

Haig

Liddell Hart's first "Impressions of the Great British Offensive on the Somme," written in September 1916, are positive.

> Never has any military operation been so wonderfully and minutely organized or so brilliantly executed as this offensive...The chief credit of all must go to Sir Douglas Haig, who worked all through the Winter and Spring with his genius for efficiency...Every branch and department was overhauled and worked up to the highest pitch of efficiency, until finally at the outset of the offensive, Sir Douglas Haig, the greatest general Britain has ever owned, had created the finest fighting machine the world has ever known (page 84, LH 7/1916/22).*

Around the same time, he placed Haig at the top of a list of "Really Great British Generals." A popular tabloid published this reassurance (Regimental Officer, "Great Generals of the War," *The Daily Express*, 21 December 1916, LH 7/1916/35). In 1917, he rebutted "armchair critics" of attrition.

> The strategy of genius is to wear him [the enemy] down to the breaking point by a constant succession of heavy blows at varying points in his far-flung line and then, when that decisive moment has arrived, the coup de

---

* In memoirs, he admits to being "amazed at the enthusiastic praise I gave to the British higher commanders, Haig above all, in my account" (1965: I, 26). Luvaas (1964: 378) realized that "his account of the Somme written while on sick leave is far more generous with the British high command than any of his subsequent studies." To Bond (1977: 9, 5) he "was perfectly willing to talk about" his "experience of the carnage in the battle of the Somme," and to grant access to "his schoolboy notebooks and letters to his mother...and an unpublished account of the Somme campaign." Bond was amazed to read "a rather unexpectedly romantic and patriotic subaltern lavishing praise on the British High Command."

grace will be given...[O]nly those who have attacked and conquered that wonderful fortress line which stretches across France...can realize the magnitude of the British achievement and the difficulties overcome ("The Somme and Its Sequel," LH 7/1917/5).

Yet, he later admitted, his critics were fellow soldiers, not "armchair critics."

As a regimental officer who preserved such faith in those days, one has better reason than a member of GHQ to know how much one was in the minority. The bulk of the Army, if that term be held to embrace the troops, had lost confidence in the Higher Command by the Autumn of 1917 (1938e: 289).

While he soured on most soldiers, his admiration for Haig survived for another 12 years. In 1927, he finished a book that places Haig among the top ten generals of the Great War, "a great gentleman," "a noble character," and "more spotless by far than most of Britain's national heroes" (1928a: 123).

In January 1928, Haig died, prompting a burst of obituaries and less-restrained critique. Still, Liddell Hart did not join in, until prompted by David Lloyd George at their first meeting in April 1929 (see Chapter 11). Later in 1929, he completed his first history of the Great War, when "I began to discover facts which compelled an increasing modification of this view" (1938e: 155-156). The first edition concludes that the war "has shattered our faith in idols, our hero-worshipping belief that great men are different clay from common men" (1930b: 471).

In fact, he had not discovered any new facts. Rather, he had caught up with the consensus. For instance, on Haig's intent for the Somme offensive, he speculates that Haig "does not seem to have foreseen the case of mixed success and failure – always the greater probability in war." As for British unreadiness for the German counter-offensive in March 1918, "Haig seems to have underrated the infinite value of surprise" (1930b: 229, 390).

He was still coming to terms with prior hero-worship after the second edition...

I am afraid that there has rarely been a young soldier so prone, in uncritical loyalty, to think the best of his superiors, or so eager to credit them with military genius ("Peccavi Contra Veritatem," 1935, LH 11/1935/160).

...and after the third edition.

I intensely admired many of my superiors, and even hero-worshipped a number ("Thoughts jotted down – to be expanded," 17 July 1936, LH 11/1936/2-25c).

His fourth history of the War scolds "the last generation" (and "humanity" in general) for needing "a great man," "idols," and "a suitable hero." Paraphrasing private letters from the official historian, he characterizes Haig as intelligent but blinkered and taciturn, blames "the essentially irrational basis of his plans" on his optimism and increasing religiosity, and concludes that Haig "was an embodiment of the distinctive characteristics of his class and his country" (1938e: 30, 43-44, 48).

Professional Soldiers

Before Liddell Hart soured on Haig in particular, he soured on professional soldiers in general. The transition year was 1921, when his doctrine came under fire, for unreal premises and impractical conclusions (on which more in Chapter 7).* His first book on warfare is nominally about *The Future of War*, but is peppered with criticisms of the last war's costs, principals, and strategies.

> The Great War caused the direct sacrifice of 8 million lives, to which the British Isles alone contributed three-quarters of a million. So ineffectual was the treatment prescribed by the military practitioners who were called in that the illness took over four years to run its course, during which the financial temperature mounted daily, until for this country alone it reached a cost of £8,000,000 a day. Our total war expenditure was nearly ten thousand million pounds (1925: 3).

He blames a dogma to destroy the enemy's army, started by Napoleon Bonaparte (1769-1821), amplified by Carl von Clausewitz (1780-1831), and implemented by French and British commanders during the Great War. However, he caricatures their prescriptions.

> What is the tenor of this doctrine? First, that there is only one true objective in war – "the destruction of the enemy's main forces on the battlefield"…Second, that the means of gaining this objective is to pile up greater numbers than the enemy (1925: 3-8).

He was correct to turn against "attrition" and "progressive butchery," but incorrect to characterize the principals and strategies as unnuanced and unchanging (1925: 21, 74). In the 1960s, he gave Brian Bond (1977: 58) the sense that *The Future of War* was motivated to avoid the high costs of the Great War, which "mattered far more than his historical accuracy and fairness." "Liddell Hart was already forcing history to yield the appropriate lessons" (1977: 44).

Within a couple years, Liddell Hart published a book about current armies, except that it is anchored in yet another critique of the Great War's professional soldiers (1927b: ix). The editor of *The Fighting Forces* (a quarterly magazine) urged him to focus on future mechanization.

> We don't want analogies of the past to emphasize the one essential "there bloody well must and shall not be another Somme and Passchendaele in the future" (Lieutenant-Colonel Richard M. Raynsford to LH, 24 September 1928, LH 9/3/7).

Nevertheless, Liddell Hart's subsequent books treat the American Civil War and Great War as similarly attritional for the same root cause: the principals were too stupid (except William T. Sherman) to break free from Napoleon's and Clausewitz's focus on destroying the enemy army. His histories of the Great War similarly reduce all strategies and operations of the Great War to "attrition," except expeditions against Germany's peripheral co-belligerents. He reduces the causes of this attrition

---

* Gordon Corrigan (2003: 14) attributes Liddell Hart's turn against "the generals" to his realization that he had "been found wanting in physical courage" and to his rationalization that "it is not courage but intellect that wins wars." This realization and rationalization might be necessary but neither was sufficient, given that the turn occurred in 1921, rather than 1916. Corrigan seems to think it happened in 1916.

to the low character and intelligence of the strategists, particularly Joseph Joffre (French Army chief of staff, 1911-1916), John French (BEF commander, 1914-1915), Douglas Haig (French's replacement, 1915-1919), "the Italian command," and Erich von Falkenhayn (German Army chief of staff, 1914-1916) (1925: 21, 74; 1929a; 1929b; 1930b: 116, 118, 185, 200, 205, 243, 298, 306; 1935a: 56; 1938e: 96).

Official Historian

Liddell Hart's growing antagonism to professional soldiers helps to explain his stormy relationship with the lead official historian of the Great War. Brigadier-General Sir James Edmonds (1861-1956) had spent most of the Great War at BEF GHQ, within the intelligence and engineer staffs. Edmonds came away both critical and defensive – particularly of Haig, who had been his chief mentor since they coincided as students at the Staff College in 1895. There, Edmonds acquired the nickname "Archimedes" for his intellectual pursuits outside the College – a reputation that appealed to Liddell Hart. Edmonds' nervous breakdown within months of joining the front was something else they shared in common (French 1991: 70; Green 2003: 24-25).

Effective in April 1919, the Cabinet's Committee for Imperial Defence put Edmonds in charge of a Historical Section. Liddell Hart made contact a year later, when the first volumes were released (produced mostly before Edmonds' appointment). They influenced and consumed each other's work. During Liddell Hart's campaign for doctrinal influence (see Chapter 7), he encouraged Edmonds' (1927: 53) remote claim that "[t]he lack of training manuals which could be understood and correctly acted on without explanation by an expert was a grave cause of delay and error." Liddell Hart later quoted this claim as one of Edmonds' insights into their superiors' "errors of outlook" (1938e: 241).

Liddell Hart's own histories quote and paraphrase the official histories, but do not cite. His first edition acknowledges "one unnamed whose knowledge of sources was as boundless as the trouble he took to aid me" (1930b: vii; 1959c: 435). Nevertheless, Liddell Hart grew irritated with Edmonds' unwillingness to publish what he revealed privately. In 1930, Edmonds admitted, "I have to write of Haig with my tongue in my cheek. One can't tell the truth. He really was above the average – or below the average – in stupidity." In 1933, Lloyd George's first volume of "war memoirs," which Liddell Hart advised, influenced Edmonds' release of a revised edition of the volume covering the war in France from August to October 1914 (the only volume ever revised), which admits that "Haig momentarily lost his head" when II Corps retreated from Mons on 23 August. Liddell Hart privately took Edmonds to task for being too kind to Haig and other Generals, but Edmonds replied that although they were "ignorant and did dishonest tricks [they] were good fellows in a tight place." Liddell Hart publicly hinted at errors of omission. "Not a few military historians have admitted that they feel compelled by position, interest, or friendship, to put down less than they know to be true" (8 December 1930, LH 11/1930/15; 27 October 1933, LH 11/1933/26; 1933c: 173).

Their angriest correspondence developed in the following year, when Edmonds drafted the volume covering the German counter-offensive of Spring 1918. Here, Edmonds (1935: 128) criticizes Maxse's "over-hasty withdrawal" of the XVIII Corps. Edmonds was well informed, having surveyed almost every surviving commander down to unit echelon, after repeated resistance to cooperation from Maxse himself. Liddell Hart blamed the commanders of the 5th Army (General Sir Hubert Gough) and BEF (Haig).

> No one has given me clearer evidence of the deficiencies of our higher leaders as individuals than you have, yet you are inclined to pretend that, collectively, they were up to the problem they had to face...

> What one is given in this volume is a purely Trade-Union point of view – it is not merely "patriotic" history but parochial history...The facts necessary for judgement are given with few exceptions, but they are warped in interpretation – a subtle twist is given to them...There is scarcely a flicker of that penetrating insight...by which you have illuminated for me not only the fundamental limitations of Haig, Robertson etc. but the causes (to Edmonds, 17 May and 6 November 1934, LH 1/259).

> [M]any of your points passed through my mind but I had always space and the views of my comrades to consider...I become more and more inclined to lay weight on the difficulties of the fighting soldiers' task and sympathize with them, whilst you are becoming more and more critical and see their blunders larger than their achievements (Edmonds to LH, 9 November 1934).

> Soldiership cannot be divorced from loyalties[,] and loyalty to anything but the truth makes scientific enquiry farcical. So the succession of errors must go on and the lessons remain unlearnt (to Edmonds, 13 November).

Edmonds was a weak opponent. In his next letter, he wrote, "You are a far more dangerous antagonist that L.G., which is saying a good deal!" (20 November).

Liddell Hart pushed Lloyd George's self-serving criticisms of the Generals, but Edmonds rightly refused to replace one spin with another. Between the fourth and fifth volumes of Lloyd George's "war memoirs," Liddell Hart renewed the pressure, but Edmonds revealed that "what ammunition I will use will depend on what L.G. says in his next volume" (to LH, 4 February 1935, LH 1/259/109). Lloyd George's next volume denies his insistence on the dismissal of Hubert Gough from command of 5th Army. Instead, he blames Haig and the CIGS. Edmonds (1937) rebutted with an article – a risky undertaking for an active official historian, except that Lloyd George was no longer in the mainstream, and Edmonds was able to quote Lloyd George's own War Secretary.

Still, Liddell Hart depended on Edmonds. At Liddell Hart's request, Edmonds sent copies of documents disproving Haig's claim that his cautious advance to the River Aisne (in September 1914) was due to the neighbouring corps, and permitted Liddell Hart to "use what I have enclosed provided you don't quote me." Liddell Hart dedicated his final book on the Great War to Edmonds, "who knows more of the history of the War than he will ever write, but to whose guidance all others who would write of it will ever be indebted." Reviewing the latest official histories, Liddell Hart praises the "skill and delicacy which we have learnt to expect from General Edmonds." However, he complains that the volume on the Somme "finished on the familiar note of extenuation and justification," and that the volumes covering 1918 "reproduced with a sympathetic or antipathetic twist" certain facts from the appendices (Edmonds to LH, 5 January 193[5], LH 1/259/64; 1938e: v, 272, 262, 273). His review of the revised volume (1933) tries to have it both ways.

> Personal inclination as well as the discretion required by his position seems to have led him to evolve a method of writing for the student who can "read between the lines,"* and of covering the more sensational facts by delicate implication (1938e: 233).

Elsewhere in the same book, he quotes Edmonds' private letters, without identifying Edmonds.

> I have known generals who proclaim [Haig's] infallibility in public, yet in private confess that they act thus "for the sake of the Army" or of friendship, and remark that he was "really a very stupid man"...
>
> For the historian loyal to his calling it would be impossible to put forward the suggestion, such as one has heard from distinguished participants in the last war, that certain episodes might "best be glossed over" in war histories (1938e: 31, 213).

Just after Liddell Hart submitted the above for publication, Edmonds revealed by letter that he had omitted the story of how Maxse's absences from XVIII Corps HQ had contributed to its order to retreat (on 23 March 1918) and its confused execution of the order. Liddell Hart effectively broke contact, even though Edmonds continued in post until 1948. Edmonds' death in 1956 did not mellow him. He told Fuller that Edmonds was a "spiteful old gossip,"† fraudulent historian, apologist for Haig, and neglecter of the Tank Corps. His second wife heard him "saying that sometimes the word 'official' cancelled out the word 'history'"‡ (note, 11 November 1937, LH 11/1937/88; note, April 1963, enclosed in letter to Fuller, 6 May 1963, Rutgers New Brunswick; 1970: vii; Travers 1987: 233; Baynes 1995: 198).

Liddell Hart's Histories

From May 1930, Liddell Hart published four histories of the Great War within eight years. The first edition has a revisionist title: *The Real War*.§ It promises not "to gloss over disturbing facts so that individual reputations may be preserved at the price of another holocaust of lives." It repeatedly implies that all previous

---

* "He used to say that he could not tell the truth frankly in an official history but hoped that it would be evident to those who could 'read between the lines'" (1965: I, 211).
† Here he is paraphrasing what a professor of modern history at Oxford said ("[C.R.M.F.] Cruttwell's opinions," 2 October 1936, LH 11/936/80).
‡ David French (1991: 70) interprets a letter to Edmonds (13 November 1934) as a characterization of the volume on the war in Spring 1918 as "'official' but not 'history'." Andrew Green (2003: 55) counters that the letter "warned that was how future historians might view his work." I find Green's counter a distinction without difference.
§ The title echoes *Realities of War*, a memoir by journalist Philip Gibbs (1877-1962), published in 1920, although Liddell Hart did not correspond until 1933 (partly because Gibbs criticized Lloyd George). Strachan (1991: 49; LH 11/1930/23) interprets an archived note as a list of alternative titles: "No Napoleon," "War of the Blind," and "The Headless Monster."

histories protect "individual reputations." "The historian's rightful task is to distil experience as a medicinal warning for future generations, not to distil a drug." He declares his "pursuit of the truth" (1930b: ix).

His task is righteous but his "medicinal warning" fails. He under-specifies what the principals did and should have done. He reduces the "causes of the conflict" to "fear, hunger, pride," but does not prove any. He works backwards from outcomes: many soldiers died, for little ground, therefore the principals and strategies must have been wrong. He is correct to criticize attrition, but his alternatives are inconsistent. He offers, at different times, distraction, surprise, or simultaneous offensives across multiple theatres (exactly what the Allies tried in Summer 1916). His alternative to war in France is to divert against Germany's peripheral co-belligerents (exactly what the Allies tried every year from 1915). These expeditions were indecisive, yet he claims "that decisive offensives [in France] were vain until the enemy's reserves had been attracted elsewhere"; "distraction of the enemy's force has ever been an essential complement to concentration – of one's own effort." He does not admit that peripheral theatres divert friendly resources (1930b: 4, 228, 347).

Eventually, he relegates peripheral expeditions behind naval blockade as the main cause of victory. Empirically, his conclusion is a *non sequitur*. The first edition contains at least 33 chapters (they are not conventionally numbered or termed), of which only one is naval – and this focuses on the Battle of Jutland (1916). Yet the book concludes that the Royal Navy contributed "more than any other factor towards winning the war for the Allies. For the navy was the instrument of the blockade…" His second edition adds no evidence. His third edition does not mention blockade at all. Yet he used the blockade as evidence towards his theoretical "British Way in Warfare," in every edition from 1932 to 1942, and his theoretical way to win the Cold War in the 1950s. Yet his engagement with the naval and economic aspects of the Great War never improved (1930b: 471; 1932c: 41; 1935a: 45; 1952: 12; 1954a: 358). In fact, Germany received trade from overseas through neutrals until late in the war, and from eastern Europe throughout. If Western forces had not advanced on Germany in 1918, Germany would have been able to continue fighting. Blockade certainly reduced some supplies (particularly foods), but was not decisive (Ferguson 1998: 252-253; Sheffield 2001: 92-93; Kennedy 2014: 343; Mick 2014: 156).

His attitudes were fashionable, but selective. He focused on the years and theatre that coincided with his war service (France, 1915-1916) and the peripheral theatres (Italy, Greece, Rumania, Serbia, Turkey, Mesopotamia). His chapters on Germany's war with Russia, Russia's war with Austro-Hungary, Italy's war with Austro-Hungary, and Russia's war with the Ottoman Empire are short. He ignores the great battles of 1915 between Russia and the Central Powers in favour of two battles in France and the landings at Gallipoli. His chapter on Germany's Eastern Front in 1916 barely surpasses two pages. By contrast, his chapter on Rumania's short fight on the Allied side, in Autumn of the same year, extends to six pages, because he interprets it as an indirect approach to Germany that could have won the war (if the Allies had inputted more resources).

He unashamedly focuses on Britain's war, but races through Britain's most mobile theatres and operations. He races through the year before he got to France. He dwells on the bloodiest, longest operations of 1916 and 1917. As for the final year, he dwells on Britain's struggles against the German counter-offensives in France, from March to June, but almost ignores the successful Allied offensives thereafter. He laments missed opportunities to break stalemates in Italy, Greece, and Turkey, but skims the advance from Egypt to Syria, except to overstate the mobility and contribution of Arab insurgents and Lawrence, who was only one of thousands of the Arabs' British co-belligerents.

He under-states joint/inter-service operations, new technologies (such as tanks and fighter planes), new techniques (such as creeping barrages), and even old technologies (such as artillery in general).* These under-statements seem intended to make British professionals look bad. Take artillery. In early 1917, he had written of his "pride" at "being present at the introduction of the creeping barrage and knowing of its invention in June 1916." Late in 1917, his defence of Haig's "strategy of genius" against "armchair critics" praises the "creeping barrage" as a thoroughly British invention. Yet his history of the Great War contains only one reference to a creeping barrage – in a German attack ("The Somme and Its Sequel," 1917, LH 7/1917/5; 1930b: 396; Strachan 1991: 46-47; Danchev 1998a: 106; Bond 1977: 27, 51; Reynolds 2014: 329; Bond 2015: 34-35).

His histories admit that the tank is "an antidote to the defensive obstacle of machine-guns and barbed wire," and that the British were first to introduce it, but obsesses about supposed professional obstruction of its development, and Haig's haste to deploy the first batch.† He overlooks the techniques and technologies of tank warfare. For instance, although he admits their great impact in 1918, he credits only numerical preponderance (1930b: 245).

He ignores aircraft, except to acknowledge briefly the transition from unarmed scout planes to armed fighter planes, Germany's launch of Zeppelins against Britain (he had seen one attacking Hull on 5 March 1916), and Britain's launch of strategic bombers against Germany in the final months of the war (1930b: 313).

Seniors naturally regarded Liddell Hart's history as unpatriotic and harsh. Not just soldiers said so. The novelist and fellow journalist Edmund Clerihew Bentley (1875-1956), who had been too old to join the fighting, told readers of *The Daily Telegraph* that the book belongs to the literature of "distress and disillusionment." A fellow infantry Captain (Herbert Edward Read, 1893-1968) characterized it as a "shoddy piece of rhetoric" – in the literary magazine *Criterion*, no less (LH 9/8/6). An American academic described it as "a mosaic of criticisms," No other author has "been able to create an attitude of such complete and unerring 'critical infallibility'." The "book stands out by the dialectical skill with which hostile criticism is presented as a narrative of fact" (Thomas 1931). The CIGS (George Milne) asked whether "it occurred to you to ask yourself 'How would you have conducted the Great War?'" Liddell Hart denied the task.

---

* Strachan (1991: 52) speculates that Liddell Hart was too focused on psychology to notice technology. In fact, in other contexts Liddell Hart asserted each equally strongly.
† He misdescribes the tank as "evolved" from Benjamin Holt's "agricultural tractor," and misreports a "lack of any exact specification of the military requirements" (1930b: 250, 254; 1936a). In fact, Winston Churchill had hidden his landship projects from the War Office, until he was removed from direction of the Admiralty. The Holt tractor and the landships projects were not necessary to the eventual tank, which was specified, designed, and developed by soldiers and business partners, without the Admiralty (Newsome 2021a: chapter 1).

> I have, in fact, tried to do what you suggest – although it is not really a test, as I know, from the enemy's account, what course would have paid. Further, it is really no part of an historian's job to argue what should have been done (LH to Milne, 6 September 1930, LH 1/512).

Juniors were most sympathetic. Enoch Powell (later an irascible Conservative politician) was six years old at the end of the War, lonely and sensitive to the wartime deaths of teachers and relatives. He consumed Liddell Hart's first history of the Great War when he was nearly 18 years of age and plotting an academic career.

> The generation who lived under the shadow of the Great War being resumed under similar conditions felt an affectionate gratitude to Liddell Hart. He enabled them to believe what the horrific follies of 1914-18 had been analysed and understood and would not be repeated (in Liddell Hart 1992: v).

Bernard Newman met Liddell Hart in 1931, after reading the first edition. He held similar dissonance about the Great War in France, where he had served longer (although at lower rank). Newman wrote a novel peppered with citations and quotes from *The Real War* as context to the fictional hero's experience. The novel is written in the first person. In the introduction, the fictional hero claims a non-fiction memoir, along with "about one per cent" of "several hundred books on secret service [that] have appeared since the war" (1935: 5). The story is preposterous enough to persuade most veterans otherwise,* but not necessarily most civilians. The hero starts in 1914 as a lowly despatch-rider, before his German fluency earns him a mission behind German lines to sabotage a railway yard in Lens, during the Battle of Loos, around the cusp of September/October 1915. Sometime in the next weeks, the hero is on leave in London, at "a party," where, he was promised, "there would be a good many well-known military men present." He meets a "Captain Liddell Hart" (who, in reality, was then a Second-Lieutenant, convalescing in a French hospital, unrelated to the Battle of Loos).

> Sometimes he quoted from military authorities, but more often he was expounding his own ideas. I particularly remember a kind of sermon which he preached from the text of Napoleon's axiom – that the aim of an army was the mind of the enemy commander – that is to say, that the object of a general is not merely the defeat or even destruction of the forces opposed to him, but loss of nerve and confidence in the mind of his opponent. A war is not won until you have persuaded the enemy commander he is beaten. To do that it is not always essential to defeat his army (Newman 1935: 113-115).

Liddell Hart's next book blames Britain's strategy during the Great War on Marshal Ferdinand Foch's supposed misinterpretation of Clausewitz and Napoleon as advocates of constant direct attacks on the enemy's core army. It gave a reviewer the "impression that most military reputation is vanity," and that Foch acted with

---

* The British hero spends three years posing as a German staff officer in the German GHQ in France, liaising between the commander-in-chief and the Kaiser, until, in August 1918, he, still wearing a German officer's uniform, escapes into the jaws of a British attack.

"faith rather than knowledge" (1931a: 519; 1932c: 111; Updegraff 1932). Liddell Hart confirmed this impression in review of Foch's posthumously-published memoirs.

> The known character of Marshal Foch inclines one to the view that, in conveying a similar suggestion of omniscience and omnipotence, he was guided by genuine belief. Faith was his greatest quality, and often blinded him to facts (1938e: 182).

Liddell Hart's first history of the Great War promises that all the evidence had been published that ever would be necessary. Nevertheless, four years later he expanded and revised it as *A History of The World War* (1934a). The new preface pretends that the first edition "has met no serious challenge" as "a summary of the significant facts of the war." Contradictorily, the same preface admits that "new evidence that has come out in the past four years has led me to modify my view of" several issues. Further, "the time has come, as well as the justification, for adopting a title that has no longer a contemporary note." He added only one chapter on the Eastern Front, which covers a battle in 1914, rather than the epic battles of 1915.

Two years later, he released a third edition, with a third title (*The War in Outline*, 1936a). Disappointed with official attention, he claimed that the Royal Military College at Sandhurst had standardized the first edition as a textbook, until, in 1932, Milne insisted on Winston Churchill's autobiographical *The World Crisis* (note, 28 July 1936, LH 11/1936/16). In fact, the latter had been published seven years earlier.

Although disappointed with official and professional reception, he revelled in "lay" or "common" reception. The second edition sold 23,000 copies, the third 22,000, making them his best sellers of the inter-war period, until his biography of Lawrence of Arabia (34,000 copies) (Higham 1966: 95n). Still, he was not satisfied. With his biography of Lawrence, he released a fourth history of the Great War (*Through the Fog of War*), prompted by recent memoirs,[*] and earlier memoirs that his first history had skimmed.[†] Other chapters are biographies of the principals, sandwiched between conventional chronological chapters. He rationalizes that a fourth history is necessary as a warning against a Second World War (1938e: vii).

Otherwise, the sources of Liddell Hart's histories are vague. Each book ends with a list of sources, organized by chapter. The most frequent item is: "private evidence." During the Second World War, he claimed to have read "some of the newspaper files of 1914-1918" before writing the first edition. Probably, he means the files of *The Daily Telegraph*, where he took up full-time work in 1925. In any case, he was amazed "that so many serious students of war could have been so often wrong and so rarely right in their calculations," which inevitably sounds like a dig at *The Daily Telegraph*'s prior correspondents[‡] (1941a: 7; 1942a: 9). In the 1950s, he

---

[*] John J. Pershing (commander of the American Expeditionary Force) in 1931; Peyton C. March (US Army Chief of Staff, 1918-1921) in 1932; Lieutenant-General Émile-Joseph Galet (military adviser to the King of Belgium) in 1932; Joseph Joffre (French Army Chief of Staff, 1911-1916) in 1932; Ferdinand Foch (French Army Chief of Staff, 1917-1918; Supreme Allied Commander, 1918-1920) in 1936; David Lloyd George (Britain's Minister of Munitions, 1915; War Secretary, 1916; Prime Minister, 1916-1922) in 1938.

[†] Henry Wilson (British Army CIGS, 1918) in 1927; and Max Hoffmann (Chief of Staff on Germany's Eastern Front) in 1929.

[‡] Likely he was thinking of Repington's (1924: 197-206) rejections of peripheral expeditions.

persuaded Luvaas (1964: 390), whom he was paying to organize his papers, that his histories reflect "conscientious research among the documents, diaries, and memoirs, lengthy conversations with the actors, and voluminous correspondence." Presumably, Michael Howard (1970b: 42; 1984: 207) was thinking of this when he wrote that "as a historian his reputation rested on his still irreplaceable studies of the First World War." However, Brian Bond (1977: 53) admits that "Luvaas exaggerates somewhat." Liddell Hart "hardly ever visited archives and only occasionally saw the original documents," although "he was able to circumvent this barrier to some extent by indefatigable correspondence and discussions with the official historians" (1977: 52). Strachan (1991: 51-52) judged that Liddell Hart read few of the sources in his "very full" reference list, least of all the many sources in foreign languages, which he likely knew only as summarized in the *Army Quarterly*.

Self-Revision

Months into the Second World War, Liddell Hart offered the First as foundation and justification for his critical thinking (1940b: 174-175). However, within years, he U-turned on naval blockade and strategic bombing, although not peripheral expeditions. By the middle of World War II, he characterizes blockade and bombing as attritional, having previously sold them as decisive, efficient, and ethical.

> That will at least be a natural continuation from the last war, where it was the Germans who showed the only skill of generalship that was seen in Europe, yet the Allies who wore them down by sheer attrition – with shells on the battlefield and hunger in the home ("A Reflection arising from the Cologne Raids," 2 June 1942, LH 11/1942/40).

He was right to realize the indecisiveness, inefficiency, and unethicalness of naval blockade and strategic bombing (see Chapter 15), but wrong to continue to praise peripheral expeditions as decisive "indirect approaches" (1941b; 1946c; 1954a).

Popular Culture

After the Second World War, Liddell Hart was too busy reinventing his record on the Second World War to retell the First, until the 1960s. Then he contributed more than anyone to Britain's popular cultural obsession with two "Battles," as if representative: Somme (July to November 1916); and Passchendaele (July to November 1917). The ledger against both campaigns was already clear. The first day of the Somme was the British Army's costliest. Passchendaele was the muddiest campaign. Liddell Hart's ethos for peddling these images was tenuous: he did not participate in the first day of the Somme, although he followed up after dark. Passchendaele (also known as Third Ypres) started a year after he had left for England, when he paid little attention. Nevertheless, his memoirs pretend that by 1918 he had realized a mission "to ensure that if war came again there should be no repetition of the Somme and Passchendaele" (1965: I, 33).

Charles à Court Repington (1858-1925) was military correspondent at *The Times* (1904-1918), *The Morning Post* (1918), and *The Daily Telegraph* (1919-1925). Liddell Hart met him in July 1924, while touring field training

In fact, through 1928, he was still praising Haig's strategy, command, and staff, particularly with regard to the Somme and Passchendaele. His inter-war writings are slap-dash in their references to the Somme and Passchendaele. His first history of the Great War has more to say about Passchendaele than the Somme. He states that "the Third Battle of Ypres" was "so fruitless in its results, so depressing in its direction...that 'Passchendaele' has come to be, like 'Walcheren' a century before, a synonym for military failure" (1930b: 337). In most mentions of Passchendaele, he attaches the metaphor "swamps." He states that "the offensive," which started on 31 July 1917, "was finally submerged in the swamps of Passchendaele in early November" (302). He complains that tanks were thrown "into the swamps of Passchendaele" (259). He offers stupidity as the root cause (337-339, 343-348). He blames "Passchendaele" for the decline in ready soldiers over the next months. Thence, he blames Germany's advance in March 1918 on Passchendaele. Contradictorily, he praises Lloyd George for curbing "the flow of reinforcements" from Britain (388).

In justifying his "British Way in Warfare," he declares that the "dual cost of the Somme and of Passchendaele...sunk the faith that created the Empire," and that British and French senility reached "its ultimate destination in the swamps of Passchendaele." In 1939, he published doubts that men would want to fight another war given memory of "the Somme and Passchendaele." He scolded his editors at *The Times* newspaper for leading Britain back to "Passchendaele-follies." His first anthology of post-war writings (1950) "distils in[to] everything that he writes the horrors of the Somme and Passchendaele" (1932c: 14-15: 1935a: 18-19; 1939b: 112, 434; LH to Geoffrey Dawson, 9 May 1939, LH 3/109; Crossman 1958: 223).

John Terraine (1959: 173) criticized Liddell Hart's (1930b: 126) long-standing speculation "that Haig's real motive [for Passchendaele] was a strange belief that he could defeat the German Army single-handed in Flanders." Liddell Hart did not admit the criticism. Instead, he scolded Terraine for relying on official histories, instead of Liddell Hart's archive. (Terraine later explained that Liddell Hart was seeking to prejudice him.) Liddell Hart repeated his prior estimates that British losses were 50 percent greater than German losses, and that Edmonds had exaggerated German losses by 33 percent, and underestimated British losses by about 20 percent, to make respective losses look equal (1959c: 436-438).

A superior officer, who had served throughout both world wars (albeit not in France), seconded Terraine's doubts about the "the swamps of Passchendaele." The semantics did not deserve controversy. (The terrain is reclaimed marshland; the preliminary bombardment destroyed the drainage, and churned clay and water into a product resembling swamp.) Liddell Hart was right to confirm the metaphor, but wrong to imply first-hand knowledge.

> It is astonishing that any soldier, let alone a Staff College graduate, should write as Brigadier F.A.S. Clarke does in his letter on "The Battle of Passchendaele" in the May issue of the RUSI Journal. There he states: "the offensive did not 'bog down' in the swamps...Passchendaele is on the Ypres ridge and the legendary swamps are 20 miles away." It is evidence that he did not fight on that front. There are many thousands of soldiers still alive who did, and will know that his statements are ludicrous (1959c: 433).

Liddell Hart defended the semantics partly because, ironically, the prior forty years ago had produced "no clear and compelling popular narrative of 1914-1918" (Reynolds 2014: 330). The official histories were still in production: the last to be edited by Edmonds was released in 1949, the last volume in 2010. Former official historian Cyril Falls did not release his history of the Great War until 1959, too late and too balanced to be popular. Controversy garnered more attention, even when both sides were equally biased, just in opposing directions (epitomized by Terraine and Liddell Hart, respectively).

In 1958, Leon Wolff, an amateur American historian, released a history of the war of 1917, focusing on the Passchendaele campaign. Wolff relied on secondary sources, particularly Liddell Hart, even for characterizations of Haig (whom Liddell Hart never met) and Lloyd George (whom Wolff misreported as Haig's consistent critic). Fuller was one of Wolff's few primary sources for Passchendaele itself. Wolff asked Fuller to write the introduction, which notes that Lloyd George was "mercurial" and supported attrition, until Lloyd George retrospectively blamed Haig. In 1959, Liddell Hart wrote to coach Wolff away from Fuller's account. In 1963, Wolff released a new edition, with an additional introduction by Liddell Hart (Wolff 1958: vii-viii, 26-29, 32-35; LH 1/760).

Alan Clark's (1961: 12) biography of *The Donkeys* (a term invented by Clark, but which he attributed to the German chief of staff, to caricature British commanders who had ordered a costly offensive in September 1915) acknowledges "an immense debt to that acknowledged master of military history, Captain B.H. Liddell Hart, who has allowed me access to his private files on the period and has been of the greatest help at every stage in the development of the book." Indeed, Liddell Hart vetted the draft. Clark cites only two sources by Liddell Hart: his short, vicious biography of Foch (1931a); and the second edition of his history of the Great War (1934a). Liddell Hart seems to have been sufficient for Clark's sweeping condemnation of Britain's senior officers. The title, at least, became part of popular culture, and introduced the conventional narrative of the inter-war period to a new generation (Reynolds 2014: 325-326).

Liddell Hart became a fashionable commentator on the Great War, in a decade when most surviving combatants were reaching the end of their natural lives. A publisher asked Liddell Hart's to vet A.J.P. Taylor's flippant history of the Great War (1963). He advised Terence Rattigan's play about T.E. Lawrence, entitled after one of Lawrence's post-war pseudonyms ("Ross"), first staged in 1960. He advised the romanticized movie about "Lawrence of Arabia," first broadcast in December 1962, although he criticized its depiction of Lawrence's war crimes. He advised the ironically-titled play "Oh! What a Lovely War," one of whose co-writers (Raymond Fletcher, subsequently a Labour MP) described it as "one part me, one part Liddell Hart, the rest Lenin!" The first tour ran from 1963 to 1964, when, at a regimental reunion, Liddell Hart and fellow contrarians proposed toasts to the tune of the titular song. Also in 1964, he advised the BBC on a quickly-produced but long-running documentary (1,040 minutes were broadcast that year), entitled "The Great War," although he resigned when Terraine became the principal scriptwriter. In a letter to *The Times*, he complains that the script blames the incapacity of the lower ranks more than the Generals. The product is dissonant: it condemns the attrition, but denies that senior officers were stupid (LH 13/104/2; LH 5/19; to George Sewell, 20

July 1964, LH 1/629; Danchev 1991: 282; Morris and Raskin 1992: 149-156; Crawford 1998: 145-148; Reynolds 2014: 326-336; Bond 2002: 59-70; 2015: 38).

> The effect of the 1960s clashes, which thanks to John Terraine has continued to determine far too much of the debate even in the 1980s, was to challenge the orthodoxy laid down by Liddell Hart, not to revise the basic framework within which he operated (Strachan 1991: 67).

Legacy

In the 1950s, Luvaas (1990: 18) found that "Liddell Hart lived in the shadow of the Somme." In the 1960s, Brian Bond (1977: 82, 5) found that the Great War is "the largest single subject" in his archive.* In 1965, Liddell Hart finished his memoirs and turned to various histories of the Second World War (see Chapter 20). Shortly after Liddell Hart's death in 1970, his *History of the Second World War* was published. Almost simultaneously, the second edition of his history of the Great War (1934b) was reissued, without revision, as *History of the First World War*. Admirers who met him later in the 1960s decided that this is his magnum opus, at least next to his *History of the Second World War* (James 1970: 55; Thorne 1985: 51).

Yet admirers have skipped over most of the content. Initially, Bond (1977: 5) eschewed Liddell Hart's "influence in shaping public opinion about the First World War." Danchev (1997; 1998a) dwelt on Liddell Hart's experiences but not histories of the Great War. Both men ignored prior refutations of his histories, of which the most professional to date was by General Shelford Bidwell.

> The popular notion is that an erroneous strategy led to a direct attack on the Western Front instead of an indirect approach elsewhere, and erroneous tactics to "attrition" instead of more imaginative methods of waging war. The campaign (it is believed) was stabilized by a combination of wire and the machine-gun; a deadlock was finally broken by the tank, whose use was ignored and opposed by obscurantist generals. This is a mistaken view. The generals of the First World War and their staffs were men of great intelligence and ability, only too aware that they had suddenly been projected into a wholly alien and unforeseen military environment (1973: 51).

Michael Howard (1991: 41) belatedly refuted any "skilful and painless 'strategy of indirect approach'" available to Britain during the Great War, except to withdraw to its own territory, wait for France and Russia to be defeated, and to make peace before Britain starved (from interdiction of trade by German submarines). This drastic alternative sounds like Liddell Hart's "British Way in Warfare" (1932c), which Howard (1966: 59) had praised during Liddell Hart's lifetime, but repudiated thereafter (1970b: 39; 1972a: 58; 1975: 15, 58; 1983: 200; 1984: 180, 202; 1989: 8, 58).

Strachan (1991: 53) complained that "the shadow of *The Real War* continues to obscure the light."† Correlli Barnett (1999: 63) complained that Liddell Hart "bears

---

* Strachan (1991: 43-44) wrote that the "First World War was the main force in shaping Liddell Hart's military thought."
† Strachan (1991: 47-48) described *The Real War* as "a deeply personal statement" and "a very

a major responsibility for the false Anglo-Saxon folk memory about the Great War and the Western Front. That is, the war as futile, and the British high command as butchering incompetents." Andrew Green (2003: 2) found that "Liddell Hart's *The Real War* [and the like] helped to reinforce the great cultural mythology of the war." David Reynolds (2014: 329) judged that "he offered a very partial and partisan view of the conflict."

Bond, to his credit, belatedly admitted that Liddell Hart is most responsible for a polemical interpretation of the war, particularly the Somme and Passchendaele campaigns (2002: 45, 58-59; 2015: 25, 33, 47). The most recent reissue of Liddell Hart's history of the Great War (1934a) dates to 2014, when Bond wrote a fair explanation.

> We can begin to place him as a late Victorian autodidact with a polemical approach to history, grandiose ambitions, and excessive confidence in his own judgment…But, due to his immense readability, his Olympian tone, and his politically appealing message for a generation which assumes the First World War to be the epitome of vain slaughter and pointlessness, his histories are still reprinted, widely translated, and read uncritically (2015: 38).

---

partial and selective look at the First World War."

Liddell Hart sits at the top table for the Royal Tank Regiment's celebration of the 34th anniversary of the Battle of Cambrai, 20 November 1951, at Bovington Camp, Dorset (RACTM).

6

Historian

Liddell Hart's histories are readable and thought-provoking, but polemic. His academic training was incomplete. He valuably garnered information from private sources, but otherwise regarded sourcing as pedantic. His methodology is idiosyncratic and usually unreplicable. Unknowingly, he took up the role of applicatory historian, in that he glorified and memorialized favourite commanders, strategists, or strategies, but demonized others, and allowed for few alternatives in between.

Academic

In June 1914, Liddell Hart passed the first-year exams in the History Tripos at Cambridge, but at the lowest grade in all four subjects, including the lowest passing percentage point in Constitutional History. Liddell Hart's formal education ended in December 1914, when he was commissioned as an officer of the British Army, aged 19 years. He later admitted "only slight growth between 14 and 20," and "a year by year development of mind since the age of 20." Why then? He does not explain. Perhaps the trigger was his first nervous breakdown, suffered within days of his 20th birthday (note, 15 July 1932, LH 13/4/1).

In 1919, the British Army Staff College restarted its peacetime courses, but Liddell Hart never applied for staff training. Instead, he petitioned for entry into Cambridge's doctoral program, years before his current term of service would end. He was unsuccessful. He eschewed also the courses in military studies that had restarted at civilian universities. These were endowed by national government to promote public understanding and military recruiting, and were taught by retired senior officers with war experience. By 1925, these men were leaving academia, but Liddell Hart did not apply to replace them. In the same year, he started his long and lucrative career as a full-time military correspondent (see Chapter 9).

After criticism of his short and flamboyant books on future war (1925) and Scipio Africanus (1926a), he soured on academics. He described the members of the Royal Historical Society, after his first attendance, as "fossils" and "cloistered dons." He described his schoolfriend Maurice Bowra, then instructor in classics at Oxford University (since 1922), as "a strange mixture of first class brains without experience." In fact, Bowra had travelled further (to China and Russia in 1916) and served longer on the frontlines (1917-1918) (note, 11 February 1926, LH 11/1926/1; note, 2 March 1931, LH 11/1931/1).

As Brian Bond (1977: 60) admitted, "in terms of academic scholarship his historical works possessed obvious shortcomings, but with the exception of the elderly Spenser Wilkinson, who had retired in 1925, there were few if any university teachers in Britain at that time qualified to sit in judgment." John Mearsheimer (1988: 9, 14, 217, 224) found few objective or informed "defence intellectuals" or "scholars" of "military affairs" during Liddell Hart's professional life. Brian Holden Reid (1998: 10, 93) noted that "military subjects, including military history, were not studied or taught in universities" during his peak years.

Sourcing

Liddell Hart read only English and French, and rarely sought primary sources, although he did correspond with principals. His doctrinal publications make unambiguous claims from ambiguous sources. He claims to have induced from all of history (1922e: 298), "the main campaigns of history" (1922e: 302), "universal experience, as contained in history" (1922e: 298; 1923a: 323; 1925: 1), "reason and experience – as embodied in history" (1925: 4), and "the decisive wars in history" (1929a: 4). In each case, he over-relies on a few undeclared secondary sources about three ancients (Alexander the Great; Hannibal; Scipio Africanus) and three early moderns (Napoleon; Clausewitz; Sherman).

He developed the chapter on Scipio into his first biography (1926a), but it is short, quick, and citation-free. Most of the historiography on Scipio was in Italian and German, which he could not read. The book alludes to only one source (Livy: the Anglicized name for the Roman historian Titus Livius). He admitted privately that his sources were "hardly adequate as a basis for an analysis" (to Scammell, 31 May 1937, LH 1/622). He persuaded Luvaas (1964: 388) that he had made "a careful reading of the primary sources," and persuaded Bond (1977: 44) that he had "brilliantly exploited the limited sources available in English," to make "Scipio...an admirable vehicle for his own military views." Richard Gabriel (2008: 18) describes the book as "not a scholarly or accurate account," but rather a "propagandistic" vehicle for his "pro-Scipio bias." This bias is a search for an alternative approach to war other than the attrition of the Great War, which he traced back to Napoleon (the book is titled *A Greater Than Napoleon*), and for an alternative ancient hero to Hannibal (the subject of several recent biographies). However, Hannibal was less attritional and more expeditionary than Scipio, and was defeated only after being recalled to the defence of Carthage.

In 1928, Fuller pointed out that Liddell Hart was publishing his fifth book and 30th journal article without references. Liddell Hart replied that archival research is "pedantic" (11 March 1928, LH 1/302). Still, perhaps Fuller's criticism prompted his decision to finish his biography of Sherman with references. It is the first of only five books (of at least 35 unique books published) in which he declares any references. At the end of the book is a list of 64 "general" references – a rate of one source per seven pages. Each chapter concludes with references, although some overlap the general list. No page numbers are given. He dismisses citations as "untidy and irritating" and "only of value to a small proportion of readers," although he expects complaints (1929b: 432; 1958: 432). A historian of the war characterizes this excuse as "specious." "Liddell Hart was too knowledgeable not to know it." Thus, he must have avoided citations in order to discourage checks on his scholarship (Castel 2003: 410).*

Liddell Hart's concurrent book on *The Decisive Wars of History* (otherwise known by its prescription for "indirect approach") (1929a) contains no references, despite its claim to review all decisive wars. The final and longest edition of this book runs to more than 400 pages, still without references (1954a).

His first history of the Great War (1930b) ends with a list of references, but not citations. After revision and expansion (1934a), it lists 485 references – a rate of

---

* Reid (2006: 403) judged it "seductively persuasive despite its paucity of original research."

about 1 reference per page, although many are repeated across different chapters. No page numbers are given. His final history of the Great War ends with a "selected bibliography," with 37 sources – a rate of 1 source per 10 pages (1938e: 315).

Immediately following the first edition, he released an article claiming a "British Way in Warfare." "The questions I shall raise are the outcome of study in the history of the last war that has been proceeding side by side with an extension of a personal study of other wars and of the general history of warfare" (1931b: 486). Yet he provides no sources. In the following year, he published a book-length version, with the same claim, still without sources (1932c).

His short book on modern military thought (*The Ghost of Napoleon*) is his fourth with references. Its "bibliographic note" contains 28 items – a rate of 1 source per 6 pages (1933c). These sources are mostly secondary. Yet he starts the book by complaining of others' inattention to the "influence of thought on thought," which is "less perceptible than the effects of action" (1933c: 11). Hyporitically, he complains that most historians and "professional soldier[s]" use a "method of concentrating on a few campaigns without a background, without acquiring a broad knowledge of all warfare," and reading only "some of the published accounts of and commentaries upon those campaigns" (1933c: 181).

Liddell Hart's longest book before the Second World War runs to 444 printed pages, without any references (1939b). His first new book after the Second World War (best known as *The Other Side of the Hill*) quotes and paraphrases captured German officers. His sudden reliance on primary sources is worthy, although he usually paraphrases, usually fails to indicate what he asked, and never specifies the when, where, or how of the communication (1948).

His official history of the British Army's tank arm runs to more than 1,100 pages, without references, and without acknowledgements to the dozens of officers, research assistants, friends, and principals who contributed (1959a; Newsome 2024: Chapter 12).

His memoirs excuse his failure to cite, because "too much so-called research is slipshod, and the habit of footnote references is often a snare and delusion merely intended to impress the reader" (1965: I, 169).

His *History of the Second World War* is his fifth and last to list references. It lists 35 sources,* one per 20 pages of main body text. It does not acknowledge a dozen assistants, and dozens of other contributors by correspondence. It reports his direct observations, but some turn out to be fabrications (see Chapter 20) (1970: 715-716).

Bond (1977: 60-61, 212) admits that Liddell Hart's books were "rarely the product of original research in the strictest sense." However, they "were based on wide reading[,] supplemented wherever possible by interviews and correspondence." with "a wide range of personal contacts."

Methodologist

Liddell Hart's methodology was energetic but idiosyncratic. So far as he ever described it, his most frequent term is "creative imagination." Early on, he had declared that "imagination" is necessary to the "art" of war (1924c: 40; 1928d: 728; 1928e: 244). Soon, he made imagination necessary to history and thence theory too.

---

* The 35 books include 45 volumes, working out at one volume per 16 pages

"The practical view of history lies in projecting the film of the past on the blank screen of the future" (1925: 73). He first referred to "creative imagination" in the same letter in which he rebuffs Fuller's sourcing as "pedantic."

> Your historical knowledge is uneven. So, I quite admit, is my own, but in such conditions I am more inclined to tread lightly and only step out when I have made sure of my foothold. You, in contrast, are sometimes too bold. On the other hand[,] I consider that the creative imagination is often more likely to arrive at historical truth than the pedantic burrower in documents – and that you have this creative imagination in exceptionally high degree (to Fuller, 11 March 1928, LH 1/302).

Again, he seems to be projecting on to others what he was denying of himself. In *The Decisive Wars of History*, the only description of method is his "impression" of history (1929a: 4). He heads off criticism of his biography of Sherman by dismissing the accuracy of maps, and noting that Sherman himself often commanded without accurate maps (1929b: 20). "I learned from my work on this book that the value of personal examination of the terrain is apt to be overrated" (1965: I, 169). Referring to this book, his second wife recalled him as "a brilliant map reader" (1970: vii). His memoirs declare "that seeing a battlefield is less effective than careful study of the maps, and the use of creative imagination, to produce in the mind a clear picture of its features" (1965, I: 170). His final history of the Great War refers to "the imaginative insight which marks the great commander" (1938e: 132).*

In late 1940, when his ethos collapsed, he wrote a new description of "method": "philosophical geometry – to get a projection of the experience of the past through the present pointing to the future" (1941a: 8). This "projection" sounds like trend analysis or forecasting, which is not necessarily philosophical, and certainly not geometrical. A year later, he drops the term "philosophical geometry" in favour of "historical judgment" (1942a: 12). These books sold poorly, as did his reprint of *British Way in Warfare* (1942b). Robert Graves reached out, but with a kick:

> My criticism of your history is that you have (in the past) tended to accept school textbook accounts of generals or religious disputes or campaigns which you have not yourself studied in intimate detail (18 August 1943, LH 1/327).

In 1944, he published a pamphlet that claims to be methodological. It is titled *Why Don't We Learn from History?* but, as Danchev (1998a: 215) admits, this is "a question never answered." In practice, it is a commentary on the current war, with occasional claims to have predicted everything. The closest he comes to answering the titular question is to revert to his false claim to objectivity: "The student must first learn to approach the subject in a spirit of doubt" (1944b: 11). Revealingly, his next book categorizes *Why Don't We Learn from History?* in the "General" section of his opus, rather than the "History" or "Military Science" sections (1946b: 2). That book revives his claim to forecast by "understanding, and applying, the lessons of the past" (1946b: 76).

---

* The sentence states that German Army General Alexander von Kluck (1846-1934) "certainly had no trace of" it.

During the Cold War, he revived his suggestion that "[c]reative imagination is the essential characteristic of genius" (1959b: 20-21). He persuaded Bond (1977: 7) that he had discovered a set of "keys"* to the "lessons of history," although Bond later realized a "clutch of principles, formulas[,] and plain prejudices."

Applicatory Historian

Most military historians favour "applicatory" history, although most do not realize the term. Liddell Hart was unaware of it. The applicatory approach (often miscategorized as a method) views war as a duel between two competitors – reduced to the most important or interesting states, premiers, commanders, or strategies (Pennington, Hough, Case 1943: 9-49). Liddell Hart (1925: 75) once declared that "[w]ar is a but a duel between two nations instead of two individuals," although he always focused on individuals. This reductionism imposes homogeneity on each side: i.e., each side is seen as a unitary actor whose behaviour perfectly obeys its national character or principals or strategies (Cohen and Gooch 1990: 37).

At operational levels, the applicatory method tends to "battle piece narrative," ending in "sycophancy or hero-worship," in which the only controversy is about which commander is best (Keegan 1976: 27). This sycophancy is illustrated by the competitive publishing of Liddell Hart and Fuller. In one year, Liddell Hart and Fuller published admiring biographies of rival Union Generals William T. Sherman and Ulysses S. Grant respectively. While each author disputed the other's choice, they both attributed military performance to the commander's "personality." Liddell Hart wrote his biography of Sherman like a direct observer. His preface predicts criticism of lack of military "details," but justifies this lack as an "exercise in human psychology, not in upholstery…For the issue of any operation of war is decided not by what the situation is, but by what the rival commanders think it is" (1929b: xiv; 1958: viii). His book on *The British Way in Warfare* repeats that only the commander's "psychology" matters to "military history" (1932c: 108; 1935a: 93).

By then, Liddell Hart was aware of criticisms of his reductionism. His next book caricatures other historians (particularly British historians) as story-tellers who set out "to glorify achievements rather than to discover the facts." (For no given reason, he terms their choice "evolutionary history.") His "facts" are that military innovation is less likely to be "a flash of inspiration" than a "development" from previous "ideas" or practices (1933c: 147-149). Later on, he focuses the blame on former professional soldiers.

> For the soldier, "My country," right or wrong, must be the watchword. And this essential loyalty, whether it be to a country, to a regiment, or to comrades, is so ingrained in him that when he passes from action to reflection it is difficult for him to acquire instead the historian's single-minded loyalty to truth (1938e: 213).

---

* Liddell Hart himself never published the word with this meaning, although Bond was correct to describe the word as "a favourite metaphor." Perhaps Liddell Hart (or Bond) recalled Fuller (1936: 461), who had described the "principles of war" as "a set of keys upon which may be played, so to speak, any war tune, so long as the player possesses a little skill. If not, they are of no value at all."

Despite his discreditation during the Second World War, he rebuilt his reputation partly by offering himself as the provider of "truth," in opposition to the increasing "desire to create idols" and a "great man" (1959b: 18).

He is correct that military historians tend to idolatry, but also hypocritical. His focus on the psychology of commanders was not counter-idolatry, just idolatry with different idols. His approach was applicatory, at the level of commanders, and thus not holistic enough to find the "truth" he sought.

Legacy

Luvaas (1964: 389) reported that Liddell Hart "was careful to avoid abusing history in his efforts to use it for constructive purposes," but Luvaas is alone in this opinion. Theodore Ropp (1962: 271) characterized Liddell Hart and Fuller as "military critics" and "expert polemicists." Robert Rhodes James (1970: 56) observed that Liddell Hart was "less a historian than a participant." Brian Bond (1977: 38, 212) characterized Liddell Hart's histories as "primarily…polemics or tracts," although he "excelled at communicating complex issues to a wide readership." During questioning by a live audience, Bond described him as "primarily a journalist, a military critic, a wise-man, a military historian," who "wrote exciting, very readable history that in his day had a tremendous impact," but "usually had a polemical as well as a scholarly purpose." In the audience, Adrian suggested that Basil was motivated more to be a part of history than to observe history (Howard 1979: 26, 30).*

Robert O'Neill (1990: 105) admitted that Liddell Hart's "works are not to be regarded as objective expositions but rather as strongly didactic." Strachan (1991: 47; 2020: 538) decided that "[f]or Liddell Hart, military history was didactic," "to instruct for the future," and "a tool to communicate ideas about war that had present application and future implication more than a help to understand the past." Russell Weigley (in Liddell Hart 1996: xi) described Liddell Hart as "more a polemicist than a military historian and a biographer." Albert Castel (2003: 425) concluded that "almost all he wrote…is propaganda in the guise of history, his purpose throughout his career being not to understand the past but to shape the future." Brian Holden Reid (2006: 402) found that Liddell Hart's thinking on the American Civil War, at least, "had a contemporary, polemical rather than historical, source." Subsequently, Bond (2015: 33) admitted that Liddell Hart "conspicuously lacked some notable scholarly attributes: such as an interest in past events for their own sake or a willingness to make substantial alterations in the light of later evidence."

---

* Adrian had given the opposite impression in the preface to a posthumous edition of one of his father's books, in which he held a stake. Here Adrian claims that his father "was a historian who strove for rigorous objectivity and maintained intellectual detachment throughout the crises of his life and despite the official, commercial or personal pressures to which he was inevitably exposed" (1972: 2).

7

Doctrinist

In 1918, Liddell Hart turned his adjutancy of the Cambridgeshire Regiment's home battalion into a training role, focusing on the platoon. At the end of the war, he transitioned from platoon trainer to regional educator, but spent his spare time turning himself into doctrinist. Through useful analogies and social networking, he was invited to contribute to the next edition of the *Infantry Training* manual. He loved the role, but soon was disillusioned by declining influence and inclining criticism. He denigrated manuals, without giving up his claims to have authored some.

Platoon Trainer, 1918

In January 1918, Liddell Hart joined the (volunteer) Cambridgeshire Regiment, as adjutant, although he based himself at a university college, and focused on the University's Officer Training Corps. Coincidentally, the War Department issued a manual on *The Training and Employment of Platoons*. He was obliged to utilize the manual, although none of his publications admit it. Instead, they condemn Britain's wartime manuals and training.

> The writer's own experience has led him to the view, shared by others of vastly wider experience, that the majority of the failures of the troop leading [sic] in modern battle are due to the junior commanders' haziness of mind as to the correct action to take in any particular tactical situation (1921d: 619).

> The confusion resulted from the unclassified mess of precepts and reservations which they had imbibed from the textbooks and manuals…I freely admit that I floundered in common with the rest (1922e: 307).

He pretends that he discovered how to train without official guidance, that the "infantry was the least trained," "the most difficult to train," and "differently trained according to the whims and prejudices of its temporary commander," who is likely "to concentrate on the more concrete factors of drill, musketry, and bayonet fighting." He recommends "a man of wide capacity and deep study," to generalize the lessons of history (1922b: 467; 1923a: 323). In memoirs, he dates to 1918 his disillusionment with British force employment, professional soldiers, and even combat veterans, and claims to be a better trainer too, thanks to his removal from operations in 1916 (1965: I, 33, 37-38). In fact, his disillusionment waits until 1921, as shown in the final section of this chapter. In 1918, he applied official drills (both tactical and ceremonial), although he thought he was a better communicator. In the summer, Cambridge University Press published his first pamphlet, which applies official drills to "volunteer forces," in fewer pages than the official manual. His memoirs claim that this pamphlet was "adopted" by "other officer training corps." Yet it was not satisfactory: in October, the Press released a revised edition, without the first edition's reference to volunteer forces (1918a ; 1918b; 1965: I, 31-35).

The pamphlet's thunder was stolen by a leaflet on *Attack Formations for Small Units*, released in September 1918 by the Inspectorate-General of Training. The Inspectorate distributed 41,496 copies, accounting for more than 20 percent of the Inspectorate's products, even though it is only one of its 14 leaflets. In the next month, the Press released Liddell Hart's version: *Battle Drill, or Attack Formations Simplified* (1918c; Baynes 1995: 211).

Platoon Doctrine, 1919

After the armistice (in November), most wartime volunteers sought to demobilize, but Liddell Hart took yet another short-term opportunity, this time at London District HQ, to administer education (of mostly reservists). Within a month, he realized that he preferred training (of skills) to education (of knowledge), and started to write an article on platoon training. In content, it reads like *Attack Formations for Small Units*, although it does not admit the leaflet. Nominally, he addresses both the "training" and the "theory" of the infantry platoon, implicitly in anticipation of the War Department's new edition of *Platoon Training*, although he does not refer to this either. In February, the new edition was released, and he submitted his article to the *RUSI Journal*, which agreed to publish, in May (LH 7/1920/20 to /31; Baynes 1995: 211).

He took sick leave from April, to try to leverage his subject into less specialist outlets, as incongruous as *The Spectator* (a weekly topical magazine). He sought a new billet too. In June, he sent a copy of his article to Lieutenant-General Sir Ivor Maxse. Liddell Hart's approach was belated. Maxse had advocated for more training at sub-unit echelons since February 1918, when the BEF's defensive phase was supposed to be coming to an end. Maxse turned his corps from fortifying to training. A month later, XVIII Corps proved resolute against the German counter-offensive, although Maxse was criticized for starting a retreat on the next day. In June, Maxse was effectively kicked upstairs, and home, as Inspector-General of Training. There his primary activity was to advocate for more sub-unit training. However, his call for training every day (even on operations), and criticism of prior training, did not appeal to most officers, although it did imply excuses for his own failure. Liddell Hart was not yet prepared to endorse him. The Inspectorate expired in December. In January 1919, he took command of a temporary corps in Germany, which looked like his last hurrah, until June, when he took charge of Northern Command and a doctrinal team carried over from the Inspectorate. The news prompted Liddell Hart's approach. Months later, Maxse replied with praise, but no offers (LH 1/499; Griffith 1994: 184; Baynes 1995: 186-188, 195, 217).

In August, the Army threatened Liddell Hart with invaliding, so he returned full-time to London District HQ. He had already completed a second article for the *RUSI Journal*, which adds to his first article by admitting the utility of a small, unarmed tracked carrier for the infantry platoon's heavier weapons and equipment. Since 1917, such carriers had been developed from and officially categorized as "tanks," hence his subtitle: "The Tank as a Weapon of Infantry." He was actually claiming that all tank requirements could be reduced to small, unarmed carriers, in opposition to the extant manual on *Infantry and Tank Cooperation and Training* (March 1918). Nevertheless, in later decades, he would misrepresent this article as foresight of Blitzkrieg (1919b; 1965: I, 35; Newsome 2024: Chapter 1).

Official manuals, 1920-1921

In April 1920, Liddell Hart's third article was published, this time in the *United Service Magazine*. Here he marries his platoon doctrine with official principles of war. In March, he sent a copy to Maxse, who appreciated it more than the first. Both men railed against their seniors, were prone to analogies and slogans, pretended to offer training that nobody had thought to offer before, and hoped to restore the infantry as the dominant arm. Maxse forwarded it to the two officers revising the *Infantry Training* manual: Brigadier-General Winston Dugan, who was now commanding a brigade; and Captain John "Jack" Evetts, a staff officer. That same month, Liddell Hart visited them at Northern Command HQ, in York (1965: 1, 37-48; Griffith 1994: 7, 100; Baynes 1995: 223, 238; Danchev 1998a: 105).

> Maxse seized the salient points of any idea with lightning quickness, although occasionally misjudging some point because of too hasty examination. His fierce manner concealed a very warm heart, and he particularly liked people who showed that they were not afraid of him. He was always ready to encourage and make use of new ideas (1965: I, 43).*

Maxse handed over a draft of the manual, dated to 1919, and seconded Liddell Hart to Dugan's HQ in Lichfield, remotely and part-time. Liddell Hart's full-time billet remained in London. There, he was absorbed into the Army Education Corps (AEC), when made permanent in June 1920, at the substantive rank of Captain. Like his time in the infantry, his years with the AEC are poorly documented. Nominally, he was co-writing press releases, official histories, and training documents, but his archives suggest he was spending most of his time convalescing and writing for private publication. His private publications commercialized his public work.

Public exposure began in November 1920, when Maxse arranged for him to lecture to the Royal United Service Institution, chaired and introduced by Maxse himself. Maxse's only two justifications are Liddell Hart's juniority and youth (he had just turned 25): "Others have written about infantry tactics, but some of us who have done so are too old to have had regimental experience of our own in the late war" (1921a: 1). Maxse did not allow the audience to comment.

From 1920 to 1921, Liddell Hart published seven articles, in magazines as far away as America, thanks to Maxse's influence. Each is a reprint or reframing of any other. Increasingly, they claim to be generalizable at any echelon. In so doing, they become less specific. They offer at least five memorable analogies: boxing (1920a); a man in the dark (1920b; 1920c; 1921a; 1921b); an (offensive) expanding torrent; a (defensive) contracting funnel (1921a; 1921c); and a pillar of fire in the dark (1921d). The fourth article (published by RUSI in February 1921) offers man-in-the-dark and expanding torrent as variants of each other. He arranged for this to be reprinted as a pamphlet in May, mistitled as *Framework of a Science of Infantry Tactics*. This was twice republished in "simplified" editions (1921a; 1921e; 1923b; 1926c). Meanwhile, he lectured on the same to the School of Military Engineering, of all places, thanks again to Maxse's influence (1921b; 1921c). The seventh of the seven articles is the most incongruous. It admits criticism, but does not cite any. It reframes the previous articles as an intellectual beacon (the titular "pillar of fire") (1921d).

---

* He paraphrases his obituary published in *The Times* in February 1958 (Baynes 1995: 234).

The pillar of fire never reappears. "Expanding torrent" became his favourite analogy, while "science" became his favourite disciplinary claim. The analogical terms were new, but the tactics and principles were not, despite his many claims to novelty. His only "maxim" that clashes with doctrine is his requirement for liaisons and runners from every battalion HQ to every subordinate company and neighbouring unit, and from every company HQ to every subordinate platoon and neighbouring company. In a later article, he clarifies that the inspiration is the French infantry manual (1921b: 180; 1922a: 246).

The instability and contradictions in these publications help to explain Liddell Hart's declining influence on official doctrine. In 1920, Evetts wrote to Dugan that they should "pick Liddell Hart's brains but need not trouble to do anything for him in return." (Liddell Hart did not see the letter until 1922, after Dugan's HQ moved to a new camp.) The War Department released its new edition of the *Infantry Training* manual late in 1921. Liddell Hart was one of many anonymous contributors, subject to revision, editing, and approval, all the way to the CIGS. Publicly, he admitted that his own doctrine is "outlined" across only two pages, but privately he claimed to "have written the whole tactical half of the official British infantry manual" (LH 7/1921/68; 1922d: 292). Once separated from the Army, he claimed to be "the author of the post-war Infantry Training [manual], and of various unofficial treatises on infantry tactics" (1929c: 96; 1935a: 297; 1965: I, 40-48), "jointly responsible for the post-war doctrine" (1932c: 271; 1935a: 315), author of training drills "incorporated complete in the official Infantry Training manual" (1939b: 388), author of "the official British 'Infantry Training,' and...editor of the 'Small Arms Training'" (1952: 29; Howard 1965: 373),* author of "a study of infantry tactics in 1917" that developed into the "Infantry Training Manual in 1920" (1956b: 2), writer of "the post-war official manual on Infantry Training" (1956a: 463), and author of "the new Infantry Training manual" (1965: I, 59). The frontmatter of his books lists prior publications, ending: "certain of the General Staff manuals." Correspondents and disciples published the same fiction (Gibson 1943: 377; Ropp 1959: 29; Luvaas 1964: 401; Stearns 1972: 5; Bond 1979: 25).

Disillusionment, 1922

Liddell Hart betrayed his claims to authorship by re-lobbying for incorporation of his offerings, while denigrating the manuals that he claimed to have authored. In 1921, he was shocked to see rebuttals of his articles, some in the same magazines. In Spring 1922, Dugan's brigade left Northern Command for its pre-war station (Shorncliffe Camp, Kent), in Eastern Command. There, General Sir Henry Horne,† who had contributed to Haig's dismissal of Maxse from operational command

---

* Luvaas (1964: 379) heard that Liddell Hart wrote only the "vital sections" of *Infantry Training*, and the "attack drills" of *Small Arms Training*, and that he edited the latter.
† Horne (1861-1929) commanded XV Corps, in which Liddell Hart had served, during the Somme offensive. Liddell Hart's first reflection on the offensive praises Horne, in common with Haig. Later in 1916, Horne took command of the 1st Army. When XVIII Corps transferred to 1st Army in May 1918, Maxse refused the dispositions assigned, until Horne threatened to relieve him. Haig promised to relieve Maxse if Horne insisted, which was agreed in June. Horne took over Eastern Command in 1919, retired in 1923, and died in 1929 (LH 7/1916/22; Baynes 1995: 209).

in June 1918, was unimpressed with Liddell Hart's demonstration of tactics on a sand-table. Liddell Hart's description of Horne's reaction is limited to the word "obtuse," which itself is obtuse. Later in 1922, Dugan recommended Liddell Hart for accelerated promotion, for "instructive pamphlets on military tactics and training." Horne replied that writing "on military subjects does not justify accelerated promotion" (1965: I, 58).*

Liddell Hart's articles of 1922 to 1924 denigrate British official doctrine. The first champions the French.†

> [The introduction to the French infantry manuals] stresses the fact that if the Regulation is written in such a wide manner as to cover every possible case, it will be so full of vague generalities and reservations as to be unintelligible to the bulk of officers; an accusation which can be levied against our own manuals, in the past at any rate...The writer has always pleaded for a more definite tone in the manuals, and for the introduction of a framework upon which the junior officer can develop his knowledge as his experience widens. Hence it is especially gratifying to find that the French authorities have recognized the need (1922a: 238).

Liddell Hart condemns Britain's current manuals, trainers, professional soldiers, and even war veterans.

> To give the ordinary manual, with its mass of unclassified precepts and considerations, into their hands is simply to give them mental indigestion. Nor are they likely to gain a clear grasp of the principles from the highly imaginary conditions of a tactical exercise in peacetime or from the narrow range of their experiences in war (1922e: 308).

Even though he had trained and published drills in 1918, he now denigrates drills as the stuff of intellectual inferiors, particularly Foch (1938e: 53).

> The correct tactics must be based on human nature, as they have been by every master of war, and not on mechanics or mathematical calculation. Yet military history is one vast graveyard of geometrical evolutions deduced from the unreal experience of the drill square and the rifle range (1922c: 714).

In 1924, he brought his charges and prejudices together on one page.

> [A] comparison with the French suggests that there is still room for improvement in clearness and classification of matter...
>
> How often does one hear the confession made, as if it were a source of pride, that the speaker never reads a military manual or book. Yet the manuals should be an epitome of military wisdom, and a "pillar of fire by night" to the aspiring junior leader...It would greatly help if the authorities withdrew their veto on any breaking away from General Staff

---

* Liddell Hart archived no notes about or correspondence with Horne.
† Years later, he would claim to have received a "request" in the early 1920s to "critique" the French Army's first post-war manuals (1941a: 83). His archives contain no evidence.

language. A clear and definite tone should replace vagueness and reservations; metaphor, word picture, and sketch should lighten the path of the leader; the interpersonal "it will be done" might be substituted by the more vivid "You will do this" (1924c: 49).

That year, he separated from the active Army, and lobbied for influence on later editions of the *Infantry Training* manual, which would be published in 1926, 1931, 1935, and 1937.[*] However, his inputs to the edition of 1921 were not included in the edition of 1926, even though the project leader (Lord Gort, John Vereker) was friendly and keen for advice. Privately, he admitted that his offerings "were criticized by the then DDSD[†] as an idle dream. Even when he passed papers for circulation he used to scribble caustic comments in the margin" (to Ogorkiewicz, 6 April 1954, RACTM E2015.2015.62). Publicly, he repeated his charge from 1922 that the "French Infantry Manual of 1920 pointed the way...from the forge of war experience" (1927a: 81).

The edition of 1931 similarly ignores him, despite his lobbying of another friend (Bernard Law Montgomery). In 1932, he complained that "the excessive crop of manuals...will never help officers to a real understanding of war nor teach them to reason tactically." His alternatives then were military biography and fiction (1932c: 278; 1935a: 322). In 1934, he complained that British "manuals, by the nature of their compilation, are merely registers of prevailing practice, not the log-books of a scientific study of war" (1935a: 238).

In 1932, "a committee of half a dozen of the more distinguished younger generals,"[‡] as Liddell Hart described them, reported on lessons from the Great War. One recommendation was for the simplification of infantry drills. Initially, Liddell Hart reported the committee without the recommendation. In early 1937, he misreported the recommendation as an endorsement of his wartime drills. By his own account, Edmund Ironside[§] (Eastern Command) prevailed on Clive Liddell (4th Division) to try his wartime drills that training season.[¶] In July, platoon drills were demonstrated to the CIGS (Cyril Deverell), without credit to Liddell Hart. Deverell authorized company and battalion drills across all infantry units in Eastern Command, for the remaining two months of the training season. Afterwards, Deverell authorized a "field drill" for the whole army. Liddell Hart claimed this was his drill from 1918. Yet be betrayed himself in 1939, when he lobbied yet again for incorporation of his

---

[*] In 1921, the manual was provisionally issued in two volumes, on "Training" and "[The Principles of] War," respectively. Both volumes were re-editioned in 1926. Volume 2 was re-editioned in 1931. Volume 1 was re-editioned in 1935. In 1937, the manual was issued as one volume again. By then, it was effectively supplanted by new editions of the *Field Service Regulations* and by new manuals for duty cycles at lower echelons.
[†] Ernest Ord Lewin (1879-1950) had been commissioned into the Royal Artillery in 1900. He served mostly as a staff officer, in India, Britain, France (where he spent most of the Great War), and Russia, through 1918. He was billeted as Deputy DSD from 1923 to 1927. He retired as a Major-General in 1938
[‡] They were chaired by Lieutenant-General Sir Walter Kirke, commissioned by Milne, and prompted by the first part of Edmonds' official history of the Somme offensive (1932).
[§] Ironside later expunged and restricted his papers, so his role cannot be verified.
[¶] He persuaded Luvaas (1964: 423) of the same, for which Luvaas cites letters to Clive Liddell (5 June) and the novelist C.S. Forester (15 March), not Ironside.

drill of 1918 into the manuals (1935a: 248; 1939b: 389, 393-394).

Also in 1939, he published a complaint about "sundry alterations made, in subsequent revisions of the drill-book, by some who had not fully grasped the underlying principle, perhaps for lack of practical experiment on their part" (1939b: 388). Liddell Hart's next published explanation comes in the Second World War.

> The War Office and the Staff College authorities raised objections on the ground that it was not written in "General Staff language." I pointed out in reply that Infantry Training was intended for the enlightenment of the junior officer and NCO, not for the instruction of the General Staff. The force of this argument, apparently new, was admitted by authority – but it was then too late to restore the simpler phrasing of the original draft, and the word-pictures which had been cut out (1941a: 50n).

In the 1960s, Liddell Hart claimed, for the first time, that his influences on the Kirke Committee are to be found in recommendations for surprise, night attacks, and exploitation of breakthroughs. He claimed to have drafted the *Infantry Training* manual, in 1920, with "the value of night action, of smoke, and of surprise in every form," only to see these values "watered down by the War Office" (1960a: 203, 206; 1965: I, 31, 216; Luvaas 1964: 394). In fact, the man-in-the-dark is an analogy to decision-making with imperfect information, not fighting in the dark. It does not prescribe night action or smoke. It lists surprise as one way to aid the principle of "economy of force," (one of eight principles of war in the *Field Service Regulations*). Different articles give different ways to achieve surprise. His first recommendation is an unexpected place and time (1920a: 32; 1920b: 474). Later, he lists "ground, night, or fog" as "aids" to "assault from an unexpected direction or at an unexpected moment" (1922b: 459). In reaction to criticism of the expanding torrent, he adds "smoke" as useful to outflanking manoeuvres (1922c: 718). This was after *Infantry Training* had been issued. By his own account, he did not call for "revival of the night attack," "artificial fog," or "flood-lighting the battlefield" until a lecture to Southern Command in early 1931, written in November 1930 (1933b: 62; 1944a: 284; 1954b; 1960a: 205). Nevertheless, in 1960 he persuaded a young friend that he had emphasized them without interruption since July 1916 (Walters 1961: 25). His memoirs pretend that he had invented "artificial moonlight" (reflecting electric light off clouds to the ground) in November 1930, as implemented from 1944. Yet Bernard Law Montgomery had already claimed to invent it in 1942. Before that, Fuller had documented artificial moonlight back to the Great War, and electric flood-lighting of the battlefield back to the siege of Fort Wagner, Charleston, in 1863 (Fuller, "Historical Notes on the Use of Searchlights in War," 30 May 1939, Rutgers New Brunswick).

To Luvaas (1964: 378) and in memoirs (1965: I, 226), Liddell Hart claimed that he had invented infantry "battle drills" at Cambridge University in 1918. However, his last self-biography dates his invention to 1917 (1969: 172). Whatever the date, a historian of the Great War found the claim "particularly irritating" (Griffith 1994: 100).

General Siegfried Westphal, Eugene Hinterhoff (exiled Polish journalist, co-founder and honorary secretary of the Military Commentators Circle), and BHLH, at the Naval & Military Club, Piccadilly, London, 17 January 1956 (LH 13/104/13).

Hinterhoff, Field-Marshal Montgomery, and BHLH at a meeting of the Military Commentators Circle, at the Dorchester Hotel, Park Lane, London, on 27 November 1958 (LH 13/104/13)

8

Strategist

From doctrinist, Liddell Hart remade himself as "strategist." He offers many insights and axioms, in memorable language, such as his reminder to approach "indirectly." However, his high-mindedness belies his conflicted definitions, his conflation of the conventional levels of analysis into "grand strategy," and the instability of his recommendations. Some of the variance can be explained by shifting agendas, such as his keenness for quick decisive wars at one time or long indecisive wars at another. Further, his strategies were undermined by his reliance on analogies – not just as means of communication, as he justifid them, but as premises. He preferred abstractions over study of technologies and techniques. His strategies are thought-provoking, but require practical development.

Definitions

A strategy is a way of achieving an objective (Newsome 2023a: 162). Liddell Hart initially defined strategy, bizarrely, as "the science of communications," or "movement [as] a simpler word for communications" (1924a: 90, 92).

Later, he folded Clausewitz's definition of war ("policy with other means";* or "an act of force to compel the enemy to fulfill our will") into his definition of strategy: "the distribution and transmission of military means to fulfil the ends of policy" (1929a: 150; 1932c: 98); or "the art of distributing and applying military means to fulfil the ends of policy" (1954a: 335). These are useful definitions, but he was dishonest about their uniqueness.† Clausewitz's "principles of war" (1812) describe strategy as "the combination of individual engagements to attain the goal of the campaign or war" (1942: 15, 45). Clausewitz's *On War* (1820s) defines strategy as "the use of fights towards the objective of the war" (1873, I, 43-44; 1943: 61-62; 1984: 127-128). Liddell Hart's first published mention of Clausewitz misreports that Clausewitz's concept of strategy "intrudes on the sphere of policy." He contradicts himself immediately by complaining that "it narrows the meaning of strategy to the pure utilisation of battle" (1929a: 147; 1954a: 333). His first statement misreports Clausewitz's definition of war as a definition of strategy. His second statement is based on Clausewitz's real definition of strategy.

Increasingly, Liddell Hart used the word "strategy" to mean "grand strategy." He differentiated "pure strategy" as "strategy on its original and true basis," and "the art of the general." He defined "grand strategy" as "policy in execution," or "to co-ordinate and direct all the resources of a nation towards the attainment of the political object of the war – the goal defined by national policy" (1929a: 150-151, 1932c: 98; 1935a: 83; 1954a: 336). He uses the term "higher strategy" as a synonym.

---

* The German word *"mit"* has usually been translated, misleadingly, as "by" rather than "with" (Clausewitz 1873: I, 12; 1943: xxiv, 16; 1984: 87).
† Similarly, Reid (1999: 69) quotes the latter definition, and implies that it is a product of his "indirect approach." In fact, it is 25 years younger.

He defines both as "to co-ordinate and direct all the resources of a nation, or band of nations, toward the attainment of the political object of the war." He still differentiates policy as the "goal" for "grand strategy," as he had for "strategy." Belatedly, he differentiates the goal of "grand strategy" as winning the peace, whereas the goal of "strategy" is winning the war (1954a: 321-322; Walters 1961: 23).

Raymond Aron (1970: 14) quoted Clausewitz's definition before complaining that "modern [current] authors contrast strategy not with tactics but with policy." Martin Kitchen (1988: 34) found that Liddell Hart meant grand strategy to be "predominantly political," other strategy to be "essentially technical and military." In any case, "the line between the two was never clearly drawn." Still, almost all definitions of "grand strategy" in English "are some offshoot of Basil Liddell Hart's rendering" (Sayle 2011).

Michael Howard (1972b: 1; 1991: 31) paraphrased Liddell Hart's definition of "grand strategy" in an official history of the Second World War, but later admitted that it is "prescriptive rather than descriptive."* Paul Kennedy (1991: 4) defends Liddell Hart's definition of "grand strategy" as "concerned with peace as much as (perhaps even more than) with war." Similarly, Robert Larson (1980: 70) appreciates that "Liddell Hart's definition was designed to re-emphasize the subordination of the conduct of war to its objective." However, Clausewitz had already done that.

Another appreciation is that Liddell Hart wanted the ends adjusted to the means (Howard 1983: 36; Kennedy 1991: 2; Unterseher 2023: 44), although Clausewitz and others had wanted the same. Liddell Hart himself was better at the ideal than the practice of adjusting ends to means, such as his expectation of victory in World War II through raids, economic blockade and sanctions, defence-dominance, "moral pressure," and political revolution (see Chapter 15).

Levels

Liddell Hart sometimes differentiated grand strategy from strategy, and sometimes defined tactics,† but otherwise conflated the conventional levels of force employment (policy, grand strategy, strategy, operations, tactics) and thence the conventional echelons of force structure (from army groups down to platoons). For instance, he recommends his "expanding torrent" as "an automatic and interchangeable system of attack...applicable to all units and formations from the platoon upwards" (1921a: 13; 1921c: 216). Contradictorily, he complains of professionals applying platoon tactics upwards, instead of studying strategy downwards.

> A professional soldier is rarely a professional strategist. His training is concentrated on the mechanism of tactics and military organization, and in his peace exercises he is far more concerned to see that his own mechanism works properly to upset his opponent's. Even if he finds time to

---

* Howard (1970c: 47) had already adopted Liddell Hart's definition. His paraphrase in the official history (1972b: 1) is uncited. Later, Howard (1991: 31) pretended that his paraphrase was of Clausewitz's definition.
† Liddell Hart defined tactics as "the domain of weapons" and "of destruction" (1924a: 90), the "actual fighting" (1929a: 150), or "the province of fighting" (1929a: 153), which is practically indistinguishable from Clausewitz's definitions. These definitions are useful conceptually but not operationally, because of the difficulty of defining where battles begin and end.

study strategy he has no real practice until war comes (1938e: 161-162).

Worse, he often conflates force employment with force structure (then called "military organization"). He ends up using "strategic" as a synonym for all things military. This is a familiar conflation now (as in the field "strategic studies"), but was not conventional in the era of "military studies" and "military science."

Agendas

Liddell Hart came up with memorable strategies or, at least, terms for strategies. However, his preferences were unstable, often contradictory. This biography lacks space to detail all the strategies, but here is a chronological summary. He offered an "expanding torrent" of pedestrian light infantry, to solve defence-dominance ((1919a; 1919b; 1920a; 1920b; 1920c; 1921a; 1921b; 1922a; 1922b; 1922c; 1922d; 1922e; 1922f; 1923b), until adopting Fuller's promise that aircraft and AFVs could race into enemy territory quicker than pedestrians could defend it (1924a; 1925). "Indirect approach" is a worthy reminder to avoid the most defended or expected approach, and to keep the enemy guessing about alternative objectives, but also a fantasy of bloodless victory through psycho-social ruses (1929a: 153; 1932c: 100; 1935a: 85; 1967: 26). His "British Way in Warfare" is unilateral, defensive, deterrent, and retaliatory, via raids in the enemy rear by distributed light tanks and heavy bombers (1931b; 1932c; 1935a; 1939a; 1939b). In World War II, he realized attacks on civilians as unethical and indecisive, and reduced the "British Way" to an economic, moral, defensive war (see Chapter 15). After the war, he reinterpreted everything he had written as foreshadowing Germany's sustained breakthroughs by concentrated combined-arms (known in English as "Blitzkrieg," a word used in German as a metaphor for the ideal quick war) (Newsome 2024; 2025a). At the same time, he reframed economic, moral, defensive war as the "good manners" that would end the Cold War (1950; 1960a).

Unstable strategies are inevitable with unstable agendas. His hopes for deterrence and victory at lower cost were stable, but other ends were not. He wanted to save the infantry from fighting (by relying on artillery) (1915-1917), to restore the infantry's dominance (1918-1922), to reduce the duration and casualties of future warfare (1922-1930), to avoid British commitment of ground forces to a continental war (1931-1939), to negotiate a way out of the Second World War, without justice, restitution, or regime change (1939-1945), and to deter war with conventional rather than nuclear armaments (1946 onwards).

Critics realized the instabilities and impracticalities, and usually tried to be helpful, but you would not know of them if you read only Liddell Hart and disciples. Critical insight is best illustrated by academic responses to his plagiarism[*]

---

[*] Fuller had shared drafts of *Reformation of War* (1923a) since 1922. Liddell Hart reviewed it as "the book of the century," but never admitted his plagiarism. Biographers who accessed Liddell Hart's correspondence found clear evidence of plagiarism (Reid 1987: 66-67; Mearsheimer, 1988: 33-36; Harris 1995: 207-208; Gat 1998: 75, 147, 150; 2000: 2-3, 36-37). In contrast, Ogorkiewicz claimed that "Liddell Hart's 1924 article is sufficiently different from Fuller's 1919 [sic] essay not [to] warrant being regarded as 'plagiarism'" (to author, 27 July 2016). Ogorkiewicz had received several letters from Liddell Hart asserting as much. Ogorkiewicz does not seem to have read the article itself. He never corresponded with Fuller.

(1924a; 1925) of Fuller's long-standing prescription (since 1918) for rapid invasion by aircraft and AFVs, which Liddell Hart developed into the somewhat contradictory "indirect approach" (1928d; 1929a; 1929b; 1929c). He published the former in a short book (*Paris or the Future of War*), which plagiarizes Fuller's *Reformation of War*, but mentions Fuller only once, to praise his plan of 1918 for a decisive combined-arms offensive in Spring 1919 (1925: 76-77). Liddell Hart's book errs towards hit-and-run raids (what he later termed "in and out" approaches). The book starts with a small, mechanized army, with its own tactical aircraft, dropping mostly toxic gas bombs, in order to incapacitate the enemy efficiently and humanely. It ends with a strategic bomber force, targeting mostly civilians, who soon agitate for peace. By then, armies are superfluous. Liddell Hart's horror at the Army's casualties during the Great War motivated his search for victory without ground fighting, and to misrepresent Napoleon and Clausewitz as bloody direct approachers (1925: 10-18; 1929a: 147; 1933c: 129, 144; 1965, I: 75, 280).

An anonymous reviewer for *Army Quarterly* criticized the book's confidence in avoiding enemy forces to get at enemy civilians, and for reducing Napoleonic warfare to destruction of enemy forces. Liddell Hart and thence Brian Bond (1977: 44, 62) speculated that the reviewer was Spenser Wilkinson (1853-1937), the first Chichele Professor of Military History at the University of Oxford (1909-1923). Wilkinson had already criticized Liddell Hart in public articles and private letters, before seeing the book. Wilkinson privately warned Liddell Hart that Clausewitz "quite understands that you must break the enemy's will, for which he suggests three processes: first to crush his army, and then to take his capital[,] and, if that is not enough, to occupy his territory" (to LH, 14 June 1924, LH 1/748). After the book was released, Wilkinson publicly rebutted its contradictions, bad assumptions, and misrepresentations. Wilkinson (1927: 15) realized that Liddell Hart was in search of "victory without battles or bloodshed" – "a paradox."

Separately, Victor Germains (1927: 147) characterized Liddell Hart's avoidance of enemy forces as indecisive, and praised "the principle of Clausewitz, viz.: that in war, your first and paramount objective is the enemy's main fighting force, for once you have decisively beaten this everything else is at your mercy."

The next year, Wilkinson wrote to a mutual correspondent, perhaps with hope that the mutual correspondent would have more success with the message.

> Liddell Hart is a keen fellow whom I am disposed to like. But he writes too much and is in a hurry. The right way to get there (wherever he is going) is to go quietly. Slow and sure (Wilkinson to J.M. Scammell, 18 January 1928, LH 1/622).

Liddell Hart then published his indirect approach. Wilkinson repeated his criticism to Liddell Hart himself.

> The criticism I should be disposed to make of your history is that it is doctrinaire rather than historical. By that I mean that you set out to teach dead generals how much better they would have done if they had been imbued with your views of the indirect approach, whereas I think the historical method consists in finding out in each case, as far as possible, how it was that they acted precisely as they did (Wilkinson to LH, 28 December 1928, LH 1/748).

Four years later, Wilkinson made the same point to the mutual correspondent.

> I think Liddell Hart is a little too much the salve of his own theories which he makes into dogmas. But he is clever and knows a good deal...

> War is always an affair of state and part of the changes in war are changes in the constitution of the state. There never were and never will be recipes for victory (Wilkinson to J.M. Scammell, 9 February and 30 June 1932, LH 1/622).

Analogies

Liddell Hart used analogies helpfully to communicate complex concepts, but fallaciously as premises and proofs. The habit goes back to his first doctrine. He imagines lighter infantry moving faster and more dispersed. He confuses reduced exposure with invulnerability, which he analogizes to "armour." Thence he analogizes the infantry unit to a "human tank," and implies that such infantry do not need real tanks (1921a: 7; 1921b: 175; 1921d: 623).

At the same time, he claimed to have "deduced from the action of a man fighting in the dark a definite formula of the essential principles which govern all fighting," and "to establish a theory of offensive infantry tactics deduced directly from these fundamental principles" (1920c: 693-694). A few months later, he presented the "expanding torrent" as an offensive "system." He "endeavoured to deduce such a system by examining and analysing Nature's method of attack" (i.e., water erosion) (1921a: 13; 1921c: 216). This claim to "deduce" turns the analogy into a premise, which is justifiable as a convenience, but not as a proof.

Vague but complex premises and proofs leave readers to imagine different things. His early critic, Colonel Bond, quoted the following paragraph:

> In battle the only true objective is the enemy. But his actual strength and dispositions can only be ascertained by fighting. Hence certain geographical objectives must be allotted beforehand in order to serve as stepping stones by means of which the artillery can co-operate with and support the infantry advance...We shall fulfil the principle of economy of force by concentrating our efforts on the only true objective – the enemy (Liddell Hart 1921a: 12, 15; 1921b: 181).

The Colonel opined:

> [This is] a paragraph which is typical of the method of his lectures. Readers who care to refer to it will find that it consists of a handful of jargon strung together on an argument of amazing inconsequence. There is in it nothing of experience; nothing of the practical outlook. We want something better than that to convince experienced officers...But if he would be convincing, he must abandon altogether the methods of his lectures. He must deny himself the use of catchwords and the easy path of flap-doodle. He must put away his "man-in-the-dark," his "expanding torrent," his "human tank," and his other dummies (Bond 1922: 162, 163).

Liddell Hart mischaracterized the Colonel's argument as deductions "from the 'man-in-the-dark' or the 'expanding torrent'," and thus proofs of the analogies.

> I admit that there is a certain danger in similes or parables, but I think that in most cases their illustrative and teaching value more than counterbalances such possible defects...It is to be remembered that the ordinary British officer or NCO has not the hypercritical mind which examines such parables meticulously. Similes might possibly be used with advantage to lighten their paths through the morasses or sterile deserts of the ordinary textbook (1922e: 302).

The above is true as a defence of analogies in general, but not his analogies in particular. He never intended them to be merely illustrative. He used them as premises. He was often misled by these premises, such as to promise that attackers perpetually expand the breach because water erodes soil, without admitting that defenders erode attackers (1921a: 13; 1921c: 216).

He criticized Clausewitz's comparison of imperfect information, communication and execution to mechanical "friction," even though Liddell Hart used the concept of "friction" routinely (1921b: 619; 1923a: 319, 323, 325; 1930b: 363, 431; 1950: 288-289). He criticized Foch's "irritating" "parable – of the rings made by dropping a stone into water, the successive rings growing less marked until the water became still" (1930b: 409),* even though it is as natural as "expanding torrent."

His "expanding torrent" provoked enough criticism to cause him to lay off until 1929, when he analogized the fix-and-flank process (which he had previously analogized mostly to a man-in-the-dark) to a trident and a net. However, in one publication the trident is fixing (1929b: 258), in another the net is fixing (1933c: 98). In the former, he analogizes the actions of William T. Sherman in the 1860s, but in the latter, he analogizes Napoleon in the 1790s. And in the latter, he uses the three prongs of the trident in yet a third way: to analogize three pre-Napoleonic French innovations (skirmishers; field artillery; moving on the enemy's rear).

His analogies became wilder. He characterized current "military thought" as a housing policy that "has embraced the larger offices and the workmen's dwellings but concerned itself little with the question of middle-class habitations" (1935a: 78). Later, he analogized force employment to a car, whose "strategic axle" turns against a target, while the "tactical axle" drives the car forward. From this dubious analogy, he concludes that offensives would fail (because the defender is quicker to turn and drive) ("The Military Situation in Europe," 6 December 1937, LH 12/1937/10; 1939b: 51). In the next month, he complains that the Army Council† "is like a motor car provided with propeller shaft, axles and cylinders, but without ignition, carburettor and pistons" (note, 29 January 1938, LH 11/HB/1938/1; 1965: II, 89).

Liddell Hart's most frequent analogy is chess:

> Between logistical strategy and chess there is a distinct analogy (1926a: 256).

> Battle is at best but a means, a move on the chessboard of war (1927b: 112).

---

* Foch said the parable in April 1918, when he first chaired as Allied commander-in-chief.
† The War Office's principal two ministers, civil servant, and General Staff.

And the comparison with chess may help us to realize the difficulty of cornering an opponent when only two pieces exist on the board (1933c: 27).

To illustrate the point by a board-game analogy, with chess – air-mobility introduced a knight's move, and tank-mobility a queen's move, into warfare (1952: 14; 1954a: 358).

However, when excusing inattention to battles in his biography of Sherman, he concludes that "a battlefield is not a chessboard" (1929b: xiv). Later, he criticized Joffre's memoirs for giving "the impression that he viewed the battle-zone as a chessboard, without contemplating such inconvenient facts as machine-guns" (1938e: 191). Similarly, when German officers complained about a colleague as a hard-charging "bull," he interpreted the colleague as "chess-like" (1948: 95n).

Yet in 1960 an interviewer found that "he saw every war as a sort of game of chess, played on a world scale, according to set rules, in which victory comes to the cleverer, more cunning, and stronger participant" (LH 13/80). Bond (2015: 37) pondered whether he had "perhaps come to see tanks almost as chess pieces or symbols which would again make possible a conflict between small, high-quality forces in which there would be the opportunity for the superior mind to triumph."

Liddell Hart filed warnings from trusted correspondents against over-reliance on analogies, but continued to over-rely on them, and to receive criticism. A final defence in memoirs ironically draws attention to yet more analogies.

> Instead of operating as a single body, an army or force should "become an octopus with waving tentacles, any one of which could grip on to the opponent, whereupon the others would automatically close upon him also." Better still, it "might be compared to a fluid body, a loose grouping of divisions which, like blobs of quicksilver, would suddenly flow together, and coagulate on striking an obstacle." Or to "a widespread net whose corners are weighted with stones, when one of the enemy's columns impinged on it then closed in [a]round the point of pressure and the stones crashed together on the intruder." This "self-protective formation" would thus "on impact" become "a concentrated offensive formation." Another simile I used was that of the retiarius in the ancient gladiatorial arena, pitted against the apparently better-armed secutor, or swordsman, with merely a net and a trident (1965: I, 182).

Bidwell (1970: 63) countered: "Analogies must only be used for illustration, and not for proof." Luvaas (1964: 389, 422) admitted that "his analogies seem a little contrived," his "catch phrases...oversimplification[s]." Bond (1977: 53) admitted "that once he had made his mind up and recorded his view in a striking phrase or paragraph, he was apt to repeat it without reappraising its validity in the light of new evidence." For Strachan (2020: 538), he "wrote trenchant, clear prose, enlivened with telling metaphors and simple, not to say simplified, analogies."

Abstractions

Liddell Hart preferred to deduce abstractly rather than induce practically, technically, or experimentally. He worked backwards from ends, to find strategies to fit the ends, rather than forwards from capabilities, towards ends that are practical.

The closest he came to experimentation was wargaming. In his own archive, the oldest rules of his own design date to 1912, stimulated by a few simple rules for a lower-echelon tactical game, published in a magazine, and written by H.G. Wells (who was never a friend). Liddell Hart's next rules date to 1917. However, his memoirs date his first use of wargames to 1919, to validate his "expanding torrent," for which he archived no evidence. His son remembered wargames in the 1930s, "on summer afternoons…or in my father's study of an evening." His youngest rules in his archive are dated to 1937, when Adrian turned 15 years of age (LH 13/56; 1965: I, 43-44; 1976: 2).

> I continued to like war-games which I used to play with my father and sometimes with his friends, whether they consisted of stalking through the woods or moving divisions [a]round the board. But they were apt to end in recriminations (Adrian Liddell Hart 1953: 18).

Liddell Hart neglected technologies and techniques, despite his current claims to know them better than "conservative" soldiers, and retrospective claims to foresee the offensive potential in artillery, tanks, and missiles. Although he plagiarized Fuller's promise of a small, fully-mechanized army with its own aircraft (1924a; 1925), his enthusiasm was short-lived. Later in 1925, he promised that militaries could be reduced to bombers for deterrence, two-man tankettes for raids, and motorized machine-gunners and pedestrian garrisons for defence. The Second World War proved him wrong, but he repeatedly wished for a return to smaller, lighter all-tank formations during the Cold War (Newsome 2024: Chapter 3).

He belatedly recognized the capacity of airborne forces after interviewing German prisoners in 1946. However, he seems to have over-compensated: in 1952 he imagined that the USSR could conquer Britain with paratroops flying from Russia. Years later, when prompted to remember Western Allied airborne landings around Arnhem in September 1944, he admitted that airborne operations should "be quickly followed up either by overland reinforcements or by a landing from the sea." At the same time, he excused himself from a question about the capacity of helicopters for airborne operations: "I'm a tactician and a strategist, not a technician, and this is really a question for the technician" (1960a: 6-10; Walters 1961: 25).

Liddell Hart struggled with nuclear warfare from 1949 until giving up in 1960. He applied prior ideals (especially limited warfare) to worthy strategies, such as a mix of conventional defensiveness, insurgency, and political influence. However, he failed to engage technically. Nuclear weapons flit through his writings as words without definitions, without nuances by readiness, reliability, portability, stealthiness, range, accuracy, or delivery vehicle. In 1945, he had written about German V2 and V1 missiles as evidence towards "automatic warfare" (remote strikes). He did not conceive nuclear warheads in 1945, or even in 1949, when he wrote of these missiles as vehicles for only bacterial and radiological warheads (mistermed as "radioactive spray") (1946b: 36-37; 1950: 79). He wrote of nuclear warheads in aerial bombs and artillery shells, until, in 1960, he admits Soviet earth-orbiting satellites (since 1955) and inter-continental missiles (since 1957). Hypocritically he complains that Western shock at both introductions is "too characteristic of the way that the leaders of the Western countries, then headed by France and Britain, ignored the revolutionary implications of mechanized warfare a generation earlier" (1960a: 41).

Technical disinterest permits unstable and false expectations and prescriptions. He expects ballistic missiles and nuclear warheads to die out – thanks to Western "manners," not defence or deterrence. His writings on nuclear deterrence want to have it both ways: he longs for peace through mutual deterrence, but will not allow for mutual deterrence with weapons that could be used offensively. His writing about nuclear war as "suicidal" sometimes implies mutual deterrence, sometimes self-deterrence, sometimes unilateral disarmament, sometimes just casualties. For Liddell Hart, nuclear weapons do not deter non-nuclear war, even between nuclear superpowers. He allows for mutual deterrence to break down with quantitative or qualitative superiority on one side, or inferior infrastructure and superior space. He expects more restraint and disarmament from the West than the Soviets. He fancies the process would end in perpetual peace and mutual disarmament. However, this expectation is contradicted by his assessment of the USSR as least vulnerable to nuclear attack, which implies that the Soviets would be left as the hegemon (once all the less armed, less spacious, and more developed countries have abandoned nuclear weapons, out of good "manners"). Liddell Hart's perpetual peace is an unadmitted Russian hegemony and nuclear monopoly (1950: 73-74, 78, 145-147, 155, 161; 1954a: 15-17; 1960a: x, 10, 12, 15, 19, 21, 23; Walters 1961: 24).

Legacy

By 1933, an instructor at the Royal Military Academy Woolwich was telling cadets that Liddell Hart is "the cook who wants to make omelettes without breaking any eggs" (Bidwell 1970: 63). Wavell warned him privately against searching for "the military philosopher's stone" and "some formula to win wars without fighting" (to LH, 15 March 1934, LH 1/733). A separate officer complained that his strategies neglect capabilities, tactics, sustainment, and administration.

> Liddell Hart does not understand that...strategy like wisdom has no permanent form, but may have to be applied differently in every case (Beadon 1936: 760).

Another soldier complained that "the view it gives of war is that of a game played with rules and with certain maxims which must be observed if one is to win" (Bidwell 1973: 5, 214). Barnett (1999: 62) lamented that Liddell Hart saw war as "a game of skill, a battle of wits, a psychological contest, almost bloodless: and himself as the commentator awarding points for clever footwork and stroke-play," without attention to industry, technology, communications, sustainment, and administration. Kennedy (1991: 4) admits "Liddell Hart himself showed little interest in the financing of war, or even in such a critically important field as the logistics."

David Lord (1997: 57) stated that "his most valuable and enduring contribution [is] his early and fundamental theorising on the abstract nature of war," but mistook enduring peace as an abstraction (it is an end). Reid (1998: 93) notes that "academic writers are more interested in Liddell Hart's writing because it reflects their own predilections for discussing strategic questions [that] deal with more abstract matters rather than with the bloody and messy inconvenience of fighting."

Certainly, we should carry forward his desire for post-war peace to be better than pre-war peace. However, we are carrying forward an idealistic end, which his strategies did not achieve, although they deserve development towards it.

BHLH with Leslie Hore-Belisha (centre) and Major Sir Sydney Frank Markham (1897-1975) during their shared political unpopularity in 1950. Belisha and Markham had been voted out of Parliament in July 1945, as Liberal and Labour MPs respectively. They failed to win return as Conservatives in February 1950. This photograph was taken on 8 October, after the unveiling of a war memorial in Markham's home town (Stony Stratford) and county constituency (Buckingham), which Markham would win by a few votes one year later (LH 13/104/9).

9
Journalist

The role that best describes most of Liddell Hart's working life, that produced most of his writings, and that paid most of his income, was journalist. Yet he never described himself as journalist, rather as "critic." With energy and some deception, he started as a freelance sports reporter. With merit and Maxse's help, he graduated to a term-limited role as military correspondent for *The Morning Post*. With the help of a new CIGS, desperate for good press, *The Daily Telegraph* hired him full-time. He soon manoeuvred for more official influence at *The Times*. The end of his full-time journalism was self-inflicted and unintended, after playing brinksmanship in opposition to Western confrontation of Germany. Thereafter, his journalism was limited to piece work, which ebbed and flowed with his reputation.

Sports

Liddell Hart's interest in journalism started in secondary school, when he started writing provocative letters to newspapers and magazines, usually on sports and aviation. In June 1919, he posed as British correspondent for the magazine *American Lawn Tennis*, to gain free entry to the Wimbledon championship. He speculatively sent a report, which the magazine published (LH 14/56).

By the end of the Great War, he preferred to write on military doctrine. In April 1920, Ivor Maxse passed Liddell Hart's third article (1920a) to his brother Leo, editor of *The National Review*, a monthly magazine. While Ivor recommended the military content, Leo bonded over a shared interest in tennis. *The National Review* published Liddell Hart's reports on tennis, and serialized his article in two parts (1920b; 1920c), for the inflated pay of £1 per page, i.e., £20 (what he had paid for his first car, second-hand, the year before).

In 1922, he wrote to the owner of *The Times*, *Daily Mail*, and *Sunday Dispatch*. Lord Northcliffe (Alfred Harmsworth) had used these newspapers to campaign for Lloyd George to replace Herbert Asquith as premier in 1916 and to stay in power in 1922. Northcliffe's opinions and editorials otherwise focused on social sports and military progress. Liddell Hart tried to appeal to all these interests.

> In my brief seven years in the Army, I have established a reputation in both Europe and America as a writer and inventor of new ideas, but with the cutting down of the Army opportunities for new brains and new ideas are ever more limited. Placid mediocrity is preferred at the top as more soothing to politicians. You seem to be the only Napoleon of the present century, and like him, the only great leader in these days who has the far-sighted imagination to hold out the chances of a Marshal's baton to all who can prove they have the ability to grasp it...Please forgive the self-advertisement, but modesty and brevity are poor bedfellows (to Northcliffe, c. March 1922, LH 7/1922/29).

Northcliffe did not reply. He was already ill, and died in August.

From 1923, Liddell Hart persuaded *American Lawn Tennis* magazine to accept reports from Britain year-round, although it still paid him by word-published.

Variants of his reports were syndicated by the *Manchester Guardian* and *Yorkshire Post* (from 1923) and accepted by *The Observer* (from 1924) and *Westminster Gazette* (from 1925). He started reporting on rugby too. His subjects include games he had never attended (LH 3/100; 3/119; LH 14/53; LH 14/56; 1965: I, 41-42).

Morning Post

By 1923, Liddell Hart was insecure about his employment by the Army and newspapers. This helps to explain his criticisms of both soldiers and journalists.

> It is the professional hack, incapable alike of personal research or critical judgment, who disparages without examination the views of the outside student (1923a: 320).

Ivor Maxse came to the rescue with a temporary job at *The Morning Post* newspaper, where he was one of the directors. Liddell Hart was appointed assistant military correspondent for the next training season, whose field phase would start in March 1924. In the year, he made about £300 a year from freelance writing, on top of his Army salary of £550. However, *The Morning Post* accepted his last article in February 1925. In March, he accepted a temporary contract to report on tennis for the *Westminster Gazette*, established the Lawn Tennis Journalists' Association (with himself as President), and wrote a book on *The Lawn Tennis Masters Unveiled* (LH 14/56; 1926d).

Daily Telegraph

This is where Liddell Hart's military corresponding might have ended, if *The Daily Telegraph*'s long-standing military correspondent (Charles Repington) had not died in May 1925, at the age of 67 years. *The Daily Telegraph* was conservative, but had been founded as an explicitly "independent" newspaper, and was unusual in being owned by partners who did not own any other national newspapers.

The editors were keen to follow the fashion for younger, more provocative reporters. Liddell Hart was aged 29. The editors shared the list of candidates with the incoming CIGS. George Milne chose Liddell Hart as the most likely candidate to promote the Army. Liddell Hart preferred to credit the editor's assistant and nephew (Fred Lawson, later Lord Burnham), who recalled his "particularly able account...of a rather unimportant tactical exercise" (interview of Thomas Jacomb Hutton, 1977, IWM 895; 1965: I, 75-76).

In July, Liddell Hart started at *The Daily Telegraph*. He effectively left the active Army, but took half-pay* (see Chapter 10). His gross income practically doubled, to over £1,000 – more than Major-Generals and professors earned. At the time, "military correspondents" were well-read gazeteers to the general public. They reported senior promotions, annual manoeuvres, weapons acquisitions, and new doctrinal publications, which today would be covered by only professional journals. He went further. "I assumed the role of tactical analyst and military critic" (1956b: 2). He

---

* Half-pay is a misnomer. His Army salary dropped from £550 to £150.

shifted from observational reports to what were known then as "think pieces" or "turn-over pieces" (if typeset overleaf). Liddell Hart tended to be published on the centre pages of the broadsheets. Today we would know them as in-depth reports. He called them "articles" – appropriating an academic term. Each ran to thousands of words, sometimes more than 20,000 words. The longer pieces were published in up to four parts, over as many days or weeks. He later estimated that he wrote an average of 120 articles or reports each year from 1925 to 1930, and around 180 per year from 1931 to 1934. Thereafter, his writing for newspapers declined slightly, as he got involved in more direct lobbying and advising, and fell out with his final full-time employer (*The Times*) (1959a: I, 257).

The Times

Liddell Hart never clearly explained his disaffection with *The Daily Telegraph*, although certainly he was ambitious for influence and pay. Initially, he was unsure about his career as military correspondent, given Milne's cautious tenure as CIGS from 1926, the War Department's deletion of his contributions to *Infantry Training*, and official discovery of his leaks of information, which ended his half-pay status with the Army, in 1927 (see Chapter 10). Still, he let the Lawn Tennis Journalists' Association expire in the same year, leaving the military as the only scope for his journalism and books. Yet he wanted to correspond for the closest newspaper to government.

In 1928, he heard that *The Times* was hiring more foreign affairs editors, so he sent a speculative letter. The newspaper's unconventional structure takes some explaining. Geoffrey Dawson had edited *The Times* from 1912 until falling out with Northcliffe in 1919. The new owner (John Jacob Astor, Lord Astor) invited Dawson back in 1923. Dawson was close to both Stanley Baldwin (leader, Conservative Party, 1923-1937; Prime Minister, 1923-1924, 1924-1929, 1935-1937) and Neville Chamberlain (Baldwin's Chancellor of the Exchequer; Prime Minister, 1937-1940). The other press barons were critics of Baldwin and Chamberlain, for taking conservatism in a liberal and populist direction.

Dawson was also school friend and near neighbour to Lord Halifax, Edward Wood (War Secretary in the first months of Baldwin's third administration; Leader of the House of Lords, 1935-1938; Foreign Secretary, 1938-1940).

Dawson set the Baldwin administration's policies as editorial policies,[*] of which the most appealing to Liddell Hart were: opposition to any British commitment to continental allies ("continental commitment"); and rearmament, except for the RAF's strategic bomber and anti-aircraft forces. Baldwin regarded Dawson as so important that he asked Dawson not to travel during Parliamentary debates on the India Bill in summer 1935. By the time of Chamberlain's administration (1937-1940), Astor was hosting appeasers, including Dawson, on most weekends, at his country estate at Cliveden, Buckinghamshire.

The Day-Editor and Associate Editor (Alfred Gordon Robbins) was hired in 1922, although Dawson delegated little. In any case, in 1927, Dawson replaced

---

[*] Dawson and his foreign news editors coordinated policy with the Foreign Office's News Department (Reginald "Rex" Leeper). They appointed their first diplomatic correspondent (Arthur Barker) in 1936, just to coordinate with Leeper.

Robbins with Robert "Robin"/"B-W" Barrington-Ward. In 1914, B-W had served as secretary to the editor, before joining the Army. In 1917, Maxse came to know B-W as a Brigade Major in his chain of command. In August 1918, Maxse hired B-W into the Inspectorate-General of Training. B-W left the army in October 1918 for a legal career, but returned to journalism in 1919. He became assistant editor at *The Observer* newspaper, which, from that year, was owned by Waldorf Astor – brother of John. The brothers allowed their respective newspapers to poach each other's employees. In 1927, B-W joined *The Times* as Day-Editor and Associate Editor. He did not get along with the older, more conservative Deputy Editor (George Murray Brumwell), but the latter retired in June 1934, and was replaced by B-W. In the same month, the editor of *The Times Literary Supplement* (Sir Bruce Richmond) declared that he would like to retire at the end of 1935, so B-W took temporary responsibility for that too (McLachlan 1971: 49-50, 82-83, 154-157; Baynes 1995: 201-202).

Dawson and B-W wrote, compiled, or edited all foreign reports. The foreign editor (Harold Williams) had died in November 1928, the principal leader-writer (Wolfe Flanagan) in November 1929. They retained a Foreign News Editor to assign correspondents and handle news agencies (Ralph Deakin, from 1922 to 1952).

Liddell Hart was under-qualified for foreign affairs, but the foreign editor's death prompted a speculative letter, just three-and-a-half years into his tenure at *The Daily Telegraph*. In subsequent years, he was assuaged by his growing audience, but resented *The Daily Telegraph*'s "independence" of government. In mid-1932, he drafted the following complaint to his general manager.

> 1. When I came to the Daily Telegraph in 1925 I had a comparatively narrow reputation. I was appointed at a salary of £1,000 per annum.
>
> 2. Now I receive £1,100. And I think I can claim to have become, in the interval, the best known military writer in the world.
>
> 3. The growth of the reputation is due more to my books than my Daily Telegraph connection (to Fred Lawson, c. 7 June 1932, LH 3/97).

Subsequently, *The Daily Telegraph* paid him £50 per year for entertainment expenses, and £100 per year for his use of his own car, for a package worth £1,250, excluding other reimbursements. Adding article fees elsewhere, book royalties, and advising, he earned more than £3,000 by 1934.

The influence of *The Times* grew as Baldwin took more control of the National Government (1931-1935) from the man who nominally led the coalition (Ramsay MacDonald, Labour). Coincidentally, the Military Correspondent was working part-time and signalling his wish to retire. George Aston was then aged 73 years. (He would die in 1938.) He was so rarely in the office that a foreign correspondent, who joined in 1933, mistakenly wrote that *The Times* had "no one to look at defence as a whole" (McLachlan 1971: 154). In fact, B-W and Dawson wrote on defence as a whole, and employed correspondents for each of the services.[*] By then, none

---

[*] Retired Rear-Admiral H.G. Thursfield was Naval Correspondent from 1932 to 1952, and editor of Brassey's *Naval Annual*. Edwin Colston Shepherd was Aeronautical Correspondent from 1929 to 1939. The Military Correspondent (Aston) was the army correspondent. No newspaper then dedicated a correspondent to defence as a whole. The Ministry of Defence

worked routinely in office. In Autumn 1934, the CIGS (Archibald Montgomery-Massingberd) said he would welcome Liddell Hart's appointment, as did others whose names B-W failed to record. B-W telephoned Liddell Hart.

> The time has come for the paper to have a [full-time] military correspondent once more. The years of experiment are over and the Army is beginning to take its post-war shape. Whether we like it or not, questions of defence are coming to the fore...Liddell Hart is almost alone, by his own exertions, in that field. He has undoubtedly won many readers for the D.T. Six years ago he asked me to let him know when a vacancy should occur on TT. Today I told him it had. He is frankly ready to come. The methods of the DT have grown too catchpenny for his liking, though they have treated him well...I was glad to hear from him that his objective is peace. I like him and he is undoubtedly able (diary, 26 November 1934, in McLachlan, 1971: 155).

The last two lines of that quote are most revealing. Dawson, B-W, and LH were determined to avoid war, to blame older and more conservative men for war, and to cast Baldwin and Chamberlain as young, thoughtful, sober liberal-conservatives who would not make the mistakes of their predecessors.

The Daily Telegraph's General Manager received Liddell Hart's resignation with regret and appreciation, but ended with "a slight and very friendly dig at your very justifiable vanity" (Fred Lawson to LH, 29 November 1934, LH 3/97).

Liddell Hart started his career at *The Times* just as he finished: duplicitously. In December 1934, a misunderstanding took another meeting to resolve. Managers offered a salary of £1,500 and expenses of £650, but he wanted to write for other outlets too, so held his salary at £1,200. T.E. Lawrence urged him to do something rigorous.

> On The Times you will be permanent and safe and dignified and opulent. Most admirable. You are now on the treetop of the profession.
>
> The power over your naval and aerial colleagues is rather astonishing. It must be a concession to your personal efficiency; for the Army today is the Cinderella service. I am sure that you will be able to correlate the three Defences and Offences to the general benefit.
>
> So I can only wind up by hoping that you are as pleased as myself.
>
> I implore you not to blow the extra salary on a new car (or a new hat, if Mrs. L.H. is in the ascendant) but to use your new enlargement for some unprofitable but worthy book. Give us some reflections upon the relations of [force] density to type of war: working out the influences of much or little land-room upon tactics. So doing you will put [Ernest] Swinton out of joint at Oxford and earmark his chair [Chichele Professor of Military History] for yourself. The Times and All Souls [College] have a historical connection (January 1935, LH 9/13/5; 1938g: 228-229; 1965: I, 352).

---

was not departmentalized until 1964.

Liddell Hart did not take Lawrence's advice. Whether he knew it or not, he was a decade away from rediscovering his ambitions to write a "philosophy of war" and to join academia. He blamed the pressures of current German-French and Italian-Abyssinian disputes. Within months, he accepted a salary of £1,700 in return for giving up work for other newspapers. In June, Lord Halifax took over the War Department, and asked for advice. In August, he bragged to Robert Graves that he expected to earn £3,400 a year from *The Times*, Halifax, and books (1965: I, 258; Graves 1990: 248).

Nominally, the Military Correspondent was anonymous, but Liddell Hart drew attention in other writings. Liddell Hart memorialized his position as "military critic and correspondent of *The Times*." "[I] at once made full use of this position to conduct a campaign for a more effective co-ordination of the efforts being made in matters of national defence." In memoirs, he describes himself as "officially the strategic adviser of *The Times*" (1956b: 2; 1965: II, 160).

His first article for *The Times* is entitled "Defence as a Whole," to B-W's delight. Yet, on the same day it was published, he recorded dissonance about *The Times*.

> I breathe pleasantly in its atmosphere, but I am not quite sure that I shall be able to breathe freely, I delight in the signs of its sense of values, its pose, its restraint – in a noisy age. But I have a doubt whether its sense of responsibility is accompanied by a sense of humour. There is an air of reasonableness within the limits of certain conventions. I wonder if its members can laugh at themselves – or, rather, at their collective self. They seem to be remarkably free from personal affectation or dignity, yet show a distinct collective conceit. One of the things that drew me most strongly to The Times was the way it maintains a sense of proportion, but this operates within limits – an Oxford-don-cum-English General's sense of proportion (note, 14 March 1935, LH 11/1935/3).

This dissonance avoids the only necessary reason for his dissatisfaction: the newspaper's and government's drift towards confrontation of Italy's expansionism and Germany's rearmament, and towards Britain's re-armament, beyond the anti-aircraft guns, light tanks, and strategic bombers that he prioritized.

He complained also of leaders and opinions published without his approval. His memoirs quote excerpts from his letters of complaint as if they are in opposition to appeasement and non-alignment. In fact, they expect Britain to divest from the continent, except to defend France's airspace if France would eschew offensives.

For now, Liddell Hart rationalized that "a channel where what one says tends to have a much bigger effect...is what matters most" (to William Lloyd-Jones, 6 March 1936, LH 1/451). Yet he got in the habit of writing long memoranda to the editors, usually demanding an answer by the end of the working day, and sometimes threatening to resign or to publish privately. His memoirs date his first thoughts of resignation to March 1938, and his first letter of resignation to 10 August. The latter coincides with his final separation from his first wife. His letter states that he had "no mind or heart to continue writing about military preparations that are likely to prove futile." The Deputy Editor was on vacation that month, but wrote a soothing reply. Over lunch on 24 August, Liddell Hart withdrew his resignation. They would repeat this drama many times.

In October, after the settlement of Germany's claims in Czechoslovakia, he started speaking publicly against the supposed warmongers and opponents of air defence. He vainly submitted his scripts as articles. By November, he counted eight submissions not published in ten months, but this is normal for any journalist who is otherwise published every couple days. On 8 November, he revived his letter of resignation. He proposed to forego £200 (12 percent) of salary, in return for permission to publish 12 articles a year in the evening and Sunday newspapers. B-W and Astor agreed. Liddell Hart's priority was to influence government, not to make money, or to influence popular opinion, as proven by his refusal of an offer from Lord Beaverbrook (Max Aitken) of £3,000 per year to correspond for the most popular of the tabloids (*The Daily Express*). Of Beaverbrook's other newspapers, *The Evening Standard* was the one most likely to be read in government, and the one with which Liddell Hart first published. This started in January 1939. Only five of his articles appeared in newspapers other than *The Times* from then until the start of the Second World War (LH 3/108; 1965: II, 125, 145, 157, 160, 179-181, 197; McLachlan 1971: 155-158, 160).

His letters of resignation became most frequent after the government and *The Times* effectively repudiated appeasement and non-alignment, in late March 1939. Partial conscription in late April added another grievance. He wrote a letter in opposition to his newspaper's supposed belligerency, and promised his resignation:

> Years ago I reached the conclusion that the only hope either of preventing war or of conducting it effectively lay in applying the scientific method to the study of war. Having devoted myself to this task for so long, my only interest is in trying to present as exact an estimate of the situation as I can. I do not see how it will be possible to do this in wartime. Not only will it be very difficult to ascertain the truth, but practically impossible to write it, especially in the atmosphere natural to the early stages (to Dawson, 9 May 1939, LH 1/309).

He later quoted this letter in support of his false claim to "abstain" from writing out of "conviction" (1942a: 9-10; 1965: II, 236-237, 251-252). In fact, he continued to submit to *The Times* and other newspapers.

Liddell Hart escalated to the owner. Over dinner on 10 May, Astor promised to talk with Dawson. In June, after seeing into print his largest book to date, based on his talks and articles since 1937, he broke down. After sick-leave, he returned to *The Times*, in mid-July, but remained unreconciled. He departed on a self-appointed tour of annual reserve training. Three weeks later, he returned to confirm rumors that the Cabinet was meeting to discuss war, which prompted another breakdown. On 25 August, he resigned for the final time, by reinvoking the part of his letter from May that is conditional on war (when "truth" supposedly would be impossible to write).

The editors had already hired a substitute: an official historian, Cyril Falls. Liddell Hart continued to correspond, in hope that the editors or owner would beg him to return. On 27 August, B-W wrote: "The absurd Liddell Hart infested the office, breathing pessimism and complaining that neither his health nor his conscience would allow him to do any work" (1965: II, 251; McDonald 1984: 44). Even after war broke out, he continued to submit articles to *The Times*. Rejected, he reframed his idleness as righteous.

> I am struck by the ominous growth of a Balaclava-like mood here. All my best work for The Times has been done after a long period of reflection, and has often taken several days even in the writing. And in the last year or two I have often found it more necessary to think it out somewhere isolated from noise and disturbance...But to elucidate events of far-reaching importance on the spur of the moment is a task I should certainly be reluctant to attempt (to Dawson, 7 September 1939, LH 3/109).

B-W had enough.

> LH seems to be playing for safety all round. For himself he wants to be wise after the event...He is a monolith of egotism and vanity (diary, 2 October 1939, in McDonald 1984: 45).

The editors suggested that his resignation should become permanent by the end of the year. He countered with the end of November. He was not employed again until February 1940, and only for piece work, and only with the consent of Lord Beaverbrook, as properly told in Chapter 13.

Legacy

In letters to gullible correspondents (e.g., Icks 1952: 26), in person to gullible disciples (e.g., Luvaas 1964: 413), and in memoirs (1965: II, 229-238, 241-242), Liddell Hart claims that he left *The Times* in opposition to appeasement. In fact, appeasement had been reversed five months earlier.[*]

He persuaded Brian Bond (1977: 119) that he resigned "partly because he had disagreed with the paper's editorial policy, but also because he took a strict view of the need to tell the truth in wartime and did not believe that he would be allowed to do so in *The Times*." In fact, he continued to submit to *The Times* after the war began.

Liddell Hart's writings for *The Times* mark his peak influence. He never repeated his high-living of the interwar period, even after reinventing himself as the unsung inventor of Blitzkrieg. Notably, he quoted little of his journalism in this reinvention. For the victims of his post-war influence, such as Richard Aldington, who rebutted Liddell Hart's (1938) hagiography of T.E. Lawrence, he remained "a journalist hack" (Aldington to Lawrence Durrell, 6 November 1958, in Crawford 1998: 134).

---

[*] Presumably this is why William Manchester (1988: 405) misdates Liddell Hart's resignation to 31 March 1939.

10

Army Insider and Outsider

Liddell Hart stayed in the active Army for a total of ten years, despite spending most of the time in convalescence or civilian employment, excluding another three years on half-pay, despite never drilling with the reserves. His service was both privileged and conflicted. The period is more complicated than he and his disciples rationalized. This chapter is organized around his own self-contradictions: both a commander by practical experience and a commander by historical study, both a Generals' pet and an anti-professional, both a recovering convalescent and an involuntary invalid, both a propagandist and a leaker, both a forced retiree and a "Great Captain."

Commander by Practical Experience

Liddell Hart's highest operational command was of a company, temporarily, in July 1916. At home, his highest command was a training company. As adjutant he administered a unit. He gave up units in November 1918, when he transferred to London District HQ, and gave up the arms in June 1920, when he transferred to the Army Education Corps. By then, he was playing to the fashion for juniority. In November 1920, Maxse told RUSI's auditorium that "Captain Hart has commanded a platoon, he has commanded a company in France, and he was adjutant of his battalion over a long period of time" (1921a: 1). The marketing went to his head. In the next month, Liddell Hart recorded his readiness to command a brigade now, a field army later:

> I realise fully that opportunity and luck play a great part in a successful career, but I do feel that given health and opportunity I could at the present time handle a brigade at least with distinction in battle and that with experience I could prove myself one of the "masters of war." But under modern conditions it looks as if the opportunity, if it ever comes, will only come – under the rigid rules of seniority – when my intellectual keenness and agility is dulled by time. I feel quite certain that even at the present moment I could command an infantry brigade in war at least as well as any brigade commander at present, and I believe that with more experience of the conditions and capabilities of the other arms I could command an army equally well if given the chance ("Some personal impressions," December 1920, LH 7/1920/32).

Colonel Lionel Bond rebutted the published versions of his talk, with a question about Liddell Hart's personal experience.

> I presume that Captain Hart writes from experience. And I shall certainly not accuse him of proposing what he knows from experience to be impossible. I must presume, therefore, that these conditions were found on the Western Front in 1918. I am glad to know it. It is news to me…

> We wish that Captain Hart would give us something of his experience on which his views are based...
>
> What were the experiences of a certain platoon of Captain Hart's battalion on a given day? (Bond 1922: 161, 163).

Liddell Hart turned around the Colonel's question without answering it.

> Colonel Bond has no hesitation in speaking in confident terms of the European theatre of war; which, so far as I understand, he never saw... My own small experiences as a platoon and company commander in France were, I freely admit, far less than those of many others – even less a foundation, possibly, than those of a senior RE officer on which to build a theory of infantry tactics. They were, however, sufficiently painful to show the defects of the existing tactics (1922e: 298).

Commander by Historical Study

Colonel Bond's and other criticisms pushed Liddell Hart into condemnation of current and past British commanders and their professional class. His preference for "amateur" commanders is paradoxical. He attempts to square the circle by caricaturing professional soldiers as too "practical" and insufficiently "historical."

> They lay stress on the assertion that in battle no two situations are ever alike, and therefore they aver that both textbooks and previously taught principles are of little use. Surely this rule of thumb method of training is unscientific and hopelessly slow even if it were sound, which may be doubted (1921d: 620).

He denies "that actual experience in the field is superior to study as a means to a mastery of war." Personal experience "is restricted to certain phases and localities," whereas "universal experience" comes from reading "military history." He adds a condition: "capacity for reflection, analysis, and originality of thought." Given such capacity, he allows for either "an amateur or a professional soldier" to gain "universal experience," although he continues to doubt the professional. Even allowing for the condition, his theory is far-fetched. We know that reading military history can introduce, remind, and stimulate ways to employ forces, but he went further. He promised that reading is as good as practicing: that reading military history produces "mastery of strategy and tactics," without practice (1923a: 320, 323).

This theory was not a temporary flash of anger. He continued to prescribe "military history" for "the training and mental development of a soldier," and to promise that reading history is more practical than soldiering. He claims that practical soldiering includes what we know now as "negative training" (unintended training of the wrong behaviours) (1929b: 2). He does not admit that negative training can be excised. Further, he never admits, in this context, that military history sometimes contains negative lessons, even though, in other contexts (see Chapters 5 and 6), he characterizes most military history as idolatry and untruthful.

He often claimed that the government could have drawn the same lessons from his histories (of the Medieval Mongols, particularly) as from the Experimental Mechanized Force in 1927, the Experimental Armoured Force in 1928, and the temporary tank brigade in 1929 (1928d; 1932c: 201; 1935a: 175). He claimed the same of the manoeuvres in 1930, when he dropped "understanding of mechanical conditions" as a condition (1930c: 684; 1932c: 208; 1935a: 182).

By then, Liddell Hart (1932c: 278; 1935a: 322) prescribes military biography and "certain works of fiction,"* without explaining why military history is no longer sufficient. In a subsequent book, he prescribes history (mischaracterized as "hard realities") over practical training (mischaracterized as "pure theorizing on make-believe and on fragmentary personal experience") (1933c: 179-181).

Liddell Hart reported from French and British manoeuvres every year from 1925 to 1939. Increasingly, he badgered the commanders on how to command. Yet when offered opportunities to command manoeuvre forces, including in the open-terrain of Egypt, he refused. Nevertheless, he and biographers pretended he was denied opportunities to command after 1916 (to Burnett-Stuart, 21 December 1933, LH 1/132; 1965: I, 34, 215; John Burnett-Stuart's unpublished memoir: 117, 144-145, LH-CMA; Bond 1977: 5-7; Winton, 1988: 157-166; Danchev 1998a: 71; Newsome 2025a).

Generals' Pet

In September 1916, while convalescing in England, Liddell Hart estimated "that 90 per cent of our general staff officers are really brilliant men, with quite a large number of men amongst them who have a genius for war...We have produced fully a hundred first-rate generals" (LH 7/1916/22). His giddiness peaked a month after his lecture to RUSI: "I can safely say that everything I have done has been in spite of the luck being dead against me" ("Notes for an Autobiography," LH 7/1920/38). He resented rebuttals printed in 1921, but by the end of the year felt better, after seeing another five articles in print (mostly reprints, some counter-rebuttals). He wrote a list of "what I have achieved by the age of 25."

> 1. I have lectured on tactics at the Royal United Services Institute [November 1920] and the Institution of the Royal Engineers [January 1921]...
>
> 2. I have written the whole tactical half of the official British infantry manual [released from November 1921].
>
> 3. I have written the article on infantry tactics for the new edition of the Encyclopaedia Britannica [Maxse 1922] which, as the announcements say, "is written by the greatest living authorities on each subject."
>
> 4. I have invented a new method of attack ["expanding torrent"], a new method of defence ["contracting funnel'], a new system of battle control [presumably his drills of 1918] besides 70 lesser ideas on infantry tactics [unspecified] (LH 7/1921/68).

Fifteen years later, he confirmed professional indulgence.

---

* He specifies recent novels by friends John Buchan (1875-1940), Bernard Newman (1897-1968), and F. Britten Austin (1885-1941), but these authors, although veterans of the war, romanticized and sanitized war and espionage.

> I have received far more friendliness than hostility from Regulars...
>
> [In the early 1920s] the leading generals treated me as an equal in military knowledge ("Thoughts jotted down – to be expanded," 17 July and 4 August 1936, LH 11/1936/2-25c).

Anti-Professional

Liddell Hart's appreciation of professional indulgence was subsumed by resentment of his critics, whom he caricatured as elders and seniors.

> In the past the training manuals have been usually compiled by senior officers who have grown grey in the slow pursuit of knowledge, and not unnaturally they have been apt to forget that what to them is self-evidence or second nature is to the aspiring young leader-to-be an unknown country littered with unfamiliar signs (1921d: 621).

In 1922, he wrote a whole article in criticism of Army personnel and culture. He sent it to *Army Quarterly*, under an imperfect pseudonym ("Bardell" – a contraction of his full name). The article promotes "amateur" soldiers as more intellectual and less conservative in studying military history, and caricatures "professional" soldiers as over-reliant on experience and practice. Ironically, he resorts to analogies.

> Even field training...is a palliative, not a cure for ignorance, a peptonized tactical food for "infantry" officers who are not intellectually mature, and hence not capable of digesting the pure food of military science. This can only be gained by study of and reflection on the lessons of military history and their application, in the light of new weapons and conditions, to future war (1923a: 321-322).

This pseudonymous article combines ageism with anti-professionalism.

> Few, indeed, have been able to devote even a year or two during their career to intensive study. In the case of the majority, study has been desultory. Thus where, as so often happens with genius, the intellect ripens early, the young student may have spent more hours in reading and reflection by the time he is 25 or 30 [Liddell Hart turned 27 during production of this article] than most men spend in their whole lifetime (1923a: 324).

"Bardell" stimulated a dozen letters of complaint and two rebuttals that the *Army Quarterly* published. In response, Liddell Hart hinted further at his true identity, but otherwise backtracked.

> My article was certainly not inspired by any antagonism to the regular soldier, nor was it "redolent of spite" – for I am deeply grateful for the large measure of courtesy and encouragement I have received in regard to my own military theories; far more probably than any other profession would have shown to a comparatively junior officer ("Editorial," Army Quarterly, April 1924, 8/1: 8).

The editors allowed his rebutters to respond.

> We feel that had "Bardell's" article been written in the same tone as this letter, his views would not have aroused so much hostile criticism, for, although his arguments were not always convincing and his deductions not always conclusive, there was yet much in his article with which any reasonable man could agree. However, there is no doubt that if one wishes to arouse controversy, there is nothing like an overstatement of his case (ibid: 10).

Liddell Hart was not as contrite as his rebutters thought. Coincident with yet another transition to half-pay (free from military repercussions for private publications), he chose to publish, under his real name, what he had written to self in 1922.

> It is foolish, also, to leave out of account the natural conservatism and prudence of military hierarchies or the parsimony of governments in regard to expenditure on military experiment in peacetime (1924a: 90).

During the final manoeuvres of the year, Liddell Hart met the outgoing CIGS (Rudolph Lambart, 10th Earl of Cavan), who turned to his Military Assistant with the instruction, "Keep that man away from me." Although usually presented as evidence for Cavan's conservatism, it might as well be used as evidence for Liddell Hart's provocation (1965: I, 64; Thorne 1985: 51n). Within the next month or two, he wrote his first proper book, which, although entitled *The Future of War*, is peppered with criticisms of "traditional," "conservative" or "orthodox" soldiers (1925: 7, 17). He offers himself as their victim and nemesis.

> The traditional military mind is notoriously sensitive to any breath of criticism, and any attempt to tear aside the veil of its mystery is apt to be greeted by the cry of "sacrilege." Occasionally some daring soldier has done so – and has paid the penalty for exposing to lay[-persons'] eyes the emptiness of the shrine (1925: 4-5).

Coincident with publication of this book, he joined *The Daily Telegraph*, saw his income and readership leap ahead, and became bullish with his value to the CIGS as Army propagandist (see the section below). In a later book (published in Spring 1927), he revealed himself as the "Bardell," who, four years earlier, had published about "the widespread prejudice of the professional soldier against even examining the suggestions of an amateur" (1923a: 321; 1927b: 178). Within a few months, his leaks and criticisms provoked the War Office to cancel his privileges. He quit the Army entirely. His journalistic reports became repetitive attacks on supposedly conservative seniors. He claimed to have provoked them into experimentation in 1927 (despite his claims that experimentation is unnecessary for those who read his histories), but to suffer banishment for doing so. In 1929, he finished his first history of the Great War, which rails against the supposed conservatism and stupidity of the soldiers who had preferred to fight Germany rather than reinforce failed expeditions in Italy, Greece, Turkey, and Mesopotamia.

> Perhaps the underlying factor was that service tendency of mind which sentimentally values things more than lives (1930b: 153).

The CIGS (Milne) complained of "a distinct tone of hostility to the regular officer," which "does not help to encourage a devotion of service to country in the hard-worked and under-paid professional soldier" (Milne to LH, 2 September 1930, LH 1/512).

In *The British Way in Warfare,* he revives his self-characterization as both victim and "critic" of nebulous "Generals."

> For in retort as in assertion they have a double advantage. If he deals with the present or the future, they declare that he is "an armchair critic"; if he deals with the past, they discount him as being "wise after the event" (1932c: 42).

Liddell Hart sent a copy to General John Burnett-Stuart, then commanding British Troops in Egypt, who called his bluff, by inviting him to command a mechanized force in the next manoeuvres.

> Imagine yourself the responsible head of the Army and read your book from that standpoint. Wouldn't you rather resent your own accusations of incompetence and rather contemptuous assumption of superiority? And wouldn't all sorts of difficulties confront you, which as a critic you make no allowance for? (to LH, 20 September 1932, LH 1/132).

Liddell Hart doubled down. Three months after publication, he contrasted himself with "soldiers, who as a class are of limited education" (note, 7 June 1932, LHCMA AJLH 4). Two months later he added some memorable parallelism:

> The Army is continually wobbling between self-discipline and serf-discipline. Serf-discipline so stunts the intelligence that it repeatedly causes the breakdown of the action it is intended to facilitate (14 August 1932, LH 11/1932/30).

He was writing this diary entry as he completed a new book, to be published in the Spring, in which he again characterizes Army officers as stupid (1933c: 179-181). He blames everybody in the War Office for the Army's "grave deficiencies."

> It is not so much the inertia of individuals in authority, as the inertia of a system. Anyone who has ever been in the War Office will know what is meant without explanation. Against the immense inertia of the machinery, with all its interlocking cogs, progressive individuals are apt to struggle in vain, until they grow tired of the effort (1933a: 110).

His publications are not just attention-seeking. His private notes continue to blame professional soldiers.

> Soldiers as a class have in some ways the highest standards of honour; in other ways the lowest. They are usually the soul of decency – where their class prejudices are not aroused. But it is rare to find a soldier who has a sense of the importance of intellectual honesty, or who puts his duty to the higher cause above his class loyalty (note to self, LH 11/1933/28).

In January 1934, he released a biography of T.E. Lawrence, which repeatedly compares the British Army's other officers harshly, although it remains vague about Lawrence's thoughts and practices. One of Liddell Hart's correspondents (Archibald Wavell) had been promoted to Major-General a couple months earlier. This promotion had benefited from both Liddell Hart's recommendation and the

Army's indulgence of "unorthodox" soldiers. Now, Wavell was awaiting a division to command, and defensive of his peers.

> His own comments display, as usual, a deep knowledge of military history and theory, and much shrewd thought for the future, spoiled at times by an over-shrewish girding at the professional soldier. Lawrence himself was less intolerant and had a better understanding of the qualities and difficulties of the regular (Wavell 1934: 404).

On the day of publication, Liddell Hart wrote privately to rebut Wavell. Wavell was unpersuaded, so Liddell Hart wrote to self.

> The thoughtful soldier is a contradiction in terms. Custom, convention, and prejudices naturally arising from them, hinder the soldier thinking freely about many subjects, even professions. Scientific habit of thought is impossible. Army never yet ready for any war emergency, nor can it be – suppression of truth (note, LH 11/1934/58).

Liddell Hart returned to the counter-rebuttal eight years later, after Wavell had been removed from Middle East Command, but Wavell was not cowed.

> I'm sorry if my remark upset you, but I meant what I said. You spoil your writing sometimes by failing to make allowance for the Regular's point of view, which is a great pity, because you are, as I said, the most stimulating and thoughtful writer by far that we have...You claim you are fair to the Regulars. I can only say that it is not the impression you leave on me who is comparatively free from class-consciousness (Wavell to LH, 22 January 1942, LH 1/733).

Meanwhile, Liddell Hart published a second version of *British Way in Warfare*, which extends the first edition's criticism of "conservatism" from "Generals" to all soldiers (1932c: 130, 138; 1935a: 61). Ultimately, the second edition counters "conservatism" with intellect and youth (even though he was beyond middle age).

> From observation, I am inclined to think that, apart from certain minds of exceptional adaptability, we may not find officers capable of handling high-mobility forces until the new generation, born in the motor age, has grown up (1935a: 302).

The weekly *Army, Navy & Air Force Gazette* published an anonymous review. He objected. Two regular contributors to the *Gazette* teamed up in rebuke.

> Liddell Hart fails to appreciate the forbearance vouchsafed [to] him by those practised in the profession of arms since he commenced his literary career. But perhaps, even in a small measure, this discussion may assist towards enlightening him that his interpretation of history, and his knowledge of the technique of military operations unbuttressed by the hard facts of personal experience or practical training, do not justify a pontifical attitude of contempt to any reasoned criticism (Beadon and Kennedy 1935).

Liddell Hart complained to self that "the root of the trouble is the Army's rooted fear of the truth" (LH 11/1935/37). Within weeks, he convinced himself he had been too tolerant.

> My fortieth birthday – what is my dominant impression? That I'm just beginning to see – and, in seeing, to conceive how much lies ahead. Looking back I realize better how much that progress in seeing has been hindered by environment, by pressure of activity, and by moral timidity (a genuine dislike of hurting others' feeling but also a fear of being hurt myself in consequence) (note, 31 October 1935, LH 11/1935/42).

Subsequently, he admitted that some "Generals, pricked by some criticism, are moved to suggest that I write as I do because it pays." He listed "facts" that are supposed to prove them wrong, but his "facts" are actually grievances against official neglect (note, 28 July 1936, LH 11/1936/16). One of his rebukers from the previous year pointed out that Liddell Hart, as an "amateur critic," has the advantage of "decry[ing] what is commonly termed 'the military mind'," while military professionals are forbidden from public response (Beadon 1936: 747-748).

In the next year, Liddell Hart finished his final history of the Great War, which reasserts his paradox that professionalism counters professional competence. He offers Lawrence as the competent amateur.

> His youth helped him. They had spent so many years in rising to command that, naturally, they could not hope to have intimate experience in using the weapons upon which tactics are based. The machine-gun which dominated the battlefields of 1914-1918 was a development since their youth, and the light automatic, scarcely less important in its influence, had only been introduced since the War began. All these he mastered, showing an aptitude rare even in receptive youth, and adding something of his own to their tactical use. Aircraft was another novelty that he came to understand through actual flying experience that no other commander of land forces enjoyed. He also overrode the barriers that in former days prevented infantry and cavalry soldiers from intruding into the sapper's or gunner's field; thus he added to his equipment an expert grasp of demolition and a working grasp of gunnery (1938e: 80).

In the same book, his favourite commander becomes Lawrence's regional commander (Edmund Allenby, 1861-1936) (1938e: 96). Allenby was 57 years old at his triumph, the same age as Haig, but Liddell Hart blames all wartime failures on "that system which chooses leaders by seniority and prefers safe men to men who are bold in thought and action" (1938e: 302).

Liddell Hart's demonization of elders and seniors was hypocritical. He had been advising War Secretaries since 1935. Most influentially, in 1937, he influenced Leslie Hore Belisha's purge of the General Staff. Perversely, he would blame the purge's beneficiaries for Belisha's fall from ministerial office more than two years later.

> Contact with the military hierarchy is a liberal education in philosophy. During my own service, as a young officer, I was on the whole very fortunate in my experience of generals, though often puzzled at the way in which the mere fact of having earned the good opinion of one of them seemed a sure introduction to the initial disfavour of another, belonging to a different set or school of ideas. But my experience became more ex-

tensive after I had been invalided from the Army and became a military critic. I was often to recall the friendly warning of my old chief [Maxse], wise among his kind – "You'll soon learn, like Repington did, that we generals are as sensitive as prima donnas!" (1940b: 174).

He used similar language 18 months later to a rediscovered regimental comrade.

> There is nothing so disillusioning as close contact with generals. That may explain why…I was such an enthusiastic young soldier – for I did not see generals "in undress" until later (to Vivian Gaster, 19 July 1941, LH 1/309).

Recovering Convalescent

Since July 1916, Liddell Hart had spent his military service in convalescence or light duty. In 1919, he reported for his first post-war review of his health.

> [He is] suffering a moderate degree of DAH [disordered action of the heart] with fair exercise tolerance. He complains of attacks of tachycardia [a heart rate over 100 beats per minute], irregular pulse[,] and dyspnea [laboured breathing] on exertion. He has lost considerable weight since he was gassed and it is obvious that at present his weight and general physique are much below what they should be (Army medical board, 21 March 1919, LH 8/129).

In notes to self, he claims to have experienced heart attacks in both 1921 and 1922 (LH 8/317), although his memoirs admit only the first. "Dr. Frederick Price, then the foremost specialist in London…[said] I must resign myself to a half-speed life." Soon he suffered angina (pain caused by reduced blood flow to the heart). He consulted a second specialist, who encouraged exercise. "I improved so much that by the summer of 1922 I was able to start playing lawn tennis again" (1965: I, 62). Although he returned to tennis, he stayed in military convalescence or light duty.

Involuntary Invalid

By February 1923, he was prospecting freelance journalism in America, but in August, he agreed to correspond for *The Morning Post* for the next training season. In the same month, he persuaded a medical board to confirm light duty, although in March he went on half-pay again, to start corresponding from the field (to J.M. Scammell, 22 February 1923, LH 8/301; to Fred Lawson, c. June 1932, LH 3/97; 1965: I, 66). Given that this one-year appointment expired in February 1925, the War Office scheduled a new medical examination in March. The medical board ordered permanent half-pay, effective in July, when he would start full-time at *The Daily Telegraph*, with the approval of the incoming CIGS. The timing was convenient, but Liddell Hart's memoirs imply an inconvenient conspiracy. "This was somewhat curious as the previous board, while reporting that I was unfit for general service, had suggested that I should be re-examined after a further 12 months. The new medical board was asked to report whether I was fit for duty 'in a tropical climate'" (1965: I, 64).

Most wartime officers retired without pay or pension. The option on half-pay was for officers temporarily incapacitated or promoted without a commensurate billet or post. Even on half-pay, officers sought official work, such as revising doctrine (Wavell's choice). Liddell Hart did nothing for the Army while on half-pay, except to promise "propaganda," which he betrayed (see the section below).

Liddell Hart misrepresented his voluntary half-pay as involuntary "invaliding." In July 1934, he noted: "When I was invalided out of the Army I was sorry to leave, because I loved the service. But I have come to see, more and more, that it means sealing up part of the mind." One of his third-person biographies claims that "his active military career was denied him when he was invalided out of the service in 1924 as a result of the wounds received during the war." His memoirs include three pages of narrative about his supposed efforts to stay in the Army. He blames the prior CIGS (Cavan) for ruling that all officers must be fully fit, but this ruling was not directed at officers on "light duty," and preceded Milne's accession in February 1926. He claimed also that the War Office used earlier reports of his unfitness rather than later reports of his fitness, but none was necessary to his separation (1944a: 102; 1956b: 2; 1956a: 463; 1965: I, 63-65).

Historians have been confused or complicit. By private correspondence, he persuaded one American historian he had been "invalided out of the army in 1924" (Ropp 1959: 293). He persuaded another that ill-health was an excuse to deny his requests for promotions, transfers, and re-enlistment (Luvaas 1964: 378). He persuaded a third that "medical reasons" were mere excuses for "the anti-intellectual CIGS" to get rid of him (Higham 1966: 48). He persuaded Brian Bond (1977: 20) that his position in the "Army was precarious because of his impaired health." He persuaded Robert O'Neill (1990: 103) "he had not sought…to leave the Army in order to become a public commentator," and that his job of military correspondent "was both insecure and financially straitened." Some historians misdescribe ill-health as the only reason for his switch to half-pay (Swain 1990: 41; Danchev 1998a: 71). Some misdate his half-pay from 1920, and his full retirement from 1924, because of conservatism (Barnett 1970: 414; Reid 1998: 3), war-related ill-health (Stearns 1972: 6; Bond 1977: 20; Bond 2015: 32), or an unspecified "wound" (Baynes 1995: 223).

To be accurate, Liddell Hart did not separate from the Army in 1924, rather he shifted from full-time service into inactive reserve. The shift was not "enforced." He reported his medical complaints, frequently sought leave for convalescence on half-pay, and chose his moment to retire from active service – at the same time as he started an indefinite full-time job in journalism. He made a rational choice between opportunity cost and a more rewarding career.

Hypocritically, during his peak power as adviser to the Secretary of State for War, in late 1937, he instigated the abolition of half-pay. He touted the abolition as a blow against incumbency (1939b: 329).

Propagandist

The Army was desperate for good press, next to the senior service (the Navy) and the modern service (the Air Force), each of which was smaller in personnel but larger in budget per person. By 1938, the RAF was larger in absolute budget too.

Publicization of the Army was known within the War Office officially as "public relations," colloquially as "propaganda." Milne was sufficient to promote Liddell Hart as propagandist. Milne, then at Eastern Command, had met Liddell Hart in

1924, without effect. Milne already saw Fuller as the Army's great thinker. Milne urged Fuller to stay in the Army and join him as Military Assistant (an adviser, in contrast to the Military Secretary, who is an administrator). Milne remembered Liddell Hart in May 1925, when the editors of *The Daily Telegraph* gave Milne a vote on its next military correspondent. Milne confirmed Liddell Hart as the candidate most favourable to the Army (interview, Thomas Jacomb Hutton, 1977, IWM 895).

In July, Liddell Hart started work at *The Daily Telegraph*. In the same month, his first proper book (*Paris, or the Future of Warfare*) was published. His memoirs falsely claim that this book influenced Milne to approach him for help with the mechanization of the Army, and that by reply he advised Milne to appoint Fuller as adviser.* Liddell Hart gave American correspondents yet another account: that Trenchard (then Chief of the Air Staff) had handed a copy to Milne (1965: I, 99; Ropp 1959: 293; Higham 1966: 86). In fact, Milne and Ernest Swinton (just appointed as Chichele Professor of Military History at Oxford) had conferred about Fuller's appointment in June. The earliest letter from Milne to Liddell Hart is dated 8 July: it responds to Liddell Hart's offer to meet about his role as propagandist.

> I want to be quite frank with you. I fully realise that without the support of the Press of the country it is quite impossible for the Army to carry out many reforms, as a good deal must depend on the education of popular opinion. You know as well as I do that I dislike advertisement, but self-advertisement and propaganda for a good cause are two quite different things. I hope therefore that we may be able to work together during the next few years for the purpose of achieving the end which I am certain we both have in view (Milne to LH, 8 July 1925, LH 1/512).

Later that month, Liddell Hart saw Milne on a tour of Territorial Army camps in Sussex. (Milne was still chief of Eastern Command.) Surely this is when Milne revealed to Liddell Hart his appointment of Fuller as Military Assistant. Liddell Hart left contradictory accounts. In Liddell Hart's first story, he suggests that Milne should establish a department to research future operations, but Milne responds with complaints about "the pressure of routine business," and suggests that only his Military Assistant is free of such pressure. "He subsequently made good use of it by choosing for the post the most brilliant and unorthodox speculative mind then in the Army, Colonel JFC Fuller." In Liddell Hart's second version of the meeting, Milne approaches him to praise *Paris*, asks how to implement its prescriptions for mechanization, took his suggestions for an operational research department and experimental mechanized force, but complains that only his Military Assistant could act without Treasury approval. (In fact, all proposals for new establishments went to Treasury for approval.) In this second story, Liddell Hart claims to suggest Fuller as Military Assistant, and to help Milne to gain "confidence" in his convictions (1939b: 342; 1959: 233-234; 1965: I, 99; Martel 1949: 52).

Liddell Hart's frequent reports of Milne's lack of "confidence" were self-serving. Milne was rightly concerned that Fuller and Liddell Hart were pushing for immediate mechanization without due specifications and experiments. He expressed the same concern to Fuller (1936: 421) upon first meeting (in September, during the

---

* John Wheldon (1968: 35) and Danchev (1998a: 138-139) perpetuate this account.

corps-on-corps exercises).

Liddell Hart's priority was not mechanization, but to get his pedestrian drills and doctrine into the manuals. Milne distanced himself, particularly once he began shadowing the outgoing CIGS in January 1926. In the same month, Liddell Hart heard that Milne had recommended Fuller for a CBE.* He asked Milne to suggest someone to recommend his own petition. Milne replied that he could not think of anyone, but volunteered to review it, after acceding as CIGS (on 19 February). Months later, Milne still had not committed, so Liddell Hart asked for Milne's recommendation. Milne properly replied that such awards "are given for outstanding merit over a long period and not for specific tasks of work" (Milne to LH, 16 January 1926, and Milne to LH, 28 April 1926, LH 1/512).

Milne still tasked Liddell Hart with propaganda. Milne granted free access to the War Office, despite complaints from other journalists.

> As I went there so frequently – to visit officers I knew in the various branches, as well as Milne's own office – the customary and time-wasting requirement of getting a visitor's pass from the enquiry desk at the side-entrance had been waived, and I always went in by the front door (1965: I, 118).

Liddell Hart's casualness in the War Office was risky, given Milne's scepticism and Maxse's retirement (to establish a fruit distribution company). Liddell Hart did not predict that Milne's appointment would be extended. (It was extended twice, until 1933.) He was already playing with Milne's eventual successor: Archibald Armar Montgomery (known as Montgomery-Massingberd from October 1926, as a condition of his wife's inheritance). In September 1916, Liddell Hart had described Brigadier Montgomery as one "of the brilliant Chiefs of Staff of the two armies on the Somme" (LH 7/1916/22). In March 1926, the former brigadier was promoted to lieutenant-general rank, without a requisite billet. He took half-pay, drafted a book on "The Lessons of the Last War," and sought Liddell Hart's help. At the time, he shared Milne's misestimation of Liddell Hart as foil to Fuller's impatience. Liddell Hart asked if Massingberd had read *Foundations of the Science of War*, released in February, coincident with Fuller's accession as Milne's Military Assistant.

> No, I have not read Fuller's book! And don't expect I ever shall. It would only annoy me! There are two classes of people I have no time for. Those who run down and crab everyone above them and those who think that because they have read a little military history everyone else is an ignoramus and has never done likewise. Fuller comes into both categories (to LH, 27 April 1926, LH 1/520).

Liddell Hart chose not to reveal his alignment with Fuller. Still, his relationship with Massingberd did not develop well, despite Massingberd spending two years on half-pay.

Liddell Hart, by then, was insecure about his half-pay from the Army and his salary from *The Daily Telegraph*, given his critical tone. Milne gave him a new

---

* Commander of the Order of the British Empire – an annually-awarded honour for public service outside the civil service. Fuller received the award in July 1926. Liddell Hart never received it, although he would be knighted 40 years later.

professional venue: the Army & Navy Club. Milne proposed his membership. The Inspector of Artillery (Webb Gillman) seconded. Milne eschewed memoirs, but his Military Secretary confirms the intent.

> [Liddell Hart] had a good many enemies at that stage, so the fact that he was proposed by the CIGS made quite sure that he wouldn't be turned down. He wanted to educate the public and the Army in the modern military equipment and tactics, particularly the public (Thomas Jacomb Hutton,* interview, 1977, IWM 895).

Liddell Hart noted the news in November, and confirmed that he wanted to use his journalism as a "platform for launching a campaign for the mechanization of the Army" (LH 11/1926/1).

Leaker

Liddell Hart's privileges were undone, little more than one year into Milne's tenure, by leaks of information and conflicts of interests.

> [I released] a stream of what Fleet Street called "scoops," and was usually able to inform the readers of The Daily Telegraph about coming appointments before they were announced by the War Office (1965: I, 83).

Major Giffard le Quesne Martel (1889-1958) had been leaking to Liddell Hart since June 1925, when they first met, at his own home, to seek Liddell Hart's help in publicizing a tankette of his own design and assembly. For the training season of 1926, Martel was in the unseemly position of marketing tankettes (produced in partnership with Morris Motors) while commanding a company of Royal Engineers that was trying tankettes (Newsome 2024: Chapter 4). Liddell Hart over-relied on him for opinion in the War Office too, even though both were of junior rank. That summer, Milne issued a warning to all officers against writing about Army Council decisions, even in private. He described such correspondence as "subversive propaganda." Once, when Martel was entering the Army & Navy Club, Milne asked what Martel was carrying in his attaché case. Martel laughed it off as "subversive propaganda," which was true. In December, Martel leaked plans to appoint an Experimental Mechanized Force for the following training season. In April 1927, Liddell Hart reported delays. During his next visit to the War Office, the Director of the Press department warned that the Army Council had discussed a court martial, but settled for cancelling his free access. Liddell Hart retorted with a threat of bad press, and his intent to retire from half-pay (Martel to LH, 14 December 1926, LH 1/492 Part 1; Martel 1949: 54; Liddell Hart, "An Army Mystery – Is There a Mechanized Force?" *The Daily Telegraph*, 22 April 1927; 1965: I, 120).

Massingberd committed to writing what Milne could not:

---

* Thomas Jacomb Hutton had known Milne since early 1914, when Hutton was an artillery subaltern in the division in which Milne commanded the artillery. They continued in these roles when the division went to France. Hutton served in France throughout the war, while Milne took a command in Greece. When Milne took over the Allied force in Constantinople, he called for Hutton as a staff officer. When he took over Eastern Command in 1923, he did the same. In 1925, he selected Hutton as Military Secretary to the CIGS (effective February 1926). Hutton was not Milne's only Military Secretary, but longest serving (until 1930).

> In my opinion you have made the gravest mistake in adopting the line you have and have thereby sacrificed a position in which you might have been of great value to the Army. No doubt you will not agree with me or pay any heed to what I say, but I feel that the line you have adopted will lead you nowhere, will estrange you from all those who hold high positions in the Army, and will largely reduce your value as correspondent of the DT...
>
> You will be dropped by senior military officers and only encouraged by the disgruntled and disappointed. Many of the things you have attempted to criticize you evidently don't know the inner history of or the real situation and you can't expect people like the CIGS, AG, etc., to take such criticism lying down from a young inexperienced and very self-satisfied junior officer (Massingberd to LH, 16 May and 9 June 1927, LH 1/520).

Retiree

Liddell Hart retired fully from the Army, effective 9 July 1927, after three years on half-pay, two years before his allowance would have run out. By the time it would have run out, he went public with criticisms of Milne's "instinctive caution." Nine years later, he told himself he was forced out but not aggrieved: "For I loved the Army all the years I was in it, and my perception of its faults has developed subsequently to leaving." In the next year, he reported his retirement as "the result of war injuries, not personal opposition" (1929c: 99; "Thoughts jotted down – to be expanded," 17 July 1936, LH 11/1936/20; to R. Simmonds, editor, *The Herald* of Melbourne, 3 May 1937, LH 9/15/7).

Yet this magnanimity disappeared by the time of his reinvention. He persuaded Luvaas (1964: 385) that he "was too critical of mind and critical in outlook to serve the Army as publicist," or to keep to himself "his knowledge of what went on in the War Office." In memoirs, he blames Milne for forcing him out of "the profession which I loved" (1965: I, 64-65, 118; 1969: 201).

Liddell Hart's retirement from half-pay in 1927 was as unnecessary as his retirement from full-pay in 1924. Milne had cancelled his free access, but he could still enter the War Office with an escort. Milne ignored him for only a month. Milne rebuked Fuller for sharing his views without approval, then wrote to Liddell Hart with hope that they could re-establish their "former pleasant relations" (30 May 1927, LH 1/512). Milne invited a meeting in the War Office.

> [Milne] gave authority – whether formally or informally, I don't remember, but he encouraged the staff to talk to him pretty openly about what they were doing, and he saw him himself on several occasions, to show that at that period they were pretty close (interview of Thomas Jacomb Hutton, 1977, IWM 895).

Now degraded to normal journalist, Liddell Hart was, ironically, free to publish whatever he wanted about the Army, without accountability, except from criminal courts (for leaking secrets), civil courts (for defaming), his civilian employers (for bringing them into disrepute), and the few other retired soldiers with a public channel (for reporting inaccurately or unfairly).

One veteran with a channel to rival Liddell Hart's was Richard Montague Raynsford (1877-1965), former infantry officer, veteran of the war in France, retired Lieutenant-Colonel, and editor (1926 to 1954) of *The Fighting Forces: A Quarterly Magazine for the Royal Navy, the Army, the Royal Air Force*. In March 1927, Raynsford reviewed Liddell Hart's latest book (*The Remaking of Modern Armies*), with objection to its caricature of "the widespread prejudice of the professional soldier" (1923a: 321; 1927b: 178). Raynsford suggested reestablishment of the norm that military correspondents should be loyal veterans of at least Brigadier rank. Liddell Hart wrote to complain.

> Come, come, my lad, you write I think in haste...You have an assured position in the eye of the public and will, no doubt, continue to appoint divisional commanders and inspire CsGIS – more power to you. Nor is there any danger of your being supplanted for many years to come by a military correspondent such as I visualize. But don't shriek like a jealous prima donna because I venture a plea that the military correspondent of the future may be one who will have a more sympathetic hearing from the regimental officer of his day (Raynsford to LH, 12 October 1927, LH 9/3/7).*

Liddell Hart was still stewing weeks later, when Fuller pointed out that a journalist has more influence than a General.

> People are jealous of you. Look at your position between 1922 and 1927 – five years. In 1922 you had to say "Yes Sir" and "No Sir" to a twopenny halfpenny Captain, now you can put the wind up the Army Council (to LH, 5 December 1927, LH 1/302)

Liddell Hart corresponded with Massingberd, until a private denunciation, in 1930, of "the high priest of humbug," who is "only positive in stamping out originality." By then, Massingberd was in charge of Southern Command. Liddell Hart's denunciation came one day after the close of the annual manoeuvres. Within days, Liddell Hart publicly criticized Southern Command's use of a temporary Medium Armoured Brigade in combination with other arms. (Liddell Hart preferred light tanks to raid independently of other arms.) Within a couple months, Liddell Hart criticized the manoeuvres for lack of ambition, without naming any commanders, but the most responsible commander was Massingberd, as any regular reader would have known (note, 13 September 1930, LH 15/3/81; 1930c: 684; 1932c: 208, 209-210; 1935a: 182, 183-184; Mearsheimer 1988: 23, 103).

Massingberd was looking forward to promotion to full General on 1 October, without billet, free to pick up his draft of "Lessons of the Last War," although in March 1931 he took up the post of Adjutant-General. In February 1933, Massingberd acceded as CIGS. Massingberd expressed the same caution as Milne about Liddell Hart's and Fuller's calls for a smaller, fully mechanized Army. Bear in mind that Liddell Hart then required light tanks and trucks as the Army's only automobiles, and assigned most active soldiers to largely static garrisons, and assigned most reservists to static anti-aircraft batteries.

---

* Raynsford was a fair reviewer. See, for instance, his positive review of *Europe in Arms* (1937b), in *The New Commonwealth* (April 1937, 5/7: 128).

Massingberd retired in May 1936. He never finished his "Lessons of the Last War" or memoirs. In 1940, after German victories from Norway to France, Massingberd publicly blamed Liddell Hart's influence in the West. In rebuttal, Liddell Hart blamed their break-up in 1930 on Massingberd's refusal to second his criticisms of their seniors' failings during the Great War. This is contradicted by Liddell Hart's failure to record this explanation in 1930, when he was already recording the same explanation for other break-ups ("Captain Hart Answers Lincolnshire General," *Lincolnshire Echo*, 3 June 1940: 3; 1965: I, 102-103; Newsome 2024: Chapter 6).

Great Captain

While Liddell Hart posed as a "military critic" and unwilling outsider for civilian ethos, he continued to pose as an insider for military ethos. He routinely published as "Captain." This was normative while he was nominally retained by the Army, but not after he left for good in 1927.

Captain is a middle commissioned rank in the navy (equivalent to Colonel in the Army). Indeed, Liddell Hart's *nom de plume* echoed the greatest naval theorist – Alfred Thayer Mahan, who always published as Captain, even after promotion to Rear Admiral (on the US Navy's retired list). Mahan died in December 1914, leaving a vacancy, as it were, for a captain to be feted by Anglophones.

Liddell Hart initially referred to great commanders as "masters of war." Fuller (1923a: 76), when ranked Colonel, was first (of the pair) to use "great Captain" as a term for the model junior officer. Fuller added that such a "great Captain" would not be promoted in a typical conservative military. In the following year, Liddell Hart wrote: "Difficulties, as the great captains have repeatedly told us, are made to be overcome" (1924c: 37). Here he is conflating "great Captains" as both junior victims of military conservatism and great commanders of senior rank.

Liddell Hart's (1925: 16) first proper book declares that "the moment is ripe for those who do not hold that the advent of Napoleon was the Year One of military history, who are disciples of earlier Great Captains" (Hannibal and Scipio). Fuller's (1926a: 87) next book ranks Napoleon the greatest of the "great captains." Liddell Hart (1927c) responded with a book titled *Great Captains Unveiled*, none of whom is Napoleon.* On promise of a copy, Burnett-Stuart replied: "I know that in your serious moments you unveil great captains with the same skill as that with which in your lighter moments you go about unveiling little ones" (24 September 1927, LH 1/132). This helps to explain why Liddell Hart undertook a wider review of past military commanders, although he took years to finish. In any case, it elevates "men of thought" over practitioners (1933c: 11).

Storm Jameson (1949: 78), whom he met in 1931, depicted him, during a fictional war, mobilized unwillingly as a Major in the Intelligence Corps. "With an offensive boredom, he said, 'I'm a writer, not a soldier'." In the same year, Liddell Hart (1932c: 278; 1935a: 322) started quoting Napoleon's advice to read "the campaigns of the Great Captains." He did not finish his review of wider commanders for another couple years. His product is mostly an attack on Napoleon, Clausewitz, and

---

* Genghis Khan (1162-1227), Sabutai (1175-1245), Marshal Maurice de Saxe (1696-1750), Gustavus Adolphus (1594-1632), Albrecht von Wallenstein (1583-1634), and James Wolfe (1727-1759).

Foch (*The Ghost of Napoleon*).

> But men of thought who produced ideas of a more concrete nature, whose thoughts more directly influenced the course of history, have been comparatively overlooked (1933c: 11).

Having shifted to thinkers, his writing on "great captains" tailed off. In 1934, he drafted a book on the "great military geniuses" or "men of war," but came up with only four. One he had championed before (Alexander the Great), but one he had previously condemned (Napoleon). The third (Admiral Horatio Nelson) replaces his prior British favourite (Major-General James Wolfe). The fourth had founded the Soviet Red Army (Leon Trotsky). It was never published. In that decade, he was preoccupied with current policies and alternatives, such as his "British Way in Warfare" (1932c; 1935a; 1939b).

In the 1950s, he reinvented himself as the maverick neglected by executives, except German executives. He started to use "great Captain" with negative connotation. For instance, he wrote that although "originality is generally regarded as a sign of genius," it is generally neglected by "great Captains."

> This is a reminder that there are two forms of military genius, the executive and the conceptive…Creative imagination is the essential characteristic of genius, in the military as well as in other spheres. When coupled with dynamic energy, it produces an executive genius. When balanced by cool calculation, it makes a Great Captain (1959b).

By then, Liddell Hart coached correspondents to refer to him as "the Captain who teaches Generals." The earliest archived writing of this phrase is on a photograph of the Israeli soldier-politician Yigal Allon, mailed after their first meeting, in 1949, in London. Liddell Hart displayed it prominently in his office. Luvaas (1964: 377) and Lewin (1971: 79) used the phrase to title publications. Yet, Liddell Hart had not taught Allon, except indirectly through snippets translated into Hebrew by other Palestinian Jews. Allon's English was probably not good enough to come up with the phrase by himself (see Chapter 18). Chris Bassford (1994: 129) claimed that US President John F. Kennedy[*] called him by this phrase, but later admitted, "I took the line off of some dust-jacket blurb," and "I always thought that JFK's alleged comment was so over the top that it probably originated with Liddell Hart himself." Brian Holden Reid (1999: 69) repeats the claim, but similarly cites no source, and later wondered whether he had seen it on a portrait that Kennedy sent to Liddell Hart in 1960. In fact, the phrase does not appear on the portrait or in Kennedy's writings (1940; 1960). Certainly, servants and mentees referred to Liddell Hart as "The Captain," but they left no evidence that Generals did (Lewin, 1971; Bond 1977: 1; Danchev 1998a: 284; Reid, emails to author, 2024).

Shelford Bidwell (1973: 5), one of the Generals, criticized "the great Captain" as "one of the most misleading concepts in classical military studies," and a reductionism typical of applicatory historians – Liddell Hart and Fuller most of all.

> Wars are not decided by "great captains" riding the storm of battle and taking decisions based on intuition. "Generalship" is concerned with the

---

[*] Luvaas (1964: 376) remembers Liddell Hart displaying a portrait.

deployments of resources and weapons, and decisions are taken by large staffs (1973: 214).

Legacy

In 1960, Liddell Hart told a mentee that "the longer [and] deeper one thinks" about or experiences war, "one ceases to be a militarist" (Walters 1961: 22).

> Experience in conducting operations or in military administration during that [Second World] War can be even more a handicap, because of the habits of thought and practice developed in those conditions. Even the worst bombing, and resulting dislocation, were not comparable to the probable effects of nuclear warfare. Reason and imagination can hardly bridge the gulf (1960a: 47-48).

What is his alternative to reason and imagination? His answers are chaotic, but reduce to objectivity. He selects some historical cases, from which he induces, unpersuasively, that the solutions to the Cold War are nuclear disarmament, non-nuclear defence-dominance, and perpetual peace. He criticizes "old habits of thought" and "soldiers [who] still think in terms of a lengthy war" (1960a: 46), without admitting he had forecast a lengthy Second World War (see Chapter 15).

His memoirs amplify his contempt for soldiers generally, and senior officers particularly – but deny any prejudices.

> I was not an instinctive "rebel"...The heartening experience of being called in, when so junior in rank, to draft the post-war tactical manual for the infantry was accompanied by the disillusionment of finding how barren of ideas most of the generals were (1965: I, 60).

Michael Howard unadmittedly parrots the above:

> Liddell Hart was not a natural rebel...It required supreme self-confidence to believe that a young man whose active military experience consisted of a few weeks commanding an infantry platoon in France and who had never even attended a staff college should lay down the law to men who had had to master the hideous complexities (1999: vi).

Brian Bond corrected the record.

> [I]f not an "instinctive rebel," he later liked to stress his individualism and unorthodoxy (Bond 1977: 35).

Bond (1977: 38, 113) admitted that Liddell Hart under-estimated the War Office's competences, partly because he took no interest in administration or staff work. Robert O'Neill (1990: 104) admitted that Liddell Hart "felt no small enmity," and "was not always fair," towards sceptics in the Army.

Less substantive is Bond's (1977: 6, 20) caveat that "he did not, like a radical minority, reject the system to the extent of becoming anti-military." In fact, Liddell Hart was the most read of the anti-military veterans of the Great War.

11
Political Sage

Liddell Hart leveraged his publications and correspondence to lobby for policies and politics of personal appeal. He identified his politics as liberal. His disciples amplified his liberalism. None defined it. In fact, his politics were unsettled at best, mercenary at worst. He was politically opportunistic, within some idealistic boundaries. He played all the parties, and particularly the ruling party, as would serve his ideals and interests. His political ideal was liberal, but he was also elitist and anti-democratic, which previous biographers have ignored. He admired fascism in the 1920s and apologized for Nazism from the 1930s. He self-identified as socialist before August 1914, and courted the socialist governments of the 1920s, the increasingly progressive Liberal Party of the late 1920s, and the Labour Party from the 1940s. Indeed, it was the socialist consensus of the 1960s with which he settled.

Liberal

Liddell Hart and biographers never defined his liberalism, except to claim his tolerance (1972: 3; Bond 1977: 3, 9, 275; Mearsheimer 1988: 156; Danchev 1998a: 66). Tolerance is not sufficient for liberalism, although it is necessary. Classical liberalism prioritizes liberties (freedoms from restraint, such as freedom from censorship), and limits government to whatever is necessary to enforce contracts and protect the individual from the mob (Newsome 2023a: 145).

Liddell Hart's understanding of liberalism was under-developed. In November 1914, he recalled his pre-war self as "a socialist, a pacifist, an anti-conscriptionist." His opposition to war and conscription would qualify as liberal if motivated to protect the individual from being forced. Indeed, he described himself as "disapproving of all state checks on the liberty of the individual" (LH 7/1914/10). Yet socialism is incompatible with classical liberalism. Socialism aims for equality of outcomes. While liberalism emphasizes equality of opportunity, socialists intervene to correct inequalities of outcomes – for instance, by redistributing affluence. His socialism overlaps progressivism, which is usefully introduced here, but detailed later. Progressivism is change-seeking, sometimes with liberal ends (e.g., equality of opportunity), sometimes at the expense of liberties (e.g., equality of outcomes). Classical liberalism is incompatible with later use of "liberalism" as a synonym for socialism or progressivism.

Liddell Hart has been described as liberal given his support for international institutionalism (Reid 1998: 191), but the Labour Party was more international-institutionalist than the Liberal Party of Liddell Hart's era. The Liberal Party's origins are in the free trade movement: economic liberals are not necessarily international-institutionalists.

To confuse the picture further, three biographers have described Liddell Hart as a "Whig," although "mainly sympathetic to the Liberal Party" (Reid 1998: 187; Gat 1998: 124; Bond 2015: 33). Liddell Hart himself did not use the term. Historians deploy "Whig" to mean anything from liberal to conservative. The Whigs emerged in the late 1600s, in opposition to restoration of monarchial power, an issue that Liddell Hart never raised. The Whigs were succeeded in the 1800s by the Liberal Party. Both the Whigs and the Liberals of that century would be considered conservative by most self-described liberals today.

To disentangle Liddell Hart's liberalism, this section needs sub-sections. Liddell Hart's liberal partisanship rose with his admiration for David Lloyd George, fell with the factionalism of John Simon, rose with Leslie Hore Belisha's receptivity to policy advice, rose with Winston Churchill's political exile, and with the discussion group "Focus," which stimulated his own "Movement for Freedom," but fell into fuzziness in wartime, and clarified as progressivism in peacetime.

Lloyd George

By the time Liddell Hart called himself a liberal, the Liberal Party was factious. His favourite politician was David Lloyd George (1863-1945), who led a coalition government from 1916 to 1922, without yet leading the Liberal Party. Lloyd George was forced out by scandals, economic difficulties, and policy ambiguities, yet 1922 was the year when Liddell Hart sought to correspond. Liddell Hart's admiration was not necessarily liberal, but coincided with both men's turn against professional soldiers. His admiration was conflicted, because his favourite soldier, General Ivor Maxse, knew that Lloyd George was responsible for the diversion of British forces from France to peripheries, and for the resignation of the CIGS (Sir William Robertson) in February 1918 (Baynes 1995: 185).

From 1922, Lloyd George blamed his wartime failures on military autonomy, and exaggerated his efforts to curb military autonomy and the military's consumption of soldiers. Lloyd George's posturing against "orthodoxy" also appealed to Liddell Hart. However, he rebuffed Liddell Hart's efforts to correspond that year, preferring to communicate publicly in the House of Commons (where he was protected by Parliamentary privilege) and anonymously through liberal journalists.

Nevertheless, Liddell Hart took up Lloyd George's narrative in his first history of the Great War. Liddell Hart's account falls into contradiction. His account of the German counter-offensive of March 1918 praises Lloyd George for "a firm check on the flow of reinforcements to France lest they should be poured down another offensive drain-pipe," but blames Haig and the War Office for reserving soldiers in Britain.* The same paragraph imagines Lloyd George to be "infinitely adaptable," "as receptive to ideas as he was critical of the pretensions of hierarchical wisdom," "with a magnetic power of drawing even the unwilling to him," and with "speech and thought so closely coincided that they became fused." Liddell Hart's memoirs recall Lloyd George's "most distinctive qualities...as...immense vitality; an exceptional capacity to keep himself informed; extraordinary quickness of mind; extreme pugnacity, and dynamism; a mesmeric ability to charm and persuade people, both

---

* He gives no relevant sources in his history, except "unpublished documents" and "private evidence" (1930: 494). In memoir, Liddell Hart's only sources are Lloyd George and Colonel Cecil Allanson, a staff officer in DSD in 1918, and a partisan defender of Lloyd George. They did not meet until 1937 (LH 11/1937/69; 1965: I, 369). Amazingly, his memoir is the only source for some academic retellings of the controversy (Woodward 1967: 322). Better sourced historians had already blamed Lloyd George (McEntee 1937: 470; Falls 1959: 331; Terraine 1978: 34-35; Mick 2014: 146).

in speech and personal contact" (1930b: 388; 1965: I, 372).

Lloyd George led the Liberal Party from 1926 to 1931, by when at least three factions were caucusing in Parliament. Lloyd George's political decline, and focus on his memoirs, explain why he wrote to Liddell Hart in April 1929. His first letter baits Liddell Hart with endorsement of his wish (recently published by *The Daily Telegraph*) for a friendlier America. Liddell Hart's long reply explores his own politics, while searching for commonality. He criticizes the Foreign Office for "short-sightedness and adherence to outworn conventions," and the Liberal Party for "the outlawry of war."* In the next paragraph, he suggests that the best argument against war "is the stupidity" of military professionals. Still, Lloyd George waited until September 1932 before their first meeting. Then, Lloyd George described every wartime British military principal as either stupid or dishonest. Lloyd George was testing Liddell Hart's sympathy, before he revealed (at the end of the visit) that he had written 40,000 words towards his memoirs and would like Liddell Hart to check the chapters with military subjects (correspondence in LH 1/450; note to self, 24 September 1932, LH 11/1932/42; 1965: I, 357-359).

Still, Lloyd George needed more convincing. They met again in November, when he said he had written another 90,000 words. He did not contact Liddell Hart again until 7 April 1933 – and through an intermediary. Maurice Hankey (Cabinet Secretary, and thus the custodian of the official documents that Lloyd George had borrowed) telephoned to ask Liddell Hart to quote a fee for "vetting" the draft. The next morning, Lloyd George telephoned directly, to ask him to collect the draft of what would become the first two volumes of Lloyd George's *War Memoirs*. (He never wrote the life memoirs he had intended.) Liddell Hart returned comments on the draft, and appended notes from his own history of the Great War, plus a few quotes from others' memoirs. They met again on 21 May. The first two volumes were published in September. In February 1934, Hankey wrote to ask Liddell Hart to vet the next two volumes, so they met on 28 June. The third and fourth volumes were published in September. On a copy, Lloyd George wrote: "Captain Liddell Hart – I regard him as the highest and soundest authority on modern war whom it has been my privilege to meet." The fifth and sixth volumes, covering the final year of the war, would occupy more of Liddell Hart's time. By then, Liddell Hart was milking Lloyd George for information towards what would be Liddell Hart's fourth book on the Great War. They met on 21 March and 25 November 1935, and 27 January and 27 April 1936, to discuss the final two volumes. These were published in September, when Lloyd George flew to his first meeting with Adolf Hitler. He and Liddell Hart had expected his return to coalition government by then, and continued to expect so through the Second World War. However, as Liddell Hart's memoirs partially admit, Lloyd George's dishonesty and pugnacity in memoirs, and his apologism for Hitler in newspapers, scuttled his remaining reputation for good judgment and honest brokerage (1965: I, 360-364; Owen 1955: 724).

Lloyd George's war memoirs are most disappointing for their lack of *mea culpa* for wartime mistakes. Lloyd George was the only person to serve as minister throughout, including as Minister of Munitions (1915-1916), Secretary of State for

---

* Liddell Hart analogizes international laws against war to treating a fever instead of killing the germ. In fact, post-war international legalism was focused on preventing war. Pre-war international laws had already addressed the conduct of war.

War (1916), and prime minister (1916-1922), but blames everybody but himself. His memoirs contain three lies that Liddell Hart perpetuated: he claims to have been enthusiastic for the development of tanks from 1915; to have forced tanks on sceptical soldiers; and to have stopped soldiers from deleting tanks after first misuse in September 1916 (Lloyd George 1938: 381-385; Liddell Hart 1938e: 164; Newsome 2021a: Chapter 1). Lloyd George fairly accuses Haig of poor force employment, mishandling of tanks, and insubordination, but raised an obvious question. Why did he not dismiss Haig? He blames political deference to military autonomy. Liddell Hart seconded these claims in his reviews of the volumes, in both 1934 and 1938 (Lloyd George 1938: 388, 1271, 1298, 1334-1335, 1672; Liddell Hart 1934a: 260; 1938e: 155-156; Bond 2018: 23-24). Nevertheless, Liddell Hart's final review is knotted with contradictions.

> Lloyd George...has a rare honesty, if frequently some lack of accuracy. He is too intent to make his point to weigh his words with the exactness required for scientific truth or for fairness to those whom his point affects. But he does not hide his faults any more than his thoughts; with entire disregard of the consequences he exposes his own mind, with no more attempt to hide its defects than the weaknesses he sees in others, and in their actions. This comment may seem questionable – why, it may be asked, do his War Memoirs scarcely ever suggest that he himself was at fault? He would have been wiser to insert the admission of mistakes on his own part, but he would have been less true to himself had he admitted, for the sake of effect, faults that he did not see (1938e: 133-134).

Liddell Hart concludes that Lloyd George's critics are just militarist and partisan opponents (1938e: 153-154).

Simon

Lloyd George refused to join the National Government of 1931, although other Liberals did. Herbert Samuel led most of them out of government in 1932 (in protest against "imperial preference," and in favour of free trade). In 1935, Samuel lost his seat, so Archibald Sinclair took leadership of the Party. Liddell Hart ignored them, except for brief engagement with Sinclair in Autumn 1938 on the back of Churchill's outreach (see the section below).

Five Liberals stayed in ministerial roles when Chamberlain succeeded Baldwin as leader of the Conservative Party and Prime Minister in May 1937. The most senior was Sir John Simon, but Simon did not endear himself to Liddell Hart. They had coincided at All Souls College, Oxford, in the late 1920s, where they sometimes dined, as, respectively, a Fellow of law and a guest of correspondents. Liddell Hart retained no notes of their conversations or correspondence. One explanation is that Simon postured as needless of advice. Another is that Simon indicated disloyalty to Lloyd George. Simon resigned the Liberal whip in June 1931, caucused with Conservatives, accepted the Foreign Secretaryship in August, and formed the Liberal National caucus in September. In May, MacDonald had appointed a cross-party sub-committee to develop a policy for the disarmament conferences. Leaders of all three main Liberal factions were included (Lloyd George, Simon, and Herbert Samuel). The Foreign Secretary was ultimately responsible for presenting Britain's proposal, but Liddell Hart preferred to advise Lloyd George, the (mostly liberal) international lawyers delegated by the Foreign Office, the international lawyers working for the League of Nations, and the leading Conservative minister involved (Samuel Hoare, otherwise Secretary of State for India). Liddell Hart's memoirs describe Hoare as his source for what Simon was thinking. Liddell Hart's proposals (such as a ban on armoured vehicles over 5 tons) look ridiculous now, and seemed ridiculous to many at the time, but even in memoirs he blames their failure on Simon's presentation (1965: I, 183, 190, 205, 206, 210; Dalton, 1957: 175; Noel-Baker 1979: 74-76; Colville 1985: 35).

Simon served as Home Secretary from 1935 to 1937. He was appointed Chancellor by Chamberlain in 1937, by when he was Chamberlain's most loyal minister. Liddell Hart was aligned with their policies, but never reconciled with Simon's rejection of Lloyd George.

Belisha

Liddell Hart should have treated Leslie Hore Belisha the same as Simon, for caucusing against Lloyd George. Indeed, Liddell Hart ignored Belisha's first two ministerial roles (Financial Secretary to the Treasury, 1932-1934; Minister of Transport, 1934-1937). However, in May 1937 Chamberlain promoted Belisha to War Secretary. Liddell Hart had advised both Conservative predecessors (Halifax; Duff Cooper), and the inaugural Minister for Co-ordination of Defence (Thomas Inskip).

Chamberlain shared Liddell Hart's determination to avoid another world war and another commitment to fight on the continent. Of the military services, he resented the Army most, for its agitation for clarity on expeditionary policy. On 28 May, Chamberlain told Belisha he wanted "drastic changes" from the Army's seniors. On the same day, Cooper copied to Belisha Liddell Hart's latest recommendations for senior promotions. After being sworn in, Belisha was met by the Military Secretary (Lieutenant-General Sir Charles Deedes), who sought approval for the Selection Board's recommendations for promotions. Belisha refused, without a review of the Army List (all officers in active service or eligible). On 31 May, Inskip lunched with Liddell Hart, bringing a verbal request from Belisha for help to refocus the Army on imperial defence, but Liddell Hart pivoted to senior officers. He proposed compulsory retirement at 60 years of age, which would naturally reduce the Army List.* Cooper arranged to introduce Belisha over lunch on 7 June, when Belisha asked for written advice on reforming the Army. This was the beginning of what Liddell Hart privately termed "the partnership," although once their relationship broke down in 1938 he misattributed the term to Belisha. Publicly, he described himself as Belisha's "personal adviser" or (less often) "private adviser" (1952: 29-30; 1956b: 1960a: 191; 1965: II, 1, 10, 29; Minney 1961: 54-55).

Liddell Hart's eagerness to make Belisha his partner was partly self-interested, partly prejudicial, partly policy-driven, partly partisan.

> Hore-Belisha's eagerness for information reminded me of Lloyd George's searching mind. I was impressed by his keen desire to foster and stimulate the citizen-soldier spirit embodied in the Territorials (1965: II, 13).

No minister more welcomed, relied upon, or executed Liddell Hart's advice.

---

* After repeated controversies about his influence, he reported the issue as "how the army might be reorganized to fit its functions better" (1939b: 166).

The influence peaked in November, with their purge of the General Staff, and promotion of unconventionally young favourites. However, the appointees did not turn out as loyal or progressive as Liddell Hart and Belisha had expected. Other recriminations built up. Belisha often distanced himself, and played the General Staff and Liddell Hart against each other. Liddell Hart considered their "partnership" over by July 1938. He courted Lloyd George again, who, when fantasizing about taking the premiership, said, "I hope to see you Secretary of State for War" (1 September 1938, LH 11/1938/91). However, as a war scare developed that same month, Liddell Hart returned to the "partnership," in furtherance of appeasement. This provoked Winston Churchill's most proactive effort to dissuade him of both appeasement and Liberal partisanship.

Churchill

Liddell Hart already was favourably disposed to Churchill. The first explanation is Lloyd George's favour. Lloyd George appointed Churchill as Minister of Munitions (1917-1919), Secretaries of State for War and Air (1919-1921), and Secretary of State for the Colonies (1921-1922). A second explanation is that all three men accused the Army of too much autonomy, carelessness with soldiers and tanks, and obstruction of the development of tanks.* A third is Churchill's appointment of T.E. Lawrence, as a vague adviser, in 1921, which is when Liddell Hart started to correspond with Lawrence (Graves 1938: 54). A fourth is their shared admiration for Benito Mussolini (although for different reasons: Liddell Hart appreciated him mostly as a progressive, Churchill as an anti-Bolshevik). A fifth is their preference for peripheral expeditions and raids, particularly by sea and air. A sixth is their Francophilia, a seventh their reliance on the French Army and British warships and bombers for balancing continental adversaries. Indeed, a critic grouped Churchill's policies and Liddell Hart's writings as equally foolhardy (Germains 1927: 154).

Liddell Hart responded by categorizing Churchill and himself as biographers of "great persons." He wrote that "distinguished soldiers have, for example, derided Mr. Churchill as an 'amateur,' forgetting that he had spent more years in soldiering, seen more active service, and probably read as profoundly as Napoleon at the outset of his 1796 campaign" (1927b: 175). In fact, Churchill had spent most of his active service away from his regiment – in journalism and politics – and read little beyond memoranda, Parliamentary records, and family records, as useful for politics, journalism, memoirs, and biographies of his ancestors. Indeed, Liddell Hart and Churchill were kindred in their love of rhetoric and history, disinterest in other disciplines, disdain for formal education, and preference for military corresponding over soldiering (Ashley 1968; Plumb 1969; Weidhorn 1974).

In 1922, Churchill lost his seat in Parliament, and started to write both a memoir and an autobiographical history of the Great War, whose many volumes Liddell Hart ignored. In November 1924, Churchill returned to the Conservatives (20 years after he had defected) and to Parliament, and was appointed as Chancellor of the Exchequer. Both Churchill and Liddell Hart realized that Baldwin's second administration would be stronger and longer-lasting than the first. Liddell Hart started to

---

* He later realized that Churchill's published claim to have invented the tank is based on his misdescription of a wheeled, unarmoured bridge-pusher, which he unnecessarily ordered into development from December 1914 to June 1915 (1969: 195; Newsome 2021a: 18).

correspond. They met in September 1927, as observers of the final exercises of the Experimental Mechanized Force. They met in March 1928, over lunch with the War Secretary (Laming Worthington-Evans) and two retired Generals, all of whom were looking forward to the Experimental Armoured Force that was being assembled that month. However, Churchill's austerity (in contrast to his profligacy at prior ministries) included his resistance to further mechanization, and his assumption of no war for ten years. Yet Liddell Hart continued to blame the Army's shortages on its Generals. After the Conservative government was voted out in May 1929, he brought to Churchill a proposal for a smaller, cheaper Army, mounted in tankettes and trucks alone. Unusually, he archived no notes, likely because Churchill (and Fuller, who also was present) criticized the idea. Certainly, Liddell Hart ceased to defend Churchill around then. His only published explanation, published 40 years later, is Churchill's U-turn on full mechanization and on more experimental mechanized forces. "His traditionalist instincts were always in conflict with his progressive impulses." In any case, Churchill's career, like Fuller's, was in decline (note, 9 March 1928, LH 11/1928/13; 1957: 8; 1969: 202).

Churchill and Liddell Hart did not meet again until 1932, when they ran into each other in the House of Commons or Lloyd George's home. They met next in February 1933, when Churchill made clear he preferred penetrations over raids, and doubted the survivability of light tanks, although they both preferred fast tanks. Later, Liddell Hart pretended that he "still thought of them in the slow-motion terms of 1918," while he preached "Blitzkrieg" (LH 1/171/22; 1969: 204).

The next time he visited Lloyd George, he quoted T.E. Lawrence as saying that Lloyd George was the only man he knew who could dominate Churchill (diary, 27 April 1936, in Stevenson 1971: 322). In memoirs, he makes the saying his own.

> L.G. made a habit of giving breakfast parties; Churchill a habit of late-night sessions...He was skilled at "squeezing the lemon" – and a good listener, unlike Churchill...Churchill's mind was apt to focus on a phrase, while L.G. seized on the point and followed on to the next...Moreover, Churchill liked to do most of the talking in any discussion, whereas L.G. liked to gather information first...L.G. usually dominated Churchill wherever the two were present together. This was astonishing to see – for in any other company Churchill was dominant (1965: I, 372-374).

Later in 1936, the Spanish Civil War broke out. Liddell Hart wanted Britain to arm the Popular Front, but Churchill rightly opposed any further empowerment of what was really a Soviet front. Liddell Hart pretended that Churchill's "sympathy with the Francoists tended to blind him to the purpose and dangers of Hitler's and Mussolini's support of that side" (note, 14 February 1936, LH 11/1936/40; 1969: 202).

Focus

On 28 September 1938, near the climax of the crisis over German threats against Czechoslovakia, Churchill invited Liddell Hart to a private discussion group. Churchill's motivation is unclear. He may have wanted to shake things up. The invitation was belated: Churchill and Oliver Locker-Lampson had launched the group in June 1935. Churchill called the group "Focus," although attendees had different interpretations. The first meeting had decided against formal rules, membership, or mission, beyond "defence of freedom and peace." One unifying commitment was to the League of Nations, although for the founders this was a means to their ends.

The founders were Conservative MPs, but conservatives were in the minority. Most attendees were liberals or progressives. The Conservatives prioritized rearmament (of Britain) and containment (of Germany, Italy, and the USSR). Most of the others did not favour rearmament or containment, and were not ready to abandon appeasement. They tended to express their priority as "peace" or "freedom."

Liddell Hart was in this majority. After communicating to Lloyd George his opposition to "the outlawry of war" (in April 1929), he had U-turned. He joined the League of Nations Union as an executive, and corresponded with Britain's most vocal international-institutionalists.* Through them, he already knew most of the liberal and progressive members of "Focus."

Liddell Hart's memoirs misdescribe his initial interest in "Focus" as opposition to appeasement, misdescribe the attendees as "people who shared his views about the German danger," and misdescribe his own role as "military adviser" (1965: II, 248; 1969: 205-206).

Movement for Freedom

In his speeches of October, Liddell Hart calls for a vague political "movement inspired by the idea and ideal of freedom." His "idea and ideal" were means to an end: British resilience against air attack.

> If there is one distinctive feature of English history it is the love of freedom...Its preservation offers a true foundation for patriotism...the one basis of patriotism which offers a hope of rallying the people as a whole ("Reflections on the Situation, its Future and Our Policy," talk to Youth Movement Conference, 12 October 1938, LH 11/1938/114; 1939b: 85).†

On 30 November, Liddell Hart brought the idea of a "Movement for Freedom" to a "Focus" meeting. Duncan Sandys (Churchill's son-in-law, and a Conservative MP) championed the idea, partly to balance the liberals and progressives. They invited members to a meeting on 22 December. However, Liddell Hart resented Sandys for bringing four surprise guests, of whom the least popular was Randolph Churchill (Winston's only son). The attendees agreed that Liddell Hart, Sandys, and Vernon Bartlett (Independent Progressive MP) should draft aims, and that these aims should be agreed by all attendees on 2 January. They agreed another 33 invitees for an inaugural meeting on 4 January. The Drafting Committee met on 29 and 30 December, but split over Sandys' desire to convert the Drafting Committee into an Executive, and to turn the "Movement for Freedom" against appeasement.

---

* Norman Angell (journalist and Labour MP), Violet Bonham Carter (Asquith's daughter and sometimes Liberal candidate for Parliament), Robert Cecil (President of the League), Hugh Dalton (Labour MP), David Davies (Liberal peer), Julian Huxley (biologist; eugenicist), Gilbert Murray (classicist and sometimes Liberal candidate for Parliament), Philip Noel-Baker (Labour MP), Eleanor Rathbone (independent MP), Arthur Salter (independent MP).

† In memoirs, Liddell Hart credits the inspiration to Lord Sankey (John Sankey), a Labour peer and former Lord High Chancellor. Sankey corresponded after hearing Liddell Hart address the student union at University College London. Liddell Hart recalled his subject as "my personal philosophy and concept of freedom." Sankey suggested a movement for the development of liberalism, Still, Liddell Hart did not act for seven months, suggesting that the war scare was necessary (Sankey to LH, 19 March 1938, LH 2/S/16/1-4; 1965: II, 207).

The meeting of 2 January ended with only Sandys and Liddell Hart remaining from the original group. Sandys insisted on re-naming the group "The Hundred Thousand" (a nickname for the BEF of August 1914) (notes, LH 11/1938/123; 1965: II, 207-208).

The next day, newspapers reported the group. The sufficient leaker was Randolph, then an itinerant journalist for *The Evening Standard*, whose front page was captioned "Hundred Thousand Against Premier is New Group's Aim." This newspaper, and most newspapers, named Sandys and Liddell Hart as founders. *The Daily Telegraph* named Bartlett too. *The Times* (Liddell Hart's employer) named only Sandys and Randolph. Most newspapers reported the group as anti-appeasement. Belisha officially broke relations with Liddell Hart, who protested his ignorance and sought to restore their "partnership." Meanwhile, the Director of Artillery heard rumours that *The Times* would dismiss Liddell Hart.

> I'm afraid that L-H's talents are those of the pure mathematician – a very talented performer in a restricted sphere, who should not attempt to give practical effect to his investigations (Major-General Sir Campbell Clarke to Major Gordon Macleod Ross, 31 January 1939, Ross papers, IWM).

On 4 January, a couple hundred people showed for the inaugural meeting, at Caxton Hall, Westminster. Sandys took charge. Liddell Hart withdrew. Within weeks, Conservative Party Central Office retaliated against Sandys and Randolph, so they withdrew. In April, "The Hundred Thousand" were absorbed into "Active Democrats" – another anti-appeasement group. Liddell Hart's memoirs explain his withdrawal as opposition to Sandys' duplicity. In fact, his notes of the time, and a letter to *The Daily Telegraph*, make clear that he feared the shift against appeasement (LH 5/23; 1965: II, 210-211; Mearsheimer 1988: 127-131, 141-150).

Conscription

One of the few liberal positions Liddell Hart maintained was opposition to conscription, although his position was not entirely liberal: it was convenient to his opposition to foreign wars. His policy contributed to a skewed distribution of personnel that was not entirely resolved in World War II.

He had opposed conscription before the Great War, and returned to opposition sometime thereafter, even though he resented "regulars" (peacetime volunteers). He was most public on the issue in October 1938, after partial military mobilization in response to German intervention in the *Sudetenland*. In a paper for Belisha, public lectures, and journalism, he proposed to separate a largely-reservist AA service from the Army. Conveniently, he wanted the government to release resources by defunding the Army's expeditionary capacity, and even some of the RAF's future retaliatory bombers (1939b: 82-84).

Over the previous year, Liddell Hart and Belisha had structured AA defence at home as reservist (apart from a few full-time administrators). Now, he revealed that he had, a year earlier, proposed that full-time soldiers should man "a skeleton line" of AA guns. His "village green principle" implies one gun and one searchlight per village, or more than ten times as many heavy AA guns as currently authorized (1939b: 182-183). The day after *The Times* published this revelation, Belisha used a speech in Cardiff to oppose such "a great addition to our standing forces." Liddell Hart's next article for *The Times* estimates that only 2,000 active soldiers would be required (1,500 for the guns, and 500 for the searchlights). He allows 2.5 regular soldiers for each of the more than 600 guns required for currently raised batteries, and promises that this rate could be reduced to 1 regular soldier per future gun to his specifications. In fact, each 3-inch gun required 11 crewmen, and each 3.7-inch gun required 7, excluding the target predictors and service and support. In 1939, the War Department would add more than 1,000 full-time administrators to the AA force. Thus, the true requirement was at least 8,000 full-time soldiers per 8-hour shift, and 21,000 to sustain defence 24 hours-a-day. Liddell Hart suggests that guns and searchlights should be left unattended, except on one evening per week, when the active cadre and the reservists would converge to train, but this suggestion contradicts his demand for full-time defence and security (1939b: 183-184).

The General Staff properly required a larger active component to meet Army obligations, and welcomed partial conscription if recruiting would not produce enough volunteers (which almost everybody estimated it would not). Belisha was duplicitous, leaving Churchill to identify most publicly with the need for partial conscription for some roles, after October 1938. In January 1939, he was interviewed by Kingsley Martin, editor of the left-wing weekly magazine *New Statesman & Nation*, with whom Liddell Hart had corresponded since 1937 (during Martin's isolationist phase), enclosing copies of his speeches and articles against conscription. Martin pressed Churchill on the tension, as Liddell Hart articulated it, between liberalism (conflated with democracy) and preparedness for war. "Captain Liddell Hart has remarked that to have conscription to combat fascism is like cutting our throats to avoid a disease." Churchill denied this false choice, but went away fully informed that they were opposed on conscription, even though they still aligned on strategic bombers, warships, and anti-aircraft guns as priorities for rearmament (LH 1/492; Lh 3/82; Gardner 1970: 12; Allport 2020: 154-155).

The unreadiness of the AA force was proven by its second partial mobilization, in response to Germany's occupation of the rest of Czechoslovakia on 15 March. On 11 April, the General Staff advised that the Army could not maintain AA readiness without conscripts. On 15 April, Churchill endorsed the War Office's proposal. He won Belisha and Halifax (Foreign Secretary) on side by 18 April. Chamberlain (partly in deference to labour unions) persisted with the delusion that reservists could man AA guns nightly without giving up their day jobs. Liddell Hart agreed. In May, Parliament legislated for limited conscription of males aged 20 to 21 years old (with many exceptions), for six months full-time military training before transfer to the Territorial Army. Liddell Hart countered that Britain's higher objective should be "the continuance of liberal civilization – those larger ideals which we epitomize when we speak of 'England'," but offered no practical alternative (1939b: 43; Colvin 1971: 218-220).

Despite the failure of this limited and belated conscription to produce enough trained soldiers when they were needed on the continent in Summer 1940, Liddell Hart continued to oppose any conscription. Even shortages of trained personnel to replace casualties in Africa in 1941, and Asia in 1942, did not persuade him. Some formations spent the whole war unready at home, being periodically combed for soldiers ready for commitment overseas, without ever meeting the demand in the arms, while Liddell Hart cried alarm about combing of the AA force.

In Summer 1944, he developed a short book, which betrays a dilemma, between the classical liberal's freedom from conscription and the centralizer's promotion of genius. He conflates freedom with meritocracy (here termed "efficiency"), and does not admit the merits and efficiencies promised by free-marketeers.

> There is only too much evidence that the temporary adoption of conscription by England had a permanent effect harmful to the development of freedom and democracy. For my own part, I have come to my present conviction of the supreme importance of freedom through the pursuit of efficiency. I believe that freedom is the foundation of efficiency, both national and military (1944b: 22).

Peacetime Liberalism

After the defeat of Germany in May 1945, the Labour Party withdrew from Churchill's coalition, and forced a general election (July). Liddell Hart campaigned for the Liberal Party in general, and his son's candidacy in particular, but expected and welcomed a Labour government.

He joined the British Liberal International Council in 1947, presided over the North Buckinghamshire Liberal Association from 1948 to 1954, campaigned for his son in the general election of 1950, appeared with and defended Belisha (including in memoriam, in 1957), kept a portrait of Lloyd George (who had died in 1945) on his wall (the only British politician so honoured), and advised Liberal MPs into the 1960s. His memoirs list Lloyd George and Lawrence as "the most interesting and most gifted" of the people he knew. Nevertheless, by then he favoured the Labour Party, as explained below (LH 5/21; 1965: I, 339).

Anti-Democrat

Liddell Hart was always an elitist, even during liberal and socialist phases. Like Fuller, Liddell Hart regarded "the modern mob, miscalled democracy," as wrong-headed. His *Decisive Wars of History* complains of voters choosing disloyal and stupid representatives, from ancient Greece to Edwardian Europe, and praises the autocrat's detached approach. "But the strategist who is the servant of a democratic government has less rein." Given a draft to review, Lawrence commented privately that the "suggested difference between autocratic and democratic warfare is very fruity" (1923a: 320; 1929a: 18, 131; 1938g: 15).

Liddell Hart's elitism was amplified in political, journalistic, and artistic echo-chambers of his own selection. From first meeting in 1932, Lloyd George blamed Britain's constitution and popular will for military autonomy, and blamed military autonomy for military stupidity. After their third meeting, Liddell Hart realized his most explicit objection to democracy – as anti-meritocracy.

> We learn from history that democracy has commonly put a premium on conventionality. By its nature it prefers those who keep step with the slowest march of thought, and frowns on those who may disturb the "conspiracy for mutual inefficiency." Thereby this system of government tends to result in the triumph of mediocrity – and to entail the exclusion of first-rate ability, if this is combined with honesty. But the alternative to it, dictatorship, almost inevitably means the triumph of stupidity. And of two evils the former is the least (28 June 1934, LH 11/1934/41; 1944a:12).

Here, he is making a false choice between democracy and dictatorship, as if options do not lie between and within. His note indicates political immaturity for a man aged 38 years, of which the last 20 years had been spent in privileged contact with politicians. To be fair, his immaturity is depressingly typical of his generation. To his credit, he rejected dictatorship as the worst of two bad choices, and never embraced communism as the best of three bad choices. In a published rehash of the note above, he specifies Britain's "freedom" as "worth defending" and "the guarantee of its vitality." By "freedom," he does not mean anything democratic (such as free elections), but instead anti-conformity and thence meritocracy: "Our civilization, like the Greek, has, for all its blundering way, taught the value of freedom, of criticism of authority – and of harmonizing this with order" (1938e: 362).

In April 1936, when he discussed Lloyd George's last two volumes of memoirs, Lloyd George was entering his fourth year of public praise for Hitler's decisiveness, and plotting a first meeting (September). Liddell Hart disagreed with Lloyd George's proximate admiration for Hitler, but shared his resentment of democracy – for amplifying commoners and marginalizing philosopher-kings.

> He was in very good form and talked largely of general matters. He remarked that the tragedy of today was that the only three statesmen of real force – Hitler, Mussolini, and Stalin – were non-democratic. (His comments threw light on his own non-democratic tendency. Yet he is essentially consistent in that he remains now, as ever, a true "Man of the Left" – as he emphasized himself) (note, 27 April 1936, LH 11/1936/54; 1965: I, 370).

In the next year, Liddell Hart met Margaret Storm Jameson, who recalled him (in fictionalized form) as "so charmed to be living in what he thought of as our last civilized years before the worm of democracy began eating into manners and government, bringing on us the meanest of tyrannies – of the stupid many against the elite – bringing on democratic wars" (1949: 31).

Liddell Hart's argument against democracy remains contrived despite years of development. He manages to blame democracy for both the outbreak and the inefficient prosecution of wars. His causal process starts with Napoleon's reasonable principle of concentrating friendly strength against enemy weakness. This was already in British Army doctrine as "the principle of concentration." Liddell Hart misrepresents it as an expectation that "mass" always wins. He complains that the principle encourages democratization – as a way to legitimize military "mass." This proposition is theoretically and empirically robust, but his next proposition is not: that democracy encourages fights to the death.

> The wave of democracy in the 1840s fostered the growth of this mass theory. The idea of the nation in arms appealed to the democratic mind. Other minds, also short-sighted, were quick to take advantage of it (1939b: 28).

> The history of ancient Greece [actually an oligarchy] showed that, in a democracy, emotion dominates reason to a greater extent than in any other political system, thus giving freer rein to the passions which sweep a state into war and prevent it getting out – at any point short of the

exhaustion and destruction of one or other of the opposing sides (1946b: 64).

Clearly, Liddell Hart appreciated the non-democracy's potential for unpopular control and progress. This helps to explain his attraction to fascism and national socialism, which previous biographers carefully ignored.

Fascist Admirer

In November 1914, Liddell Hart repudiated his prior socialism and "internationalization." "Socialism and its forms are an impossibility unless human nature radically alters." He did not repudiate benign dictatorship. In December 1920, he wrote that he would "like power, but to wield it for the good of those under me" (LH 7/1914/10; LH 7/1920/32).

By 1922, Liddell Hart was disappointed in his influence on the Army, and dissonant about his wartime nationalism, traditionalism, and militarism. He shifted back to socialism and internationalism. From there, he discovered national fascism and national socialism. These alternatives remain confusing. Both apologists and critics tend to false differentiations. Traditional socialists promise that transnational solidarity and supernational institutions would end everything from war to hunger. By the 1920s, splitters asserted national variations, but still called for international cooperation against their opponents. Even domestically, the competitors are confusing. By 1922, Britain alone had at least five socialist parties competing nationally: Labour, Independent Labour (which, despite the title, was not entirely independent), Socialist, Socialist Labour, and the Communist Party of Great Britain.

Liddell Hart was then acutely Anglophobic, which helps to explain his preference for Italian fascism. He recorded no explanation, except that the National Fascist Party was then the most successful of the socialist parties west of the USSR. It administered Italy's government from 1922. British copy-cats perhaps encouraged his curiosity. The "British Fascists" formed in 1923, in explicit opposition to the Soviets and thence the Communist Party of Great Britain. The "Imperial Fascist League" split off in 1928, with a more pro-Italian and antisemitic bent. In the same year, Liddell Hart visited Italy, at the Italian government's expense. It arranged demonstrations by the army and air force, visits to the War College, and interviews with the Prime Minister (Benito Mussolini, 1883-1945), War Secretary (Ugo Cavallero, 1880-1943), Air Secretary (Italo Balbo, 1896-1940), and principals of the Fascist militia. He wrote for *The Daily Telegraph* a series of three reports, admiring both Mussolini the person and his politics:

> That he enjoys possession of this power he does not conceal, but to a student of human nature he gave the impression that he enjoys it basically for the power it gives him to improve and advance his country and his ideas for that country...

> The freely offered and even joyous subordination of the self for the good of the cause, combined with a discipline of the reflexes – a rigorous repression, not merely of contrary opponents, but of contrary instincts in themselves...

> Fascism knows that the source of the greatness of ancient Rome lay in her discipline. And with this, perhaps from this, moral root has grown another utilitarian virtue – honesty...
>
> Whatever the future may bring, it is at least certain that it will be different from the present, for Fascism, responsive to the law of life, is all the time changing its system, and adapting its ideals progressively to fresh conditions (1928b; 1928c: 113, 116, 117, 119).

Here Liddell Hart explicitly associates fascism with honesty, discipline, collectivism, and progressivism. His admiration for Mussolini the man is less clear. His memoirs contain three explanations. Mussolini rose to greet him, disproving what he had heard about Mussolini sitting silently behind a remote desk while visitors approach. Second, Mussolini displayed a photograph of Sir Austen Chamberlain (Foreign Secretary, 1924-1929), whom he recalled as "an English gentleman." Third, Mussolini claimed to read Britain's greatest liberal newspaper (*Manchester Guardian*) daily (1965: I, 105-106).

Liddell Hart's admiration persisted. Writing at the end of 1931, he looked to Italy as the primary foreign inspiration for his "British Way in Warfare." Italy prioritized bombers and tankettes, as he had prescribed since 1925. On mechanization, "Italian authorities take a view free from conservatism" (1932c: 136).

Italy's political appeal is subtle. He presents autocraticness as aristocraticness, elitism as meritocracy, socialism as preparedness. "Among Italy's present leaders are acute minds who, in reviving the Roman tradition, have remembered the fact that Roman statesmen understood war as well as politics." He admires Mussolini for "picking his ministers" by "expert qualifications." He claims that Italian officials offer more "common sense" and transparency than those of any other nationality. "To the courtesy, cordiality, and unrestrained facilities offered me I cannot pay high enough tribute." He credits fascism for increasingly active, healthy, and egalitarian Italians. "Italy, like France, has shown a full understanding of the fact that a modern war calls on the whole resources of the nation, which should be organized beforehand." He credits fascism for a "new spirit" and "a real pride of service," and assesses the Italian army's progress as more "moral and physical" than "mental" or "material" (1935a: 122; 1932c: 280, 284, 285).

In 1931, Oswald Mosley, other members of the Labour Party, and a few Conservatives formed the New Party. In 1932, most of them formed the British Union of Fascists (BUF), with Italian aid. In January 1934, Liddell Hart accepted Mosley's invitation to join a discussion group (January Club). Around May, he accepted Fuller's invitation to visit the BUF's headquarters. He was repelled by the BUF's militarist policies and paramilitarist symbols, given news of Germany's rearmament and Nazi paramilitary violence. Nevertheless, he continued to admire current dictators as progressives and meritocrats.

> A successful dictator is apt to be more of a realist than is the relatively cloistered member of a General Staff. Even if of military origin, he is less embedded in the professional grooves. By his circumstances, he is dealing every day in the fundamentals of strategy, instead of soaking in theory for most of a lifetime before he had a chance to practise against opponents. Also he is usually younger. A significant symptom is the marked increase

of attention which has been given to military aviation and army mechanization in Italy since Mussolini, and in Germany since Hitler came to power. Under these dictators[,] Balbo in the one country and [Hermann] Goering in the other have also been giving strategy a fresh direction – skywards. Here, certainly, is a warning of danger for democratic countries where military doctrines have been dictated by the heads of a professional class, autocratic within their own sphere and cut off from others (note, 13 November 1934, LH 11/1934/30; 1944a: 108-109).

Liddell Hart was harder on British than foreign fascists. For the rest of his life, he kept a signed photograph of Mussolini on a side table (Bond 2018: 20).

Nazi Apologist

In 1937, Fuller mailed a copy of a booklet he had authored: *What the British Union Has to Offer Britain*. By then, the BUF turned to Germany for inspiration. Liddell Hart had always compared Germany harshly to France and Italy. He dismissed the BUF as disloyal.

> I can admire those who criticize this country for any failure to live up to its own principles of justice – even in condemning its action they are upholding its honour. I can sympathize with those who, as convinced pacifists, feel that they cannot defend their country by force. But I can only regard as double-dyed traitors those who wish to import methods of government that are contrary to the English traditions of justice and freedom, and uphold the aggressive policies of Great Powers which can be a danger to us – thereby playing into the hands of the enemies of England. Old friends of mine like Fuller and Britten-Austin are among them besides men like Graham Seton Hutchinson (note, 26 April 1937, LH 11/1937/31).

The above is admirably liberal, but also self-interested. He told Fuller that he expected both men to be targeted by foreign authoritarians. He also belatedly recognized foreign illiberalism.

> What I observe in watching the growth of Communism, Fascism, and Nazism is that they are alike in developing a growing habit of denying or distorting facts, even where the facts can so easily be checked that the untruth of the denial or assertion is obvious; or where what is asserted as a certainty is inherently improbable. By sealing up so many aspects of life as undiscussable they are bound to produce a creeping paralysis of the mind, together with a gradual poisoning of decent feelings (to Fuller, 6 May 1937, LH 1/302/282).

Fuller did not correspond from then until the Second World War, by when Liddell Hart needed more rehabilitation than Fuller, although both needed some. Liddell Hart repeatedly defended Hitler's rationality and negotiability. His histories hardly mention German war crimes. His chosen biographers explain his attitude as professional and moral equivalency, not political sympathy (Bond 1977: 153-56; Danchev 1998a: 230-232), but there was political sympathy.

It is too simple an explanation to describe the Nazis as bad men. Their social aims were inspired by good ideals, but even there the means distorted the end, and still more so in the political sphere. The Nazis might more truly be defined as a party where bad manners were carried to the extreme (1946a: 62).

Progressive Socialist

Progressivism is change-seeking. Politically, progressivism demands government intervention to reduce risks, at the expense of individual autonomy. While liberals emphasize liberties, progressives emphasize rights. Some progressives share the classical liberal's emphasis on equality of opportunity. Otherwise, progressivism looks increasingly like socialism, in their quests for equality of outcomes and centralized protections. The difference is that progressives do not necessarily aim for equality of outcomes (Newsome 2023a: 145).

Socially, culturally, and politically, Liddell Hart was change-seeking. In the 1920s, he revived his pre-war counter-orthodoxy, anti-traditionalism, ageism, celebration of youth, and bias for change. He took up the terms "progressive" and "far-sighted" in opposition to "conservative" and "orthodox." However, he represented the progressive elite against the "orthodox" or "conservative" elite, while pretending to be anti-elitist (1921d: 621; 1923: 321; 1924a: 90; 1925: 7, 17).

Further, progressivism belies his demographic prejudices, political opportunism (particularly with Conservative ministers and employers), and policy regressions (to static defences, pedestrian garrisons, non-alignment, and unilateralism).

His progressive-socialism embraced Ramsay MacDonald's ascendancy of the early 1930s, the Independent Progressivism of the late 1930s, Clement Attlee's landslide of the 1940s, and Harold Wilson's socialist revival of the 1960s.

MacDonald Socialist

Liddell Hart welcomed the Labour Party's first general election success, in January 1924, given its policy of international disarmament and institutionalization, and Lloyd George's difficulties with the Liberal Party. However, he was not committed. When Ramsay MacDonald's first administration collapsed in October, he pursued Conservatives, such as Churchill.

MacDonald's return to the premiership in 1929 clarified his self-interests and his politics. Publicly, he admitted that his lobbying for international legal restraints on war, disarmament, defensiveness, and "rational pacifism" were closest to MacDonald's policies (1932c: 8, 165; 1939b: 9). He regressed to neutrality and unilateralism, even as he appealed for transnationalism. Without admitting his prior opposition to international legalism and institutionalization, he sets himself against "conservatism." He nests his criticisms of military conservatism within criticisms of Britain's political and cultural conservatism, which he traces back to the 1600s (1932c: 130, 138; 1933c: 166, 172; 1935a: 61). From 1931, MacDonald formed a National Government, in which conservatives took more ministerial positions, usually in replacement of Liberals. Liddell Hart equated political trends with military conservatism.

> Why is that soldiers are so often the most passionate resisters of Socialism? For when one hears a soldier, sailor, or any other government servant denouncing Socialism – especially if he be a staunch upholder of his

own service – one is struck by the astonishing illogicality and incongruity of his attitude. What a reflection it is on the self-contradictoriness of mankind! For the more he maintains the moral values of his own service the more he is testifying to the moral benefits of a Socialistic State. It is only by admitting the moral flaws of a State Service, its detrimental effects on mind and character, and by recognizing that they may outweigh its benefits, that one can reasonably justify an argument against socialism (note, 13 November 1934, LH 11/1934/30; 1944a: 109).

Independent Progressive of the 1930s

His distaste for small "c" conservatism explains his tumultuous relationships with Conservative administrations from 1935 to 1940. He happily advised their ministers, but his favourite was a National Liberal (Belisha). Even that relationship became recriminatory by early 1938. Soon the government shifted from his preferences. He opposed Chamberlain's acceptance of rearmament later in 1938, The Hundred Thousand's turn against appeasement (January 1939), and Chamberlain's switch to (partial) conscription and an effective alliance with France (April). He and the Labour Party (led by Clement Attlee since 1935) confirmed preferences for international institutionalism, non-alignment, non-aggressive defence, and rearmament with only defensive and retaliatory weapons.

Two Liberal international institutionalists – Lord (Robert) Cecil (President of the League of Nations Union) and Richard Acland MP (later a defector to Labour) – persuaded the Liberal and Labour Associations in the Westminster Abbey constituency to invite Liddell Hart to run as an Independent Progressive in the by-election of 17 May. The by-election was called after the death of Sir Sidney Herbert, who was a Conservative, but a critic of appeasement, and a long-time ally of Churchill. Polling suggested a cut in support for the Conservative government, in an otherwise safe constituency.* However, Liddell Hart was stressed by months of public campaigning against supposed warmongering, and an overdue book (his largest to date). The government's U-turn against appeasement gave him extra motivation, but undermined the main reason for conservatives to rebel against Chamberlain.

> They have been trying to get me into politics but I do not feel inclined to do so – there is not much scope for the exploration of truth there, and still less for its observance (to Graves, 5 April 1939, LH 1/327).

Liddell Hart turned down a separate invitation from the Liberal and Labour Associations of Rye, East Sussex, to run as an Independent Progressive against the incumbent government ally, in the general election, expected later in 1939 (correspondence in LH 13/43; 1965: II, 212).

Attlee Socialist

On 10 May 1940, Attlee and most of the Parliamentary Labour Party unambiguously abandoned its pre-war policies by joining Churchill's coalition government.

---

* The Liberal and Labour Associations persuaded the communist candidate to run as an Independent Progressive, who cut the Conservative majority from 13,000 to 5,000.

Liddell Hart did not abandon those policies, but he welcomed Labour as the dominant party, although he wished for Lloyd George to take over as premier. By the end of 1940, he embraced the new consensus for a socialist state, to win the war and secure the peace. He went public in the Labour Party's semi-official newspaper.

> We must create a new order in Britain, ready for extension abroad, that will be superior in nature and attraction to the Nazi order. We must give men a new vision, and a new hope. To beat the doctrine that the individual exists for the state it must be shown that we can evolve a scheme of national life in which the state of every individual is better than it could ever become in a totalitarian system. The new "free state" must secure its citizens all the benefits that the National-Socialist state promises them, together with the advantages that the latter, of its very nature, cannot even offer. In other words, our new order should combine a guarantee of economic security, based on the free provision to every one of the material necessities of life, with the largest possible measure of individual freedom outside the economic sphere ("Can We Take the Offensive in 1941?" Daily Herald, 7 January 1941, in 1941a: 406).

By 1945, he and the Labour Party were spinning their peacetime records as anti-appeasement. Labour won a landslide victory in July, including in the constituency where he campaigned for his son's candidacy with the Liberal Party. In 1951, he lobbied Attlee's administration for a peerage and a ministerial role. His most senior interlocutor was Lord Pakenham (1905-2001), then the First Lord of the Admiralty (notes, 20 and 23 June 1951, LH 11/1951/5). That government was voted out in October, before it could grant his backup wish (a knighthood) in the new year honours. Winston Churchill returned to power. Liddell Hart again equated revived political conservatism with supposed professional conservatism.

> In sum over the last 30 years, my own country had only made use of a small fraction – perhaps 20 percent or less – of my capacity for service to it. It has also left its opponents abroad to get the most profit out of my published products ("A Reflection," November 1951, LH 11/1951/14).

In fact, Conservatives had administered government for a minor part of his life.

Wilson Socialist

From 1951, Britons confirmed an unusually long-lasting Conservative administration (13 years), partly because the economy rebounded. Nevertheless, Liddell Hart decided the West was not offering "sufficient prosperity" to counteract communist promises. Given that he assessed the West as offering sufficient "liberty," his argument was progressive more than liberal (Walters 1961: 26).

From 1962, Liddell Hart corresponded with Harold Wilson, before Wilson took the Labour Party's leadership in 1963, and won the general election in October 1964. Wilson's administration invited policy advice. The period coincided with his most energetic advice to left-wing satirists of the Great War (see Chapter 5), and the success of his reinventive memoirs (see Chapter 20). In 1966, Wilson's administration granted his request for a knighthood. It stayed in power throughout his remaining life.

Legacy

Liddell Hart contrived with a friend to be asked whether his commitment to "truth" explains why he "never aligned…with a political party." He replied, "Yes" (Walters 1961: 29). Brian Bond (1977: 274) claimed that Liddell Hart "held aloof from party politics."* Danchev (1998a: 197) decided that "Liddell Hart was not much of a party man." In fact, Liddell Hart participated in party politics.

Also inaccurate are the many claims that he was liberal. Adrian (1972: 3) wrote that his father "was, in the widest sense, a liberal – while recognizing the limitations, from some points of view, of liberalism." Danchev (1998a: 197) decided that "intellectually he was a good liberal."

Azar Gat's concurrent book (1998) was meant to prove that "liberal" writings (led by Liddell Hart) were superior to "Fascist" writings (led by Fuller). Gat's differentiation is Manichean, but otherwise unclear. He synonymizes fascism with modernism, particularly technicism, but Liddell Hart saw himself as modern and technological, his adversaries as conservative. Similarly, self-described Marxists, such as Lewis Mumford (1934), whom Gat ignores, saw themselves as modernists and technicists. Even less clear is how liberalism causes superior military thought, and how fascism causes inferior military thought. Gat's evidence suffers selection and confirmation biases. Still, his evidence contradicts his repeated claims that Liddell Hart was liberal and invented Blitzkrieg, and that one had something to do with the other (Searle 2001: 345-347; Pearson 2001).

These claims for Liddell Hart the liberal ignore his elitism, anti-majoritarianism, and sympathies for fascism, Nazism, and progressive socialism. Reid (1998: 187) urged readers not to use his articles of 1928 "as evidence for any ideological sympathy with fascism," but does not explain why, and does not admit the other evidence for sympathy. Readers of only secondary sources continue to misreport that "he soon became disillusioned" with fascism after 1928 (Unterseher 2023: 30).

To be accurate, Liddell Hart was a fuzzy liberal who became a fuzzy progressive – a fuzzy elitist progressive, no less. Brian Bond (1977: 126) accurately observed that although Liddell Hart wrote "often about 'freedom' he seldom examined the concept," beyond "personal liberty from bureaucracy and compulsory service, and freedom to publish critical or unorthodox opinions." Bond is on firmest ground when writing that "in his egocentric and highly individual way, Liddell Hart was an idealist." However, Liddell Hart was not idealistic enough to eschew whatever political party was in power, or to resist illiberal centralization, or to repudiate fascist and Nazi favourites. The roots of his politics lie in his doubts about democracy, which in turn were driven by elitism. Although elitist towards civilians, he was populist towards professional Army officers. Additionally, he was an opportunist. John Mearsheimer (1988: 169) and Alan Allport (2020: 144) found that he usually told people what they wanted to hear.

---

* Bond seems to paraphrase what Liddell Hart had said verbally. "Liddell Hart also subscribed to the ideal of the philosopher-king who, having conquered the urge of personal ambition and made himself independent of all political, religious and sectional affiliations, is suited to proffer wise advice to the harassed statesman or general" (1977: 274).

BHLH and David Lloyd George in the latter's garden, 28 August 1934 (LH 13/104/3).

12

Appeaser

Appeasement is a policy of making concessions to a dissatisfied party in order to avoid conflict.* Japan, the USSR, and Italy benefited from Western appeasement from the 1920s, although British national syllabi focus on appeasement of Germany after Adolf Hitler's accession to Germany's premiership in January 1933. Liddell Hart contributed to this narrative. Japanese and Soviet aggression hardly appear in his notes at the time or his histories thereafter.

Liddell Hart defaulted towards appeasement, as a lesser evil than war. His commitment accelerated from 1935 to 1939. This period reflects two self-interests: first, he was in demand from two successive administrations (Stanley Baldwin from 1935 to 1937; Neville Chamberlain from 1939 to 1940); second, he was employed by *The Times* newspaper, which was closest to these administrations and their policies.

The issues that most stimulated his appeasement were, in chronological order, Italian invasion of Abyssinia (October 1935), German reoccupation of the Rhineland (March 1936), German and Italian support for the rebels in Spain (July 1936), German annexation of Austria (March 1938), Germany's reincorporation of its *Sudetenland* (October 1938), German occupation of the rest of Czechoslovakia (March 1939), and German threats against Poland, even after Britain and France guaranteed Poland at the end of March 1939.

Abyssinia

By 1935, after years of border disputes, Italy was openly reinforcing Italian East Africa as if intent to invade Abyssinia in the Autumn, after the rainy season. Liddell Hart was conflicted. His admiration for fascism waned with exposure to the British version, but he still admired Mussolini (see Chapter 11). He supported "collective security" through the League of Nations, of which Britain and France were the most active members. He opposed the sort of bilateral alliances that had entangled Britain in the Great War, but worried that collective security could entangle Britain in another war – a war that could "end civilization" (1935b).

He got cold feet about economic sanctions too. Since 1931, he had listed international economic sanctions within his prescriptions towards a "British way in warfare." In 1935, he supported and publicized a conference on collective security, organized by the League of Nations. From January, he reported on the national submissions to a study group on using economic sanctions to repress war, and the four meetings of the group, before the conference opened in June. However, when fellow liberal institutionalists pointed to Italy (relatively weak in natural resources

---

* Appeasers justified it as compromise and accommodation. Liddell Hart never defined it. His first published use of "appeasement" mischaracterizes it as "prolonged retreat from collective security" (1939b: 23-24). Retrospectively, he synonymized "to appease" as to "be bought off" (1952: 26-27). Almost all his published uses come after the war, always in denial of his association. His memoirs use the word "appeasement" 18 times, without definition.

and industry) as an ideal target for economic sanctions, he demurred (1932c: 37-42; LH 15/3/286).

In March, he used his first articles for *The Times* newspaper to undermine the theory of economic sanctions that he had previously championed. He exaggerates the provocativeness of sanctions and Italy's capacity for retaliation. To avoid provoking Italy, he argues against closing the Suez Canal, by which almost all Italian forces and armaments reach the combatant region. He warns of Italian aircraft devastating the Royal Navy's bases in Malta and Egypt, but imagines that British forces cannot deter or retaliate (even though they were arranged from Egypt to Kenya, on the land borders of Libya, Eritrea, Abyssinia, and Italian Somaliland). He urges British naval withdrawal from Malta to Alexandria – out of range of aircraft flying from European Italy. He wants a Soviet-French alliance to contain both Germany and Italy – but does not want Britain to confront Italy without France, even though France controlled shorter borders with Italian territories.

His first article for *The Times* prescribes "collective security" as the alternative to "isolation," but this is a false choice. He uses "collective security" to mean international diplomacy through the League of Nations, without national obligations. He recommends economic sanctions, but only to raise the costs of imports, not to block any, for fear of provoking the target into acquiring resources by force. He warns against blockading oil, specifically, even though he acknowledges oil as Italy's critical dependency. He uses "isolation" to mean Britain acting more provocatively than other states. Britain would be choosing literal isolationism if Britain were to follow his advice: to divest alliances and commitments, and invest in home defence (particularly air defence). His memoirs pretend he was arguing against the government's and the newspaper's appeasement of Italy. In fact, he, the government, *The Times*, and the League of Nations Union agreed that economic sanctions should be limited and unenforced, so as not to provoke war. His subsequent articles confirm his position ("Defence as a Whole," "Defence Against Air Attack," and "The Military Problem in Abyssinia," *The Times*, 14 March and 17 and 30 June 1935, LH 10/1935/76 and /77; 1965: I, 286; McLachlan 1971: 162-167; Allport 2020: 92-93).

Liddell Hart had been advising Samuel Hoare since 1926, when Hoare was the Air Secretary. In June, Hoare became Foreign Secretary. Liddell Hart did not call on Hoare to amplify British and French sanctions, even after Italy and its local allies invaded Abyssinia in October. He did not oppose Britain's abandonment of sanctions once Italy conquered Abyssinia, or challenge the political consensus that economic sanctions do not work. Nevertheless, by 1939, he criticized his government for not enforcing oil sanctions that "could have crippled Italy's campaign," and for not accepting the risks from Italy's capacity to inflict "considerable damage on us." His memoirs (and his disciples) claim that he had called for "full economic sanctions," and fought with his editors about their opposition to sanctions. He had not (1939b: 22, 140; 1965: I, 287; 1965: II, 125-127; Luvaas 1964: 413; Mearsheimer 1988: 133; Allport 2020: 93).

Rhineland

The Versailles Treaty (1919) demilitarized German territory west of the Rhine and within 50 kilometres east. In 1925, Britain, France, Belgium, Italy, and Germany guaranteed current frontiers, by a treaty signed at Locarno, Switzerland. However, the guarantors were left to determine for themselves what constitutes "unprovoked aggression." Subsequently, the British political consensus abhorred any continental obligations, and worried that a repeat of French punitive incursions into the Ruhr (1923-1925) or occupation of the Rhineland (1919-1930) could entangle Britain in war (Marshall-Cornwall 1935: 148-149, 158 Allport 2020: 87-91).

German forces reoccupied the Rhineland on 7 March 1936. On the same day, Liddell Hart wrote fairly that it was sovereign – *de jure* and *de facto* (at least since the Saar voted in 1935 against continuing as a plebiscite). Less fairly, he argued that the wartime Allies could not do anything about it. He did not submit this writing to his editors at *The Times*, who preferred to write the leaders on foreign affairs. Yet his memoirs pretend that they prevented him from commenting. His histories criticize Western responses as weak and enabling, but repeat his argument that the French and British could have done nothing militarily. This is a strange claim, given that the French Army was the largest in the West, and Britain sustained the largest navy and heaviest air force (notes, 7 March 1936, LH 11/1936/45; 1965: II, 126; 1968b: 740-741; 1970: 22).

In each publication, Liddell Hart assumes that the French Army could not mobilize fast enough. Liddell Hart knew the French Army better than any other British civilian, but he contrived this assumption. In fact, France readied more troops on the border than Germany did, and German commanders were under orders to withdraw if opposed. Even if French troops were late, they could have driven the Germans out. For fiscal and diplomatic purposes, French military leaders exaggerated the German Army's size, equipment, and training. They concluded that France could not defeat Germany without Britain. For domestic and international reasons, French politicians agreed. But they did not claim that the German Army was faster to mobilize (Emmerson 1977: 111-112; Schuker 1986: 304; Young 1996: 28; Ripsman and Levy 2007: 49-50).

British intelligence correctly estimated that Germany was unready for war. Most foreign intelligence was gathered from open sources by British consular staff in Berlin. For the domestic intelligence service (MI5), the most important human sources were Wolfgang zu Putlitz (a civilian diplomat in London, since 1934) and Baron Geyr von Schweppenburg (Military Attaché since 1933). Putlitz revealed the regime's intent to remilitarize the Rhineland, and its confidence that Britain would not intervene militarily. Schweppenburg revealed the Army's unreadiness, but not the regime's intent. The Cabinet ignored MI5's reports. Schweppenburg was known to Liddell Hart as the sender of invitations to observe German manoeuvres, which Liddell Hart continued to rebuff after the reoccupation.

Liddell Hart preferred Albert-Hilger van Scherpenberg (1899-1969), a consular official in London since 1928, and a contactee since 1932. Years later, Scherpenberg would join an anti-Nazi discussion group, but he never indicated this leaning to Liddell Hart or British intelligence. Scherpenberg returned to Germany in 1935, Schweppenburg in 1937. Liddell Hart never asked them about the Rhineland, perhaps because he preferred convenient assumptions over inconvenient intelligence (notes on meetings with Scherpenberg, 12 July 1932, 30 May 1937, and 15 June 1938, LH 11/1932/39, 11/1937/47, and 11/1938/65; Schweppenburg to LH, 10 August 1935, and 14 February 1936, LH 9/24/61; 1965: II, 133, 158; Hinsley et al 1979: 67; Strong 1968: 25-26; Andrew 2009: 195-196).

Spain

In July 1936, Spanish nationalists, monarchists, Catholics, and militarists, with German and Italian military aid and support, rebelled against the Soviet-sponsored coalition government (Popular Front). Liddell Hart always characterized the rebels as fascists, consistent with the Popular Front's reductionism. Similarly, he never gave up the Popular Front's myths about the preponderance of rebel armaments and crimes ("Note of Warning," 15 March 1938, LH 11/1938/35; 1939b: 38, 43, 89; 1965: II, 127-129).

Liddell Hart opposed French and British military intervention, even though he assumed Germany and Italy were motivated primarily to close the Mediterranean to France and Britain,* and thence to advance by "indirect approach" on France and Britain. He never admitted that Germany and Italy might be acting against the USSR, or that the USSR was taking an indirect approach against Western democracies. He did not admit even that the USSR was the Popular Front's enabler.

His next book (*Europe in Arms*) urges Britain to sell and donate aid to the Popular Front. Aid fulfils part of his "British Way in Warfare," made easier by Spain's maritime borders and Britain's alliance with Portugal. Also consistent with "British Way," he warns against boots on the ground. He even warns Britain against using military transportation and escorts to get the aid there. He never specified how Britain is supposed to persuade others to stop intervening without intervening itself. The book was released in March 1937. In April, he tried to persuade his editor at *The Times* that "non-intervention is the wisest policy in the Spanish War," even though he admits "more cause for anxiety" about Italy's and Germany's interventionism. He wants the British government and the newspaper to display "a firm line in insisting on genuine non-intervention." In May, he reported to the same editor that Scherpenberg had told him of Germany's despair with Franco's stupidities, and intent to withdraw, but Scherpenberg was misinformed or disinforming (1937b: 132; note, 30 May 1937, LH 11/1937/47; BHLH to Robert Barrington-Ward, 30 April 1937, LH 3/107; 1965: II, 132-33).

Chamberlain's rise from Chancellor to Prime Minister in May raised Liddell Hart's influence.† As Chancellor of the Exchequer, Chamberlain had supported appeasement and opposed any commitment to fight on the continent, on financial and fiscal grounds. Now he took on the role of chief diplomat and national security strategist too. On the same day, he appointed Belisha as War Secretary, and advised Belisha to read *Europe in Arms* and to consult the author.

> His views as to the broad lines of defence policy were in agreement with those in my book Europe in Arms, which had been published in the spring. So were Mr. Hore-Belisha's (1939b: 278).

Liddell Hart self-plagiarized from *Europe in Arms* for much of the papers he wrote for Belisha in subsequent months. In September, Liddell Hart drafted a paper that became a talk to Conservative backbenchers of the 1922 Committee (6 December) and to officers at the British Army Staff College (9 December). He said that

---

* He repeats this myth in 1948: 27.
† Alan Allport (2020: 144) found that Chamberlain "relied on the writings of Basil Liddell Hart" and introduced Liddell Hart as "an éminence grise at the War Office."

Italian victory over Abyssinia in May 1936, Italian and German support of Spanish rebels in July 1936, Japan's invasion of China in July 1937, and Germany's threats against Czechoslovakia are "indirect approaches" against France and Britain. He argued that France's and Britain's only engagement should be arms exports to the Popular Front. This might be considered an indirect approach against Germany or Italy, but he did not frame it so. In October 1938, he declared that "the second great war of the twentieth century began in July 1936." Yet he remains confident in defence-dominance and the Popular Front's victory. He still limits French and British engagement to arms exports. He does not categorize such exports as an indirect approach, although he alludes to a "super-strategic manoeuvre under cover of neutrality." In June 1939, he republished both papers, without changing or adding anything. His memoirs pretend that he had surveyed pro-rebel British journalism to reach his estimates, and that his editors at *The Times* prevented him from expressing them ("The Military Situation in Europe," 6 December 1937, LH 12/1937/10 and 1939b: 57-61; 1938e: 367; 1939b: 81; 1944a: 32; 1965: II, 128-130; Mearsheimer 1988: 130).

On 13 March 1938, he responded to Germany's annexation of Austria, by declaring that "the military key to the situation does not lie there, but in Spain." He urges the British government to sell to the Popular Front "on nominal terms enough material resources to restore the balance." He still wants to send aid without forces, without explaining how aid is supposed to reach the Popular Front through a coast controlled (by then) almost entirely by rebels. His confidence in defence-dominance helps to explain his vain hope that Germany could be tempted into attacking both France and Britain.

> If Germany and Italy were to reply by a large increase in the quantities of material that they have already sent, France and Britain are in a better strategic position than they are for such competition...If they dared to press their objections to the point of war, we should fight with all the advantages of the defensive and under more favourable circumstances of strategic geography than we could hope for once Spain has been conquered. For these reasons the risk seems less than that presented by any other contingency that can be foreseen ("Note on the Situation," 13 March 1938, LH 11/1938/30b; 1939b: 63-64; 1965: II, 142).

On 15 March, he again describes the Spanish war as the "second Great War." He characterizes Italy's and Germany's approach as "the modern equivalent of the familiar phase of manoeuvring for position before the main stroke is delivered." Now, "the enemy is within reach of gaining the decisive points without a battle, and in the most vital direction." He complains that "we" let "our" adversaries get the upper hand. He imagines that these adversaries are motivated only to weaken France and Britain. Yet for all his urgency, he has no solution except supplying arms to the Popular Front, redundant to yet another surge in Soviet supplies ("Note of Warning," 15 March 1938, LH 11/1938/35; 1939b: 65; 1965: II, 142-143).

Belisha requested a paper on policy towards the Western Mediterranean. Liddell Hart's paper urges the Cabinet to prevent a pro-Axis regime in Spain. He expects such a regime to close the land border with France, make Gibraltar "unusable" with a "few mobile batteries" of artillery, and make the whole Mediterranean unusable with land-based aircraft. He never admits that an isolationist Spain would be committing economic suicide, or that a victorious Popular Front could align with the Soviet Union to close the Mediterranean. He remains opposed to British military intervention anywhere – except by air. He wants more strategic bombers at home as deterrents, even at the expense of ground capabilities ("Western Mediterranean: Vital Problems," 20 March 1938, LH 11/1938/35; 1939b: 66-68). Belisha never presented this paper to the Cabinet, but Liddell Hart turned it into an article that was published in June. Here he admits "a strong probability that [in July 1914] a clear statement of Britain's intentions, had it been possible, would have prevented the [Great] War – by prompting the German government to restrain the Austrian." However, he does not allow the same in 1938, lest Britain would be dragged into a second Great War. He assumes that defence-dominance on land and sea, and strategic bombers in the air, are deterrence enough (1938c: 647).

His memoirs reprint parts of his papers of March 1938 with the suggestion that he wished to confront Germany and Italy militarily (1965: II, 127-130). Brian Bond (1977: 101) cited these memoirs and Liddell Hart's final peacetime book when claiming that one "issue on which Liddell Hart did believe Britain should make a stand was over the Axis powers' supply of arms and troops to General Franco's side." This is not true, except in the sense that Liddell Hart wanted to supply arms to the Popular Front.

Austria

On 12 March 1938, Germany annexed Austria. The next day, Liddell Hart wrote another paper for Belisha. He dismisses the viability of any foreign intervention except by Italy, which, despite Italian-German cooperation in Spain, he fancied as Germany's potential adversary. In any case, he declares that the way to influence Germany in Austria is to aid Germany's adversaries in Spain ("Note on the Situation," 13 March 1938, LH 11/1938/30b).

Sudetenland

As of 1937, Liddell Hart thought Germany's next national targets would be Hungary and Rumania, for access to the Black Sea. He did not expect Germany to confront Czechoslovakia directly, given Czechoslovakia's military capacity and Europe's defence-dominance. He proposes that Germany's most rational "indirect approach" against Czechoslovakia would be "to extend her grip through Hungary and Rumania." He warns against Western intervention in any country, given the Soviet ambassador's (Ivan Mikhailovich Maisky's) warning (since 1935) that Germany is already the most powerful state in Europe. The ambassador wished to provoke Western Europe to confront Germany, but his warning encouraged appeasement (correspondence with Maisky, LH 1/486; estimates, 10 December 1935, LH 11/1935/110; "The Military Situation in Europe," 6 December 1937, LH 12/1937/10; 1939b: 57-61; Neilson 2005: 128, 139, 193).

In March 1938, annexation of Austria extended Greater Germany around Czechoslovakia's southern border, as far as Hungary. MI5's best source in the German Embassy (Putlitz) predicted that Germany would move on Czechoslovakia next. Liddell Hart still expected Hungary and Rumania to be next. His main sources remained the Soviet Ambassador and selected correspondents in France.

He submitted to Belisha his concern that French guarantees entail Britain in war. He warned against foreign intervention, except by the Soviet air force and the Polish army. Either intervener was wishful: both the Soviets and Poles would need to cross foreign territory to reach Czechoslovakia. None of their neighbours was friendly to foreign military passage. Poland and the USSR suffered the worst relationship. Further, Poland had been making its own claims on Trans-Olza since 1935. Liddell Hart's notes give no awareness of these facts ("Note on the Situation," 13 March 1938, LH 11/1938/30b; 1939b: 63-64; 1965: II, 141-142; Andrew 2009: 200).

The British government's vulnerability to Liddell Hart's assessments increased in May 1938: British intelligence warned of an imminent German invasion of Czechoslovakia; Chamberlain mistakenly thought that his expressions of concern deterred Germany; and Putlitz was posted to the German Embassy in The Hague.* Liddell Hart's preferred German source remained Scherpenberg (then an international trade negotiator, based in Germany). On a visit to London, Scherpenberg said that Hitler's primary intent in the *Sudetenland* was to stop Soviet aircraft being based there. Again, Scherpenberg was misinformed or disinforming. Liddell Hart possibly encouraged or interpreted what he wanted to hear. Two days later, B-W found that Scherpenberg "put his case a little differently" (note, 15 June 1938, LH 11/1938/65; B-W to BHLH, 17 June 1938, LH 3/108; 1965: II, 158-159; Allport 2020: 103-104).

Liddell Hart's relationship with Belisha had been breaking down since December. His memoirs claim their separation after an argument on 3 July, but he did not record an argument that day. His memoirs give two explanations, starting with "Hitler's manifestly impending moves to isolate Czechoslovakia." In fact, their correspondence barely mentions Czechoslovakia. His second explanation is his real grievance: Belisha's rebuff of his demands for further investments in strategic bombers and anti-aircraft guns, at the expense of the active Army (note, 30 July 1938, LH 11/1938/89; 1965: II, 125, 157).

In August, Schweppenburg, less than one year into his command of a *Panzer* division, visited London to hand to MI5 a memorandum by Germany's foreign minister, estimating that its *Sudetenland* would be returned in the Autumn, and that Britain and France would not intervene. Schweppenburg's motivation was to stimulate Britain's resolve. He did not contact Liddell Hart, and Liddell Hart did not revive their brief correspondence of two years earlier.

On 6 September, Germany's chargé d'affaires (Theodor Kordt) bravely visited Chamberlain's lead civil service adviser (Horace Wilson) to warn that Hitler had decided to invade Czechoslovakia. The next day, Kordt returned to warn the Foreign Secretary (Lord Halifax) too. Wilson and Halifax were in denial, as was Hoare (the Home Secretary) – partly from resentment towards MI5's stance against appeasement, partly given Hoare's competitive wartime service in MI6.

Liddell Hart was unaware. Hoare was receiving Liddell Hart's estimates, but not returning any. Kordt was handled by someone whom Liddell Hart regarded as

---

* Over the summer, Putlitz and other sources confirmed Hitler's intent, but not schedule. MI6 took over the handling of Putlitz abroad, although MI6 co-opted MI5's prior go-between (Kopp Ustinov). The Germans had already identified the MI6 agents in The Hague, whom they harassed and eventually lured into Germany (and detention) after the outbreak of war in September 1939 (Andrew 2009: 200-201, 242).

a warmonger (Sir Robert Vansittart, a career civil servant in the Foreign Office, then acting as the first ad-hoc "Chief Diplomatic Adviser" to the Cabinet). Nevertheless, within a couple days, Liddell Hart heard that Chamberlain was meeting with his ministers, so he returned to London early from the Army's training cycle. He wrote a paper that he distributed to politicians of all parties. It estimates that German forces could snatch a strip of territory along the border, but not advance further. He dismisses the chances of Czechoslovakian counteroffensives, and Soviet or French offensives into Germany – even with British help, even by aircraft. He opposes Western offensiveness on moral grounds too, unless Germany bombs Britain. He pins Czechoslovakia's survival on Soviet aircraft flying from Czechoslovakia. Why cannot Western aircraft be based in Czechoslovakia? He does not explain. The paper seems contrived to avoid British involvement (paper, 9 September 1938, LH 11/1938/92; 1965: II, 161-162; Andrew 2009: 201-202, 206).

On 15 September, Chamberlain landed in Munich to negotiate personally with Adolf Hitler. On the same day, Schweppenburg shared with MI6 an updated war plan, which allows for invasion of the Sudetenland on 25 September. Every day during the week of 15 September, Liddell Hart circulated papers to politicians, and published versions in newspapers and magazines. He argues for appeasement of Hitler's rational demands. He wants most investment in anti-aircraft guns, followed by strategic bombers – for deterrence. He assumes defence-dominance on land and sea, so does not fancy Germany's chances, except by air against England.

Towards the end of the week, he separated from Lloyd George's confidence that Germany's demands could be resolved diplomatically. Likely the main prompt was news of Czech deaths and abductions at the hands of the *Sudetendeutsches Freikorps* (established 17 September). Another prompt might have been Italy's statement in support of Germany (18 September). The final prompt was a leader article in *The Times* (20 September). He wrote a response to his editors, and distributed copies to politicians. For the first time, he quotes the adage about standing up to "bullies" (although he mispresented his realization as going back to Japanese aggression in Manchuria in 1931). This sounds like a turn against appeasement, except he cannot "see how any guarantee we give the Czechs would have adequate value," given supposed defence-dominance on land, and Britain's supposed defensive incapacity in the air. His memoirs spin his paper of 20 September, and his meeting with the Focus Group on 28 September, as arguments to confront Germany. In fact, his arguments were at best equivocal ("Britain's Foreign Policy: A Reflection," 20 September 1938, LH 11/1938/98; 1965: II, 165-170).

He welcomed the news, on 30 September, of a settlement, signed in Munich by the premiers of Britain, France, Italy, and Germany. German forces occupied the *Sudetenland* on schedule (10 October). He started a public speaking tour. He used Germany's aggrandisement to justify more appeasement, thereby contradicting his adage about standing up to bullies. In December, he raised alarm at popular and official trends against appeasement and towards British-French bilateralism. He characterized the agreement in Munich as an encouragement to bilateralists. His memoirs and disciples pretend that he was raising alarm against appeasement, but in fact he remained conflicted, at best ("An army for the Continent? The effect of Munich," *The Times*, 7 December 1938, LH 10/1938/105; 1939b: 81; 1965: II, 159, 171-174, 241; Luvaas 1964: 413; Bond 1977: 102; Mearsheimer 1988: 130).

Czechoslovakia

On 20 February 1939, Vansittart (probably given a warning from Putlitz) reported to Halifax that Hitler had decided to occupy the rest of Czechoslovakia. Two weeks later, Putlitz predicted a German invasion in the week of 12 March. On 11 March, MI5 forecasted invasion by 13 March; MI6 forecasted 14 March. By contrast, Halifax and Chamberlain were confident that Hitler was appeased. Liddell Hart was confident that Hitler was deterred (by British and French economic threats). The invasion occurred on 15 March (Andrew 2009: 207-208; Jeffery 2010: 309-310).

Liddell Hart's reaction is dissonant: he both blames the West for not intervening and claims the West could not intervene.

> Over Czechoslovakia, we were handicapped by the fact that the Germans had the immediate strategic advantage – owing to geography. There it is probable that they would have succeeded in occupying the frontier belt of Czechoslovakia, though improbable that they could have conquered the country as a whole unless the Czechs were left to fight alone. And Germany lacked the resources for a prolonged war, so that the ultimate prospect would have been adverse to her.
>
> On a broad and long view of the situation it was a reasonable conclusion that the opponents of aggression still held a strategically decisive hand on the whole, even though it was marred by one inexcusably weak card: this country's state of preparedness to meet air attack (1939b: 22).

Poland

Poland, like Czechoslovakia, as delineated at Versailles in 1919, incorporated traditionally German territories and peoples. By October 1938, Liddell Hart foresaw that Germany would turn on Poland. He told Storm Jameson that the chance of avoiding war was "almost negligible." Yet he opposed any British guarantee of Poland. His chief argument was that such a guarantee would be another step towards British commitment of ground forces on the continent. (From April, he would characterize it as a "provocation" too.) Throughout, he pins his hopes on Soviet intervention. According to Jameson (1969: II, 94), he said that the "next crisis may shock our incorrigibly hand-to-mouth government into making promises to the next victim, Poland – an insanely rash thing to do unless we have an alliance with Russia." Yet he would not support British intervention even with a Soviet "alliance," because the Soviets would "impose terms on us." He wants the Soviets to intervene without Britain. His "worst fear is that the government will panic," by "flinging in masses of men," of which 500,000 would be killed before it would "learn" its mistake. In November, he met with the Soviet Ambassador to urge Soviet intervention. In March 1939, Maisky told him of Josef Stalin's supposed disgust with British and French concession of the *Sudetenland*, suspicions that Britain and France were pushing Germany against the USSR, and intent to disassociate from the West (notes, 1 November 1938 and 7 March 1939, LH 11/1938/117 and 11/1939/19; 1965: II, 167, 222, 241; Aster 1971: 335-339).

One week later, Germany occupied the rest of Czechoslovakia. That afternoon, Chamberlain declared the Munich agreement void, although he rebuffed calls to guarantee Poland's sovereignty. The next day, Liddell Hart noted "the wave of hysteria... here." Days later, he wrote that "our government are [sic] making it impossible for Hitler to draw in his horns without losing 'face,' and also making it impossible for themselves to withdraw" (16 and 20 March 1939, LH 11/1939/24).

In that week, Chamberlain committed to "collective security," without specifying whether he meant international institutions or bilateral alliances (even though he had, on 6 February, committed Britain to "cooperation" with France against any threat to France's "vital interests"). On 27 March, Belisha invited Liddell Hart to lunch, to complain that Chamberlain's commitment was weakening. Liddell Hart urged Belisha to encourage the weakening. On 31 March, the French government reaffirmed its defensive alliance with Poland. The British government promised "to lend the Polish government all support in their power," in the event of any threat to Polish independence, and started to plan with the French for bilateral defence of France. Liddell Hart disagreed. He remained confident that Hitler could be appeased, and characterized the guarantee as "far more provocative than would have been an earlier declaration that we were resolved to fulfil our obligations under the League Covenant...[O]ur sudden reversal of policy makes it far more difficult for Hitler to save face" ("A Reflection," 2 April 1939, LH 11/1939/35b).*

In June, he rightly but hypocritically criticized the government for "clinging to hopes of appeasement" until March. He now mischaracterizes appeasement as "prolonged retreat from collective security," only to contradict himself in the same paragraph, where he inadvertently admits that Britain's guarantee of Poland is properly categorized as traditional balancing ("a counterpoise to Germany's power of concentration in the west"). In a final contradiction, he criticizes "collective security" for offering "more danger of war" (through entanglements) (1939b: 23-24).

He broke down within days.† A month later, he returned to *The Times*, but continued to argue against "actual war." He objected to supposed British imitation of German "irrationality" and "insanity." "It is bound to lead to a clash and likely to produce a struggle in which the true purpose of our policy, that of curbing aggression, will be forgotten in the urge to give blow for blow regardless of the consequences to humanity and civilization." He urged investment in defence-dominance, as deterrence enough. *The Times* refused to publish this offering. He would publish it a year later, when he reframed it as a prediction of Britain's unpreparedness ("Spread of Irrationality," 4 August 1939, LH 11/1939/71; LH 3/109; 1941a: 140).

Liddell Hart's theory of Western provocation is undermined by Hitler's continuing indecisiveness. On 23 August, Germany disclosed a mutual non-aggression and trading pact with the USSR. Neither party disclosed an agreement to divide Poland.

---

* Liddell Hart's (1969: 205) attack on Churchill's record blames Churchill as well as Chamberlain for an "irrational guarantee." Liddell Hart's (1970: 11) history of the Second World War ignores the rational arguments for containing Germany. Instead, he speculates on the "indignation" and "humiliation" behind Chamberlain's "impulse" or "gesture." These words are quoted with the same ignorance by American historian Simon K. Newman (1976: 193), American journalist-historian William Manchester (1988: 405), and US Presidential candidate (1992 and 1996) Patrick J. Buchanan (2008: 255-256, 266).
† Liddell Hart's memoirs (1965: II, 248) and disciples (Luvaas 1964: 414; Bond 1977: 89) claim a heart attack.

On 25 August, Britain joined the French-Polish defensive alliance, but Hitler still was not provoked: he postponed invasion from 26 August to 1 September, while he sent diplomats westwards. Chamberlain and Liddell Hart remained confident that Hitler was deterred in the West and would seek a peaceful settlement. Liddell Hart argued that Hitler was not deterred in Poland, but for the wrong reason, i.e., that Western states lacked capability. In fact, by 1939 the Cabinet's Joint Intelligence Committee had realized that Germany's air force could not overwhelm Britain, and that Britain and France could defeat Germany on the continent (although it preferred to wait until Autumn 1940, when accelerated rearmament of the "Field Force," i.e., expeditionary force, was scheduled to complete). Other than Chamberlain, Cabinet members now preferred to fight than appease. German military principals warned Hitler of Western capability, but Hitler (and some members of the British Cabinet) expected Chamberlain to capitulate again. Hitler was correct to predict that the British and French premiers would not respond to Germany's invasion of Poland by invading Germany, which was their most effective but also costliest option (Andrew 2009: 204-213; Allport 2020: 115-119).

On 27 August, Liddell Hart circulated another paper, which argues that defence-dominance applies to only Germany's western frontier. Thus, he concludes that Poland cannot defend itself, and Britain and France cannot influence Germany. He urges them "to press the Polish Government to compromise" (1939c: 147). Hugh Dalton, who had collaborated with Liddell Hart in arms control since the 1920s, and as the Labour Party's chief spokesperson on foreign policy since 1935, objected.

> It is ironical that now, when The Times, in my view, is shaping very much better, you should have become an appeaser! (Dalton to LH, 31 August 1939, LH 11/1939/85).*

Liddell Hart struggled to develop a rebuttal.

> It is impossible to deny...the comparative reasonableness of Hitler's suggested terms for a settlement with Poland (note, 1 September 1939, LH 11/1939/75b).

Even three years into war, he maintained that Hitler could have been appeased.

> The profound psychological truth of experience [is] that "burglars do not commit murder" unless they are deprived of any way out...Hitler was remarkably reluctant to get into war – considering his military assets – and...he repeatedly tried to get out of it from the first afternoon onwards...in accord with the underlying doubts revealed in Mein Kampf (to Esmé Wingfield-Stratford, 5 October 1942, LH 1/757).

In every book, from 1939 to 1970, Liddell Hart characterizes Britain's guarantee as a "provocation," without which Hitler would not have invaded Poland (1939b: 94-95; 1941a: 137; 1941b: 301; 1954a: 230; 1950: 165-166; 1960a: 163, 254; 1965: II, 214; 1968b: 742; 1969: 205; 1970: 7, 11, 704). He persuaded Brian Bond (1977: 122, 124) that "he believed that Britain and France had chosen an emotional and unconvincing cause for which to go to war."

---

* His memoirs mischaracterise Dalton's objection as "anti-Polish" (1965: II, 255).

Legacy

Chamberlain gave up the premiership in May 1940. His career and health were broken, but he did not repudiate appeasement. Instead, he claimed that appeasement had given Britain time to prepare for war – the same excuse the Soviets used to justify their pact with Hitler. His chief adviser contradicted him.

> Our policy was never designed just to postpone war, or enable us to enter war more united. The aim of our appeasement was to avoid war altogether, for all time (Horace Wilson, in McDonough 1998: 55).

Chamberlain died in November, while Liddell Hart compiled an anthology of selected, redacted articles. He inserted a claim that he had "considered the importance of administering a check to aggressive policies" when Italy invaded Abyssinia in 1935 and again when Italy and Germany intervened in Spain in 1936.

> Over Abyssinia, and again over Spain, our strategic advantage in case of war was so clear as to be a deterrent to war, and to outweigh the tactical risks if it came (1941a: 137).

In his next edition of "indirect approach," he pretends that he had wished to check Germany over Austria in March 1938, the *Sudetenland* in September 1938,* and the rest of Czechoslovakia in March 1939 (1941b: 300; 1954a: 229). Yet he continued to claim that war could have been avoided over Poland in September 1939.

> To blame Hitler for the war is to exaggerate both his guilt and his importance. Hitler and the war are but episodes in a Political-Economic Revolution that is in progress in our time. They are eruptions on the skin ("Hitlerism," November 1942, LH 11/1942/59).

After the war, Liddell Hart pretended to have been against appeasement all along.

> The warnings I gave about the Nazi menace, and the emphatic line I took in opposing the policy of "appeasement" will be known to most of those who, in America as well as in Europe, followed my pre-war writings (1948: x).

> It is folly to imagine that the aggressive types, whether individuals or nations, can be bought off – or, in modern language, "appeased" – since the payment of Danegeld stimulates a demand for more Danegeld. But they can be curbed. Their very belief in force makes them more susceptible to the deterrent effect of a formidable opposing force (1952: 26-27).

When challenged in interview, he admitted that he had supported appeasement, but only from 1938 to 1940, in order to allow for rearmament.

> I went on urging from the moment Hitler came in until the Munich crisis in 1938 that we should make a stand while there was time. When we failed to do this over Munich, I pointed out that it was folly to make a

---

* Later, he blamed appeasement in 1938 on the "French and British governments," and their unreadiness for war (1948: 33).

stand until we had restored the balance (in Walters 1961: 27).

His memoirs claim that he had urged military confrontation with Germany and Italy throughout the 1930s. Contradictorily, he claims that all aggressors could have been accommodated peacefully (1965: II, 125-126, 137-144). His final histories blame Baldwin and Chamberlain for provoking war by trying to "curb" Hitler from 1935 (1968b: 740; 1970: 6). In between times, he blames Churchill's warmongering, since 1938 (1969: 203-205).

Michael Howard (1970b: 40; 1984: 204) admitted that the only way "any war against Nazi Germany could be limited" was "that she could be appeased," but did not explicitly associate Liddell Hart with appeasement. Brian Bond, citing nothing but Liddell Hart's memoirs, pretends that Liddell Hart was unfairly associated with appeasement given his association with the government and *The Times* (1977: 100, 112-113, 120). By contrast, David Lord (1997: 61) admitted that Liddell Hart was "guilty by prominent association (if not shared sentiment) with the appeasing Chamberlain and Hore-Belisha." Similarly, one of Bond's students, Brian Holden Reid (1998: 174), with no evidence or sources, wrote that Liddell Hart "was appalled by the appeasement of Germany." Another of Bond's students, Alex Danchev (1998a: 203), quoted Liddell Hart's private doubts about pacifying bullies, as written on 20 September 1938, as if evidence that "Liddell Hart was an appeaser only after war was declared...His inter-war record was spotless." Mearsheimer (1988: 131) judged Liddell Hart an appeaser until Summer 1939, which perhaps explains why a reviewer of Danchev's book reported the same (Campbell 2000: 457). In fact, Liddell Hart was an appeaser from 1935 until 1945, through the Second World War – the subject of the next three chapters.

Liddell Hart and Lloyd George at Portmeirion, North Wales, 6 September 1940 (LH 13/104/3).

13

War Official

The outbreak of a Second World War capped a dreadful half-decade for Liddell Hart, although his nadir was still to come. His military ideal (T.E. Lawrence) died in a motorcycle accident in 1935, his father in 1937, his marriage in 1938 – although he entertained hopes of reconciliation with Jessie, while he continued his affair with Kathleen. His son was rebellious, resentful, directionless, and looking forward to emancipation in 1940. He suffered breakdowns in June and August 1939. In September, war broke out. In October, he agreed to quit *The Times*. He feared turning 44 years old, on 31 October – the age at which his only sibling had died (in 1932).

War disproved Liddell Hart's promises of appeasement and deterrence. The collapse of Germany's western and northern neighbours disproved his promises of defence-dominance on land and sea. The inability of British strategic bombers to navigate at night, to counter air defenses by day, or hit targets smaller than cities by day or night disproved his confidence in both deterrence and victory by bombing. The German bombing of British cities from Danish, Dutch, Belgian, and French airfields disproved his claims that Britain should not contain Germany to its borders.

Fear of German bombs and shells prompted a move to south-western England. Fear of German landings prompted his move to north-western England. He was lonely and dependent on private charity, without full-time employment, with expenses beyond his royalties. He lived with Kathleen but failed to divorce Jessie until 1942. He continued to clash with Kathleen's relatives. By 1944, he gave up hopes of reviving his military ethos, and wrote mostly on female fashion and manners.

Liddell Hart's archives prove that he remained an energetic writer, although his contacts in government dwindled. The recipients of Liddell Hart's first wartime recommendation to negotiate include Lloyd George, Belisha, Lord Halifax (Foreign Secretary, 1938-1940; Ambassador to the US, 1940-1945), Anthony Eden (Secretary of State for Dominion Affairs, 1939-1940; War Secretary, 1940; Foreign Secretary, 1940-1945), Lord Beaverbrook (Minister of Aircraft Production, 1940-1941; Minister of Supply, 1941-1942; Minister of War Production, 1942; Lord Keeper of the Privy Seal, 1942-1945), Arthur Salter (Parliamentary Secretary to the Ministry of Shipping, 1939-1941; to the Ministry of War Transport, 1941-1945), Clement Attlee (leader of the Labour Party), Lord Cecil (President of the League of Nations Union), Hugh Dalton (Under-Secretary for Foreign Affairs, 1929-1931; Minister of Economic Warfare, 1940-1942; President of the Board of Trade, 1942-1945), and Stafford Cripps (Ambassador to the USSR, 1940-1942; Minister for Aircraft Production, 1942-1945).

In search of official opportunities, his correspondence narrows to Lloyd George, Belisha, Churchill (First Lord of the Admiralty, 1939-1940; Prime Minister, 1940-1945), Beaverbrook, James Grigg (War Secretary, 1942-1945), and soldiers he had championed before the war (such as Lord Gort), as explained in sections below.

Lloyd George

Lloyd George and Liddell Hart closed ranks once Chamberlain guaranteed

Poland in April 1939. "Only Lloyd George pointed out the practical difficulties and the dangerous folly of offering such a pledge without first securing Russia's adhesion" (1965: II, 219; 1968b: 742). Lloyd George held no hope for a role in Chamberlain's administration, given their implacability in the Commons since the Great War, but hoped to replace Chamberlain once a Second World War would expose the prime minister's incapacity (as the First had exposed Herbert Asquith in 1916). He welcomed Liddell Hart's proposal for a quick negotiated peace, and argued as much in the *Sunday Express* on 10 September, the House of Commons on 3 October, and his constituency on 21 October. He was associated with the Peace Aims Group, twenty of whose members published a call for an armistice in November. Lloyd George took pride in the backlash.

> [The Daily] Express have [sic] done me the honour of putting me in the same category as yourself as a man who tells too much of the truth about the war to be encouraged in their columns. I am afraid that the realists are in for a bad time for at least some months but I think our chances will come when the nation begins to understand the utter futility of this ghastly struggle (to LH, 20 November 1939, LH 1/450).

The "phoney war" failed to discredit Chamberlain. Indeed, Chamberlain felt validated. Nevertheless, Liddell Hart still counted on Lloyd George's rise. Effective in April 1940, he started writing features for the daily *News Chronicle*. This newspaper was part of no newspaper group, and low in circulation, but was edited by a partisan Liberal (Walter Layton), and influenced the Liberals whom he expected to dominate the next administration.

Lloyd George's hopes for a return to premiership increased with Chamberlain's unready response to Germany's invasion of Norway on 9 April. He was stoked by an agreement over the phone between Lords Beaverbrook and Rothermere that he should be prime minister if Norway collapses. Rothermere promised to turn his newspapers to the cause, and wrote to this effect to Lloyd George on the same day (26 April). Liddell Hart had already urged him to start a parliamentary debate, but he waited for the opposition party (Labour) to table it. He hid from Liddell Hart his assent to an offer from Churchill (via an intermediary), on 5 May, to serve in any coalition formed by Churchill. Liddell Hart wrote talking-points for the first day of the debate (7 May), but Lloyd George did not rise until the second day. When Churchill rose to take responsbility, Lloyd George replied that he "must not allow himself to be converted into an air-raid shelter to keep the splinters from hitting his colleagues" (notes, 6, 7, and 8 May 1940, LH 11/1940/32-33 and /36; Addison 1971: 371-372). Liddell Hart remained naive of these machinations.

> [O]ne heard on all sides a growing volume of support voiced for the recall to office of Lloyd George, as the man who had triumphantly ridden the storm in World War I. That might well have been the outcome if the political crisis had lasted a few more days. But early on May 10 the German invasion of the West was launched (1965: II, 279).

Churchill took over the premiership late on 10 May, but waited almost three weeks before he invited Lloyd George, and he did it by letter. Lloyd George replied by the same medium, to complain that Chamberlain and Halifax remained in Cabinet. Churchill replied he could not abandon Chamberlain. Cabinet friends suggested other offers, but Churchill confirmed none. Months later, Churchill invited Lloyd George to take the Ambassadorship to the US (prompted by the death of the current ambassador). Lloyd George refused, so Churchill sent Halifax. Lloyd George's acceptance would not have helped his or Liddell Hart's ambitions, although it added to Liddell Hart's musings about emigration. Lloyd George's excuse (age) undermined his claim to any future offer, as did his speeches against government policy (from 1941), for a compromise peace (through 1942), and against Western expeditions to Western Europe (although he would flip-flop once Western Allied forces landed in Normandy in June 1944). In 1944, he rapidly declined, physically and mentally, and rarely attended Parliament. His regular visitors dried up. Liddell Hart used the excuse of geographical remoteness (diary, 29 May and 12 and 19 December 1940, in Colville 1985: 143, 309, 320; Addison 1971: 372-375, 384).

Belisha

Belisha remained in government, but "the partnership" with Liddell Hart was rocky. They suspended it in May and October 1938.* They cooperated on the annual Army budget that Belisha delivered to Parliament in March 1939, but Belisha subsequently distanced himself again. Their last peacetime meeting was on 26 July 1939. Days after the outbreak of war, Belisha's assistant telephoned to invite "any ideas about the war and its conduct." Liddell Hart said he hoped to help "as a military scientist." Belisha got on the phone to express interest, but, later, would come back with a familiar excuse (the Army Council's opposition). Liddell Hart included Belisha in the circulation for his papers, but Belisha sensibly demurred (LH 11/B/1939/1-17; 1965: II, 252, 266).

In mid-September, two Army generals invited the editor of *The Sunday Express* to discuss the ousting of Belisha. John Gordon telephoned Liddell Hart to prepare an article in case the plot were to succeed. Liddell Hart's memoirs portray this plot as the necessary start to Belisha's ruin, but Belisha ruined his career months later, by intervening in fortifications with technical naivety, self-promotion, and Francophilia. Belisha toured the BEF from 18 to 20 November. He inspected troops on the roads, without visiting their fortifications, most of which were camouflaged so as to be invisible from the roads. He told the Cabinet of the BEF's unready fortifications (but not its unready mechanized force). He compared fortifications occupied by a French brigade on the BEF's left, without realizing that the British had built them. Edmund Ironside (CIGS), Chamberlain, and the King toured separately. Ironside returned on 2 December, to tell the Cabinet that Belisha was wrong. Ironside hoped this would end Belisha's Secretaryship. Ironside was seconded by Lord Gort. Gort's accelerated promotion to CIGS in November 1937, and to commander of the BEF in September 1939, had necessarily involved Liddell Hart and Belisha, but they found Gort less progressive and grateful than expected. They did not realize that Ironside was briefing against Gort, in hope of replacing him. Ironside was senior and better qualified: his final peacetime role was to prepare expeditionary capacity. However, Liddell Hart opposed that role and Ironside, partly because Ironside was Fuller's

---

* Reid (1998: 7) misreported that "Liddell Hart worked as an informal adviser...for less than a year," due to his "passion for retaining freedom of expression."

most senior champion. Still, Liddell Hart accepted hearsay from Ironside's chief of staff that Gort was the main plotter (Colonel Roderick "Rory" Macleod to LH, 5 December 1939, LH 1/481; Kennedy 1957: 40; Portway 1971: 159).

Belisha was desperate for good press, so, once Liddell Hart was published by Beaverbrook's newspapers again, he invited Liddell Hart for lunch. Belisha denied any trouble with Gort, but wished he had chosen Ironside ahead of Gort. That evening, Liddell Hart wrote, imaginatively, that "in conferences, Hore-Belisha is rising much in the opinion of some who disagreed with him before the war" (note, 11 December 1939, LH 11/1939/136; 1965: II, 264-265).

Chamberlain defended Belisha, until 4 January, when he suggested resignation, due to "prejudice" elsewhere, which he refused to specify. (His diary suggests that Gort's distrust was sufficient.) Chamberlain offered the Ministry of Information, which had been the best match all along (given Belisha's prior career as a journalist), or the Board of Trade,* but Belisha refused everything. On the evening of 5 January, the Prime Minister's office announced his resignation. Vague explanations at the time helped his former colleagues at *The Daily Express* and Paramount Films to accuse senior military officers of anti-semitism. They misreported that Belisha planned to overturn a ban on officers and other ranks dining together. Liddell Hart added the falsehood that Belisha was dismissed for criticizing French strategy (1965: II, 271-274; 1970: 41; Feiling 1946: 434; Minney 1961: 258-276; Colville 1972: 157-159; Colville 1985: 68-69).

Churchill

On 27 July 1939, Liddell Hart attended the last meeting of the "Focus" group. He noted nothing of the meeting at the time, but his memoirs recall alienation from Churchill's willingness to confront Germany and cooperate with France militarily.

> In discussion I felt, not for the first time since the Polish Guarantee, that Churchill's pugnacious impulses were getting the upper hand of his judgment, and that he was fostering people's exasperation with Hitler in a way that might tend to precipitate war when there was still a reasonable chance of averting or postponing it (1965: II, 248).

Presumably he used this event to persuade an American correspondent of the following false but often quoted biography.

> In 1939 he was associated with Churchill but resigned because he felt Churchill's bellicoseness and attitudes were premature in the existing state of Britain's defences (Icks 1952: 26).

Upon war, Chamberlain returned Churchill to the Admiralty, where he proved as adventurous in the Second World War as the First. Liddell Hart opposed such adventurism. Hearsay from officials about Churchill's proposals to intervene in neutral Scandinavia encouraged Liddell Hart's mistaken assessment that Belisha "has impressed them more than Winston Churchill, who is too wordy, and whose grasp of problems is uncertain" (note, 11 December 1939, LH 11/1939/136; 1965:

---

* The incumbent was Oliver Stanley, whom Chamberlain had already instructed as the next War Secretary.

II, 264-265). Liddell Hart blamed Churchill for Belisha's removal in January, and claimed to predict the betrayal back in June 1938. Churchill was indeed complicit,* but Liddell Hart did not report the real plotters (1965: II, 273).

The debacle in Norway, from April, encouraged Liddell Hart's hope that both Chamberlain and Churchill would be deposed in favour of a coalition government led by Lloyd George. On 6 May, he justified his goading of Lloyd George partly with exaggerated hearsay about Churchill: "Most of the naval staff…complain that he is slow and confused," and "alternates between recklessness and panic," "due to too much old brandy." Churchill's accession to the premiership on 10 May shocked him. However, he still hoped that Allied failure in Norway would catch up with Churchill (although he remained confident in Allied defence of France) (notes, LH 11/1940/31 and /37).

Within weeks, the administration proscribed the BUF and detained (without trial) Mosley, his immediate family, and many political co-travellers. Liddell Hart believed that only Churchill's favourable experience of Fuller in the War Office in the 1920s saved Fuller from internment. Liddell Hart was not politically aligned, but he was certainly philosophically aligned. He started a file of press reports and opinions on the persecution of the Mosleys, and rightly referred to these government actions as evidence for an "illiberal" turn that undermined British righteousness and motivation (LH 15/3/190; Skidelsky 1990: 433-434, 501).

He drew up a list of poor policy-makers, probably prompted by the recent best-selling book *Guilty Men*, to whom he adds Churchill. He hoped Churchill would over-reach and be replaced by Lloyd George or Beaverbrook. In subsequent years, he reported that several of "Churchill's closest assistants" told him they rated Lloyd George as more "gifted."† Finally, he speculated that Churchill's insecurity about his intellect, due to his father's and school's low expectations, "may help to explain why he later tended to surround himself, unlike Lloyd George, with colleagues and assistants whose minds moved more slowly than his own" (Cato 1940; LH 11/1940/142; 1965: I, 339 1969: 174).

By then, Liddell Hart had U-turned on strategic bombing (see Chapter 15). In May 1941, a correspondent on the Air Staff (Richard Peck)‡ named the drivers of strategic bombing as the prime minister and the Chief of Air Staff (Air Marshal Sir Cyril Newall, since 1937). Peck later revealed that strategic bombing was costlier and less effective than the government claimed. With these data, among others, Liddell Hart admonished the Bishop of Lichfield (Edward Woods) for praising Churchill. "[H]is almost unique egocentricity, his dramatic sense, his lack of scruple, and his lack of judgment, made a combination that might be destined to lead

---

* Churchill had foreknowledge, but left for France on the day that Chamberlain informed Belisha. Beaverbrook persuaded Churchill to telephone his home, where Belisha was waiting. Churchill advised him to take the Ministry of Information (Minney 1961: 273).
† Addison (1971: 377) identifies Edward William Macleay Grigg (1879-1955), Parliamentary Under-Secretary of State for War (not to be confused with James Grigg, Permanent Under-Secretary) and Maurice Hankey (Paymaster General) as revealing to Lloyd George their doubts about Churchill, after their dismissal from government in February 1942.
‡ Liddell Hart started to correspond in 1936, when Peck was in charge of RAF India. In 1939, Peck returned to the Air Ministry as Director-General of Operations. Liddell Hart (1965: II, 247) credits Peck for the decision to expand Fighter Command in October 1939.

this country to disaster" (notes, 30 May and 19 December 1941, LH 11/1941/26 and /78; to Woods, 12 April 1942, LH 1/764).

Another leaker of official data was "Tim" Pile – who retained a position that Liddell Hart had helped to create in July 1939 (Anti-Aircraft Command). In July 1943, Pile revealed Churchill's intent to escalate strategic bombing, including from mainland Italy, which, he revealed, would be invaded in September.

> Winston is pinning all his faith to the bombing offensive now. The devastation it causes suits his temperament, and he would be disappointed at a less destructive ending to the war. Having seen him at close quarters on many occasions, particularly in the Battle of Britain, Pile feels that he is a "masochist" – danger and destruction are the breath of life to him (note, 4 July 1943, LH 11/1943/41).

Within days, Liddell Hart developed a paper to send to Churchill. It argues that enemies would fight to the end if aggrieved by bombing, and if denied opportunities to negotiate. He decided that Churchill would not be receptive. Peck agreed, adding that Churchill was "not a good psychological strategist." Liddell Hart sent it to the War Office, perhaps thinking it would get to Churchill indirectly. Churchill received it with urgings to punish Liddell Hart for "defeatism" (which had been criminalized in July, to Liddell Hart's righteous objection). Churchill replied, "He seems more a candidate for a mental home than for more serious action" (7 July 1943, LH 11/1943/43; Gilbert 1983: 964).

Liddell Hart abandoned hopes of influencing Churchill privately, and took off the gloves publicly.* He complained of Churchill's "instinctive pugnacity and complete intentness on beating Hitler – regardless of what might happen afterwards." He blamed Churchill for post-war political instability (as an after-effect of wartime anti-German insurgencies) and economic insecurity (due to bombing and blockade) (1950: 63). Writing in 1954, after Churchill's welcome of the US policy of massive retaliation, he tied Churchill to the Napoleonic "belief that our problems could be, simply, solved by victory" over the enemy's core forces (1960a: 22). His histories of the Second World War describe Churchill as "restless and dynamic," the author of overly-aggressive proposals to intervene in Finland in 1939 and Norway in 1940, the pusher of offensives in general, the person most responsible for "a prolonged war" (which left "Europe....exhausted and under the shadow of communist domination"), and the person most responsible for unwarranted escalation of bombing against civilian targets (1968b: 746-747; 1969: 209; 1970: 65, 594). His criticisms are fair but somewhat hypocritical.

Beaverbrook

Beaverbrook became Liddell Hart's greatest political champion, and Liddell Hart's hope for permier, as Lloyd George declined. Although they had always tended to similar policies and politics, they did not cooperate until late in 1939, due

---

* His son observed that "his opposition to some of Churchill's war policies led to his eclipse in Britain – although his ideas remained influential in other countries, especially Germany" (1976: 315). Bond (1977: 7-8) found that wartime "papers reveal him as a virulent critic of Churchill and virtually all he stood for." Danchev (1998a: 102) described Churchill as Liddell Hart's "nemesis." None of these writers admits Liddell Hart's early admiration.

to differing views on Lloyd George. Beaverbrook had entered the House of Commons as a Unionist (1910), but supported the Liberal administrations of the Great War, took a peerage from Lloyd George in 1917, and served as the first Minister of Information in 1918. Nevertheless, Beaverbrook (1956: xvii, 190, 301, 328, 340) found Lloyd George unsupportive of his complaints against soldiers and ministers, and of his campaign for imperial trade preferences. Latterly, he found him unreliable and dictatorial. He resigned within a couple of weeks of the end of the war. In 1922, Lloyd George frustrated Beaverbrook's attempts to force a general election on imperial commercial union, so Beaverbrook campaigned for Lloyd George to step aside. Liddell Hart sided with Lloyd George's antagonism towards the Generals, but took no notice of the dispute over free trade.

Meanwhile, Beaverbrook decided, for unclear reasons, that Hoare would lead the Conservative Party someday. Liddell Hart was advising Hoare by then, but Hoare did not suggest Liddell Hart's approach until 1932. Liddell Hart wrote express support of Beaverbrook's published opposition to any British commitment to a continental state. (Beaverbrook opposed commitments to any international institution too.) Implicitly, Liddell Hart was asking for work. By then, Beaverbrook was the mightiest press baron in both Britain and Canada. *The Daily Express* newspaper was the most read in the world. However, Liddell Hart chose *The Times*, putting official influence before popular reach. Still, he negotiated a permit from *The Times* to publish occasionally in other outlets (albeit ineffective until 1939). In between times, he corresponded with Beaverbrook's editors and leader writers, such that Beaverbrook heard a complaint about a leader in *The Daily Express* (dated 11 March 1938) being from "the Liddell Hart school." On 19 May, Belisha complained of *The Daily Express* parroting Liddell Hart's under-estimates of British anti-aircraft guns (as an argument against cooperation with France). Liddell Hart repeated this argument in his first opinion-piece for *The Evening Standard* (in January 1939) (LH 1/52; 1965: II, 104, 113, 181; Chisholm and Davie 1993: 322-325, 351-353).

Beaverbrook, like Liddell Hart and Lloyd George, opposed Chamberlain's undertakings, in April 1939, to guarantee Poland and cooperate militarily with France. They continued to write leaders promising "no war" through August. Beaverbrook imagined that if he had not been visiting Canada for part of that month, he might have prevented war. He wanted his newspapers to appear patriotic, but also to give voice to campaigners for peace, including Lloyd George, whom *The Sunday Express* published again on 8 October. He was less keen to publish Liddell Hart, although he encouraged Liddell Hart to keep circulating proposals for peace and to publish them elsewhere. He took a week to consider the paper of 8 September before referring it to *The Sunday Express*, only to have second thoughts. (The editor wrote on 4 October to blame "several…executives.") In November, Liddell Hart mailed similar opinions, especially in opposition to any British support for Finland against Soviet invasion, but on this issue Beaverbrook preferred to publish himself and his favourite Socialist MP (Aneurin "Ni"/"Nye" Bevan). In December, Liddell Hart asked for employment. Beaverbrook beat around the bush, cycling between enthusiasm and despair, between rude health and hypochondria. Still, he was in no doubt about Liddell Hart's righteousness. In private letters, he often refers to himself as Liddell Hart's "disciple," and urges Liddell Hart to be more critical. He employed Liddell Hart as a weekly opinion-writer from February 1940, met privately with Liddell Hart from March, and purchased his opinions daily once Germany invaded France on 10 May (LH 1/52; 1965: II, 275-276; Chisholm and Davie 1993: 354-356, 370-371).

Beaverbrook expected to be called into government, but Chamberlain appointed a conservative as Minister of Information – Lord (Hugh Pattison) Macmillan, whom Beaverbrook had known as an underling in the Ministry of 1918. Beaverbrook turned his newspapers against the revived Ministry, especially (to Liddell Hart's delight) its censorship. In January, Chamberlain replaced Macmillan with the BBC's director (John Reith). Beaverbrook campaigned against him too, despite Reith's agreeable politics. By March, Beaverbrook was entertaining anti-war campaigners from the Independent Labour Party, and courting Bevan as potential premier. He continued to propose Hoare as a Conservative leader, but hedged his bets with Churchill. On 1 May, he congratulated Churchill on being appointed as chair of the Military Co-ordination Committee. Beaverbrook was the one with whom Churchill chose to lunch on 10 May, before he was summoned by the King to form a new government. Churchill intended to appoint Beaverbrook as the first Minister of Aircraft Production. A few hours later the King wrote to warn of opposition, particularly in Canada. The King had probably voiced similar in person, although Churchill was not shown the letter until the day he confirmed the appointment (14 May) (Colville 1985: 131; Chisholm and Davie 1993: 372-374, 380-382).

Churchill was keeping the most powerful press baron on side, rather than giving a friend what he wanted. Churchill passed over Beaverbrook for the Ministry of Information, in favour of Duff Cooper, who kept his distance from both Beaverbrook and Liddell Hart. Churchill exiled Hoare by appointing him ambassador to Spain. Hoare resented Beaverbrook's failure to help, and rebuffed Liddell Hart.

Beaverbrook liked self-aggrandizement, but not administration. He worked from home (Stornoway House in St. James, London), absorbed the production staff from the Air Ministry, poached resources from other ministries, and appointed employees from his newspaper empire – who simultaneously propagandized his role. He kept Liddell Hart as a nominally-independent propagandist in the pages of *The Daily Express* and *The Evening Standard*. Liddell Hart wanted official employment. In replies, Beaverbrook treats him as an agony aunt. Typical subjects are the inadequacies of colleagues, the likelihood of defeat, the need for a negotiated settlement, and ill-health. Meanwhile, Beaverbrook was the most senior member of Britain's wartime government to leak secrets to Liddell Hart. Beaverbrook's propaganda includes the slogan "urgency and speed," which evokes Liddell Hart's semantics. He took credit for changes planned months earlier by the Air Ministry. He manipulated statistics to claim incredible jumps in production. Then and later, Liddell Hart misreported Beaverbrook as most responsible for victory in the Battle of Britain. In fact, although production accelerated exponentially through June (given policies before his appointment), it decelerated from June to July, and fell in August – one month before any enemy intervention in production (LH 1/52; 1970: 92; Bond 1977: 142; Deighton 1977: 164-165; Chisholm and Davie 1993: 377, 384-396).

Beaverbrook submitted his first resignation on 30 June, another three by December, at least 14 for the war as a whole. Churchill could not allow an outsider with so many channels, so kept refusing the resignations, but often allowed him to rove as Minister of State without portfolio. In the first such period (May to June 1941), Beaverbrook urged the Cabinet to focus on oceanic and homeland security, to abandon expeditions overseas, and even to cut foreign aid, all in line with papers that

Liddell Hart had been circulating (see the next two chapters). However, the Axis invasion of the USSR in June intensified his strange admiration for Stalin, whom he had met in 1929. He agreed to take over the troubled Ministry of Supply,* but enshipped for Moscow on 21 September, as self-appointed head of a British delegation, additional to the diplomatic and military missions already there. Before he returned, he repudiated his former "isolationism," as he himself described it, and embraced the Soviet call for a "second front" (a Western Allied invasion of Europe). Liddell Hart opposed any landings in Europe, but Beaverbrook kept him friendly with indiscretions about his diplomacy in the USSR (September to October 1941).

Similarly, Beaverbrook leaked secrets about his first official tour of America (December 1941 to January 1942). In February, within a period of just 15 days, he accepted and quit the first Ministry of War Production, and returned to Minister of State without portfolio. Officially, Beaverbrook blamed asthma. Privately, he resented appointees with more credibility of liaising with Stalin and leading the government (notably Sir Stafford Cripps, socialist MP, then another minister without portfolio). He again estimated Churchill's administration as within months of collapse. Still, he remained in Cabinet. Churchill sent him on a vague mission to America to coordinate supplies. Instead, Beaverbrook planned to lobby Americans for a Western invasion of Europe in 1942 (1943 at the latest), and recognition of the Soviet borders inside Poland, Estonia, Latvia, Lithuania, and Finland. On 17 March, he wrote to Churchill of his intent. He told Liddell Hart in person.

> Beaverbrook remarked that Winston was a great man, very difficult to deal with and impossible to control. Whatever anyone might think necessary, or wish to do, they had to remember that "this is Churchill's war." Unfortunately, he thought of it in terms of fighting "the wars of Marlborough" [and] cannot grasp mechanized warfare (note, 19 March 1942, LH 11/1942/15).

Churchill proposed that Beaverbrook should stay in America as ambassador. Beaverbrook had foreseen this, ignored the proposal, and returned to London on 5 May (Chisholm and Davie 1993: 427, 430-435, 440-441).

Later in May, he leaked to Liddell Hart the Allied intent to land forces in North-West Africa, coincident with a counter-offensive from Egypt (eventually launched in November and October respectively). In June, when British forces were retreating furthest into Egypt and India, Beaverbrook again forecast the end of Churchill's premiership within months. In March 1943, he betrayed Allied intent to invade France. On 23 September, Churchill confirmed to the Cabinet that the "second front" was scheduled for May 1944. This took away one of Beaverbrook's hobby horses, and dashed Liddell Hart's hope to avoid more British expeditions. On 28 September, Churchill appointed Beaverbrook as the most senior minister without portfolio (Lord Privy Seal). His immediate assignment was post-war intercontinental air travel. To everyone's surprise, Beaverbrook enjoyed this appointment, and kept it through the end of the war, during which he rarely corresponded with Liddell Hart, and never met (notes, 19 March, 23 May, 11 June, 23 September, and 26 September 1942, 11/1942/15, /37, /42, /78, and /82; note, 11 March 1943, LH 11/1943/8; Chisholm and Davie 1993: 391, 397, 399, 402, 406-412, 438, 446-447).

---

* This Ministry was responsible for supplies to the Army only.

Grigg

By January 1942, Liddell Hart realized that Beaverbrook was campaigning for a "second front." He asked Hugh Cudlipp, erstwhile editor of the *Sunday Pictorial*, which Beaverbrook did not own, for an opportunity to counter. In 1940, Cudlipp had joined the Army, and was currently posted to Egypt, so could not offer any work, but urged government to employ "first" Fuller and "second" Liddell Hart.

> Liddell Hart was Hore-Belisha's adviser. And that, apparently, is sufficient reason for him to be nobody's adviser now...[but] he is a man with magnificent brain. A man of utter integrity. Not only a strategist, but a philosopher. "Oh," say the fools, "Liddell Hart said we could win the war by sitting on the defensive. To hell with that!" Liddell Hart, of course, said nothing of the sort. He has always advocated that the weaker force should not rush into action like a bull in a china shop. It should adopt the counter-offensive – to strike, that is, when the superior force has spent its initial energy ("All Change!" Sunday Pictorial, 1 February 1942: 15).

By coincidence, within days, Churchill appointed, unconstitutionally, a new War Secretary. James Grigg had worked mostly in India's department for finance. Some of that time (1936 to 1939), he worked alongside Sir Archibald Rowlands.[*] In April of 1938, Grigg wrote to the editor of *The Times*, to suggest that Liddell Hart should meet Rowlands in London, in hope of public pressure on Britain's funding for Indian rearmament. The meeting occurred in July. The two men bonded over Liberal partisanship, Lloyd George, and homeland security. Rowlands shared privileged information from the start. In late 1939, Grigg was recalled to London as Permanent Under-Secretary for War, without Liddell Hart's attention. Rowlands was recalled to serve in the Air Ministry, with Liddell Hart's enthusiasm. In May 1940, Beaverbrook selected Rowlands as Permanent Secretary to the Minister of Aircraft Production. That ministry's turbulence was covered up by Beaverbrook's newspapers, while Liddell Hart drew public attention to tumult in the War Office. Desperate for more control over the War Department, Churchill promoted Grigg to Secretary, in January 1942, even though, by precedent, at least, the Secretary should be a Parliamentarian. Churchill arranged an uncontested by-election to a seat in the House of Commons. In February, two months before this could happen, at a time of military disasters from Africa to Asia, Rowlands suggested that Grigg should invite Liddell Hart to advise on senior Army appointments. They duly met, but Grigg was wary of repeating Belisha's mistakes. In March, Liddell Hart met with Rowlands to revive his proposal of 1938 for a "scientific" department of the General Staff. Rowlands urged Grigg to put Liddell Hart in charge of a team of "scientific" experts to advise Home Forces and each expeditionary force, even though Army Operational Research Sections had been appointed since 1940. Liddell Hart asked for support from the Soviet Ambassador (Maisky) and Lloyd George, who reported Maisky as saying: "We regard Liddell Hart as the best military brain in England, and the only one." By April, the scheme had fallen through; Liddell Hart heard that soldierly opposition was the reason, but Rowlands had blamed the same in 1938

---

[*] Rowland was then Financial Advisor to the Defence Department. Rowlands had served as the War Department's Permanent Private Secretary from 1920 to 1936.

and 1940. Liddell Hart's memoirs misreport that Maisky initiated the meeting, that Maisky raised the issue of his under-employment, and that Maisky's intervention ruined his opportunity (note of talk with Rowlands, 18 March 1942, LH 11/1942/14; note of talk with Maisky, 20-22 March 1942, LH 11/1942/18; note of talk with Lloyd George, 23 March 1942, LH 11/1942/22; note of talk with Rowlands, 30 April 1942, LH 11/1942/30; 1965: II, 183-184).

In May, Rowlands organized a discussion between Liddell Hart and Grigg, on senior promotions and force structure. Grigg declined further meetings. Rowlands again blamed soldierly opposition, although he himself continued to meet with Liddell Hart (increasingly to slander Churchill and other Conservatives). In 1943, Rowlands was sent back to India. Grigg stayed at the War Office through the end of the war, occasionally answering Liddell Hart's correspondence, but refusing to meet (notes, 30 April, 1 May, 11 June, 27 September, and 4 November 1942, LH 11/1942/30, /32, /43, /73, and /95).

Soldiers

Liddell Hart pinned his professional hopes on the Generals he had helped to promote since November 1937. The trouble is, none did as well as he had promised. The most senior was Gort, who rocketed to CIGS in 1937, but became disillusioned with Liddell Hart's influence by 1938, and was happy to leave the War Office to take command of the BEF in September 1939.

All three men who served as CIGS in wartime (Edmund Ironside from 1939 to 1940; John Dill from 1940 to 1941; Alan Brooke from 1941 to 1945) had been rejected by Liddell Hart and Belisha for the same role in 1937. Brooke was longest serving and most powerful, but most antagonistic (Brooke had taken command of the Mobile Division in 1938, in opposition to Liddell Hart's recommendation – Percy Hobart) (note, 22 November 1937, LH 11/1937/96; 1965: II, 44, 48).

Like the CIGS, the DCIGS (Ronald Adam) thanked Liddell Hart for influencing Belisha's choices in 1937, but soon resented Liddell Hart's influence on policies. In the BEF, Adam commanded a corps. After evacuation, he was shifted laterally to Northern Command, but returned to the General Staff in June 1941 as Adjutant General. Here he found his calling. He was engaged and competent enough that no War Secretary could justify Liddell Hart's help with promotions. Adams was the one whom Rowlands blamed most for blocking Liddell Hart's wish to serve the War Department in 1942 (note, 1 May 1942, LH 11/1942/32).

The Adjutant General that Belisha and Liddell Hart had agreed in November 1937 (Clive G. Liddell) was demoted to command of Gibraltar upon war. He retired in 1943 as Inspector-General for Training at home. The next most powerful job in the General Staff was the DSD. The person (Ernest Squires) was unaffected in November 1937, but left for a job in Australia in 1938 and died there. The next DSD (Laurence Carr) had resisted Liddell Hart's approaches, partly because Carr wanted tanks of all classes, while Liddell Hart wanted only light tanks. Liddell Hart (1965: II, 35, 80-81) misreported his appointment as a backwards step. In November 1937, Liddell Hart had taken comfort that Percy Hobart took the Directorate of Military Training (nominally ranked equal with DSD). In 1938, the DMT was taken over by Hugh R.S. Massy. Massy was promoted to DCIGS upon war, but his combatant commands (from 1940) did not go well, and he retired in 1943.

Maurice Taylor, who had been selected in November 1937 to take over as Master General of Ordnance, saw the portfolio reduced to inconsequence in 1940, when folded into the Ministry of Supply. He retired in 1941.

Thus, by 1941 the General Staff were directed by persons who owed nothing to Liddell Hart, or repudiated him, or saw their portfolios reduced into irrelevance.

His protégés performed no better as commanders. Gort abandoned France in 1940, disappointed in his own performance but also the government's inadequate resourcing and unclear guidance. Gort was given the Inspectorate of Training and the Home Guard, which involved a lot of foreign travel. After that, Gort was shuffled as Governor of Gibraltar (1941), Governor of Malta (1942), and High Commissioner for Palestine and Transjordan (1944) (Kennedy 1957: 5, 37-38; Minney, 1961: 69; Liddell Hart 1965: II, 67; Colville 1972: 80-81).

The BEF's Chief of Staff was Henry Pownall, formerly DMO&I (since 1938), with no thanks to Liddell Hart, and no love lost. Pownall had foreseen and planned for a continental commitment that Liddell Hart had opposed. Pownall went from strength to strength: from Inspector-General of the Home Guard to commander of Northern Ireland in 1940, VCIGS in May 1941, commander Far East in December 1941, and chief of staff to the inter-Allied regional command in 1942, which eventually became South East Asia Command in 1943.

Ironside welcomed the invitation to escape the War Office for command of Home Forces in May 1940, which then was constituted as both expeditionary and defensive, but lacked the political and bureaucratic intelligence to survive the new regime. He took retirement in August, and was replaced by Brooke.

Hobart failed in his first divisional command (Mobile Division Egypt; later 7th Armoured), in 1939. Although Hobart and Liddell Hart blamed conservatism, their emphasis on raids by light tanks behind enemy's lines resisted combined-arms. Hobart's reputation as a trainer justified his recall to command the nascent 11th Armoured Division, within Northern Command, in March 1941. Liddell Hart moved to Westmorland in June. Still, their residences were about 100 miles apart, and Hobart was not as friendly or successful as before, whatever Liddell Hart claimed retrospectively. They barely acknowledged each other until after the war (in Macksey 1967: xiii-xv; Bond 1977: 120; Newsome 2024: Chapters 6 and 12).

Liddell Hart's most frequent soldierly contact during the Second World War was Frederick "Tim" Pile, who owed Liddell Hart for his appointment to Director of Anti-Aircraft Defence in early 1938, at the rank of Brigadier, and elevation to Anti-Aircraft Command in July 1939, at the rank of Lieutenant-General. Pile was the only British soldier to hold one command throughout the War. Pile betrayed scurrilous information on every echelon of government, from the Prime Minister to minor officials at the Air Ministry. However, like most wartime correspondents, he was keener to influence than be influenced. Pile did not suggest Liddell Hart when authorized to hire a military scientific adviser in February 1940. In June, Liddell Hart offered to work for Pile "in an advisory or inspector capacity," but Pile made clear that superiors were opposed (1939b: 169, 187; 1965: II, 115; Pile 1949: 39; Pile to LH, 22 June 1940, LH 1/575). Still, Pile continued to leak secrets, including the first products of the first Army Operational Research Section, in August 1940.

> I was sent daily charts of the [air] raids by General Pile in the hope that I might be able to find a clue, but could perceive no clear indication of

pattern or purpose (1970: 98n).

Within months, Liddell Hart pushed Pile as a potential CIGS. Beaverbrook shared Pile's antagonism towards the Air Ministry, but Beaverbrook quit the Ministry of Aircraft Production in April 1941. As Minister of Supply, from June, Beaverbrook resented the War Office's complaints about failures of supply, and held the CIGS (John Dill) most responsible. When returning from Moscow in October 1941, he told Hastings "Pug" Ismay (the Prime Minister's Military Assistant) that he would recommend Pile in place of Dill. On 20 October, Dill informed Brooke (then C-in-C Home Forces), who did not approve. Brooke wanted the job for himself, and would get it in December. After the war, Brooke added a hypocritical explanation.

> I have known Tim Pile for a long time, and he has got certain valuable qualities, but he certainly had not got the necessary qualifications for a CIGS. In fact, I could not imagine a worse selection, but typical of Beaverbrook. I had heard that Pile was frequently spending weekends with Beaverbrook and there can be no doubt that on such occasions he would not waste his time; he is a "climber" if he is nothing else (2002: 192).

The lesson for Liddell Hart was that his influence through Beaverbrook was insufficient to achieve the appointments he had achieved through Belisha.

By 1944, he turned to femininity as primary subject, and to Americans for validation, particularly George S. Patton, who had just returned to Britain to command the nascent 3rd Army. Liddell Hart identified with Patton's posturing as maverick and inventor of mechanized warfare, and ignored the bad press about Patton arguing with peers and slapping psychological casualties. They met on 14 March. Liddell Hart thought he had found a soul mate. Patton wrote home that he "has developed a great love for me. He is very well read but badly balanced and has no personal knowledge of the facts of life so far as war is concerned." They met on 19 June, but never again (LH 11/1944/14; Blumenson 1998: 426).

Legacy

Liddell Hart put about the myth that for several months from February 1942 he was officially and secretly employed to research "higher organization problems" (to Martel, 24 and 31 January 1946, LH 1/492 Part 3; 1965: II, 186). His American correspondents published the following spin.

> Controversy over the value of his contribution, illness from overwork, and hurt through the adverse criticism he sustained, as well as the fact that he could not tell the truth in wartime, caused him to isolate himself for a time (Icks 1952: 26).

> During the Second World War there was talk from time to time of placing Liddell Hart in charge of various operational research organizations, but either he was sent off to do [e]specially urgent work or someone else was found who needed a post (Higham 1966: 98).

Bond (1977: 142) reported accurately that "at the beginning of 1942 it looked as though Liddell Hart might be offered an official appointment as a military adviser, but in the end nothing came of it."

Field-Marshal Sir Claude Auchinleck (Middle East C-in-C, 1941-1942), BHLH, and Kathleen at a private showing of the movie "Rommel: Desert Fox," at Century Theatre, London, 3 October 1951. Belisha too attended, but was photographed with other guests (LH 13/104/10). Liddell Hart did not open correspondence until 1948, prompted by publication of Auchinleck's despatches from India in 1943 (LH 1/30).

14

Peace-Maker

Liddell Hart's policy to appease in peacetime became a policy to quit the war, unilaterally, short of victory and justice. He campaigned for quitting even before the war started, and during Germany's invasion of Poland. He urged France and Britain to take Hitler's offer of negotiated peace before they lose. He planned self-exile to America. He campaigned for Britain to keep out of Scandinavia. In 1940, he urged disentanglement from Western Europe, and even the Western Alliance. In 1941, he isolated himself in north-west England. He used Germany's turn against the Soviet Union to add to his argument for Britain's unilateral peace negotiations. In 1942, he imagined a missed opportunity for peace negotiations in Sweden. He justly opposed the policy of unconditional surrender in 1943, but shamefully invented peace negotiations in Stalingrad. He continued to argue for negotiations while the Allies advanced through Europe and Asia from 1943 to 1945, and excused Nazi aggression and other crimes. His wish for peace without the costs, vengeance, and recriminations of decisive victory deserves rediscovery, without his carelessness for justice and restitution.

Pre-emptive Quitter, Spring 1939

Appeasement and quitting share a motivation to avoid war, although Liddell Hart frames quitting as magnanimity and efficiency. He credits Lloyd George for the framing, since their first meeting in 1932.

> I noticed how often he dwelt on the drawbacks of a too complete victory and the importance of avoiding too extreme war aims, while emphasizing the folly of slamming the door on efforts to bring about a negotiated peace (1965: I, 375).

Liddell Hart warned that a Second World War, with the same emphasis on decisive victory as in the First, would "end civilization" (1935b). In April 1939, he wrote a note, which, after slight revision, became the conclusion to the first chapter of the book he published in June. He wishes to apply "a cold douche of reason" to the "emotional conviction that force must not merely be checked, but crushed."

> That notion is a mirage in the desert. It can only lead to mutual suicide, and the collapse of civilization…
>
> The chief hope for our civilization lies in nobody winning the next war. Or, better still, in everybody being brought to realize beforehand that it cannot be "won." The more widely that truth can be spread, the more chance there is that war will be averted ("Reflection," 19 April 1939, LH 11/1939/43b; 1939b: 26).

The book urges Britons to escape a ruinously long war by staying defensive and ready to negotiate for peace. He expects the enemy's economic capacity to weaken, and defence-dominance to strengthen, until the enemy realizes it could not win and should negotiate. He urged Britain to reach peace unilaterally, despite its current alliances. He characterizes alliances as restrictions on Britain's freedom to join, fight, and quit in its own way, although he allows co-belligerency (mistermed as "collective security") (1939b: 49-50).

> If war comes again on the continent there would be too much prospect of repeating the same sequence – strategic entanglement, illimitable expansion, mass conscription, futile sacrifice, and national exhaustion – leading not only to a prolonged impoverishment, but, immediately, to the weakening of our influence over the peace (1939b: 100-101; 1939f: 13).

Liddell Hart was correct to worry about a Pyrrhic victory to the benefit of other belligerents. However, his rejection of any "continental commitment" of British forces, and his wish to stay out of this particular war, put him in company with communists and fascists, even though he did not endorse them. Liddell Hart had rejected Mosley by 1937, but not the BUF's unilateralism and isolationism. By 1939, both men regarded Churchill as ruinously intent on victory at any price, were confident that dictators could be appeased and deterred, campaigned for a unilaterally negotiated settlement, and opposed entangling alliances. Liddell Hart kept his distance publicly, but privately archived the BUF's policy statements and news, and publicly championed the same policies. Meanwhile, he and Lloyd George were the Britons most engaged with the Soviet ambassador's machinations for foreign and military cooperation with the USSR, even as they opposed cooperation with France. Once the Soviet Union aligned with Germany in August 1939, and urged socialists everywhere to support Germany, Maisky told them the pact was a ruse – that the USSR was still neutral, but he also blamed Britain for forcing the USSR into the pact by refusing a UK-USSR alliance. The Communist Party of Great Britain adopted a policy it called "revolutionary defeatism" – it promised not to subvert or support the war effort against Germany. In practice, it propagandized against the effort, subverted workers and military personnel, spied on behalf of the USSR, and campaigned for a negotiated peace. The public and government naturally associated Liddell Hart (and Lloyd George) with fascist and communist defeatists and double-dealers even before the war got going (LH 15/3/186; Mosley 1968: Chapter 20; Aster 1971: 350-356; Skidelsky 1990: 285, 307, 329, 423-424; Andrew 2009: 273).

Quitter, Autumn 1939

On 1 September, Germany invaded Poland. Britain declared a state of war on 3 September. It launched bombers against Germany the same day. It sent advance parties to France on the next day. On 7 September, Liddell Hart pondered how to return Britain to unilateralism.

> The problem, obviously, is how to save the British people from the consequences of their past blindness and present gallant obstinacy – their "Charge of the Light Brigade" mood. The need is to revive a sense of reality by making them see the picture as a whole. But how can it be done? It is impossible to find a place for such a view in our [news]papers at present – and yet the earlier it could be done the better chance there would be of limiting danger and the damage. One can send memoranda

privately to various of our leaders – but in the present mood, will they make any adequate impression? The next most obvious and urgent course is to rouse the USA to the danger they will be in if we go down, and show them the vital importance of their early help – both in buttressing our position and in restraining us from dissipating our strength. If Western civilization is to be saved, we need not only support, but to be saved from ourselves (note, 7 September 1939, LH 11/1939/75).

On the same day, he drafted an argument for negotiated peace ("The problem if Hitler should make a peace offer," 7 September 1939, LH 1939/99). He edited it the next day, then noted his alarm about a "march to battle."

It is less than two months ago that the "Defence of Britain" [1939b] was published, and its warnings…were greeted in every quarter as obvious common sense. One expression of opinion after another shows complete disregard of the warnings, and an urge to march to battle in the same old way – "Blood has gone to their heads" (note, 8 September 1939, LH 11/1939/75b).

Also on 8 September, he developed his second wartime proposal for unilateral negotiated peace, without which, he warns, neutrals would bandwagon with Germany, France would quit, and Britain would be isolated ("The Need for a New Technique of War," 8 September 1939, LH 1939/100; 1939d: 157). *The Times* declined to publish. No official championed it. Nevertheless, it was one of the papers he included in his next anthology (1941a: 151-157). After the war, he quoted only its summation ("by making our stand on ground that was strategically unsound we have got into a very bad hole") as evidence for realism at a time of optimism (1957: 4; 1970: 17n). His memoirs admit that "a number of the political leaders who still showed interest in having my view considered it 'over-gloomy'" (1965: II, 236, 260). He considered giving up the struggle.

It is obviously impossible to write the truth, and to write anything less than it would only make one an accomplice in maintaining a dangerous state of illusion, so that it is better to keep silence – but how I am to earn a living I cannot see (to Geoffrey Faber, 11 September 1939, LH 1/274; 1965: II, 258).

He rebounded within a couple days. His third wartime paper urges unilateral withdrawal into neutrality.

To seek a victory in a modern "great war" is never more than the pursuit of a mirage in the desert. In the present war it may be worse – leading us into a bottomless quicksand not merely in the national sense. For the prolonged struggle made inevitable by such a fallacious aim endangers the existence of all spiritual values. Freedom itself may hardly survive such a reckless offensive "defence" ("A Personal Problem," 14 September 1939, LH 11/1939/110b).

By the end of September, he drafted a fourth version, in which the Western Allies would lose, unless Germany and the Soviet Union fight each other without Western involvement. Only Lloyd George supported the document (1939e).

Beaverbrook belatedly agreed to publish a more patriotic version. Liddell Hart edited until 4 October, when he sent it to *The Sunday Express*, entitled "The Need for a New Technique in Curing 'Hitlerism'." Ten days later, the editor (John Gordon) returned it, due to "strong opinion expressed by several of my executives that it might conceivably have a rather depressing effect on many people at a time when they are bewildered, uncertain but still fairly confident." He revised it, in which form it was published on 10 December, entitled "Is There a New Way to Fight this Strange war?" (Gordon to LH, 14 October 1939, LH 3/122; typescripts in LH 10/1939/83-92; 1965: II, 275).

Negotiator, Autumn 1939

On 6 October, Hitler spoke to the Reichstag, mostly about the triumphs of German arms in Poland, before he declared his openness to peace. On 10 October, the French Prime Minister declared that France would fight on, although he said also that negotiations would be conditional on guarantees of peacetime behaviour. Chamberlain was still circulating a draft response among selected ministers, civil servants, and diplomats. On 12 October, Chamberlain told the Commons that he was open to peace, conditional on "acts – not words alone," given that Hitler could not be trusted and had not specified any conditions. Privately, he specified a condition: Hitler's demotion (but not arrest) (Colville 1985: 34-35).

Chamberlain's public allowance for negotiations helps to explain Liddell Hart's return to London in mid-October. He and Maisky helped to develop Lloyd George's speech to constituents (21 October), proposing that the USA, Italy, and the USSR (to which an envoy of "real standing and influence" should be sent) should mediate a peace with Hitler. Liddell Hart developed his seventh wartime paper on this theme. He declares "no reason to expect that France and Britain can ever attain such a superiority as to win." He argues that they should "proffer a ladder by which Hitler can climb down." His reason is contradicted by his expectation that Western economic superiority would only increase. Only Lloyd George and Beaverbrook expressed agreement ("The prospect in this war," 7 November 1939, LH 11/1939/128b; Addison 1971: 368).

Self-Exile, 1939-1940

By 1939, Liddell Hart had been talking about emigrating to America, where isolationism remained popular. He amplified the idea on 27 August, after *The Times* rejected his latest submissions. Short of friends, he sought his 17-year-old son's validation.

> I sympathize with your feelings over The Times – better late than never – but what could you turn your hand to? If it is a case of America, though I cannot pretend to anticipate it with great pleasure, it would be better than Flanders – if it is not a longer way [a]round to it! (AJLH to BHLH, 31 August 1939, ALH/2).

Upon war, he moved further west, to Dartington, Devon, where friends Dorothy and Leonard Elmhirst gave him a furnished home at reduced rent. On 10 September, he washed his hands of Britain: "As I am unable to do anything effective now to check this fatal course, I do not care to be an accomplice in the vain sacrifice of the nation's youth and the wrecking of British civilization." After sleeping on it, he wrote to his son that he washed his hands of London alone: "While it is difficult to see anything clearly ahead, it does seem plain that London is not a desirable place to reside" ("A Personal Conclusion," 10 September 1939, LH 11/1939/108; BHLH to AJLH, 11 September 1940, LHCMA ALH/2). Yet, within weeks, he consulted Robert Graves, who had moved to America early in 1939.

> If you are over 41 and not in the active forces there is nothing to prevent you getting out, especially if you give as your reason something about explaining our war aims to America. You are only allowed to take £25 in cash but royalties can be sent to you there. I got a permit easily on my "name" as you could on yours (Graves to LH, 2 October 1939, LH 1/327).

He consulted a liberal academic, who encouraged him to raise his voice.

> I aways find that I learn from your conversation or writings, and when I do not entirely agree, you always make me think. You certainly do a valuable service in standing up to the flood of wishful thinking that war generates (Gilbert Murray to LH, 6 October 1939, LH 1/538).

In November, he and Kathleen accepted an invitation from Graves and his current partner (Beryl Hodge) to accompany their return to America (planned for March). In January, Graves U-turned, when his prior lover (Laura Riding), already resident in America, rejected him for the penultimate time (Graves to LH, January 1940, LH 1/327; Graves 1990: 326, 328). Graves rationalized that Liddell Hart should not emigrate after all, given Beaverbrook's favour.

> I think it is clear that so long as you have Beaverbrook's ear and permission to write, you are doing far more good here than (say) in America. After all, your articles are read by the troops and generals concerned, as they would not be if they were first published in America; this offsets the greater freedom of frank speaking that you would have if you wrote from America. Besides, anyone who goes to America now has the odium (unjust and absurd but inescapable) of being called a rat and the credit given to his opinions is therefore reduced (to LH, 19 February 1940, LH 1/327).

He and Kathleen stayed in Devon, but sent her daughters to Canada. Storm Jameson's later novel places the fictionalized Liddell Hart in a defeated Britain, when a General says he would be more useful in America.

> "I shall be criticized for going. Naturally. A great many people will be only too delighted to think they've found someone meaner than themselves" (1949: 80-82).

Jameson gives him an opportunity to explain to his wife.

> "No, it's myself I'm cursing. Why didn't we leave five, ten, years ago? Why wait until the last minute, and have to bolt like rats? I was a fool."

> "We talked about it often enough. Perhaps it was my fault we didn't."

> "No," he answered, "it was mine. The truth is I was afraid" (1949: 101).

Scandinavian Wars, 1939-1940

The USSR invaded Finland on 30 November 1939. Liddell Hart heard through private corresondence of Churchill's proposals for aiding Finland and intervening in neutral Norway, to interdict exports of Swedish iron ore. Liddell Hart opposed these proposals, but did not publicize them yet. He lobbied Beaverbrook for more journalistic work and against any aid for Finland.* They were prepared to accommodate German and Soviet annexations to date. They wanted Britain to negotiate unilaterally. In effect, they aligned on a policy that since 1931 Beaverbrook had called "the Empire and Splendid Isolation" (Chisholm and Davie 1993: 322-325).

By January, Lloyd George shared Liddell Hart's confidence in a stalemate. In the same month, Richard Stokes (Labour MP) shared some parameters for peace as discussed with the German ambassador to Istanbul, while the Marquis of Tavistock publicized peace terms gathered from the German ambassador to Dublin. Germany denied them, but Lloyd George and Liddell Hart kept the faith (note on conversation with Lloyd George, March 1940, LH 11/1940/15b; Addison 1971: 371).

On 31 January, Chamberlain spoke to the Commons about his satisfaction with the progress of the war, "until friend and enemy can sit down to build a happier and safer world." On 3 February, one of Beaverbrook's newspapers published Liddell Hart's response: he would negotiate with Hitler, now, although he expects years of stalemate before all parties would definitely negotiate. Like Chamberlain, he warns against challenging the stalemate.

The current stalemate was popular but negotiations were not. That month, a survey suggested that only 29 percent of Britons approved negotiations with Germany. The percentage had risen from 12 points since September, although respondents might have meant negotiations after German passivity in the West. On 4 March, the newspaper published Liddell Hart's opinion that Britain should adopt "a policy of restraint in regard to taking the offensive," and wait for Germany to reach "an agreed settlement." Beaverbrook asked him to visit on 7 March to hear of hate mail. Still, Beaverbrook hoped for cumulative impact on public opinion, and urged him to add a speaking tour (1940c; 1941a: 180-181; 1941a: 168; "Sundry notes," 8 March 1940, LH 11/1940/8; Chisholm and Davie 1993: 372; Allport 2020: 189).

Germany invaded Norway on 9 April. In one account, Liddell Hart blames Churchill's order to board a German warship in neutral waters in February (1969: 207). In most accounts, he describes Hitler as provoked by Allied sea-mines. In fact, Allied mining did not start until 8 April, hurried by Allied intelligence on German intent. Allied plans certainly contributed to German intent, but were not necessary (1948: 36; 1965: II, 278; 1968b: 746; 1970: 52; Coville 1985: 97-98; Allport 2020: 219).

Liddell Hart hoped the debacle would justify Lloyd George's return to the premiership and international negotiations. However, when Lloyd George joined the debate in the House of Commons, he criticized the response, without calling for withdrawal or negotiations. Late in the day, Lloyd George telephoned Liddell Hart, who advised, according to his note, "it was essential to be realistic, and while doing our utmost to foil the German aim, to work for an honourable peace" (note, 8 May, 1940, LH 11/1940/36).

---

* He publicized this effort after Germany turned on the Soviet Union in June 1941 (1942a: 10).

Western European Campaigns, 1940

Germany invaded France and the Low Countries on 10 May. Liddell Hart claimed Hitler had been provoked by Western offensive "talk" (1941b: 302; 1954a: 231), "threats of 'opening up the war'" (1948: 36), rejection of Hitler's proposal of October 1939 (1965: II, 259-261, 279), and "talk of attacking Germany's flanks" (1968b: 746). Finally, he blamed Churchill's plea, broadcast on 29 January, for the neutral nations to stand with Britain and France against aggression (1969: 206).

Liddell Hart's private writings of the day are dominated by dismay about Churchill's accession to the premiership. The next day, he noted that "the new War Cabinet appear[s] to be a group devoted to 'victory' without regard to its practical possibility" (LH 11/1940/37).

His daily articles for Beaverbrook's newspapers are confident in the defensive, but anxious that Britain would neglect opportunities to quit. He imagines the greatest opportunity to quit when German forces cut off the Allied salient around Dunkirk, by 21 May. German commanders had sound military reasons to avoid pressing the salient and Britain itself. Hitler also wanted to impose his will on commanders, after days of confusion, so he confirmed a halt order on 24 May. In any case, the order was rescinded on 26 May. Liddell Hart's post-war writings add a motivation to reach a settlement. His only evidence is hearsay from Günther Blumentritt (1892-1967), who, as a staff officer at Army Group A, heard Hitler say (24 May) that he would make peace in return for Britain's recognition of Germany's dominance of the continent, although Blumentritt noted also Hitler's keenness to turn against the USSR. When first publishing this evidence, Liddell Hart expressed uncertainty as to "the true explanation" for Hitler's disinterest in attacking Britain, and realized that no German flag officer was enthusiastic for invasion, given the Royal Navy, if nt the Royal Air Force. Yet in later publications, he is emphatic that Hitler's reason was Anglophilic (1948: 106-107, 135, 153; 1954a: 248-252; 1968b: 755, 758; 1970: 83-84, 87; Allport 2020: 247).

Western Alliance, 1940-1941

During nine meetings from 26 to 28 May, Churchill's Cabinet considered a negotiated settlement. At the ninth, Halifax conceded Churchill's preference to fight on, for now. After the evacuation from Dunkirk (4 June), Liddell Hart fancied an oportunity for Lloyd George to take the premiership and to negotiate peace, unilaterally. After all, Britain's withdrawal was unilateral, and France's government considered itself released from an agreement of March to negotiate bilaterally. Lloyd George received deputations from the Peace Aims Group on 20 June, 25 June, and 17 July, when he met with Liddell Hart and three Liberals-turned-socialists: the leader of His Majesty's opposition (Hastings Bertrand Lees-Smith, 1878-1941), the political editor of *The News Chronicle* (Arthur John Cummings, 1882-1957), and a columnist for *The Observer* (Archibald Gordon Macdonell, 1895-1941). Some days later, he urged Churchill to negotiate peace (LH 11/1940/73; Addison 1971: 375-377; Allport 2020: 259, 264).

Britain was never alone in this fight. All dominions and most dependencies allied from the start. Exiled European governments and forces travelled to Britain. Yet Liddell Hart (and Churchill) pretended loneliness to emphasize vulnerability (although with different priorities: Churchill prioritized American aid; Liddell Hart prioritized peace). The bombing of London (from 7 September) added to Liddell Hart's sense of vulnerability (although he was living far away). He reframed his defeatism as a general theory of war. This reduces to six assumptions or observations.

1. Every war between great powers was avoidable.

2. There are always faults on both sides.

3. The common people are always the chief sufferers.

4. Suffering is increased by the pursuit of illusory "victory."

5. Victory is rarely attained in a military sense and never in a political sense – of being ultimately more profitable than an indecisive issue.

6. Even when victory is attainable it is a bad foundation for subsequent peace ("War and Peace," 14 September 1940, LH 11/1940/87).

By October, he repeats his expectation of relative decline, unless the United States join in. He wants the Allies to focus on "the nuisance value of our air campaign and blockade," until peace could be negotiated, in about ten years' time ("Simple Arithmetic for Statesmen," 12 October 1940, LH 11/1940/90).

In November, he wrote a new paper. It clarifies that any offensive, except in the air, would ruin Britain but not Germany. It adds that propaganda might persuade Germans into revolution, once German forces have exhausted themselves offensively, although he is not confident. He urges British concessions now, given that Britain's costs grow with time. He forecasts that the costs of decisive victory would result in communism or fascism at home, or international dependency on America.* He is correct on the international dependency, and to some extent the domestic revolution (socialists would win their first landslide in the general election of 1945). He does not admit that concessions could cost Britain more than decisive victory, provoke domestic revolution, and provoke German aggression ("The Reckoning," 17 November 1940, LH 11/1940/102c). His paper passed through friends to the service ministries, of which the Admiralty forwarded it to the Prime Minister's office, with concern than he was peddling enemy propaganda. The First Sea Lord (Admiral Sir Dudley Pound) wrote upon it: "Probably no technical correspondent has more responsibility than Liddell Hart for the accepted military theories propagated before the war and which were so disproved in the Battle of France. I should have thought he would have preferred to hide his head rather than produce still yet another theory as pregnant with defeat as his former theories" (diary, 3 December 1940, Colville 1985: 304-305).

In the same month, he published an anthology of prior writings, with a plea for "a constructive and dynamic peace plan that will stir the imagination of our people and the peoples of the world" (1940i: 55). His next book warns that "both sides are losers" from most wars ("except the parasite class of war-profiteers"). "Peace by

---

* This expectation was normative, partly because Britain was indebted to America after the Great War. Chamberlain had expressed the same concern for years (Allport 2020: 128-129).

victory" is temporary, since a victory just "creates a desire for revenge." Britain's "aim should be to convince the aggressors that their pursuit of victory is likely to bring them more loss than gain, and they can only regain peace on a basis of common agreement" (1941a: 141). His absolutism denies an obvious antinomy: victory is necessary to enduring peace.

Self-Exile, 1940-1941

In October 1940, Adrian left a nearby artists retreat to start the undergraduate degree that he had postponed for a year. In November, Basil saw his first wartime anthology in print, and finished his second, for publication in February. Unintentionally, they confirm his unfashionable record and attributes. He was 45 years old, a self-advertised adviser to discredited peacetime administrations, and a member of what George Orwell (1941: 55) called the "ruling class" and "the old." "A generation of the unteachable is hanging upon us like a necklace of corpses."

He had not visited London since November, for fear of bombing. When *The Daily Mail* sought him out, in March 1941, Liddell Hart was grateful,* but refused invitations to London. He feared German invasion of Devon from May, so sought to move northwards. He was relieved that Axis forces invaded Balkan states in April, but remained intent on a move, by the Summer.†

Eastern Front, 1941

The movers delivered his furniture and books on the day after the Axis invaded the Soviet Union (22 June 1941). The *Daily Mail* found him by telephone to request an article. Liddell Hart claimed nowhere to write, but nevertheless delivered on the next day. He admits that the "whole face of the war has been changed…ideologically as well as strategically," and that most German forces are in Russia. Yet he still argues for a negotiated settlement, independent of the Soviet Union ("The Great Gamble," *Daily Mail*, 24 June 1941, LH 10/1941/12; 1942a: 70). His argument further isolated him, as recalled by his son (then training with the Royal Navy at Fareham, near Portsmouth, in Hampshire).

> I recall the disruption between my father and some of his literary friends who had been fervent preachers against war, and in some cases conscientious objectors, when, after Russia entered World War II they began to write with like fervour – and with utter disregard for the strategical problems – in favour of immediately opening a second front (1976: 11-12).

In September, he circulated yet another paper urging the British government to signal conditions under which the German government could negotiate: "victory over another great power never fulfils expectations of a good and lasting peace." The *Daily Mail* and Beaverbrook's newspapers refused to publish it ("The Eternal Wisp O' the Wisp," 3 September 1941, LH 11/1941/54; to Lloyd George, 10 September 1941, LH 1/450).

---

* He explained that he was asked by "Rothermere to do a periodical commentary on events for the *Daily Mail*, starting in March 1941" (1942a: 11). Brian Bond (1977: 119) and Robert O'Neill (1990: 110) misdescribed him as the *Daily Mail*'s full-time military correspondent.
† He settled on High Wray House, near Ambleside, Westmorland.

The Sweden Opening, 1942

By 1942, Beaverbrook's campaign for negotiated settlement unwittingly confirmed Liddell Hart's wishful thinking that officials were already negotiating peace. The Bishop of Chichester (George Bell) also misled him. The Bishop's opposition to Western offensiveness had stimulated Liddell Hart to correspond since 1940. In April 1942, Bell visited church leaders in Sweden. German representatives speculated about a coup against Hitler, suggested that Germany could withdraw to borders pre-dating the occupation of the *Sudetenland* in October 1938, and hoped that the Allies would signal their expectations for Germany's opening proposal. The Bishop told Cripps (then a minister without portfolio and the leader of the Commons) and Eden (Foreign Secretary), without telling Liddell Hart. Cripps' personal assistant (David Kemp Owen) did not tell Liddell Hart when they met in May. Instead, Owen complained of Beaverbrook's briefings against Cripps. On 2 June, Owen and Cripps told a literary circle of their confidence that the Soviets would fight the Germans to a standstill by October. In August, Owen revealed Bell's experience in Sweden to Liddell Hart, but also made clear their scepticism. Still, Liddell Hart was optimistic, and wrote to the Bishop for confirmation (note to self, 28 August 1942, LH 11/1942/68; Chisholm and Davie 1993: 438-439; Davison 2012: 384).

Orwell (who had organized the literary circle, at Cripps' request) received Liddell Hart a few weeks later.

> Yesterday [I] met Liddell Hart for the first time. Very defeatist and even, in my judgement, somewhat inclined to be pro-German subjectively. Although, of course, [he is] strongly opposed to the Second Front, also anxious for us to call off the bombing (Orwell, diary 21 September 1942, in Davison 2012: 409).

In the next week, the Bishop belatedly replied to correct Liddell Hart's optimism (Bell to LH, 25 September 1942, LH 1/58).

From 1945, his interviews and correspondence with German prisoners produced no evidence for German intent to make peace through Sweden, except for a rumour heard by Günther Blumentritt in June 1940. Nevertheless, two years later, Liddell Hart published a claim that "the war might have ended three years earlier" if "Churchill and his colleagues[*] had" acted on the Bishop's contacts (1948: 145; 1950: 60). This was 15 years before he first visited Sweden, without mention of the fiction.

Unconditional Surrender, 1943

In January 1943, the Western Allies demanded their enemies' "unconditional surrender." As Liddell Hart wrote to the Bishop, it was "the most stupid and untimely step that could have been taken – and the best possible reinforcement to Hitler" (12 February 1943, LH 1/58). All the Germans he interviewed from 1945 to 1946 confirmed that the policy stimulated military resistance to the Allies, and stifled political resistance to Hitler (1948). His next book confirms his predictions.

> [U]nconditional surrender…prolonged the war far beyond its likely end,

---

[*] Here, Liddell Hart admits only Eden as the Bishop's recipient, and omits Cripps, perhaps to imply that only Conservatives failed to act.

thus leading to the sacrifice of countless lives...It...entailed immense devastation on the continent as well as the undue exhaustion of Britain... and...was bound to make Russia "top dog" on the continent...

[It] merely prolonged Germany's resistance, producing the boomerang effects that now make "victory" look such a farce (1950: 52, 166).

He was right to criticize the policy of unconditional surrender, but wrong to urge peace without regime change, criminal justice, and territorial restitution

Stalingrad, 1943

In March 1943, Liddell Hart invented a ridiculous story: that in January Hitler had promoted the commander of the besieged 6th Army to Field Marshal in order to empower Friedrich von Paulus to petition for peace. In fact, Hitler had promoted Paulus in hope of stoking his resistance in Stalingrad: Paulus received the news on the day he surrendered (31 January). Liddell Hart claimed that Hitler had proposed Axis withdrawal from Russia, concession of territory in Finland and Rumania, and financial reparations. Liddell Hart told the Bishop that the hearsay came from Swedish contacts (to Bell, 22 March 1943, LH 1/58). He never named any Swedish contacts. Post-war, he implies a leak from the German foreign ministry.

> I had an account of it from an officer who was one of the technical advisers on [Joachim von] Ribbentrop's staff. The proposal of a concealed truce had behind it the ultra-ingenious idea that it would enable Russia to go on drawing American and British supplies, and pass part of them on to Germany to help the latter in checking the American and British forces! But the Nazi leaders were not prepared to make any large concessions to Russia (1950: 36).

This post-war version contradicts his wartime claim that Hitler had proposed territorial concessions. No peace-feeler appears in his first account of the German-Russian war (1956a: 115). Yet his final history of the Second World War revives the myth, although this time the month is June and the principals are the foreign ministers of Germany and the USSR. Supposedly, they met inside German lines, at Kirovograd (now Kropyvnytskyi) in central Ukraine. Supposedly, Ribbentrop proposed a new frontier along the Dnieper (Dnipro) River (which runs through central Ukraine, less than 50 miles, north-east of Kirovograd). Supposedly, Vyacheslav Molotov insisted on the pre-war frontier. Supposedly, "the discussion...was broken off after a report that it had leaked out to the Western Powers." Liddell Hart's only explicit source is "German officers who attended as technical advisers" (1970: 488).

The United States Central Intelligence Agency had never heard the story before. The publisher claimed to have challenged Liddell Hart in December 1969, who promised evidence, but died a month later. The publisher could not find evidence in his archives, but released the book as submitted. The CIA (1972) asked its officers in Europe to ask their contacts for evidence. None was found.

Peace-Monger, 1943-1945

Liddell Hart continued to urge immediate peace, even after Axis defeat in Africa in May 1943.

> We have won the war – but don't know it: We are now stupidly fighting on to sacrifice life, wealth, health, and independence – in short to lose the peace...Victory is a possibility; stalemate a probability; loss of our purpose in fighting almost a certainty. Peace through victory in a year or two's time would probably mean that we should lose more, in every sense, than by peace through stalemate this year (note, 10 June 1943, LH 11/1943/2).

Even upon news of the Western Allied invasion of mainland Italy in September 1943, he argued against decisive victory. He argued the same during Western Allied advances in France, and Soviet advances in Poland, in Summer 1944. His legitimate justification, which he repeated most frequently retrospectively, was that total defeat of Germany would leave space for the Soviet Union, but this justifies negotiation with Germany, not Hitler. He was correct to point out the inefficiency and counter-productiveness of total subjugation of enemies, but wrong to eschew regime change, criminal justice, and territorial restitution, particularly while Allied leverage was increasing ("The Future Balance of Europe," 1 October 1943, LH 11/1943/60-63; 1944b: 53; 1948: 465; 1950: 52; 1954a: 15; 1960a: 22; 1969: 221).

Apologist for Nazism

Lloyd George's unwavering confidence in Hitler's "genius" and "shrewd[ness]," and Liddell Hart's conviction that the Allies should have avoided and settled the war without regime change, justice, or restitution, encouraged their apologism for Nazism (note on talk with Lloyd George, 22 March 1942, LH 11/1942/22; Addison 1971: 379-380). In August 1945, LIddell Hart gained access to senior German prisoners near his home. He corresponded with their peers in Germany. He bought gifts, arranged for day-release, and campaigned against trials for war crimes. One product was a book, usefully quoting what they had to say, but gullibly reporting as facts whatever they had to say. He was right to deny guilt by association, but wrong to claim that none crossed into policy.

> They were essentially technicians, intent on their professional job, and with little idea of things outside it. It is easy to see how Hitler hoodwinked them (1948: x).

He was right to ponder how war could have been avoided, but wrong to blame Westerners most.

> It sufficed for the purposes of the Nuremberg trials to assume that the outbreak of war, and all its extensions, were purely due to Hitler's aggression. But that is too simple and shallow an explanation (1970: 60).

He was right to equate the immorality and indecisiveness of strategic bombing, but wrong to portray the Germans as more restrained.

> For a surprising feature of the next war was that the German Army gained a better reputation for humane behaviour than it had in 1870 and 1914...Travelling [a]round the liberated countries after the war, one heard widespread praise of the conduct of the German soldiers – and, too

often, unfavourable reflections that of the liberating forces (1965: I, 203).

He was right to oppose the prosecution of Germans for crimes defined *ex post facto*, but wrong to deny military complicity.

> It is the job of General Staffs to explore all the problems of any future conflict...That does not necessarily imply an aggressive intent – though the legal experts of Nuremberg have chosen to construe it (1950: 201).

Brian Bond (1977: 125, 153-154) admitted "a strange quirk in Liddell Hart's mentality which caused him to be severely critical of British (and to some extent Allied) policy and actions while making every allowance for the enemy." Liddell Hart's apologism for Nazism was the only issue that drove Danchev (1998a: 231-232) to unconditional condemnation.

Legacy

Liddell Hart was incorrect to forecast defensive stalemate and a consensus for negotiated peace. Italy switched sides in October 1943 more than a month after it had been invaded by the Western Allies. Germany surrendered in May 1945 after invasions from west and east. Japan surrendered in August after atomic bombs had devastated Nagasaki and Hiroshima, and Allied forces had assembled to invade. Still, Liddell Hart argued that no belligerent should pursue decisive victory.

He was correct on the counter-productiveness of unconditional surrender, the inefficiencies and unethicalness of strategic bombing – and (a later U-turn) of naval blockade, the greater military burden of decisive victory than indecisive settlement, and the risks of post-war instability and blowback, given the ways in which decisive victory is achieved.*

> It is the combination of an unlimited aim with an unlimited method – the adoption of a demand for unconditional surrender together with a strategy of total blockade and bombing devastation – which, in this war, has inevitably produced a deepening danger to the relatively shallow foundations of civilized life (1946b: 74).

However, he was wrong to omit the risks and injustices of indecisive settlement. He did not want to change aggressive regimes, to restore the *status quo ante*, or to punish war crimes, or to disable aggression. Brian Bond (1977: 156) admitted "no new strands in Liddell Hart's thinking in the last year of the war. If possible, the tone of his memoranda and reflections becomes even gloomier."

All his post-war books assert that decisiveness was achieved at too much cost for too little gain, even though he admits some campaigns were decisive and that sometimes one decisive campaign was necessary to another. All these books blame only Western Allied policies (1948: 143, 358; 1950: 60-61, 166; 1954a: 303; 1960a: 34; 1960b: 330; 1968b: 793; 1969: 221; 1970: 141, 451, 588-589, 681).

> The British...survived the danger and in the end came through to victory, but are paying heavily now for the blindness before and during the war.

---

* In 1960, he generalized a warning that fighting without "reason" leads to unnecessary casualties and either defeat or victory in war, before "you will lose the peace" (Walters 1961: 23).

Not the least part of the price is that "victory" had brought so little prospect of peace (1950: 71).

His first explanation for "so little prospect of peace" is vengefulness. His second explanation (in the same book) is, hypocritically, "the new school which thought only of bombing" (1950: 72). One of his friends defended the book, but admitted its "defeatism" too.

> Written off as a pacifist crank or a false prophet by every respectable British general, admiral, and air marshal, he obstinately demands to be taken seriously as a military theorist...
>
> He was Mr. Hore-Belisha's one-man Brains Trust at the War Office, shared in his fall from grace, and then provided the arguments for Mr. Lloyd George's defeatism in the winter of 1939. Yet, at the very time when, in his own country, his theory of total defence seemed to be utterly discredited, he was being studied and revered by Guderian and Rommel...
>
> If he was a political defeatist in the autumn of 1939, so were von Fritsch, Beck[,] and half the German General Staff – not to mention the French and Italians (Crossman 1958: 223-224).

Even in the nuclear age, Liddell Hart forecasted and prescribed defensive stalemate over decisive victory, without admitting the imperatives for decisive regime change, justice, and restitution.

> The conservative state [defender] can achi[e]ve its object by merely inducing the aggressor to drop his attempt at conquest...
>
> While it is hard to make a real peace with the predatory types, it is easier to induce them to accept a state of truce, and far less exhausting than an attempt to crush them...
>
> The experience of history brings ample evidence that the downfall of civilized states tends to come not from the direct assaults of foes but from internal decay, combined with the consequences of exhaustion (1952: 25, 27).

His new edition of "indirect approach" repeats his opinion that the pursuit of decisive victory ruined Europe and empowered Russia and America (1954a: 237). Similarly, his final histories of the Second World War start with his old complaint about the catastrophe of decisive victory (1968b: 740, 742; 1970: 3, 36, 713).

Bond (1977: 149) biographed Liddell Hart as "a pessimist but not a defeatist." However, Bond (1978: 426) later admitted that he "continued to argue that neither side could win," which "laid Liddell Hart open to charges of defeatism." Howard (2006: 45, 154) admitted that "[i]n 1940 he had been notoriously defeatist." All biographers admit that he mistook Hitler as rational, cautious, satisfiable, and negotiable (Bond 1977: 124; Mearsheimer 1988: 154-155; Danchev 1998a: 227-228).

15

Low-Cost Warrior

Liddell Hart expected and prescribed a mostly reactive war. He promised that mechanized raids, economic sanctions, moral pressure, and defence-dominance would disable aggression. This is consistent with his *British Way in Warfare* (1932), except that by 1941 he eschewed bombing, and amplified naval blockade –although by 1945 he considered blockade too to be inefficient and unethical.

He expected all parties to go through a process of realization: offensives do not work; defensives work; defensive stalemate is indecisive; negotiated settlement is preferable. When he specified the time horizon, he suggested ten years (to Random House, September 1939, LH 3/50). He kept this horizon even after he realized that a US alliance would be necessary.

> To overcome Nazi domination of Europe we need a "Ten Year Plan" – a long term policy which, instead of pursuing the mirage of victory in a fight to exhaustion, will seek an opportunity of breaking away from the present clinch with a view to gaining the ultimate advantage in the most strength-conserving and surest way ("Simple Arithmetic for Statesmen," 12 October 1940, LH 11/1940/90; 1965: II, 258).

Ten years is a long war. In 1934, the British government had started a five-year plan of rearmament. In 1938, it added another five-year plan, through fiscal year 1942-1943. By 1939, the Joint Intelligence Committee, and thence Chamberlain, expected Western material preponderance to overwhelm Germany by 1942. The plan was accelerated upon war. By October, Chamberlain expected Western production to persuade Germany to concede by Spring 1940. In November, he repeated his expectation (Allport 2020: 115, 148, 212-214, 269).

In this chapter's sections, I trace Liddell Hart's flip-flopping on mechanization, his prescription for a largely economic war, his addition of moral pressure, his confidence in defensive stalemate, and his expectation for German political revolution, given the economic, moral, and kinetic stresses of aggression.

Mechanization

Since 1918, Fuller had promised that fully mechanized land and air forces could shorten wars. At this time, Liddell Hart was ignorant of Fuller. Liddell Hart shared the desire for shorter wars, but not the method. He promised that lighter infantry, moving on foot – except for a tracked carrier for each platoon's heavy equipment, using infiltration tactics (reframed as "expanding torrent"), would shorten and cheapen battles (1919b; 1920a; 1920b; 1920c; 1921a; 1921b; 1921c; 1921d; 1921e; 1922b; 1922c; 1922d; 1922e; 1923b; Newsome 2024: Chapter 1). After making contact with Fuller in 1922, and much argument by correspondence, he plagiarized Fuller's method. His first book expects tracked vehicles and aerial bombers to shorten wars to "a few hours, or at most days from the commencement of hostilities" (1925: 40).

While Fuller continued to expect mechanized forces (even unarmoured) to shorten wars (1931a: 42), Liddell Hart's history of the Great War contains a U-turn. He admits the possibility of a "speedy decision on land," but, "if the armies failed to secure it," he expects years of war (1930b: 43). In the next year, Liddell Hart completed his *British Way in Warfare*, which assumes long wars, mostly because of the defensive capacity of machine-guns, the greater speed with which automobiles can carry machine-guns rather than the heavier weapons specified for offensives, and the counter-offensive capacity of aircraft (1931b; 1932c). In the second edition, he fantasizes about perpetual stalemate "within a few days," thanks to congested armies and broken supply chains (exacerbated by air attacks and labour strikes) (1935a: 56). He amplifies this argument in his final peacetime book.

> Unless the supplies from the factories and oil-fields are maintained without interruption they are no more than inert masses...And in that aspect is presented the potential factor that may save the world from catastrophe (1939b: 38-39).

He argues that even the most industrialized state is "unlikely" to acquire enough "munitions" to equip its "total man-power" (1939b: 47). Mobilization would end in paralysis (armies too ponderous, bombers too capable, labour strikes too likely, munitions too short). This leads to his economic expectation of stalemate.

Economic War

Liddell Hart always wanted Britain to fight a largely economic, non-kinetic war, although his definitions and justifications are shifty and sometimes contradictory. In the years before the Great War, the British consensus expected a short war due to economic incapacity. Liddell Hart estimated its length around five months, and worried that a war of 12 months would end civilization. He was confident that infantry offered offense-dominance, despite cavalry, artillery, and machine-guns (November 1914, LH 7/1914/10; Portway 1971: 58).

By contrast, his first history of the Great War is wise after the event. He complains that in 1914 the "General Staffs of Europe...hoped for a short war," even though the American Civil War had proven defence-dominance. For Liddell Hart, "a long war became inevitable" once the French checked the Germans in early September (1930b: 78, 91). This implies, and he admits, "[h]ow narrowly Germany missed decisive victory" in August.

> But fortunately, in 1914, the tiger was held at bay, and with this breathing space gained Britain had the opportunity to exert her traditional weapon (1930b: 73).

However, his references to the Royal Navy are inconstant. Sometimes he presents Britain's navy as necessary to victory, sometimes not. He presents Germany as anaemic due to naval blockade, but admits naval indecisiveness. He theorizes that victory goes to the dominant naval power, but recognizes some of the geopolitical and economic reasons why Germany is not as exposed or vulnerable as navalists had theorized. He admits that future Britain "would starve in three months" of enemy interdiction, but assumes that Britain is economically advantaged in every sector other than food, so would win any long confrontation. A few weeks after publication, he wrote: "Economic resources rather than the armed forces may be the real point of aim in another war" (1930b: 43-44; note, April 1930, LH 15/2/11; 1944a: 56).

Within months, he came up with his "British Way in Warfare," which prescribes naval blockade and maritime trade, although it ultimately relegates naval warfare behind air bombing. In 1925, he had regarded air bombing as decisive within days (without any need for an army, once bombers mature). By January 1931, he regards bombing as attritional over years. He realizes a trade-off between quick decisive victory and his slow "British Way," but assumes that the latter is cheaper. He promises even "that one is better off after the war than if one had not made war." By "better off," he seems to mean that "British Way" is cheaper than alternatives, rather than profitable (although later he would promise "profit" too: 1939b: 25).

> Victory, in this sense, is only possible if the result is quickly gained or the effort economically proportioned to the national resources. Favoured by geography, it has been Britain's distinction to excel in this wise economy of force (1932c: 41; 1935a: 45; 1944a: 43).

Although he never admitted as much, his "British Way" is indistinguishable from American, Japanese, and Italian ways. His earlier history of the Great War had admitted that "the United States, indeed, wielded the economic weapon with a determination, regardless of the remaining neutrals, far exceeding Britain's boldest claims." He never admitted the Committee of Imperial Defence's findings, in 1932, of which he was aware, that economic sanctions would hurt Britain more than Japan, and that Japan would not be contained, except in the unlikely event that all other states cooperate.* He never admitted the Chiefs of Staff Committee's findings, by wargame, that Germany would "not fear blockade," so long as most German ports are out of range of British bombers, most German imports travel overland, and Germany's eastern frontiers remain open to trade (as would be agreed with the Soviet Union in August 1939). A "sea-borne attack against [Germany's] coast is practically impossible," given Germany's superior home forces and fortifications. Thus, the players of Germany judged that Britain's "intrusion into the war must be regarded as incidental only – to be taken into account, but only in so far as it directly affects [Germany's] plans against France" (1930b: 313; "Joint Memorandum by the CGS and CAS," March 1935, LHCMA Burnett-Stuart; Bond 1973: 9).

In May 1937, Neville Chamberlain took over the premiership. Chamberlain, like most Parliamentarians, and Liddell Hart, swallowed self-interested claims from three big lobbyists. Big corporations claimed that the extra taxation and diversion of industrial capacity to rearmament would be ruinous. Big labour unions claimed that switching workers to the relevant trades would "dilute" British skills, lower wages, and lower exports. The financial sector warned against any provocation that might trigger German default on debts. In December, Liddell Hart told the 1922 Committee and the Army Staff College that "we should not lose sight of the present inadequacy of Germany's resources – and the natural superiority of those which might be opposed to her – for a prolonged struggle." Later in the month,

---

* Instead, he reported that "Japan was extremely susceptible to economic pressure" (1969: 213). Implicitly, he is referring to Japanese dependency on imports of American oil, but Britain did not control this embargo. America did not undertake such an embargo until two years into the war.

Chamberlain led the Cabinet to retrench a long war strategy: economic stability, naval dominance, and aerial bombers to deter potential enemies, without need for ground expeditions. This was articulated by the Minister for Co-ordination of Defence (Thomas Inksip) in his report to Parliament: "This country cannot hope to win a war against a major Power by a sudden knock-out blow; on the contrary, for success we must contemplate a long war." In March 1938, Chamberlain told Parliament "that wars are not only won with arms and men; they are won with reserves of resources and credit...and...the maintenance of those commercial and industrial activities" ("The Military Situation in Europe," 6 December 1937, LH 12/1937/10; 1938d: 149, 152; 1939b: 61; Forbes 1987; Narizny 2003; Allport 2020: 147-148).

Liddell Hart and Chamberlain never admitted that Germany was incentivized to short-circuit Britain's long-war advantages, or that Britain should hedge against Germany's short-war strategy. Instead, they planned on a slow wartime mobilization that would not break the bank. Such political-economics seem less realistic to soldiers. For instance, Pownall (when DMO&I) predicted that Germany "would do her best, by air or other means, to see that it wasn't a long war," because "only in economic weakness in a long war is she at all inferior" (diary, 14 March 1938, in Bond 1973: 139). Germany's peaceful occupations of Austria (March 1938) and its *Sudetenland* (October 1938) foreshadowed its short wars of 1939 to 1941. However, Liddell Hart offered them as proof that Britain "cannot win a war against Germany except by economic pressure." To deter Germany, he wrote, Britain should concentrate on "defence of the possessions that matter most to her, while seeking to foster foreign sources of distraction" ("Reflections on the Situation, its Future and Our Policy," 12 October 1938, LH 11/1938/114; 1939b: 85).

Surely Germany's occupation of the rest of Czechoslovakia, in March 1939, was enabled by the strategy Liddell Hart had urged? And surely Germany could keep picking off continental neighbours until it was strong enough to take on Britain? In June, Liddell Hart responded with a claim that 20 commodities are essential for mechanized war and are most deficient in Germany, Italy, and Japan. He claims that "the amenities and even the necessities of life" too are short – equivalent to Germany after two or three years of the Great War.

> We should not lose sight of the existing inadequacy of German, and Italian, resources for sustaining a long war – or of the inherent superiority of the resources which could be opposed to them. In any such conflict as is now on the horizon the fortunes of the Axis would turn on the chance that the war could be settled quickly. By comparison, the problem of preventing a war being short is much simpler to solve (1939b: 42).

He rightly states that Germany's shortage of petrol alone "should give her cause to pause, unless she believes in the prospect of a short war" (1939b: 25), but does not admit overland imports from Rumania, the potential for favoured imports from the USSR (as would be agreed in August), or the potential for Axis powers to capture Western-owned wells in the Middle East, South-East Asia, northern France, or southern England.

This is where he escalates the promised rewards of his strategy. In 1931, he had promised that Britain would be "better off" by following his strategy than any alternative (1932c: 41; 1935a: 45; 1944a: 43). In 1939, he warned that "if you concentrate exclusively on victory, with no thought for the after-effect, you may be too exhausted to profit by the peace." Perhaps he was using "profit" loosely, but naturally he could be read as promising net gains.

Still, the same page betrays his weakening confidence in Britain's economic capacity for a "long war." Suddenly, he adds France's economy as necessary for Western victory over Germany. Since he allows for co-belligerency but not alliance with France (so that Britain should retain unilateral options), any weighing of the French and British economies together would be inefficient at best, ineffective at worst, although he does not admit so (1939b: 25).

In August, Britain's economic strategy weakened with Sweden's refusal to stop exports of iron ore, Norway's refusal to stop flows through its ports, and the Soviet Union's pact to favour Germany with munitions and commodities. On 27 August, Liddell Hart circulated a paper, which admits that "if Russia made war supplies available for Germany, the prospect of economic pressure would be greatly diminished," but doubts that the USSR would honour it ("The Prospect in a War Over Poland," 27 August 1939, LH 11/1939/1984; 1939c: 144; 1965: II, 253-254).

JFC Fuller opposed "long war theory," as he called it, in an official submission, at Ironside's invitation. Fuller predicted that it would encourage neutrals to side with Germany to counter Britain's naval blockade, the Soviet Union and Japan to annex Britain's imperial and friendly territories in Asia and the Middle East, and Germany to win more European territory and allies before blockade could stop its warmaking ("Our Strategic Problem and a Possible Solution," enclosed with letter to CIGS, 16 October 1939, Rutgers New Brunswick). Indeed, Germany won most of Poland in 1939, Denmark, Norway, the Netherlands, Belgium, Luxemburg, and France in 1940, and the Balkan states in 1941.

Although Britain gained a new premier in May 1940, and although Churchill and Liddell Hart were now antagonistic, Churchill remained a believer in long war theory. Liddell Hart separated from Churchill's urgency for strategic bombing, but both men realized that Britain alone could not reverse Germany's command of the continent. In October 1940, Liddell Hart added the American economy as necessary to his economic strategy, but he still did not want any military application beyond blockade by sea, and raids by air, and he preferred forces to stay far from Germany itself ("Simple Arithmetic for Statesmen," 12 October 1940, LH 11/1940/90).

Hitler turned against the USSR in June 1941, and declared war on the USA in December, thus aligning the three greatest foreign economies against him. Liddell Hart did not welcome this alliance, given constraints on Britain's freedom to quit and to avoid international debts. Still, retrospectively he had to admit that all three economies were necessary to the defeat Germany. Nevertheless, his history of the Second World War repeats his list of 20 essential commodities, and his claim that they were particularly short in the Axis states, although the book does not admit his prescription for economic war without military fighting (1970: 23-24).

Moral Pressure

In September 1938, during peak German demands for the *Sudetenland*, Liddell Hart circulated a prescription for "economic and moral pressure."

The general damage resulting from a long war – such length being in any case almost inevitable – could be minimized by restricting military effort against Germany to the frustration of her offensives, at any rate in the earlier stages. This strategy, besides being wise economy of force, would also be the most productive of demoralization in her troops and people – since nothing is more weakening to the fighting will than attacks that consistently fail. The effect of economic pressure will be greatly increased by moral pressure, especially if we abstain from the bombing of civilians or from systematic invasion (paper, 9 September 1938, LH 11/1938/92; 1939b: 76-77; 1965: II, 161-162).

The subsequent British-French-Italian transfer of the *Sudetenland* to Germany disproves the effectiveness of Western "economic and moral pressure." Nevertheless, he presented the transfer as a compromise, and used Germany's occupation of the *Sudetenland* as justification for more defensiveness at home and compromise abroad ("Reflections on the Situation, its Future and Our Policy," 12 October 1938, LH 11/1938/114; 1939b: 85).

Almost a year later, he used the Nazi-Soviet pact as justification for a "slow process of economic and moral blockade." He warned against "such an offensive as would tend to stiffen the fighting spirit of the German people" ("The Prospect in a War Over Poland," 27 August 1939, LH 11/1939/1984; 1939c: 144; 1965: II, 253-254). One week into the war, he urged Britain to "renounce military attack," thereby "strengthening our moral position" and "set[ting] us free to develop economic and moral pressure" and a defensive "cordon" ("The Need for a New Technique of War," 8 September 1939, LH 1939/100; 1939d: 157). A year later, he confirms that he meant to eschew any kinetic hostilities, except through proxies.

> The only way in which [the Western Allies] might have extricated themselves from this awkward position, without allowing Hitler to have his way entirely, was by adopting the "sanctions" policy of economic and diplomatic boycott, coupled with the supply of arms to the victim of aggression. This would have done Poland quite as much good, and done much less harm to their own prestige and prospects, than a declaration of war under such adverse conditions (1941b: 302; 1954a: 230-231).

Defensive Stalemate

Liddell Hart's economic warfare and moral pressure are premised on defence-dominance. Thence, he prescribes a passive defence (other than raids by aircraft and light tanks). He promises that defensiveness would be least costly. By cost, he means human casualties, without admitting the material and opportunity costs (and cumulative human casualties) of a longer and less decisive war.

His final peacetime book is *The Defence of Britain*. It urges Britons to learn from the Great War, when "we abandoned regard for the principle of economy of force and put our utmost strength into the land struggle abroad." He wishes for Britain to confine operations to sea and air, and reasserts "the superiority of the defence over attack" (1939b: 25, 48).

> The difficulty of a "knock-out blow" is greatly increased by the modern superiority of defence over attack. That is already established on land,

> where all recent experience goes to show that an attacker needs at least a three to one superiority in armament in order to gain even a local success. And now in the air, also, the defence appears to be overtaking the advantage that the attacker formerly enjoyed.* New developments in the technique of anti-aircraft fire are giving promise of providing an obstacle to the air menace similar to that created a generation ago in land warfare by the combination of barbed wire and the entrenched machine-gun. Thus, in sum, the soldier's dream of the "lightning war" has a decreasing prospect of fulfilment (1939b: 42).

He doubts that Germany "believes in the prospect of a short war," given Germany's "economic…handicap," and "the superiority of the defence over attack" (1939b: 25). This is where he escalates his warning from four years earlier about "the difficulty which industrial power has in producing the immense output of munitions necessary even for attempting attacks" (1935a: 56; 1939b: 38, 47).

A month after publication, Chamberlain paraphrased the same argument in a letter to his sister (his greatest confidant). Britain requires "defensive forces sufficiently strong to make it impossible for the other side to win except at such a cost as to make it not worthwhile." He opposes the alternative, proposed by "Winston & Co.," for "offensive forces sufficient to win a smashing victory" (Allport 2020: 139).

A month later, within days of Germany's invasion of Poland, Liddell Hart warns against any offensive "efforts to restore Poland's territory." Here, he assumes, paradoxically, that defence-dominance applies to Germany's frontiers but not Poland's. He warns that Western offensives would result in "the mutual exhaustion of all the warring countries, with the consequent establishment of Russia's supremacy in Europe." Here, he gets to his second unadmitted paradox. Both Western failure and Russian success would encourage "other aggressive-minded countries" ("The Prospect in a War Over Poland," 27 August 1939, LH 11/1939/1984; 1939c: 144; 1965: II, 253-254). A week into the war, he wants Britain to retreat behind a unilateral "sanitary cordon." "It would throw on the Germans the responsibility of taking the offensive, with all its disadvantages" ("The Need for a New Technique of War," 8 September 1939, LH 1939/100; 1939d: 157). Whether or not this paper reached the Prime Minister, Chamberlain still shared its confidence in defence-dominance. Chamberlain reassured the US President that Germany could not break France's frontier defences, and France could not invade Germany. A visit to the frontier in December confirmed "even more strongly than before, that neither side could or should attempt to break through the fortified lines" (Self 1988: 37).

Once France was defeated, Liddell Hart realized Britain would need America to make his "sanitary cordon" work, but wanted both to remain passive ("Simple Arithmetic for Statesmen," 12 October 1940, LH 11/1940/90).

Given Beaverbrook's switch from imperial isolationism to support for the Soviet call for a "second front," Liddell Hart's best outlet became the *Daily Mail*, from March 1941. Like Liddell Hart, Rothermere had argued for defence-dominance on the ground, offense-dominance in the air, more strategic bombers and anti-aircraft guns, and Hitler's appease-ability, deterrability, and negotiability. Liddell Hart

---

* Note the contradiction with his coincident article's warning about Britain's "vulnerability" "against a knock-out blow" from the air (1939a: 127).

added an argument for a long, defensive, peripheral war, "in conjunction with America, a combination of air and naval force with economic power that will be capable of turning the tables – even without the use of force" ("Passchendaele in the Air," 12 April 1941, Daily Mail, LH 11/1941/21).

Political Revolution

In September 1938, Liddell Hart promised that a Western defensive posture would lead to "demoralization in [Germany's] troops and people – since nothing is more weakening to the fighting will than attacks that consistently fail" (paper, 9 September 1938, LH 11/1938/92; 1939b: 76-77). By October, he worried about British resilience too, given the government's supposedly inadequate preparations for air defence, civil defence, and "rallying her own people" ("Reflections on the Situation, its Future and Our Policy," 12 October 1938, LH 11/1938/114; 1939b: 85).

By June, he expects any society on the offensive to breakdown. "It is easier to launch a nation into an aggressive war than to hold together its multitudinous components" (1939b: 124). He senses "the overstrained state of the German and Italian peoples," given that "the amenities and even the necessities of life have been curtailed in the interests of armaments" (1939b: 41).

Once war began, he promised societal before economic breakdown, due to "the superiority of defence," "growth of long-range bombing forces," and "obvious lack of any enthusiasm for war among the majority of the people in every country – a state of mind which in Germany has been accentuated by years of privation" ("The Need for a New Technique of War," 8 September 1939, LH 1939/100; 1939d: 153). He lists five Allied advantages: naval; economic; a "well-fed and unstrained" civilian population; a less "apathetic" civilian population; and the "sympathy" of neutral states (Ibid: 154-155).*

Liddell Hart expects the German population to crack first, so long as the Allies eschew offensives. He wishes for a Western "declaration that we were renouncing military attack as a means of combating aggression." This would "set us free to develop economic and moral pressure," and force Germany to take the offensive.

By contrast, Fuller doubted a German revolution even after years of "blockade and air action," and warned that democracies are more vulnerable to revolution. Within the month, the Cabinet received estimates that German morale would not collapse until after German forces had suffered existential losses ("Our Strategic Problem and a Possible Solution," 16 October 1939, Rutgers New Brunswick; Colville 1985: 50).

So it proved. Anti-Nazi rebels did not act "with any conviction until July 1944." They failed at every attempt. Germany did not surrender until after Hitler had committed suicide and Allied forces from East and West had met inside Germany (Allport 2020: 125).

Legacy

Liddell Hart expected the war to stagnate within days, as mechanized armies

---

* He warns that neutrals would be alienated by any "attempt to crush a rival rather than to uphold international justice," to reject German terms, or to "acquire the appearance of being the attacking side against a Germany keeping the defensive."

consume quicker than they could be supplied – exacerbated by air attacks and labour strikes. He prescribed economic blockade, although he later repudiated its ethics. Thence, he relied upon "moral pressure," which reduces to renunciation of aggression. He proscribed offensives, as cost-ineffective and unethical. Before the war, he had promised that raids on logistics and industry, by light tanks and heavy bombers, would be efficient and decisive (cumulatively), but in wartime he proscribed them too. He expected offensiveness to end in economic collapse, social malaise, and political revolution. He expected the war to last ten years, and end in negotiated settlement. He was wrong on everything, except Britain's indebtedness and relegation to the Soviet Union and America.

Just because Britain was on the winning side does not prove that the long war strategy was right. It played into the hands of the aggressors, which planned a series of short wars, separated by economic exploitation and recovery. Liddell Hart was confident in deterrence and defence-dominance, so did not foresee German, Italian, or Japanese aggression towards or victory over Western states.

Once Poland, Denmark, Norway, Luxemburg, the Netherlands, Belgium, and France had fallen, he hoped, perversely, that stalemate was confirmed. He offered a false choice between perpetuating the current stalemate for years or quitting now. When he suddenly opposed "long war," he was actually arguing for immediate negotiation as the only alternative to years of stalemate (1941a: 141).

The war ended four years earlier and more decisively than Liddell Hart had expected. Writing in early 1945, with victory imminent, his only explanation is that strategic bombing is not as shocking as peacetime advocates had expected. He does not admit he was one of them. A decade later, he added the lie that only he and Lloyd George dissented from the consensus that the war would be long.* He quotes from papers he had written in August 1939. In fact, they are arguments for Britain and France to avoid war or wage a long economic-moral-defensive war until the enemy agrees to negotiate ("The Prospect in a War Over Poland," 27 August 1939, LH 11/1939/1984; 1941a: 144; 1946b: 25; 1957: 4; 1970: 17n). He even reinterpreted Germany's quick victories as parts of a long war he had predicted.

> For no reasonable calculation of the respective forces and resources provided any ground for believing that the war could be "swift and short," or even for hoping that France and Britain alone would be able to overcome Germany – however long the war continued (1957: 3; 1970: 16).

He contradicts the above by admitting that the War could have ended quicker if one side or the other had handled certain opportunities differently (1968b: 794):

- the Western Allies could have defeated Germany on the continent in 1940 given the same "mobile-mechanized warfare" as the Germans (1950: 13; 1960a: 104; 1965: II, 280; 1970: 66; Walters 1961: 27);†
- Germany could have defeated Britain if it had "throw[n] a force over the Channel in the weeks immediately following the collapse in France, when the British Army was disorganized and almost disarmed" (1950: 200; 1954a: 251-252; 1960a: 10; 1970: 89-90);

---

* He blames the consensus on Halifax and Churchill.
† Contradictorily, he also wished that the French and British had held the river lines without counteroffensives (1950: 10-12, 85; 1969: 209; 1970: 33-34, 70).

- Axis forces could have conquered Egypt if Hitler had authorized regional commanders' current requirements in either 1941 or 1942 (1948: 154-156);
- the Western Allies could have cleared Africa in 1941 if Churchill had not diverted to Greece (1950: 22; 1954a: 275, 277; 1969: 211-212; 1970: 131);
- Britain could have held Malaya and Burma against Japan's surprise attacks (December 1941) if Churchill had not diverted forces to the Middle East ("The End of a Bluff," *Daily Mirror*, 23 January 1957, LH 10/1957/6; 1960a: 34);
- Germany could have retained the continent if it had not turned on the USSR in June 1941 (1948: 40; 1950: 200-201; 1954a: 253-254; 1956a: 100; 1969: 209, 212; 1970: 141);
- Germany could have occupied Russia in 1941 given more consistent objectives (1948: 166; 1954a: 258), tanks (1948: 41), "tracked transport" (1948: 167; 1950: 33; 1956a: 111; 1960a: 193; 1970: 158, 164, 170; Walters 1961: 28), or "developed" "roads" (1948: 167; 1968b: 769; Walters 1961: 28);
- Germany could have avoided defeat if Hitler had not proscribed retreat from Autumn 1942 onwards (1948: 154-155, 189; 1950: 35-42; 1956a: 115; 1968b: 775; 1970: 485, 569, 711);
- German forces could have defeated the Western landings in Normandy (1944) if they had concentrated quicker at the beaches, or withdrawn quicker behind the River Seine (1948: 243-245; 1950: 51; 1970: 550, 557).

His post-war counter-factuals are well informed and judged. The trouble is, he never admitted their contradiction of what he had assessed during the War.

Brian Bond (1977: 114) admitted that "he does not seem to have grasped that economic pressures, as well as the ideological frenzy prevalent in Nazi Germany, would inevitably manifest themselves in the style of warfare adopted." Later, Bond (1978: 426) admitted that Liddell Hart did not foresee Germany securing supplies from a friendly Soviet Union or in conquered territories. Still, Bond never admitted Liddell Hart's expectations of long war, stalemate, failed offensives, and negotiated peace. Bond's student, Danchev (1998), followed suit. Michael Howard (1970a; 1970b; 1976: 131-132) pretended that Liddell Hart prescribed and expected a Blitzkrieg. Howard's student, Lawrence Freedman (2017: 56), quoted Liddell Hart's early expectation that aerial bombardment would stop wars within days (1925: 40), as if exemplary of a consensus on short and decisive future wars, and ignored Liddell Hart's later and more enduring expectation that wars would last years, indecisively.*

Len Deighton had already worked out from *British Way in Warfare* (1932) and *Defence of Britain* (1939) that Liddell Hart's strategy for Britain was "economic pressure...naval blockade and strategic bombing."

> In fact, as Germany extended her territories and traded with the East, the naval blockade affected her less and less. Strategic bombing proved a catastrophe, and Liddell Hart's suggestion that psychological warfare might be the indirect approach that would overthrow Hitler also proved a fiasco (Deighton 1980: 118).

---

* Curiously, Freedman (2017: 61) refers to "they [who] argued for fast-moving and enveloping maneuvers" by tanks, without naming anybody. Perhaps he wished to avoid naming JFC Fuller, whom his book overlooks entirely. Freedman (2017: 51-52) names a few "internationalists" and "appeasers" that expected war to be avoided entirely, but not Liddell Hart.

16
Germany's Prophet, 1940s-1950s

Liddell Hart was naturally discredited by Britain's and his own failures. Britain failed to appease and deter Germany from 1935 to 1939, to defend Poland in 1939, Western European allies in 1940, and Balkan allies in 1941, to defeat Germany by economic, moral, and political pressure, to avoid expeditions to the continent, and to win cheaply and without American credits. He failed to regain official influence, to persuade Britain to quit, and to predict the course and duration of the war.

He generally avoided his experience of the war. His post-war books include claims to have foreseen this or counselled that, but such claims are patchy and often decontextualized. From 1954, Michael Howard (1999: vi) observed that "he craved recognition and acceptance, and to the end of his life never quite understood why he had not retained the influence and revived the high honours that he felt were rightly his due."* In the 1960s, Robert O'Neill (1990: 111) realized that Liddell Hart "believed himself to have been unfairly damned by politicians opposed to his views, wrongly excluded from influence, and denied credit." Brian Bond (1977: 121) found that Liddell Hart "seldom spoke spontaneously about the war years." Clearly "the Second World War was a period of disappointment and frustration."

Liddell Hart's memoirs avoid the war, beyond a short "epilogue," covering September 1939 to May 1940. The epilogue is mostly a reprise of others' mistakes, and ends with a claim to vindication.

> [T]here was a tragic irony in having to watch, as a mere onlooker, my ideas being applied to pierce the defence of France, my birthplace, and put in extreme jeopardy my own country (1965: II, 281).

Elsewhere, he admits that he needed "six months to recharge" and "more than two years before I was really fit again" (1965: II, 251-252). He wrote the epilogue in July 1963, two years before publication. The publisher had demanded cuts, which should have motivated a third volume. He never started it. His history of the Second World War (1970) is similarly vague but self-righteous about what he was doing. Bond (1977: 7, 119) surely was thinking about his published record when writing that his wartime "activities and beliefs" are "most mysterious." However, Bond admitted that Liddell Hart's "thinking during the war is extremely well-documented in his files." Bond's biography simply skips over his mentor's wartime record, so John Mearsheimer was first to publish an evaluation.

He had boundless energy, and it is no exaggeration to say that the over-

---

* Liddell Hart died before Howard wrote this. Howard's autobiography implies doubts since 1940. By his own account, Howard (2006: 45, 154) resented wartime peaceniks, given that he expected his Jewish mother and perhaps himself to be deported by any British government that made peace. For the same reason, he resented post-war apologists, including A.J.P. Taylor, who had taught him at Oxford in 1941. Howard does not admit that Liddell Hart (1969) cooperated in Taylor's apologism for Britain's appeasement and passivity.

riding goal in his life from the Fall of France until his death in 1970 was establishing his place in history (Mearsheimer 1988: 9, 215-216).

By 1942, Liddell Hart worked towards new and revived careers. For each, he leveraged a prior pose: neglected prophet. He tried to become an expert on femininity, to restore his journalist career, to become a professor at Oxford, and (most successfully) to reinvent himself as the inspiration for German force employment.

Femininity

The year of 1942 was a year of transition for Liddell Hart. He released another anthology of prior writings (1942a), with a negative title (*This Expanding War*). He released a new edition of *British Way in Warfare* (1942b). Publishers stopped asking for proposals. He divorced Jessie, and married Kathleen. His longer-running plan for a general "philosophy" of war would not progress beyond a chaotic collection of snippets from his writings, published in Spring 1944, as *Thoughts on War*.

In May 1944, her daughters returned, after more than four years with relatives in Canada. They were now teenagers, which stimulated his intervention in their manners and fashions, to the dismay of everyone except Mr. and Mrs. Hart. He pondered a permanent refocus. Kathleen was his model, muse, and champion.

> Basil is in the middle of a creative burst and has written a brilliant memorandum on the subject of WOMEN. [I] will send it to you. He wants to start a campaign for the refeminization of women so that they can fulfil their proper function in the world. He says he is finding it so inspiring to get on to something constructive, and he didn't realize until he started how fed up he was with war (KLH to her parents, 24 September 1944).

His experimentation on her daughters provoked opposition from her brothers, to whom he responded with the same claims to "truth" and counter-orthodoxy he had used more than 20 years earlier to justify his military and political writings.

> You may say that I am much in the minority in regard to the present issue – but that has always been the case on every issue when I arrived at conclusions that were fresh, and therefore strange, to people whose minds ran in the conventional ruts of the moment (to his brother-in-law – Barry "Matthew" Sullivan, 7 September 1948).

By the end of the war, he was distracted by a local opportunity to interview senior German officers. He continued to submit articles on feminine manners and fashions for years, but never published a book on these subjects.

Journalism

During the Second World War, Liddell Hart founded a Military Commentators Circle, but he did so by correspondence, from the Lake District. His most notable co-founder was Belisha, who had worked as a journalist before entering politics, although never as a military correspondent. Both men worried about their post-war careers. Belisha had withdrawn from the National Liberal caucus in 1942, and remained in the House of Commons as an independent, on borrowed time.

Liddell Hart's contract with Rothermere's *Daily Mail* ran out in February 1945.

In the same month, Lloyd George was ennobled, but died in March, before he could take his seat in the House of Lords. In August, Belisha realized he had been voted out of the Commons. Meanwhile, as Japan negotiated peace, Liddell Hart pressed Rowlands to prevail on Beaverbrook to hire him as a peacetime opinion-writer for *The Daily Express*. Beaverbrook did not take Rowlands' advice, so Liddell Hart wrote directly. This time he reframes his potential as "a political commentator in the wider sense." This approach also failed. More galling, Beaverbrook appointed Rowlands as a member of the board governing his newspaper conglomerate, and ignored Liddell Hart as a source or a subject in his subsequent nine books (to Rowlands, 24 August, LH 1/613; to Beaverbrook, 10 and 15 September 1945, LH 1/52).

Liddell Hart let the Military Commentators Circle expire, but also planned to move nearer to London. Thanks again to charitable friends, in Spring 1946 he moved 300 miles,* although still with no certain employment.

Belisha too failed to return to full-time journalism. He joined the Conservative Party, which helped him to win a seat on Westminster City Council in 1947, but failed to win his return to the House of Commons in 1950. He settled for a peerage, as announced in January 1954. In March, Belisha and Liddell Hart restarted the Military Commentators Circle, with Liddell Hart as founding President, although the Circle employed a Chairman and a Secretary to do the real work. In truth, most of the attendees were retired military personnel, who attended to hear each other speak. Belisha was supportive, but died in 1957. Liddell Hart resigned from the Presidency in 1960, except that he remained honorary President (LH 5/22/1 to /2).

Oxford I

In Summer 1945, Liddell Hart sought one of the three Fellowships at Nuffield College, which had appointed its first Fellows just before the Second World War. His search was vain, given that Nuffield is Oxford's smallest and only fully post-graduate college. The warden – a long-standing Professor of Economics – quickly and undiplomatically replied that the Board was seeking senior academics (Sir Henry Clay to LH, 21 September 1945, LH 13/44).

In April 1946, Oxford sought to restore the Chichele Professorship of Military History (now to be renamed "...of History of War"), which had been suspended in wartime. The incumbent (Ernest Swinton, since 1925) was 77 years old, and disinterested in returning. Gilbert Murray (1866-1957) was Liddell Hart's only academic recommender, and hardly relevant (Murray was a Professor of Greek, and acquainted as a partisan Liberal). Another referee was Maurice Hankey, who had emerged as a righteous critic of the wartime government that had dismissed him. The third was Archibald Wavell, currently Viceroy of India, although this civilian position reminded everyone of Wavell's failings as a commander. Wavell recommended two other candidates. Liddell Hart was one of 23 applicants. He was not one of the four interviewees. Hobart was one of three flag officers interviewed, suggesting that soldiering was valued over writing.

The interviewee with whom Liddell Hart could be considered most directly competitive was Cyril Falls (1888-1971): another infantry Captain of the Great War,

---

* He moved from Ambleside to a large Georgian country house (Tilford House) in Surrey, 40 road-miles from central London, 30 road-miles from the southern coast.

but also a decorated staff officer, a veteran of France from 1915 to 1918, an official historian since the 1920s, military correspondent for *The Times* newspaper (after Liddell Hart had quit), a critic of wartime Liddell Hartian thinking, and a broader linguist (English, French, Italian, German). Falls was chosen (Bond 1977: 165; Hattendorf 1990: 27-34; Strachan 1991: 62-64).

Liddell Hart gave different explanations to different correspondents. To Maurice Hankey, he blamed his opposition to government policy during the war (26 June 1946, LH 1/352). To his son, he blamed an academic-government complex.

> Universities used to prefer originality but have been acquiring more and more the colour of official institutions. Of course my views on the futility of victory were not [of the same colour]. It is somewhat ironic, however, that just as the scope of the Chair has been enlarged from "military history" to "the history of war" it should be filled by a man whose work has been confined to military history in the narrowest sense (BHLH to AJLH, 1 July 1946, LHCMA KLH).

Similarly, he persuaded Brian Bond (1977: 165) that Falls was "orthodox and 'safe' but was patently lacking in Liddell Hart's range of interests." In fact, the endowment specifies "military history in the narrowest sense."

Liddell Hart would need to rely on new books for his reinvention.

Germany's inspiration

From August 1945, Liddell Hart started interviewing nearby German prisoners of war, with the idea of compiling their memories into a book. However, he lacked a publisher for new works. In the 1920s, Liddell Hart had leveraged many publishers – of which the friendliest were John Murray and Douglas Blackwood. In 1930, his main publisher of books became Geoffrey Faber. Faber & Faber Limited was otherwise not a match: it specialized in art, poetry, and left-wing polemics. It remained his main publisher through the Second World War, although the relationship was in decline. His failure to deliver a promised "philosophy" of war was the last straw. Faber published his *Thoughts on War* in 1944 and a short book on military trends in 1946, with little oversight and no commerical success. The former gathers snippets from private notes and published writings, within vaguely themed chapters, sometimes repeated across chapters. The latter refers to the current war despite an epilogue written afterwards. Faber subsequently committed to only reprints and new editions of pre-war legacies.

In 1946, Desmond Flower (1907-1997), owner of Cassell & Company Limited, agreed to publish Liddell Hart's book on what German prisoners told him. In 1947, Flower commissioned memoirs and a history of the Second World War too. Liddell Hart would take decades to complete them. Every year, he claimed commercial, official, and medical distractions. These distractions peaked each winter, suggesting seasonally affected disorder. With the help of friends, he spent winters in seaside resorts. From 1947, he restarted his summer trips to France, now with Kathleen.

> [W]e made almost yearly visits to Western Europe to study battlefields and landing beaches, to visit old friends, and, maps in hand, to check data for this History [of the Second World War]. He loved beautiful country, cathedrals, and good food, so for our tours the Guide Michelin, battlefield

maps, and tourists' guides were always put in the car together, and careful daily notes about terrain, food, and church architecture were dictated to me for subsequent filing in the ever-growing records (1970: vii).

Liddell Hart returned to expensive tastes but not yet expensive income. In Spring 1948, he moved to a smaller home.*

Coincidentally, Cassell published his book on what German prisoners told him. None suggested he had invented German mechanized warfare. Since 1939, this had been termed "Blitzkrieg" or "lightning war" by Anglophones, but is best described as sustained penetrations by concentrated combined-arms. German use of the word contradicts his pre-war doubts that Germany "believes in the prospect of a short war," given its "economic…handicap," and "the superiority of defence over attack" (1939b: 25). German practice contradicts his pre-war reductionism to raids by bombers and (separately) light tanks, for days behind enemy lines, without the encumbrances of sustainment assets. Some interviewees required more sustainment assets than even the *Panzer* divisions had received. No interviewee could specify anything he had written, although some recalled his journalism. "Blitzkrieg" does not appear in his book (in either German or English). Nonetheless, he suggested that "most were…old students of my military writings" (1948: 113).

A Swiss edition followed in 1949, a German in 1950,† beside an anthology of thoughts on the last war and Cold War, masquerading as a coherent proposal for *Defence of the West*. Here he characterizes "Blitzkrieg" as "fast and deep armoured thrusts" and "deep strategic penetration by armoured forces." He claims to have invented them in the 1920s, as "a strategic adaptation for armoured forces of the tactical 'expanding torrent'" (1950: 33, 221). Indeed, in 1925 he had envisioned combined-arms riding automobiles into the enemy heartland. However, by 1930 he reduced ground offensives to raids by light tanks alone. He did not refer to depth or penetration until Summer 1945, when he characterizes "Blitzkrieg" as "the rapid and deep penetration of the [German] armoured divisions" (1946b: 28).

In 1950, Flower agreed to publish an edited version of Field-Marshal Erwin Rommel's papers (1953), and an official history of the British tank arm (1959a), which the Royal Tank Regiment had commissioned Liddell Hart to write in 1946. He edited Rommel's papers little, but footnoted false claims of influence. More consequentially, in 1952 he introduced an English-edition of Field-Marshal Heinz Guderian's memoirs, with the addition of a claim he had influenced Guderian too, without admitting that he had suggested what Guderian should add. The deaths of Rommel in 1944 and of Guderian in 1954, and the linguistic, political, and economic insecurities of their families, helped his fabrications (Macksey 1967; 1972; 1981: 155-156; 1988: 48; Mearsheimer 1988: 163-165, 185-191; Danchev 1998a: 224-225).

He took little interest in the official history of the tank arm, so the RTR allocated officers as writers. By the 1950s, Hobart was in charge, but he effectively gave up on Liddell Hart's compliance with his specifications, suggestions, and edits. Hobart died in 1957, by when the RTR had effectively lost influence. Belatedly, Liddell Hart commissioned friends to provide data or to write chapters, and played them

---

* He moved more than 80 road-miles north from Tilford House, Surrey, to Wolverton, Bucks.
† The Swiss edition was titled *Die Strategie einer Diktatur* (The Strategy of a Dictator). The German edition was titled *Jetzt dürfen sie reden* (Now They Can Talk).

against each other to excuse his own lack of knowledge. Yet the book itself does not admit any co-authors. Desperate for completion, the commissioners accepted insertions that misrepresent his pre-war views on tanks and even foreign policies (Newsome 2024: Chapter 12).

In the same decade, former publishers started re-publishing his pre-war books. Mr. and Mrs. Hart could afford to spend winters in tropical resorts. However, income is not the same as reputation. To accelerate his reinvention, he went to America and Israel, as explained in the next two chapters.

(Top) Manfred Rommel (Erwin Rommel's son), Frau Speidel, BHLH, KLH, and General Hans Speidel (Rommel's chief of staff, 1944), in Freudenstadt, Baden-Württemberg, 22 June 1950 (LH 13/104/9).

(Bottom) Heinz Guderian and BHLH at Guderian's home in Schwangau, Bavaria, near the border with Austria, 26 June 1950 (LH 13/104/9).

17

America's Adopted Hero, 1950s

Liddell Hart's rehabilitation in America proceeded through American editions of what German prisoners had told him, a publicity tour, Robert Icks' faithful promotion, introduction to American academics such as Theodore Ropp, Ropp's introduction to his student Jay Luvaas, Liddell Hart's false claims to influence US Army General Douglas MacArthur, and his consideration of emigration, given his dissatisfaction with his influence elsewhere.

German Generals Talk

Liddell Hart's book on what German prisoners had told him was published in Britain as *The Other Side of the Hill*, in America as *The German Generals Talk*.

The immediate American reception was sceptical. One American reviewer rightly noted that "after the First World War he drew its lessons from static trench warfare." Liddell Hart wrote to the newspaper, claiming he had "often repeated the prophecy that 'in the future we shall not again witness the stagnation of trench warfare owing to the new mobility brought in by the tank, the caterpillar tractor, the aeroplane'." Here he paraphrases the conclusion to an article written in 1922, which is not representative of his histories of the Great War, his doctrines before 1922, or his strategies and policies after 1930 (1922d: 294; William Harlan Hale, "Meeting of Military Minds," *New York Herald Tribune*, 26 September 1948: 2; LH to the editors, 5 November 1948, LH 9/24/16).

In 1949, he summarized the book for the US Army's *Infantry Journal*, which, in wartime, had republished Fuller's mechanized doctrine of the 1930s, including a new edition of his most famous book (1943). The editors wrote a fair biography.

> In the years preceding World War II, Captain Hart gained some distinction as an advocate of the idea that in modern war the defence was much stronger than the offense; a principle badly shattered in World War I[I]. Nevertheless, he had tremendous influence on military thinking in Great Britain (1949: 31).

Liddell Hart wrote a letter of complaint.

> European soldiers would be amused to hear that I am mainly known in the USA as an advocate of defence. To them I was known primarily, from 1920 on, as the exponent of armoured attack and of the future Blitzkrieg methods.

The editors printed Liddell Hart's letter in a later issue, and added an apology.

> The Journal's humblest apologies. Our statement was an editorial error which should have been caught and deleted, for we did know better. We have long regretted the fact that a completely erroneous idea of Captain Liddell Hart's actual military thought and recommendation has so long persisted ("Letters," Infantry Journal, June 1949, 64/6: 53).

In 1951, second editions of *Other Side of the Hill* were published in Britain and America, although he was disappointed with reception. The British electorate's rejection of the Labour government in October rekindled his Anglophobia. Thus, the timing was good, when the US Embassy telephoned to relay an invitation to lecture at US military colleges. Nevertheless, he decided that the invitation was insufficiently governmental, academic, and Anglo.

> In the last year I have had similar invitations from more than half a dozen countries. The prospect does not have much attraction and I have been wondering why. I feel that it is due to a basic loss of interest in military things, and even in military thought. And that, I suppose, is a natural sequel to manifest fulfilment as well as to 35 years' intensive study in this field. I ought to have cut clean out of it after 1945 and entered an entirely fresh field, as I had the urge to do. I cannot expect to produce a revolution in warfare twice in my lifetime, and anything less that I could achieve in this way would be an anticlimax ("A Reflection on Losing Interest in a Subject," 14 February 1952, LH 11/1952/2).

North America Tour

In subsequent months, Robert Icks persuaded him otherwise. Since 1929, Icks, a retired US Army Ordnance officer, had relied on him for information on British armaments, while he relied on Icks for information on American armaments, for their respective publications. In Summer 1952, Icks persuaded him to tour North America to publicize the second edition of *German Generals Talk*. That Autumn, Liddell Hart made his first visit.

For September, Icks and the US Embassy arranged talks at the US Army's Armor Center at Fort Knox in Kentucky, the US Naval War College at Newport in Rhode Island, and the US Marine Corps Schools at Quantico in Virginia. Liddell Hart advanced a long biography, in the third-person, most of whose statements are untrue.

> Liddell Hart was an early and vigorous advocate of air power, and an exponent of mechanized warfare. General Guderian, creator of the German World II armoured forces, called himself "one of Liddell Hart's disciples in tank affairs." In 1942, Marshal Rommel wrote: "The British could have avoided most of their defeats if they had better studied the modern theories expounded by Liddell Hart." General Patton told Mr. Liddell Hart, in 1944: "I have been nourished on your books for 20 years, and gained much from your ideas."
>
> Mr. Liddell Hart has been a recognized military authority for many years. He paid a visit to the French Army in 1926 and gave advice on its reorganization. In 1929 he wrote a manual governing the use of the armoured forces. In 1932, he was approached by a Russian delegation concerning his acting as military advisor to the Red Army, but he turned this offer down...
>
> In 1937, Mr. Liddell Hart was appointed personal advisor to the British

War Minister. However, he resigned his post a year later,* hoping to better arouse the British public to the urgent need for build-up and reorganization in the armed forces (1952: 29-30).

He was best received by the USMC, which was least familiar with his work. "Among the honours he received that gave him most pleasure was his honorary membership of the US Marine Corps, and until he died he daily wore the gold tie clip presented to him on that occasion," recalled his wife (1970: vii). He accepted an invitation from the USMC to edit two accounts of the last German offensive in Egypt. He biographed himself "as one of the great military minds of the century," the "author of no less than 27 volumes dealing with military tactics, history, strategy, and the doctrines of national defence..." (1956b: 2). In 1960, the *Marine Corps Gazette* agreed to publish an interview by a young friend, which starts with a paraphrase of the biography from 1952: "Liddell Hart is one of the world's outstanding military writers..." (Walters 1961: 22).

Icks

To the Armor Center, Icks said that "Liddell Hart occupies an undisputed position as a leading military historian...but whether he is a military theorist of note or a false prophet is where opinions on him diverge, often violently." Yet Icks clearly sided with the "military theorist of note."

> He has the gift of making even complex military problems simple to understand and at the same time presents them in relationship to the larger aspects of their impact on national and international situations...
>
> Try as any man will, he cannot completely divorce his emotions from facts as he sees them. But so far as it is humanly possible, I believe Liddell Hart tries with honesty (Icks 1952: 25, 27).

Along the way, Icks retold Liddell Hart's false narrative.

> Sweden, Denmark, and Switzerland consulted him on internal military problems[,] and his own country did likewise...
>
> [T]he Germans almost won World War II by following his precepts. Later the Russians, and to a much lesser and later extent the Allies, defeated Germany by following them...[A]lthough the Germans gave him credit for their near victory, the Allies never have admitted his influence on their final victory (Icks 1952: 25-27).

Icks (1952: 26) peddled at least another three lies:
1. "the French were incensed over his criticism of their military theories" (in fact, he praised French posture, force structure, and force employment);
2. his "theories of dynamic defence in 1939 represented a belief that it was necessary to buy time" (in fact, Liddell Hart promised deterrence);
3. he has written "consistently from the Twenties on."

---

* This error of commission is repeated by Luvaas (1964: 411).

Ropp

In the audience was Professor Theodore Ropp (1911-2000), then at the history department at Duke University. Ropp introduced himself, and started an energetic correspondence, and frequently visited Liddell Hart at home.

Ropp's subsequent book on *War in the Modern World* starts with a quote from Liddell Hart, relies on Liddell Hart as source (even for American history), and was proof-read by Liddell Hart (although most of his comments arrived between the first and second editions). Both editions list him as one of the Britons "more honoured abroad than at home" (1959: 291; 1962: 311).

Luvaas

Ropp introduced Liddell Hart to his doctoral student Jay Luvaas, who moved to Britain to work in Liddell Hart's archives and undertake a history of *British Military Thought*, which concludes with a hagiographic chapter, edited by Liddell Hart.

> A brilliant and prolific journalist, an imaginative, far-sighted theorist, and unselfish and aggressive advocate of army reform, and an historian of commanding stature and integrity, Liddell Hart has often despaired of ever teaching anybody anything (1964: 376).

Luvaas often seems to paraphrase Liddell Hart's recollection of a publication rather than the content. For instance, Luvaas (1964: 381, 404) misreports Liddell Hart's second article (1919b) as "integrating a section of tanks into each infantry combat unit," and "advocating infantry together with tanks as integral parts of the same combat unit." In fact, it integrates one carrier for each platoon's equipment. Luvaas (382) claims that Liddell Hart's article on "The Problems of Mechanization" (1922a) persuaded the Germans of "armoured warfare." Yet Luvaas admits that Liddell Hart did not concede Fuller's advocacy for tanks until 1922, and did not publish any plagiarism until 1924. Luvaas evades the plagiarism by claiming that "Liddell Hart was more specific than Fuller in his recommendations."

Luvaas (398, 402) claims (without evidence) that Liddell Hart persuaded the British Army to start the Experimental Mechanized Force in 1927, and the German Army to adopt "Blitzkrieg" in the 1930s. Yet Luvaas (406) admits also that, by 1934, Liddell Hart encouraged Hobart's experiments with 1st Tank Brigade, "operating independently against enemy objectives many miles behind the battle zone."

Without admitting the contradiction between all-tank raids and combined-arms penetrations, Luvaas pretends that Liddell Hart "had become deeply involved with other and more pressing problems, and time did not permit a final synthesis of his views on armoured warfare." As for defence-dominance, Luvaas (414-415) claims that "his defensive doctrines often were distorted and ridiculed," and constrained by "the policy of *The Times* and the tense political situation."

Luvaas (1965) contributed a chapter to Howard's Festschift in honour of Liddell Hart, but fortunately its scope ends in the year 1914.

MacArthur

American appreciation encouraged Liddell Hart to write to retired US Army General Douglas MacArthur, to suggest that the United Nations' landing at

Inchon, Korea, in September 1950 was inspired by a book Liddell Hart had published in 1927. In 1935, MacArthur had praised the book by letter, without mentioning any amphibious lessons (LH 1/469).

Liddell Hart took no interest in MacArthur's appointment as Army Commander Far East in 1941, or promotion to Supreme Allied Commander Southwest Pacific in 1942, or occupation of Japan in 1945, except to archive a few press cuttings about associated campaigns. His *History of the Second World War* mentions MacArthur only to criticize MacArthur's opposition to indirect approaches to Japan, so that he could return to the Philippines, which he had abandoned in 1942 (1970: 620).

Liddell Hart's interest peaked in 1951 with MacArthur's dismissal from command of United Nations forces in Korea by the US President (for over-reaching orders and criticizing the President), with which he identified as a fellow maverick (LH 15/5/551). Yet he waited until 1959 before claiming credit for Inchon. General MacArthur diplomatically replied that he was inspired by his own "imagination."

> In reply to your query with reference to the integration of the Inchon campaign with Wolfe's Quebec operation, so much time has elapsed since then that I would hesitate to attempt a categorical reply. That I have read and studied your account in Great Captains Unveiled [1927c] is unquestionable (MacArthur to LH, 12 November 1959, LH 13/37).

Nevertheless, Liddell Hart published claims that his chapter on the Mongols (1927c) "caught the imagination of General MacArthur, who emphasised it in his 1935 report as chief of staff of the United States Army." Although MacArthur's report points to the Mongols, it does not mention Liddell Hart.

Liddell Hart's memoirs (published a year after MacArthur's death) add claims that his journalism on the Tank Brigade influenced MacArthur's report in 1935, and MacArthur referred to the chapter in a press conference (1960a: 190; 1965: I, 75, 271-272). Luvaas (1990: 16) admits that at best the two men were thinking along similar lines, as proven by highlighting of certain lines on a copy of MacArthur's report, which Luvaas had found in Liddell Hart's archives, with no date of acquisition.

Depression

Liddell Hart's reception by Americans belied his insecurity in Britain. He again pondered a switch of focus to femininity, and of home to America.

> Yet a contrary pull remains. The receptiveness to my ideas that I have found abroad – greatly increased since the war, in contrast to here – does generate an incentive both to fresh activity, and to its transference to a different site. That is why I found the vitality of America stimulating (to Chester Wilmot, 27 April 1953, LH 13/32).

He was more depressed on his sixtieth birthday. He complained that no Briton in government, military, or academia was seeking his services. He doubted his prospects as a historian too. His official history of the tank arm remained outstanding since 1946, his history of the Second World War since 1947. He found the primary research tedious, despite outsourcing most of it ("A Reflection at Sixty," 31 October 1955, LH 11/955/9). He obsessed about his reinvention. For help, he now prioritized a second foreign nationality: Israeli.

In September 1967, BHLH signed this portrait for one-time author John Wheldon, "with every wish for his book and admiration for his studies of mechanical warfare." He had already written an endorsement, which was printed on the back cover, when published in Spring 1968: "Its approach is refreshingly out of the ordinary." In fact, the book paraphrases what he had told Wheldon, who does not cite anything he had written before the Second World War. Wheldon (1968: 8, 33, 85, 143) tells of struggles between stupid, conservative, attritional Generals and Liddell Hart's "logical defensive system" (unspecified), "psychological weapons" (unspecified), and "expanding torrent," "indirect approach," and "Blitzkrieg" (which, according to Wheldon, aim at the enemy's "psychology," not forces) (RACTM).

18

Israel's Inspiration, 1940s-1960s

Liddell Hart gained little interest or influence on the Zionists of Palestine during the Mandate period. However, he subsequently corresponded with Israeli principals of the Independence War (1948) and Second Arab-Israeli War (1956), which prompted his tour of Israel in 1960. Subsequently, he sought evidence for influence on the Israelis during the Six Day War of 1967. After his death, his disciples even claimed his influence on the Yom Kippur War of 1973.

Mandate Palestine

Britain administered mandates in Palestine and Transjordan from 1920 to 1948, during which Jewish immigration accelerated. Immigration provoked conflict with the largely Arab Muslim residents. The Jewish "Defence" (*Haganah*) organization (established 1920) struck back. Three men were involved and contacted Liddell Hart then or later: Orde Wingate, Yigael Yadin, and Yitzhak Sadeh.

Wingate

Liddell Hart opened correspondence with Wingate in 1934, when Wingate's participation in an archaeological expedition from Sudan into Libya was publicized. His interest was rekindled in September 1937, when Archibald Wavell took command of GHQ Palestine. By then, Wingate was on the Intelligence staff there. All three shared an interest in "unorthodox" or "irregular" warfare. Wingate had adopted Christian Zionism, which encouraged more partiality towards the Jews, in a year when Arab violence against British soldiers was peaking. He organized counter-insurgent "Special Night Squads" from members of the British Army and the *Haganah*. In November 1938, Wingate took leave in England, sought a meeting with Liddell Hart, and handed over copies of nine secret estimates and reports, dated from June to September. Later that month, at Wingate's request, Liddell Hart wrote to Winston Churchill, to suggest an introduction. Churchill had criticized the government for under-investment in the counter-insurgency, although his preference was for "air control," which perhaps explains why he did not reply. Liddell Hart too favoured air control, which perhaps explains why he subsequently ignored Wingate (LH 2W/167/1-4; LH 15/5/300; Wavell 1948: 62, 78).

In late 1940, Wavell, as Middle East Commander-in-Chief, restarted Wingate's career in "unorthodox" operations, for the invasion of Abyssinia. Liddell Hart remained disengaged. In 1942, Wavell (1948: 64-68), as commander in India, restarted Wingate's career a second time, which ended with Wingate's wilful death in an overloaded aircraft while returning from inspections of his "Chindits," during their second raid into Burma, in March 1944. Liddell Hart (1970: 368, 517) criticized the raids' cost-ineffectiveness, and traced Wingate's failings back to 1938.

> Wingate, then only a captain serving in Palestine, came to see me...and was obviously filled with the idea of giving the theory [irregular warfare] a fresh and wider application. But I was beginning to have doubts – not of

its immediate efficacy, but of its long-term effects...These lessons of history were too lightly disregarded by those who planned to promote violent insurrections as part of Allied war policy (1950: 65-67).

However, after Israel's victory in 1956, Liddell Hart claimed influence.

> He came to see me several times to discuss the training of the "SNS" (1970: 366n).
>
> Wingate told me how he had been applying the ideas in my early books on infantry tactics and my recent book on The Future of Infantry [1933b]. He also, with evident pride at that time, said that he had a family connection with Lawrence. Although I did not feel that he was intellectually on Lawrence's level, I was impressed by his force of character – which had a Cromwellian flavour – as well as by his tactical flair. His views about the Middle East situation, and the potential value of the young Zionists, also coincided with mine (1965: II, 181-182).

In fact, Liddell Hart was not impressed by Wingate's tactics, character, or Zionism – at least not enough to meet or correspond after 1938.

Yadin

Yigael Yadin (1917-1984) was a senior officer in the Haganah. In 1975, he told Brian Bond that, during the Second World War, he had translated parts of either *The Decisive Wars of History* (1929a) or *The Strategy of Indirect Approach* (1941), to impart general strategy. He found Erwin Rommel's book on *Infantry Attacks* (1937) most useful tactically. However, Israeli research found no evidence for these translations, and no evidence that Yadin was capable of translating English or German (Bond 1977: 246; Ben-Moshe 1981: 374).

No such translations were ever published by the periodical (*Ma'arakhot*) that the *Haganah* had established in 1939. During the Second World War, it published only three pieces referencing Liddell Hart, none consequential:

    1. In September 1939, it included a translation of Liddell Hart's article in *The Times* on shortening the basic training of British soldiers.

    2. In July 1943, it reproduced his journalism on British intelligence problems.

    3. In February 1945, it summarized his biography (1934b) of Lawrence of Arabia (Ben-Moshe 1981: 390).

Sadeh

Yigal Allon (1918-1980) had served the *Haganah* since 1931. From 1936, he served in the Jewish Settlement Police, as established by Wingate. Allon did not mention Liddell Hart as an inspiration for Wingate, the Special Night Squads, or Yadin. Instead, Allon remembered Yitzhak Sadeh (1890-1952) as Wingate's Jewish partner, "the father of modern Jewish fighting, the teacher of most young Israeli commanders." Sadeh was not available to confirm, having died years earlier. Sadeh left few writings. What is clear is that his command of English was no better than Yadin's, and that the "tactics" and "guerilla war" that Sadeh and compatriots developed were normative rather than Liddell Hartian. Indeed, they were indistinguishable from the tactics that Arab insurgents had used (Ben-Moshe 1981: 375).

The Haganah, and especially its field unit "Fosh" (the initials of the Hebrew words for "field companies"), learned to fight in the field, by night and by day, mostly in sections and platoons, sometimes as a company, and very occasionally, in co-operation with Wingate, within the framework of a battalion subdivided into smaller units. These units learned how to search for an enemy in hilly country and cultivated areas; to place an ambush; to carry out a raid; to outflank an enemy; and to disengage rapidly whenever necessary for military or political reasons (Allon 1965: 341-342).

Haganah's plan for defence of Palestine is equally normative. By 1940, *Haganah* was cooperating with the British in case of any Axis invasion. In 1941, Allon helped to establish *Haganah*'s "striking companies" (*Palmach*), which Sadeh commanded.

The combination of a hilly country with some access to the sea and air, fully supported by the Allied forces in the matter of supplies, defended in depth and assisted by guerilla raids against enemy lines of communication, bases, and installations was thought to carry a fair chance of survival (Allon 1965: 347).

Independence War, 1948

Three men (Yigal Allon, Yigael Yadin, Yaakov Dori) were involved in the defence of the nascent Jewish state, and subsequently credited Liddell Hart's writings, although circumspectly.

Allon

Yigal Allon, who took command of the *Palmach* in 1945, listed three principles for the security of the nascent state:

1. Remote settlements were on no account to be abandoned...

2. Direct clashes with the British were as far as possible to be avoided, in order not to impede their plans for evacuation...

3. Jewish territorial continuity was to be established in each predominantly Jewish zone...(Allon 1965: 357).

On 29 November 1947, the United Nations recommended partition of the Mandate into independent Arab and Jewish states. Israel was proclaimed in May 1948. Its neighbours invaded. Allon's account does not mention Liddell Hart until after the collapse of the ceasefire of October 1948, when Allon commanded Southern Command. Allon focuses on an offensive launched on 22 December, to clear the Gaza Strip and southern Negev. He sums up this offensive as "a combination of guerilla actions and quick moves by large bodies." Allon admits that his own ideas of "indirect approach" matured in January 1949 (Allon 1965: 365-366). In 1975, Bond (1977: 250-252) asked Allon to elaborate. Bond interpreted an indirect approach, in the sense that Allon authorized the improvement of a track to avoid the defended highways in the Egyptian Negev. However, Allon said "he had no particular textbook in mind but had worked out his movements in the light of his knowledge of the enemy forces and terrain," and "had acted more or less instinctively." Further, Allon credited Wingate for his realization that night operation is a useful indirect approach.

In late 1949, Allon and other Israeli officers toured European capitals. They met Liddell Hart in London, although they needed an interpreter. Subsequent written correspondence does not prove any necessary influence. In 1965, Allon contributed a chapter to the Festschrift in honour of Liddell Hart's seventieth birthday. Allon's chapter is long, reflective, and detailed, but mentions Liddell Hart only once: it cites the most recent edition of *Indirect Approach*, without page numbers, and without specifying any approach. In 1975, Allon told Bond that Liddell Hart was their second most influential Briton (after Wingate) (LH 2/2/1; Bond 1977: 245-246).

Israeli research identified four principles of war carried over from the *Haganah* to the nascent Israeli Defence Forces:
1. avoidance of a direct fight with the enemy's main force;
2. mobility;
3. surprise; and
4. attacks on weak spots, supplies, and command.

The principles overlap Liddell Hart's indirect approach, but were "the fruit of an instinctive evolution and of cumulative local experience" (Ben-Moshe 1981: 378).

Yadin

In 1948, independent Israel promoted Yadin to chief of operations. In Summer 1949, he wrote a reflection for the Israeli Army's weekly magazine. This contains the first mention of Liddell Hart's indirect approach in an Israeli military publication. The second was published in 1950 (Ben-Moshe 1981: 375, 388).

Liddell Hart knew nothing about them until 1953, when Yadin sent translated excerpts from the reflection he had written in 1949. Liddell Hart appended them to a new edition of *Indirect Approach*. Here Yadin praises Liddell Hart's indirect approach, but specifies it as material manoeuvres to cut enemy communications, logistics, or retreat, and ignores Liddell Hart's social-psychological alternatives.

> The days of frontal tactical attacks are fast disappearing, and the art of tactics aims at achieving the main tasks by flank and rear attacks... There is no doubt that the strategy of indirect approach is the only sound strategy; but the constitution of the indirect approach in strategy – as brilliantly defined, explained[,] and elaborated by Captain Liddell Hart – is far wider and more complex than in the tactical field (Yadin to LH, 3 March 1953, LH 2/23/1; Liddell Hart 1954a: 387).

Yadin relates that a copy of *Indirect Approach* was found in a captured Egyptian position. "But fortunately for us they did not grasp the essence of the book" (Ibid: 389, 396n). This implies that the book is not sufficient for the method.

Bond's other Israeli interviewees remembered learning of Liddell Hart's indirect approach through Yadin, but it served to rationalize what they were already doing.

Dori

Yaakov (Jaacov) Dori (1899-1973) was *Haganah*'s chief of staff from 1939. In 1947, Dori wrote to credit Liddell Hart's biography of T.E. Lawrence for Israeli use of Jeeps tactically (Dori to LH, 17 June 1947, LH 2/7/1; LH to Ogorkiewicz, 16 August

1949, RACTM E2015.2015.58). However, Lawrence's first writings (1919; 1920: 63) do not make any automobiles necessary; they portray camels as sufficient for insurgency. Liddell Hart's biography (1934b: 164; 1938g: 95-96) is vague on Lawrence's practices. It prescribes "mobility," not mechanization, and skips Lawrence's (1938: 167) belated admissions that, for the advance in 1918, trucks were necessary logistically, and armoured cars tactically. Lawrence never saw anything like the Jeep, which was introduced in World War II.

Second Arab-Israeli War, 1956

In 1956, Israel defeated Egypt again. By then, the principals of the wars of 1947 to 1949 had been purged. Three new principals (Moshe Dayan, Ariel Sharon, Haim Laskov) were subsequently connected with Liddel Hart, without proving influence.

Dayan

Moshe Dayan (1915-1981) was chief of staff from 1953 to 1958. Liddell Hart did not initiate correspondence until after the war of 1956, and elicited only about one letter per year. Bond never met Dayan, and admits Dayan's disinterest, but still categorizes Israel's victory as Liddell Hartian.

> Though he was never a disciple of Liddell Hart's, General Dayan's strategy in the 1956 Sinai campaign was very much in accord with the spirit of the former's doctrine. Rather than a direct attack on the Egyptian's fortified perimeters with the object of destroying their army, Dayan believed that the enemy's forces would disintegrate if the Israelis could penetrate deep into Sinai and cut their communications (Bond 1977: 254).

However, consistency does not prove influence.

Sharon

Ariel Sharon (1928-2014) commanded the Paratroops Brigade in 1956. In 1958, he attended the Staff College at Camberley. In August, he wrote to Liddell Hart, for help to write a paper on German and British decision-making during the Second World War. They met again in 1963, and in 1968, after Sharon had commanded an armoured division in the war of 1967. Bond (1977: 259) admitted that "it would be straining the evidence to list Sharon among Liddell Hart's 'disciples'."

Laskov

From 1953 to 1955, Haim Laskov (1919-1982) studied politics, philosophy, and economics in England, without contacting Liddell Hart. In 1956, he commanded an infantry division. At the end of the war, he was promoted to Southern Command (after the wartime commander had died in a plane crash). Liddell Hart wrote to credit him, mistakenly, for Southern Command's performance.

In 1958, Laskov was promoted to chief of staff, in place of Dayan. In the next year, Liddell Hart sent an inscribed copy of his recently-published history of the British tank arm. Nothing came of it. Laskov retired in 1961.

Eight years later, Liddell Hart wrote to Laskov with a report that David Ben Gurion (1886-1973), who had served as prime minister (1955-1963), had claimed Liddell Hart's influence on Laskov in 1956. Laskov's reply suggests coincidence rather than influence (Laskov to LH, 11 May 1969, LH 2/13/40). Nevertheless, Brian

Bond (1977: 259) misreported that Laskov "is probably the only important Israeli soldier to have drawn more on Liddell Hart's ideas about armoured warfare."

Israel, 1960

Liddell Hart visited Israel in 1960,* at the government's expense. He claimed an "official tour" (to Hamish Hamilton, 21 November 1960, Bristol University Library Special Collections, DM1352/I.i). He was booked to give five public lectures, over a couple weeks, entitled "'How military ideas shaped world history," which are remembered mostly for his nervousness and incoherence.

Laskov was his point of contact. Gurion led the official welcome. For political reasons, the other Zionists of 1938 were not present. The most notable absentee was Moshe Sharett (Chertok) (1894-1965), who had served as prime minister from 1954 to 1955 and foreign minister from 1948 to 1956, but was now estranged. Also absent was Yisrael Galili (1911-1986), who had served in the *Haganah* from 1927 until 1948, when Gurion fired him as chief of staff, prompting Galili to join a rival party.

In 1960, the receiving officers lauded Liddell Hart as "the greatest military expert of our time." Liddell Hart described them as his best disciples. Liddell Hart's memoirs claim: "I found there a grasp of military problems and new military ideas comparable to that of the Germans, and in some respects surpassing theirs." Years later, a friend wrote to relate that "[you were] mentioned several times during [my] visit[,] and at places such as the Command & Staff College I was proudly shown the visitor's book with your inscription[,] and your writings are obviously widely read" (Ogorkiewicz to LH, 26 August 1964, RACTM E2015.2015.72; Liddell Hart 1965: II, 183; Bond 1977: 260-261; Bond 2018: 87).

Six Day War, 1967

In June 1967, Israel pre-emptively attacked Egypt. Ground forces took various approaches to the Suez Canal. Israel declared victory within six days, which is how the war came to be named in the West. Subsequently, Liddell Hart wrote to three particular officers (Yitzhak Rabin, Israel Tal, Jehuda Wallach) to claim influence.

Rabin

The Chief of Staff, General Yitzhak Rabin (1922-1995), rebuffed Liddell Hart's approach. In Hebrew, Rabin reported that he had rejected proposals to outflank the enemy, given Egyptian force density. He expected and proved that direct breakthroughs were necessary to get into the enemy's rear. After breakthroughs, the "indirect approach not seldom upset the balance of the enemy's dispositions, but by itself it was not generally sufficient to wipe out his forces" (Ben-Moshe 1981: 380, 384). Rabin told Bond (1977: 248, 272) that Wingate was more influential than Liddell Hart, and that neither was necessary to his strategy of 1967.

In August, Liddell Hart reviewed a book on the war by Randolph and Winston Churchill. He criticized them for missing the indirect approach. He sent copies to Yadin and Laskov in hope of confirmation. Neither had direct knowledge of the 1967 war.† Nevertheless, Yadin seconded Liddell Hart's interpretation of "the basic

---

* Liddell Hart was in country from 20 March to 5 April.
† Yadin had jumped into archaeology since leaving the military in 1952. Laskov had been

strategic principle of Rabin's plan" as "the true strategy of indirect approach" and "a brilliant chain of tactical improvisations all based on the main doctrine of the indirect approach" (Yadin to LH, 29 August 1967, LH 2/23/67). Laskov replied that Israel had applied "your ideas on armour." "I do have a feeling that on armour you sit back, chuckle and wonder what fate and the Israelis did to vindicate a life-long teaching and preaching" (Laskov to LH, 22 August 1967, LH 2/13/40).

Tal

General Israel Tal, commander of the Armoured Corps in 1967, had always intended to make a direct approach, for decisiveness. In 1968, Lieutenant-Colonel Zeev Ayalon of the same Corps published (in Hebrew) his finding that all Israeli direct approaches in 1967 were successful, contrary to previous wars, presumably thanks to improved capabilities. At the same time, Colonel Me'ir Pa'il published his finding that a direct approach on Rafah-el-Arish in 1967 was more effective than indirect approaches in 1949 and 1956 (Ben-Moshe 1981: 382-383).

By contrast, Bond (1977: 262) selected one particular brigade as "a model illustration of Liddell Hart's concept of indirect approach," just because it travelled across country (between two brigade groups on respective highways).

Wallach

In 1967, Liddell Hart initiated correspondence with Jehuda Wallach (1921-2008), a public information officer in the Army reserves. Wallach was never a tank officer, although in 1956 he had commanded a divisional group that included tanks. He retired from active service in 1960 (ranked Colonel), and studied in Jerusalem, so was assigned to escort Liddell Hart in March. Liddell Hart's embarassing lecture probably inhibited subsequent correspondence. After a quick undergraduate degree, he undertook a quick doctorate at Oxford (1962-1965),* where Howard persuaded him that Liddell Hart had invented Blitzkrieg. Thus, when Liddell Hart wrote in 1967, Wallach assumed that the Israelis' indirect approaches were Liddell Hart's, "not in the technical concept alone, but mainly in the mental and intellectual sphere, by the intelligent selection of the time, direction, method, and power of our moves" (Wallach to LH, 27 June 1967, LH 2/22/2; Unterseher 2023: 85).

Wallach's (1968: 39-43) subsequent article does not mention Liddell Hart. It attributes victory in 1967 to air superiority, initiative, aggression, concentration of forces, leadership from the front, and superior training of tank crewmen (especially in long-range gunnery and mental endurance). None of these causes is peculiar to Liddell Hart's doctrines. Concentration is antithetical to the distribution, infiltration, and raiding that Liddell Hart had prescribed since the 1930s. Air superiority is unnecessary to Liddell Hart's doctrine, given that he expected distributed small, fast tanks to evade aircraft. And he never emphasized gunnery. Rather, he prioritized speed (Newsome 2024: Chapter 6).

Liddell Hart sought Wallach's information on operational events, before writing a short reflection on the Six Day War. This was published in a monthly magazine, eight months after the war had ended. Liddell Hart's description is undermined

---

running Israel's civilian Ports Authority since 1961.
* Wallach's dissertation is entitled "Clausewitz and Schlieffen: A study of the impact of their theories on the German conduct of the 1914–1918 and 1939–1945 wars."

by errors of fact, such as his claim that the Israelis had already settled a divisional structure with balanced arms (1968a; Ben-Moshe 1981: 383). Liddell Hart coded Israeli post-breakthrough operations as an "indirect approach" (singular), which he conflated with "Blitzkrieg," which in turn he credited to himself. He ignored the direct approaches that produced the breakthroughs. Bond (1977: 265) characterized his judgment as "pardonable hyperbole." Bond never interviewed Wallach, but Wallach told an interviewer in 1981 of methodological problems in Liddell Hart's indirect approach, and in Liddell Hart's histories generally (Unterseher 2023: 85).

Yom Kippur War, 1973

Liddell Hart died in 1970. In 1973, Israel was attacked by Egypt. Bond (1977: 267-268) coded Egypt's attack and Israel's counter-attacks as indirect approaches. However, his justification for the former was that it surprised Israel, for the latter that the Israelis manoeuvred. Ben-Moshe (1981: 385) found that the "Israeli 'indirect approach' – if indeed it existed – expired in the October 1973 War, which took the form of a frontal clash and caused swift pulverization of men and matériel."

Legacy

Liddell Hart told Laskov of ambivalence towards German praise, but "there have never been any such mixed feelings, and only pleasure, in seeing how the leaders of Israel have applied those ideas, even still better" (to Laskov, 12 September 1967, LH 2/13/40). His wife (1970: vi) remembered that "Basil often said, somewhat ruefully, that rather than his own countrymen, the Germans and Israelis were his 'best pupils'." Bond (1977: 229) recalls that "Liddell Hart made no pretence of impartiality where Israeli military affairs were concerned: indeed his attitude rather resembled that of a proud headmaster." He would "declare à propos of Israeli tributes that he had never felt wholly comfortable when praised by the Germans." However, Bond admits that this attitude was "not apparent in the 1940s."

Howard (1970b: 42; 1984: 207) misreported that the "founders of the new Israeli Army, men who could afford to run no risks, soaked themselves in his writings." Robert Larson (1984: 100) and Bevin Alexander (2000: 7) also misreported, without evidence, that he helped Israeli victories in both 1956 and 1967.

In 1975, Bond visited Israel. Initially, he (1977: 238, 270) reported that Liddell Hart "made a significant impact in Israel – the most important evidence being the tributes of several distinguished soldiers and scholars." Later, Bond (2018: 88) admitted that Liddell Hart was known mostly "second-hand from newspapers and journals," "mostly implanted indirectly, that is by means of his books, and articles, …in translation or at second hand from lectures."

Only two of his books had been translated into Hebrew by then: *Scipio* (published in English in 1926, Hebrew in 1970); and *Indirect Approach* (English in 1954, Hebrew in 1956). Few articles had been translated, and only on current policies and strategies. Ben-Moshe (1981: 373, 386) found that his "translation into practical operational effect was little more than marginal," but convenient to Israelis who wished to avoid crediting Germans and fascists, even though "Fuller's concepts matched Israeli strategy after 1956 better than Hart's." Mearsheimer (1988: 203-204) also found that his Israeli disciples were motivated to avoid crediting Germans.

19

Academic, 1950s-1960s

By the mid-1950s, Liddell Hart stopped courting senior academics and started on the next generation of historians, with a mix of altruism and self-interest. His wife remembered:

> Friendships with historians – the younger historians particularly – and students from all over the world enriched his life and he spent a great deal of time reading and criticizing the drafts of their theses and books, to the neglect of his own work but to his infinite pleasure (1970: vii)

She lists eight Britons (Corelli Barnett, Brian Bond, Alan Clark, Alastair Horne, Michael Howard, Barrie Pitt, Reginald William Thompson, and Michael Williams), one Australian (Robert O'Neill), three Americans (Peter Paret, Jay Luvaas, and Don Schurman), and three retired French Army officers (André Beaufre, Henri Bernard, and Adolphe Goutard). Howard (1970b: 37-38; 1983 and 1984: 198-199) recalled "an unending stream of disciples and pilgrims."

Liddell Hart still wanted a professorship at Oxford, but settled for an honorary degree. Through Howard and Bond, Liddell Hart influenced London University's reinstitutionalization of "Military Studies," with less military science and more social studies, rebranded as "War Studies." Through Howard's student Peter Paret, he took a temporary professorship in California, but quit within months.

Oxford II

Liddell Hart still hankered after the Chichele Professorship of History of War at Oxford, despite rejection in 1946. In 1953, Cyril Falls was succeeded by Norman Henry Gibbs (1910-1990). Gibbs was deserving: he had earned his doctorate and taught at Oxford before the war, joined a cavalry unit (armoured cars) at the start of the war, was seconded to the Cabinet Office's official historians in 1943, and returned to the university in 1946 (without giving up official history).

Yet Liddell Hart pretended that Gibbs was less qualified, even while he entertained Gibbs in hope of influence. Kathleen said that Gibbs cared about only his rose garden, but Brian Bond (2018: 18) found that "Gibbs took his teaching duties seriously." To fellow journalist-historian Chester Wilmot, an Australian, Liddell Hart blamed British society or culture.

> I have ceased to cherish hopes that any seeds I may sow will bear fruit in this soil. They may do so in a few receptive patches, but the principal part of this domain is stony ground for any fresh conceptions. There is no country where ideas – other than those of a mechanical gadget kind – are given so little encouragement (27 April 1953, LH 13/32).

This Anglophobia did not work on Wilmot, who was happily resident and employed in England.

In 1954, Liddell Hart seemed to Howard (2006: 154) "bitterly disappointed," although Howard realized later that "his pre-war writings" had discredited him. Ten years later, Howard persuaded Gibbs to contribute a chapter to the Festschrift in honour of Liddell Hart. Howard presumably chose Gibbs to balance the hagiographic chapters. Without mentioning Liddell Hart, Gibbs (1965: 191-192, 194, 210) demolishes *British Way of Warfare*. Gibbs found that peacetime Britain had idealized isolationism, defensiveness, and the navy, but wartime Britain needed to accumulate allies, expeditionary forces, and ground victories before containing the threat. Gibbs (1965: 209) mentions Liddell Hart only to point out, diplomatically, the contradiction between his proposal to reduce the expeditionary force to a small tank force and his opposition to any continental commitment.

Gibbs held the professorship for seven years after Liddell Hart's death.

London

London offered a better fit than Oxford for Liddell Hart's expertise. London University had departmentalized professional Military Science from 1848 to 1867. From 1927, the War Department paid for a lectureship in Military Studies, held by Major-General Sir Frederick Maurice, who naturally treated the field as professional. The university renamed Military Studies as War Studies in 1943, to better reflect the wartime mission. The end of World War II, divestment from Empire, and austerity justified the closure of War Studies in 1948, although the Board of Studies for Military Studies continued. The University reauthorized the lectureship in 1953, but Liddell Hart did not apply for it. Nevertheless, he would become the leading influence on the first full-time Lecturer of War Studies: Michael Howard.[*]

Like Liddell Hart, Howard admitted "to have been born into a prosperous family," indulged by his mother, given "an elite education of a kind that today would be regarded with deep disapproval," a "shamelessly affected youth," a dandy, and a pacifist (2006: vii, 37, 40).

Like Adrian, who was born a few months earlier, he realized in adolescence his homosexuality, chose Liberal partisanship ("woolly liberal that I was"), chose to stay at boarding school for an extra term (he left in December 1940, a year after Adrian), chose higher education over immediate military service (in January 1941, three months after Adrian), chose varsity (Oxford rather than Cambridge), focused on English literature and history, and suspended his education to join the military (Army rather than Navy) (2006: 48-55, 83-84).

In August 1942, he joined the Coldstream Guards, in London. He deployed in September 1943 (to Salerno, Italy). Weeks later, he joined his first assault, which he rallied, under the gaze of superiors, who recommended a Military Cross. The next day, without their gaze, he fled an artillery bombardment, until a Guardsman asked what he was doing. Days later, they rotated out of the line, when he went down with malaria, with a hint of post-traumatic stress disorder. In July 1944, he returned to command of a platoon, on a static front, with occasional patrols, during one of which he regrettably left a wounded Guardsman to die. By the time the unit was allocated to the final offensive in Italy, in April 1945, it could not catch up. His memoirs admit "a very cushy war" and occasional "cowardice." "In spite of my

---

[*] Michael Eliot Howard (1922-2019), not to be confused with Conservative politician Michael Howard (born Michael Hecht, in 1941), ennobled as Baron Howard of Lympne in 2010.

brief front-line service, my war had been as protected as my childhood" (2006: 123).

Howard was extraordinarily lucky for an academic career.* By his own account, his only training to lecture was at the hands of the Army Education Corps in Spring 1945, and his research methodology was self-taught (at least until he encountered Liddell Hart). He returned to Oxford within weeks of demobilization, "letting my energies trickle away doing nothing in particular." He scraped though his final exams in November 1946. He failed separate examinations for a Fellowship. Nevertheless, thanks to passing in the first division in 1942, he earned a second-class undergraduate degree (2006: 114, 125-127).

Soon after graduation, he was invited to replace a co-author of his regiment's official history of the recent war. Howard worked in the regiment's archives and his former secondary school (Wellington). One of the teachers there was lecturing at Kings College London (on English literature). He recommended an opportunity as Assistant Lecturer in Modern History. Howard was interviewed in May 1947.

> With a mediocre degree and no research experience, I was ill-qualified for a university post anywhere. But at that time higher degrees were exceptional, and the head of the history department was adventurous in his appointments...
>
> And as I watched them [students] dutifully taking notes of my lectures – lectures hurriedly put together from such elderly secondary sources as the Cambridge Modern History – I had a terrible vision of them teaching their own pupils from these notes, who would teach their own pupils from their notes, my platitudes and errors bounding down the generations (2006: 131, 134).

Howard focused on late Medieval and early modern English politics, until another opportunity came his way in 1953: the University of London lectureship in Military Studies. As preparation, Howard was granted a one-year sabbatical, which he spent largely in Austria, nominally to improve his German language. This hardly helped his knowledge of Military Studies, so, upon return, he approached Cyril Falls, but Falls had retired in 1953. For some reason, Howard ignored Gibbs for now, probably because Gibbs, like Maurice, treated military history as professional in utility (Maurice 1929; Howard to LH, 23 November 1954 and 10 December 1955, LH 1/384; Morgan-Owen and Finch 2022: 60-63).

In November 1954, Liddell Hart wrote in appreciation of Howard's review of the latest edition of *Indirect Approach*. Liddell Hart bought "a splendid lunch at the Athenaeum [Club]," proposed Howard's membership, and invited Howard to visit for a weekend, which became a week of illness. Within a month, Liddell Hart mailed seven papers. Some are useful bases for lectures on Military Studies (such as: "Some Notes on Military Reading"), others are self-serving ("Deep Strategic Penetration and Battles and Campaigns, 1939-1945"; "Conversations on Army Organization, 1919-1939"). Howard was receptive. He shared a resentment of the military profession and the professional bias in miltary studies. He wanted to focus on what he characterized to Liddell Hart as "war and society," later the "social and

---

* Strachan (2020: 537) lectured, in Howard's presence, that Howard would not be hired today with the qualifications he had offered in 1953, although Strachan was happy he was.

economic aspects of war." Howard became "involved in a correspondence which barely flagged for ten years, one letter of mine evoking about three from him'"* (LH to Howard, 20 November and 20 December 1954, LH 1/384; Howard 1970b: 37; 1983: 198; 1984: 198; 2006: 141, 144).

> And when one visited him, to be entertained with excellent food and wine and endless whisky – everything the heart of man could desire except sleep – he would be lying in wait with a deceptively small piece of paper on which he had jotted down in his microscopic writing a few dozen topics on which he wanted information or discussion. One was hooked; willingly bound in an exacting, exhausting, delightful[,] and immensely rewarding slavery...
>
> And he would sit up all night drinking whisky and lukewarm water arguing with his guests. And he would make himself available to any inquiring visitor who wanted to see him. And he seemed to have infinite time for the host of personal friends whom he grappled to himself, out of his huge acquaintanceship, with hoops of steel. He was a very remarkable man.
>
> Liddell Hart in fact was a sage (1970b: 37-38; 1984: 198-199).

Howard wrote the above as an obituary. A quarter century later, his memoirs downplay their relationship. Nevertheless, his self-interests are clear.

> The benefit I derived from knowing Liddell Hart extended far beyond what I learned from him personally. He introduced me around...Some I met at his home, some at a dining-club over which he presided, the Military Commentators' Circle (2006: 154-155).

Howard's memoirs claim that he came up with his methodology before 1954, when he found confirmation in Clausewitz's writings. However, his methodology sounds like Liddell Hart's (1959b; 1965, I: 170) "creative imagination."

> First, find out what happened. Then, establish a cause of causation. Finally, apply critical judgment. Before one could interpret the past, one had to recreate it (2006: 130).

Clausewitz remained Liddell Hart's theoretical and doctrinal nemesis. Howard did not reveal his intent to translate Clausewitz until 1958, and did not get going until after Liddell Hart died. In 2002, Strachan (2020: 543) spoke, in Howard's presence, with Howard's knowledge, and without Howard's objection, of "Howard's apprenticeship – here at King's, at the hands of Liddell Hart." Similarly, Reid (2009: 880) identified Liddell Hart as Howard's "most important influence." Of Howard's other two "most significant...influences,"† neither is Clausewitz. Morgan-Owen and Finch (2022: 57) confirmed that "Liddell Hart occupies a pre-eminent position as a mentor and sponsor of Howard's career." Liddell Hart was certainly the strongest influence on Howard's (successful) petition in 1955 to convert the legacy "military

---

* Howard's memoirs reduce this sentence to: "we began a correspondence" (2006: 154).
† Hans Delbrück (1848-1929) and Raymond Aron (1905-83), whom Howard read from 1953.

studies" component of the General (Studies) Degree into a less "technical," less "professional," more "academic," and more sociological component named "war studies." Howard retitled himself as "Lecturer in War Studies." In February 1958, he started to teach a course on "War and Society," which was authorized in October as a general elective, called "War Studies."

That same Autumn, Liddell Hart presided over the foundation of the Institute for Strategic Studies (later prefixed International), with Howard as one of the board members. Howard (1970a) recalled that "Liddell Hart's reputation was only just beginning to recover from nearly 20 years of neglect and misrepresentation."

That same year, Liddell Hart negotiated a tax arrangement with the government's department for Inland Revenue, on the grounds of academic and official work of national importance. This "made it possible for us to live and work in England," according to Mrs. Hart, although in fact they spent winters abroad. In December 1958, they moved a few miles, to a Victorian manor (States House) in Medmenham on the Thames (1970: ix).

They hired Edward Bond as gardener, whose son, Brian,* visited in January 1959 for help with undergraduate studies. Howard (1970a), Luvaas (1990: 19), and Bond (2018: 20) remember mentees calling Liddell Hart "the Sage of Medmenham." Mentees remember his humanity and generosity, although they admit his anger towards critics. The only time they experienced his anger was when they submitted for publication without his review, or admitted to eating poorly for want of money. Bond observed "an extremely highly-strung and sensitive person, not, on his own admission, very brave in confronting pain in himself, and easily upset by illness and suffering in others" (Larson 1980: 70; Luvaas 1990: 13; O'Neill 1990: 101-102, 111; Bond 1977: 9; Bond 2018: 21).

Liddell Hart encouraged Bond to take a masters degree in military history (against the advice of Bond's tutors), and undertook to read Bond's thesis (despite disinterest in the subject: reforms of the British Army, 1868-1874). He referred Bond to Howard. They met in March, in London, where Howard seconded Bond's ambition, although Bond suspected that Howard's motivation was to distance them both from Liddell Hart. Oxford rejected Bond's request for funding, so, in August, Howard undertook to supervise the same research. The next month, Bond started to attend Howard's seminars at the Institute of Historical Research in London, and to teach history at a secondary school (2018: 20-24).

Also in 1959, Howard persuaded Kings College London to pay for conversion of Liddell Hart's stable block into a library, and a barn into an apartment for guests. The conversions were completed in 1961, where Bond, Luvaas, and peers toiled to organize his papers and to glean material for their eventual publications.†

In November 1960, Liddell Hart lectured twice to Howard's students, on "The military balance-sheet of World War Two." However, the chair of History (C.H. Williams) resented Howard's utilization of an anti-academic. The chair's more

---

* Brian James Bond was born in 1936. He was educated at Sir William Borlase's Grammar School, Worcester College Oxford (modern history, 1956-1959), and Kings College London, culminating in a masters degree in war studies (1962). Like Howard, Bond never completed a doctoral degree. He completed National Service with the Royal Artillery (1954-1956).
† The College opened Liddell Hart's library and archive on campus in 1964, but transfers of files continued for more than a decade.

justifiable complaint was Howard's failure to publish (beyond a pamphlet on Eastern Europe, in 1958). Liddell Hart encouraged Howard to resign, which he did in Spring 1961, after submitting his first book manuscript. Howard blamed the administrative and teaching load for his slowness to publish and his resignation. Once the book was published, he was promoted from Assistant Lecturer in History to the College's first Reader in Military Studies (LH to Howard, 8 June 1959, and Howard to LH, 28 November 1961, LH 1/384).

Howard now could confer post-graduate degrees. In 1962, Bond received a Masters degree in War Studies. Liddell Hart, Howard, and Bond had changed the professional "Military Studies" of Maurice's time into an artistic inter-disciplinary field, best described as political-sociological-military history. "War Studies" is too narrow in literal meaning to capture all these disciplines. Yet military history dominated, despite denial. In 1955, Howard had described the scope of his general elective course on "War Studies" as "social, political and economic problems arising from the growth of total war," but he never engaged economics, except as socio-economics. The sociology and politics (and politicization) of history were fashionable in the new universities, government, and popular culture – as cheered by Liddell Hart (see Chapters 5 and 10). Yet none formally studied any social sciences, identified with social science,* or defined "War Studies"† (Howard 2006: 141-147, 148, 154; Reid 2009; Bond 2015: ix-x; 2018: 33-34).

---

* Howard (1970: 13) wrote: "I am unrepentantly a historian and not a social scientist." In 2002, Strachan (2020: 543) reported that "Michael has consistently described himself as an historian not a social scientist."
† Howard wrote that a "historian who studies war...cannot be simply a 'military historian,' for there is literally no branch of human activity which is not to a greater or lesser extent relevant to its subject." He contrasts "didactic and normative" and "analytic...guides to the efficient conduct of war," but military history has never been about just "conduct of war," and those adjectives are not exclusive to military history (1976: ix-x). He later wrote that "military history" should be studied "in width, in depth, and in context" (1983: 194; 1984; 197). Bond recalls Howard saying "that all the courses in the Department would be based on a broad disinterested study of armed conflict over the past two hundred years" (2015: x), or "the disinterested study of warfare in a broad social and political context" (2018: i). Strachan (2019: 229) reports that Howard "treated war as part of 'total history' and placed it in its political and social context." Yet the art of history is in tension with the science of sociology and politics. Howard urged each to become more like the other, but eschewed expertise in any. Reid (1999: 72) characterizes Howard's "war studies" as a "heuristic tool kit shaped by strategy" and "international relations," but "consistently historical in its exigesis." Strachan (2019: 225) reports that Howard "believed that war was best understood through the perspective of military history." Kitchen and Mitchell (2022: 10) found that Howard "was by education and temperament fundamentally a historian." Halewood and Morgan-Owen (2021: 49) point out that Howard's "War Studies" is so broad as to lack an "object" of study, and thus ironically keeps returning to the "fighting" that he urged studiers to escape. "Despite being unified under the 'war studies' banner, war is overwhelmingly studied with reference to society, economy, government, or diplomacy, rather than as the central phenomena in its own right." Morgan-Owen and Finch (2022: 58, 59) make the same point, although with apparently contradictory semantics: "Howard articulated a limited conception of 'War Studies' which did not extend far beyond an umbrella grouping that might allow for the co-existence of numerous disciplinary approaches to war." Later "attempts at delineation underline the lack of disciplinary clarity that has always characterized War Studies."

Curiously, Howard's promotion and Bond's graduation were not yet sufficient to reverse Liddell Hart's contempt for historians in general.

> The decline is becoming so marked and widespread that it makes me feel like abandoning the study of military history and retiring to Tristan da Cunha! (to Ogorkiewicz, 19 December 1962, RACTM E2015.2015.70).

Liddell Hart's attitude turned after he had helped Bond into academic history. By then, he referred to Bond as more like a son than Adrian. In 1962, Bond gained a temporary appointment at Exeter University. This was followed by a lectureship at Liverpool University, also on Liddell Hart's recommendation. Howard was promoted to Chair of War Studies in 1963. In 1965, Howard interviewed Bond for a lectureship in Military Studies, but it went to Wolfgang "Wolf" Mendl (1926-1999), who was ten years senior and focused on international affairs. Liddell Hart preferred Bond to stay in academia, although he also explored Bond's options in the Army Education Corps, as if replaying his own life at similar age. His letters of recommendation, which he shared with Bond, refer to Bond's "ardent interest," "great powers of concentration," "intellectual curiosity," "wide background knowledge," "extensive reading, and his historical grasp." Liddell Hart did not intend to condemn by faint praise, but, nevertheless, his praise does not live up to his rating of Bond (to Hamilton) "as the best [historian] we now have after Michael Howard." Certainly, the three men share a style: brief, quick, and pleasing reads, from one eloquent subjective impression to another, usually without citations, references, or revisions.* In 1965, the Masters in War Studies was opened for general registration, and the Department needed more instructors. In 1966, Howard hired Bond as the College's first Lecturer in Military History (letters, 5 and 7 July 1966, in Bristol University Library Special Collections, DM1352/I.i; Bond 2018: 21, 27-28, 35).

Oxford III

In December 1964, Oxford University awarded to Liddell Hart an honorary doctorate of letters. He asked to wear the associated robe, only to be reminded that a honorary degree cannot be incorporated. A year later, his former college (Corpus Christi) at Cambridge made him an Honorary Fellow.

California

Meanwhile, Michael Howard and a student (1955-1960), Peter Paret, arranged for a temporary teaching appointment in history at University of California Davis (1965-1966), where Paret already taught (since 1962). Howard was then a visiting professor at nearby Stanford University. Unconventionally, they offered Liddell Hart's honorary doctorate as a qualification. During the appointment, he prefixed his name as "Captain (Professor)," and suffixed "D.Litt."

Mr. and Mrs. Liddell Hart sailed from Southampton on 2 September, so missed the first quarter of the academic year. Nevertheless, he brought crates of books and portraits as if prepared to stay. He took a gratis home, 700 yards from campus.

---

* Strachan (2020: 550) describes Howard as "master of the short book," who "writes fluent, literate prose" and "is always right." Kitchen and Mitchell (2022: 5) agree that Howard's short books rely on "fluid prose and a remarkable breadth of knowledge to draw readers."

Kathleen acquired a cat. He celebrated his 70th birthday in the Chancellor's office and at home, where Howard handed over an especially bound Festschrift in his honour. A couple weeks later, officers of the United States Marine Corps visited to hand over a plaque and letters (dated to his birthday, but mistakenly addressed to England). The letter from their Commandant (General Wallace M. Greene, Jr.) declares him "unequalled by any living military philosopher." The Commander of Marine Force Pacific (Lieutenant-General V.H. Krulak) wrote that "your tactics and techniques…are paying dividends in the jungles of Southeast Asia." Mr. and Mrs. Liddell Hart broke their pattern of travelling to the tropics for the winter, in order to spend Christmas and New Year in Davis. He spoke to the *San Francisco Chronicle* about the war in Vietnam on 4 January. He delivered a lecture ("If you want peace, understand war") to the World Affairs Council in San Francisco on 14 January. He delivered another ("Why don't we learn from history?") to the University of California San Francisco on 16 January. He had written 27 lectures, covering history from the causes of the First World War to the courses of the Second, which would take him through the final two quarters of the academic year. He held invitations to speak and entertain through the same period. Photographs show that he entertained at home through 23 January, and wrote at home through 26 January. The photographs show him relaxed and jocular, without his typical strain and stiffness (LH 12/1965/7 to /64; LH 13/104/18).

Yet within days he was gone. His wife recalled: "This was a stimulating experience, which he thoroughly enjoyed, but unfortunately our stay was cut short by several months as he had to return to England for a major operation." His correspondence refers to an illness from late 1965, which required, in February 1966, an operation, followed by three weeks in hospital. Neither he nor his wife explains why he could not take medical care in California. Howard's memoirs reveal that "Peter and Basil were strongminded men with ideas of their own who did not get on at all well." Paret and Liddell Hart were supposed to co-teach a seminar on the world wars, but Paret does not appear in the photographs after 1 November. From England, Liddell Hart corresponded with his students, teaching assistant, and university, to reconcile paper submissions, grades, and expenses, while Howard took over the lectures for the remaining five months of the academic year. Howard recalled those months as his unhappiest in academia. Liddell Hart continued to correspond until 1969 about his desire to return, but always referred to ill-health or over-work as excuses (LH 2/26 to /39; 1970: vii; Howard 2006: 180-181).

Legacy

In 1968, Howard moved to Oxford, while Bond failed in his bid to replace him. The nascent Department of War Studies was led by a series of men without Howard's work ethic or political intelligence, so Howard remained a guide and a visiting lecturer into the 1990s. In 1996, the College made him a Fellow.

In the 2000s, the government transferred responsibility for most teaching of military officer cadets and staff officers, from mostly public servants, to mostly contractees from the War Studies Department. Yet, perversely, war studiers continue to rail against social sciences and to "counter the orthodoxy," in echo of Liddell Hart's prejudices against seniors, conservatives, and professionals.

20

Final Publications

Liddell Hart took decades to finish his histories of the Second World War and other lax projects for Cassell. Their story proceeds through Hamish Hamilton's attempts to lure him into other projects, his long-winded but glorious completion of his memoirs, his unpublicized cooperation with Howard in production of the *Festschrift* in his honour, his contributions to the *New Cambridge Modern History*, and the long-overdue completion of his *History of the Second World War* – his final book.

Hamilton

Liddell Hart first heard from (James) Hamish Hamilton (1900-1988) in 1942, but was too busy editing new editions of prior works for other publishers. Hamilton reconnected in 1954, after Cassell's success with various editions of *The Other Side of the Hill* (1948-1951) and *The Rommel Papers* (1953). Hamilton asked Liddell Hart to author a title on "Six Great Soldiers." Hamilton's motivations were both rational and biased. In the 1920s, standard print runs of Liddell Hart's short military biographies had sold out; his biography of Lawrence of Arabia (1934) had sold best. Yet Hamilton ignored Fuller, who had sold more biographies.

Liddell Hart was too busy with outstanding projects for Cassell, but Hamilton kept asking. In the meantime, Hamilton paid Liddell Hart to vet other authors. For instance, in August 1956, Liddell Hart agreed to review a draft *Story of Land Warfare* by Paul Kendall. The book is thin – no more than an accessible introduction. It does not mention Liddell Hart,* who took offence.

> [I]t tends to be a selective story of a number of the leading figures in land warfare rather than a comprehensive outline of the development of tactics and weapons – as I had hoped. In the early chapters the author keeps a balance better, but his account of modern times, particularly the last half century (with the two world wars) seemed to me rather disappointing (to Hamilton, 12 April 1957, Bristol University Library Special Collections, DM1352/I.i).

Hamilton demanded revisions from Kendall, before publication later that year.

In 1956, Liddell Hart agreed to write "Six Great Soldiers," retitled as "Six Great Captains." However, in 1957, he claimed to have been diverted by "the Suez crisis [October-November 1956] and a call to re-examine our defence organization." Months later, he blamed official "defence consultations." In 1960, he claimed to be diverted by "an official tour to Israel, Greece, and Italy," followed by "a long attack of conjunctivitis." He promised to spend the winter in the Canary Islands, "concentrating on the completion of my history [of the Second World War] free from interruption by telephone calls and visitors." In 1961, Hamilton sent increasingly

---

* Kendall (1957: 174) refers to how German forces "paralysed nerve-centres of command," but Fuller (1919; 1923a: 35-37, 41-46) was first to use such semantics.

frustrated reminders, but Liddell Hart replied that he was too busy writing "my history" and planning his memoirs. Hamilton agreed to seek another author (2 January and 12 April 1957, 21 November 1960, 13, 14 and 20 December 1961).

Liddell Hart was playing Hamilton. After completing the memoirs in 1965, he took the "Six Great Captains" project to Cassell.

Memoirs

Cassell had commissioned Liddell Hart's memoirs in 1947. By April 1963, he had completed nearly 150,000 words and fifteen chapters, bringing the story up to 1937. By July 1963 he was writing the "epilogue," taking the story to May 1940. He finished the draft at 310,000 words – twice as many as the publisher had specified (three times longer than this biography). Liddell Hart cut to 228,000 words, but refused to go further. The publisher decided to publish two volumes, so asked for restoration of the cuts. This took him through 1964, and delayed publication of the first volume until May 1965, the second until October (LH 9/30/1 to /35; to Ogorkiewicz, 26 April 1963, 8 July 1963, 11 October 1963, and 7 December 1964, RACTM E2015.2015.70 and .72; Higham 1966: 47n).

Liddell Hart's memoirs tell an impossible story, in which every positive development resulted from his conversation or correspondence, while every negative development resulted from official rejection. No evidence is given, except excerpts from his own writings.

He archived hundreds of reviews, few of them critical. No critic was a prominent historian. A.J.P. Taylor, still mired in a controversy about his apologism for Nazi belligerency (1961), described him as "the most formidable military writer of the age." "His first volume was greeted with almost deafening praise. His second is even more revealing. Now Liddell Hart has been vindicated" (1965c: 26, 27). Field-Marshal Montgomery, whose earlier memoirs moan about British ingratitude (1958), although without mentioning Liddell Hart, now wrote: "one has only to read the volumes of Liddell Hart's memoirs to realize that he was wise before the event – a prophet at last honoured in his own country" (1968: 20).

Michael Howard reviewed the first volume as if it is the best evidence for the inter-war period.

> It would be less than human if he did not remind us, at some length, of the remarkable prescience of his writings on tactics, strategy[,] and warfare in general; and he would be more than human if he could conceal his impatience with the men who so disastrously ignored his advice. But... there is no rancour. There is frank criticism, but never a trace of malice. As a result, there are few occasions when his judgments are not completely convincing (1965b: 24).

Howard reviewed the second volume as if it is the best evidence for Liddell Hart's ethos.

> His place in history is secure; not, as he might have wished, as the reformer of the British Army, but as the man who, more than any other in this century, has shown us how to think clearly and sanely about war (1966: 61).

Brian Bond (1977: 22) agreed: "When every allowance is made for the element of self-justification, Liddell Hart's *Memoirs* and archives remain an impressive indictment of the mentality of the 1914-18 generation of senior Army officers." Danchev (1998a: 247) described the memoirs as "setting the record straight down to 1940."

However, Mearsheimer (1988: 7-9, 13) found "a blatant distortion of the historical record" – helped by prior manipulation of "a network of scholars."

Festschrift

In the same year as the memoirs, Howard edited a collection of essays on *The Theory and Practice of War*, nominally in honour of Liddell Hart, unadmittedly in cooperation. Liddell Hart edited the chapters on the interwar period. Most writers were correspondents, research assistants, or mentees – or Howard's students.

Howard (1965a: ix) described the product as a gift "to a great teacher by a group of his pupils, disciples, admirers, and friends." Howard presented an especially bound copy on 1st November, the Monday after Liddell Hart's 70th birthday. In the next month, Liddell Hart asked Howard to nominate him for the Nobel Peace Prize (to Howard, 13 December 1965, LH 1/384; to Ogorkiewicz, 15 December 1965, RACTM E2015.2015.73).

The *Festschrift* was published coincident with the second volume of Liddell Hart's memoirs, and by the same publisher. Within two months came news that Liddell Hart would be knighted, for services to "military history." He had been petitioning for the honour since 1930. He pressed friends in the Labour Party once Harold Wilson formed an administration in October 1964. In 1965, he sought Montgomery's help too. Nevertheless, he pretended to be surprised and disinterested.

> When the New Year's Honours List is published, I hope that people will abstain from "congratulating" me on the Knighthood. For I have repeatedly tried to put a stop on proposals for giving me a title or other official honour, and have only now yielded, very reluctantly, to the pressure of those who have urged that I must accept it in order to establish the principle, and precedent, that military thought should be officially recognized and honoured in this way like other fields of research and scholarship.
>
> Personally, I value it only for such practical utility as it may have as a kind of "laissez passer" with minor officials and bureaucratic impediments. I appreciate far more than this "K" the Festschrift volume of essays, the Oxford Hon.D.Litt, and the Cambridge honorary fellowship at Corpus (BHLH to AJLH, 4 December 1965, LHCMA KLH).

New Cambridge Modern History

The publication of Liddell Hart's *Memoirs* and *Festschrift* left Cassell with no competing projects that could justify his failure to deliver the history of the Second World War, which they had agreed almost 20 years earlier. One explanation is his discomfort with his own experience of the war. Another is his ambition to write history for Cambridge University Press.

Since 1926, Liddell Hart had submitted book proposals to Cambridge. One was for his first history of the Great War, eventually published in 1930 by Faber

& Faber. In 1937, he proposed to add a chapter on the Great War to the *Cambridge Modern History*. At that time, the Press was planning to take its scope beyond 1910, but Liddell Hart was not part of the plan (LH 3/174).

After the Second World War, the Press commissioned the *New Cambridge Modern History*. None of the editors or contributors was carried over from the *Old*. Liddell Hart was not asked to contribute to the first edition.

David Thomson (1912–1970) edited the most relevant volume (XII), covering the two world wars. In 1950, Penguin Books had published Thomson's well-received *England in the Nineteenth Century, 1815-1914*. Liddell Hart archived press reports that year, and again when the book was reprinted. His interest remained unclear until 1952, when he wrote to critique Thomson's conventional power-and-interests explanation for the outbreak of the Great War. Where was Thomson's blame for Napoleonic and Clausewitzian cults of the offensive? He referred Thomson to his own books. Implicitly, the trouble was that Thomson had not cited or mentioned Liddell Hart. Thomson dropped the correspondence within weeks (LH 1/690).

The tenth volume, covering the years 1830-1870, was the most nepotistic. Its editorship was given to J. Patrick Bury (1908-1987), a long-standing junior faculty (since 1933). Liddell Hart had ignored him, even though he was the nephew of Liddell Hart's tutor from 1913 to 1914 (John Bagnell Bury, 1861-1927). Patrick never rose to John's rank (Regius Professor of Modern History). Patrick's (1952: 127) main contribution to the Press was a history of Liddell Hart's former College, with one mention of Liddell Hart as "a well-known writer on military matters," and a member of a cohort of "some distinction." In the same year of publication, the Press commissioned Patrick to edit the tenth volume. Patrick's only qualifications for the period 1830 to 1870 were his lectures on modern France. He needed authors for two military chapters, each entitled "Armed Forces and the Art of War," one on navies, one on armies. For the chapter on navies, in 1955 he commissioned a retiring professor at the Royal Naval College, Greenwich (Michael Arthur Lewis). He came to Liddell Hart late, in 1958, and in a hurry, before publication in 1960.

Liddell Hart had barely written on the period before. He showed a draft to Ropp and Luvaas, when they visited. Ropp criticized Liddell Hart's outdated view of the Prussian General Staff. After sleeping on their argument, Liddell Hart did revise his view, but not a self-serving claim that the "art" of "distracting" the enemy and attacking the enemy's weakest point with "mobile forces" was invented in this period, after a struggle with conservatism. Here he is reflecting his own imagined struggles from 1919 to 1939 on to an earlier period. His new interpretation contradicts his old interpretation: that in the 1800s a neo-Napoleonic cult of the offensive became an international consensus, and it caused the bloodshed of the Great War (1925: 12; 1933c: 11-13; 1939b: 28; 1946b: 64; 1960b; Luvaas 1990: 17).

The twelfth volume covers the years 1898-1945. Here the chapter on armies was written by Wavell, with homage to Liddell Hart and Fuller for supposedly inspiring "Blitzkrieg" (1960: 267). The volume contains a chapter on the First World War, but none on the Second. Four years later, the Press appointed Charles Loch Mowat (1911-1970), from the University of North Wales, Bangor, to edit a second edition. This would be published before some of the first edition volumes. Mowat repudiated the first edition's titular focus on "The Era of Violence," which is far as Mowat gets in justifying "a new kind of history and a new name." Mowat commissioned from Liddell Hart a chapter on the Second World War. Liddell Hart persuaded

Mowat to commission Brian Bond to write the chapter on the First World War – outside of Bond's prior expertise. Inevitably, Liddell Hart vetted that too. Bond recalled "the pressure he placed on me to alter even moderately sympathetic or favourable statements about Haig or Robertson…perhaps reflecting more deep-seated feelings of insecurity about his career and reputation" (LH 3/176; Mowat 1968: 2, 4; Bond 2015: 34; 2018: 21).

Mowat's commission was confirmed in June 1964. Coincidentally, the Wolfson Foundation, thanks to personal interest from Leonard Wolfson (1927-2010), agreed to fund Liddell Hart's vague theory of peace. Liddell Hart used the fund to pay researchers of the Second World War. Wolfson's funding was effective from 1965 to 1967, which is when Liddell Hart completed the chapter.

The chapter is long (62 pages) but selective. It dwells on pre-war diplomacy. The first year of war gets more attention than any of the subsequent five years. Western Europe is his favoured region, mostly to recycle old complaints about British inter-war and early-war policy. The campaigns around the Mediterranean, Africa, and Middle East are skewed towards the first months and the Egyptian-Libyan desert. The German-Soviet war is skewed towards its first year. He reduces the war against Japan to Britain's war for Malaya and Burma. His impatience with the last four years encourages ridiculous over-simplification.

> No great military errors were made on the Allied side in the years from 1942 to 1945, following America's entry into the war…and it is very doubtful whether the alternative courses that some of them favoured would have done much to shorten the war or diminish its cost (1968b: 793).

History of the Second World War

Liddell Hart's final and longest history of the Second World War took 23 years from commission to publication. He published frequently in that period, always with reference to the Second World War, but almost always to recycle claims and quotes he had released first in *The Other Side of the Hill* (1948).

The invitation from Cambridge, in 1964, to write a chapter on the war helped to focus him. In 1965, the flow of funds from the Wolfson Foundation paid for others to research the campaigns that disinterested him. The completion of his memoirs ended his greatest writing burden since the publication of the history of the tank arm in 1959. Still, he needed another commission to get him moving. In 1966, Purnell & Sons of London commissioned him as "editor-in-chief" of two series of weekly magazines, entitled *History of the Second World War* and *History of the First World War* respectively. The "editor-in-chief" was really honorary. The "editor" (Barrie Pitt) commissioned and edited all the content. Liddell Hart wrote some forewords and suggested friends for Pitt to commission. However, by then some friendly writers had died, such as Percy Hobart, or moved on to current subjects. For instance, Richard Ogorkiewicz had written on wartime German and Soviet armoured forces for a book edited by Liddell Hart in 1956, but declined to write further except on current engineering (LH 1/577; Pitt to Ogorkiewicz, 6 August 1966, LH to Ogorkiewicz, 17 August 1966, and Ogorkiewicz to LH, 8 September 1966, RACTM E2015.2015.74; Bond 1977: 10).

Cassell regarded *Purnell's History of the Second World War* as a competitor for Liddell Hart's time and for market share. Liddell Hart argued that his association with Purnell produced material for his draft book, but he was still seeking other content. In 1967, he agreed to consult on a series of books: *Ballantine's Illustrated History of World War II*. Again, his contributions were limited to suggesting writers and writing forewords. More commitment would have been impossible: the series ran to more than 150 books, each around 160 pages, published from 1968 to 1975. Meanwhile, Purnell published 128 weekly magazines on the Second World War from 1966 to 1969, and another 128 magazines on the Great War from 1969 to 1971. Liddell Hart practically gave up work for both Purnell and Ballantine in 1968.

Liddell Hart completed his *History of the Second World War* in Summer 1969, for Cassell to publish in Spring 1970, with more haste and less oversight than normal. The book itself admits none of dozens of paid researchers and unpaid contributors by correspondence. His wife named only four paid researchers: Christopher Hart, Peter Simkins, Paul Kennedy, and Peter Bradley (in her order). Luvaas and Bond had started earlier, but she soured on their competition with Adrian in her husband's affection (1970: viii; Bond 2018: 111).

Liddell Hart contributed chapters on the years before the war, and the first year of war. Paul Kennedy, then a doctoral student, contributed chapters on Western Allied strategic bombing, anti-submarine operations in the Atlantic, the war in the Pacific, and the second half of the fighting in Italy. A.J.P. Taylor was Kennedy's dissertation adviser and cooperating with Liddell Hart in a revision of Churchill's record (1969). Before the history's publication, Taylor recommended the book as "a work of great length and great learning, illuminated by flashes of insight…full of brilliant strategic analysis." However, after publication, he described it as "ponderous" and patchy (1971). Robert Rhodes James (1970: 56) gained "the impression of a bored Liddell Hart doing his duty in describing events in which he has little interest." Another young admirer admitted that it "is a disappointing and in places misleading book" (Thorne 1985: 49). Correlli Barnett (1999: 62) found it "narrowly concerned with military strategy and its implementation."

21
Biographies

Liddell Hart returned to minor projects and his normal routine: napping in the afternoon (whoever was visiting), entertaining late, working later, and rising late in the morning. On 29 January 1970, he sat down for brunch, stretched for a newspaper, suffered a heart attack, and died.

Over the next thirty years, Liddell Hart's military thought or life was memorialized or biographed by seven men most consequentially: Adrian Liddell Hart, Michael Howard, Jay Luvaas, Brian Bond, John Mearsheimer, Brian Holden Reid, and Alex Danchev. Most were intimates. Most acted with his wife's approval and constraints – and eventual regrets. Mearsheimer was the only one to propose a critical biography, but he self-admittedly failed to overcome the consensus. Liddell Hart continues to be treated faithfully by most historians and soldiers, even though few express satisfaction with any biography. Critics are many, but none has risen to Mearsheimer's rank in academia, partly because most academics, contrary to academic ideals, punish, ignore, or cancel challenges to the consensus.

Adrian Liddell Hart

Adrian started writing recollections of his father in 1970. Some of these recollections are polished (and have been quoted earlier in this book), but he remained conflicted and scattered, and never finished a biography.

In the first half of the 1970s, Adrian's writing was preoccupied with his father's outstanding projects. One was a revision of the short and inaccurately-titled *Why Don't We Learn from History?* (1944b). Adrian chose to commission an editor (1972). He edited only one of his father's projects for himself: an anthology of military writings, from ancient to modern. His father had carried it for two years. Adrian carried it for six. It was published as *The Pen and the Sword*, with Adrian's name as second author. He retained many excerpts of his father's choice, without comment, but corrected his father's dialectic view of soldiers versus writers.

> War leaders and generals and the rank and file have attacked treasonable critics and armchair strategists. Writers, in turn, have attacked stupid and bloodthirsty soldiers…
>
> Yet the antithesis is not clear-cut. Many great war leaders have owed their positions more to the influence of their pens than to any accomplishments on the battlefield…
>
> Moreover, it has been common for great writers on war, as well as many lesser ones, to show marked inconsistency and ambivalence to their subject (1976: 10-11).

This was Adrian's last book. He commented in response to Bond's lecture in January 1979, and lectured to Bond's students on "British Way in Warfare" in February 1982, but later that year stopped writing recollections, although he continued to correspond with Howard and Bond. In 1988, he started notes towards a book on penology. He wrote a review of Mearsheimer's book in February 1989, but never submitted it for publication. He died in 1991 (LHCMA AJLH).

Howard

In 1970, Michael Howard produced two obituaries, which misdescribe Liddell Hart as the "author" of both Germany's Blitzkrieg and Britain's counter-Blitzkrieg in 1939, and thus a man vindicated by the Second World War, until Winston Churchill took a disliking in 1940 (1970a; 1970b; 1976: 131-132).

Howard was best qualified to biograph Liddell Hart, but never did. Strachan believes that Liddell Hart's death allowed him to "give free rein to" a different "side of himself." "Michael could be at once charming and excoriating. When I was in need, he was wonderfully supportive and empathetic; if he disagreed with a judgement I made on a professional matter, he would be instantly dismissive." By then, he was two years into his professorship at Oxford, and pushing Clausewitz as the greatest military thinker. In 1974, Howard, Paret, and linguists not credited on the cover contracted for a new translation and edit of Clausewitz's *On War*, for publication in 1976. They certainly earned more academic ethos from writings on Clausewitz than Liddell Hart. Additionally, Strachan thinks, "the Cold War made Michael a continentalist and therefore sceptical about a British maritime strategy or the British way in warfare." In 1974 Howard lectured on his "reappraisal" of *British Way in Warfare* (1932). The next year, he published it as a pamphlet (24 pages long) (Strachan to author, 2024; Strachan 2022; Mungo 2022: 92-100).

Despite this revisionism, privately Howard continued to lead the search for a biographer who would satisfy Kathleen. He gave up the struggle only after her death in 2001. Five years later, Howard delivered memoirs that admit doubts about Liddell Hart's temperament and judgment. His motivations are not explicit, but certainly he reserved credit for his development of himself and War Studies. Some of his recollections are not true. For instance, he pretends that Liddell Hart was interested in only "operational skills," and disinterested in the politics and sociology of war – which my Chapter 11 alone disproves.* Most revealingly, Howard's memoirs omit his machinations (and disappointments) with Liddell Hart's actual biographers (2006: 141, 144, 154; Strachan 1983; Morgan-Owen and Finch 2022).

Luvaas

After Howard, Liddell Hart's longest-serving disciple was Jay Luvaas. Luvaas had hagiographed him in the last chapter of *British Military Thought* (which is otherwise objectively researched). This chapter leaves no room for the exposures to come. Luvaas (1964: 422) attributes Liddell Hart's biographies and histories to "sound and original research, careful, objective analysis, and a genuine desire to get at the truth." He describes *The Rommel Papers* as "meticulous scholarship." He

---

* Reid (1998: 233) notes that the "true significance of Fuller and Liddell Hart lies in their examination of a number of endlessly complex and fascinating connnections between strategy, operational art, and tactics (the province of the soldier) within their broader study of war as a political and social phenomenon."

describes the history of the tank arm as "a masterpiece that may become a military classic," in which "Liddell Hart has been almost as careful as Thucyidides to conceal his own efforts and treat the oposition impartially." He concludes (424) that the Germans were his "greatest practitioners," "a large number of whom have publicly acknowlegded their debt."

After Liddell Hart died, Luvaas (1970: 1573) memorialized "one of the most profound, original, and influential military thinkers of modern history." Yet he did not develop the chapter or obituary into a biography. To peers, he still seemed to be Kathleen's favourite, but she favoured Adrian. He himself was entering a lazier period, and the end of his marriage (Strachan and Reid, emails to author, 2024).

His productivity certainly slowed in the 1970s, after promotion at Allegheny College (also his alma mater) in Pennsylvania. By then, his focus was the American Civil War, and opportunities at US Army educational instiutions. Like Howard, Luvaas realized that Clausewitz was more marketable than Liddell Hart. Unlike Howard, Luvaas did not repudiate anything. Luvaas (1986) produced a comparison of Clausewitz, Liddell Hart, and Fuller, which admits they shared the principles that Liddell Hart would claim to invent as "indirect approach." Yet the same article maintains the fiction that Liddell Hart applied it to "armoured warfare" and thus invented "Blitzkrieg." Mearsheimer (1988: 15) found that Luvaas "presents distorted accounts of both his military thinking and his policy recommendations." Luvaas (1990: 13) responded with airy faith in Liddell Hart's good nature and influence on Blitzkrieg, but admitted that Liddell Hart had insisted on insertion of the word "deep" before "strategic penetration" in his hagiographic chapter. Yet this admission is missing from his proposal to categorize "indirect approach" as a "landmark in defence litertaure" (1992), and from his introduction to a posthumous edition of Liddell Hart's (1993: vii-ix) biography of Sherman. Here, Luvaas repeats the myth that it contains "the ingredients for...the concept of 'deep strategic penetration,'" and that this concept influenced Germany's Generals in the 1930s.

Bond

Late in 1969, Liddell Hart and Bond (1977: 3, 10) had started work on "Six Great Captains," which Hamilton had suggested in 1954 but given up in 1961. Liddell Hart sold the proposal to Cassell once he finished his *History of the Second World War*. However, after his death his wife transferred the copyright to her step-son, who failed to complete it.

For the time being, Bond did not reveal his plan to write a biography. He made himself busy editing the diaries of Henry Pownall (1887-1961). The work gave Bond new insight into the General Staff, and thence into Liddell Hart's perception of the Army as a whole, although Bond admitted no doubts publicly for now. The first volume was published in 1972, the second in 1973, when he was ready to ask Lady Liddell Hart for permission to write the biography. She was upset. Bond confided to friends (but not to the public) that she did not want her husband to be biographed by their gardener's son. She hoped for her husband to be biographed by David N. Dilks, who had already published biographies of Winston Churchill and George Curzon, and started biographies of Neville Chamberlain and Harold Macmillan. Dilks was a professor of International History, while Bond remained a Lecturer, despite being older. Dilks had visited Medmenham in 1963, to seek Liddell Hart's recollections of Churchill, but stopped corresponding after three letters. The Lady was surely over-ambitious. Bond (1977: 1, 3; 2018: 108-110) implies she was biased by his arrival in a Bentley touring car (although her husband preferred Rolls Royce).

In 1975, Howard persuaded her to permit Bond to write a book on her husband's "military thought," with no more biographical information than necessary for context, pending a distinguished biographer. They agreed that the manuscript should be completed within a year and published by Cassell, where Liddell Hart's long-time collaborator Kenneth Parker still worked. Parker was then at Medmenham, preparing the final archives for transfer to Kings College London. Parker agreed with almost everything in Bond's manuscript, but wasted a year searching for an American publisher, so it was published in 1977 rather than 1976 (Bond 1977: vii, 4; 2018: 111).

Despite the scale and scope of Liddell Hart's military thought, and Bond's choice to include Liddell Hart's non-military "philosophy," Bond's product is long on hearsay and short on quotes. The main body text passes 270 pages, compared to more than 600 pages of Pownall's edited diaries. He spends as much space on the historical context as Liddell Hart's writings. He rarely quotes any writings, but paraphrases or summarizes, often inaccurately (as I have cited in my chapters above). He over-relies on Liddell Hart's memories and memoirs for episodes as long-running and consequential as Liddell Hart's advice to the British government during the 1930s (1977: 60, 95, 105-106, 111).

> It is not the purpose of this study to chronicle Liddell Hart's career in detail, since that has already been admirably done in his memoirs (19).

After the memoirs, Bond quotes Howard most. In the preface, Bond is "very grateful to Howard for suggesting a way of approaching the subject," and to Lady Liddell Hart for permissions and discussions.

From the start, Bond (1977: 4) admits to an emotional relationship with his subject, but claims "to be fair and impartial." In practice, Bond tends to deify in most contexts, and to criticize excessively in minor contexts.

Most reviews were sympathetic, but Lady Liddell Hart blamed Bond (2018: 111) for John Terraine's and the Marquess of Anglesey's attacks on her husband's character and record. Kenneth Macksey (1978), who had already revealed (1972) Liddell Hart's manipulation of Guderian, without Bond mentioning him once, complained of "serious omissions," and characterized the book as a stepping stone to a proper biography: "It remains to be seen if the job is ever done or if this volume of his will suffice."

Nevertheless, the biography boosted him professionally. In the same year it was published, he was promoted to Reader in War Studies. In January 1979, Howard (1979: 21) introduced a debate between Bond and one of Fuller's biographers with a prepared description of Bond as "not only Basil Liddell Hart's biographer, but a close associate, neighbour, friend, and disciple." One of Liddell Hart's publishers (Dan Davin) commissioned Bond to write *British Military Policy Between the Two World Wars* (1980), which relies on Liddell Hart's papers more than the National Archives.

Mearsheimer

John Mearsheimer (1988: 15) found the latter book more objective, and sought Bond's help in a critical biography of Liddell Hart's military thought. A critical biography implies inadequacies in any previous biography, but Bond did help. Mearsheimer pointed out some of Bond's errors, but nevertheless described Bond's biography as "a first-rate work of scholarship, both comprehensive and insightful." Bond did not return the favour: Bond simply ignored Mearsheimer's book.

Jay Luvaas (1990: 13) and Robert O'Neill (1990: 101-102, 111) naturally took exception to Mearsheimer's documentation of Liddell Hart's disarming generosity to a new generation of historians. Their rebuttals are unsound. First, they pretend that Liddell Hart's brief enthusiasm for a small mechanized army in the mid-1920s inspired Blitzkrieg in the 1940s, omitting to mention that in the 1930s Liddell Hart discounted the offensive potential of anything except strategic bombers and two-man tanks (Newsome 2024; 2025a). In the process, O'Neill (1990: 107, 111-112) inadvertently reveals that he had not read Mearsheimer's book properly: he cites Liddell Hart's edition of Guderian's memoirs to rebut Mearsheimer. Second, they conflate Blitzkrieg with "indirect approach." Third, they misrepresent Mearsheimer as insensitive. Luvaas (1990: 13) caricatures Mearsheimer's book as "a coarse chiaroscuro," without "effort to understand the human dimension of his subject." O'Neill (1990: 106) pretends that the book lacks effort to understand Liddell Hart's intents, contributions, and generosity, and that Mearsheimer judges Liddell Hart by "the standards of professional scholars."

Azar Gat had submitted a version of his doctoral thesis, supervised by Michael Howard, for publication in 1988, before he saw Mearsheimer's scholarship. In Gat's review of military thinkers, Clausewitz and Liddell Hart are his favourites (1989). Rather than admit Mearshimer's discoveries, he re-published his book under new titles (1992; 2001), and added ever shorter, self-plagiarized articles and books to "revise the revisionists" – "especially" Mearsheimer (1996a; 1996b; 1997a; 1997b; 1998; 2000). Gat focused on Liddell Hart's claim to invent Blitzkrieg. Gat (1998: 128; 2000: ix, 1) confirms Liddell Hart's "compulsive manipulations of evidence for the purpose of self-aggrandizement," including Liddell Hart's manipulation of Guderian's memoir. Gat claims new evidence, but this turns out to be Liddell Hart's journalism. Gat claims that Liddell Hart publicized Blitzkrieg in articles, whereas Mearsheimer read only books. In fact, Liddell Hart self-plagiarized from articles to books, and Mearsheimer had cited both. Worse, Gat presents Liddell Hart's prescriptions for hit-and-run raids by light tanks as prescriptions for sustained "deep penetration" by combined arms – a misrepresentation and a term that Liddell Hart came up with only after the Second World War (Newsome 2024; 2025a).

Nevertheless, fiery rebuttals, denials, and what we now know as "shadow cancelling" were sufficient to maintain the consensus, as Mearsheimer admits.

> I think the key to explaining the cool reception to my book is that BHLH was (for one reason or another) a god to most serious students of military history in the 1950-1990 time frame, and those "disciples" and their students simply wanted to do everything possible to preserve his reputation, which meant largely ignoring my book (Mearsheimer to author, 18 September 2017).

Yet Mearsheimer had persuaded some professional historians. Chris Bassford (1994: 128), citing Mearsheimer, observed that Liddell Hart's "reputation has not weathered well." J.P. Harris (1995: 201) observed that "it is now generally realized that both his impact on the Germans and his prescience and insight concerning military developments in his lifetime have been vastly overrated." This minor consensus provoked Howard into two more attempts at a sympathetic biography.

Reid

In the 1970s, Brian Holden Reid studied for a doctorate under Bond, and became friendly with Kathleen. In 1982, he graduated to lecturer. Reid (1987: viii, 267) described Bond's book as "a model of how such a study should be written," and "an object lesson in lucid and balanced scholarship." He (1998: 13, xi) characterized Mearsheimer's book as "narrow," "weak," and "polemic," and declared "high time that Liddell Hart's life was treated within the context of the times."

> The "weight" of Mearsheimer's history is directed towards the years before 1945[,] and he makes too much of Liddell Hart's manipulation of his friends (Reid 1999: 80).

Reid looked like an expert, with a biography of Fuller (1987: 161), an article comparing Fuller and Liddell Hart (1990: 70), and eventually a book claiming the same (1998). Howard and Bond suggested Reid to write the definitive biography, but Kathleen resented Bond's students as yet more junior. In 1992, Howard persuaded her of Alex Danchev, but by 1994 she had second thoughts. In November, Howard invited her to attend Reid's lecture (at the College, but to an open audience) on Fuller's and Liddell Hart's politics. By Bond's account, she took exception to Reid's characterization of Fuller and Liddell Hart as similar, except one was fascist, the other liberal. Reid knew nothing of it at the time. He later speculated that she must have misheard something, due to deafness.

This is the most recent of the lectures that Reid revised, over the next few years, for an anthology on British military thought. Reid (1998: 169) offers it as rebuttal to Mearsheimer. However, most chapters are about Fuller. None confronts Mearsheimer's evidence. Yet he endorses Gat's (1996a) earliest rebuttal, as "likely to enhance our understanding of Liddell Hart's influence on the Germans" (13). He states upfront: "I have tried to avoid some of the more contentious areas of debate, mainly because I regard them as fundamentally unimportant" (xi). The book is mired in errors, as basic as the dates of Liddell Hart's military service and partnership with Belisha (3, 7), and as fundamental as the myth that Liddell Hart had offered "deep strategic penetration" within "indirect approach" (178). He dismisses Mearsheimer's finding otherwise as "a terminological quibble" (179).

Still, Bond (2018: 111) hoped that "Reid will eventually produce a biography that will be as nearly definitive as can reasonable be hoped for." Reid himself has not given up hope, but is otherwise retired (emails to author, 2024).

Danchev

Alex Danchev (1955-2016) was awarded a doctoral degree in War Studies from Kings College London in 1984, under Bond's supervision. He went to teach elsewhere, and took more interest in literary fiction, music, and visual art.

In 1992, Danchev finished a biography of Oliver Franks (1905–1992; professor of moral philosophy; civil servant at the Ministry of Supply; independent Liberal peer). Howard invited Danchev to lunch at the Garrick Club in London, followed by tea and cucumber sandwiches with Lady Liddell Hart in Medmenham. She picked up the biography, pointed to a passage about Mrs. Franks, and asked Danchev, politely, to explain. His reply persuaded her of sympathy to wives of male subjects. She and Danchev's agent signed a written agreement: she would act as a source, on condition that he should "consult in good faith" if she were to request changes. The correspondence between him and her runs to more than 100 letters, from September 1993 to publication five years later. Her advice is direct and firm. In response to each of three drafts (sent during the last five months of 1997), she asks for more attention to her husband's good character and contacts in Israel, although she seems uncertain of her husband's writings (University of St. Andrews, ms39008/1/1/41; Danchev 1998a: 265-266).

Howard was one of five people whom Danchev acknowledges as having "carefully scrutinized" the "manuscript." Howard had not consulted Bond or Reid in 1992. Both later denied any responsibility for the commission, characterized Howard as sufficient, and repudiated the product. Still, both were involved when the War Studies Department elected Danchev as Visiting Senior Research Fellow for the period 1993 to 1997 (to fund the research and to accommodate him in the same building as Liddell Hart's archives). At the end of that period, Reid (1998: xi) declared that "we must wait and see what he makes of it."

Danchev's product is shorter than Bond's, despite incomplete sentences, rhetorical questions, foreign idioms, and irrelevant quotes from artists and novelists. Like all previous biographers and memorialists, Danchev quotes little of what Liddell Hart published before the memoirs, rarely criticizes, follows criticisms with caveats or contradictions, and focuses his outrage on Liddell Hart's sympathies towards Nazis. Historian Alaric Searle (2001: 342) characterized the biography as more style than substance. Its "catchy phrases and purple prose serve to highlight rather than conceal the failure to produce really new material or interpretations on the phases of Liddell Hart's life which really matter." Lutz Unterseher (2023: 80) observed that the "book shows that Alex Danchev likes LH," and "does his utmost to save LH's honour," but his success "remains an open question."

Danchev (1998a: 241, 322) confirms Mearsheimer's findings of Liddell Hart's manipulation of Rommel's and Guderian's writings, but otherwise ignores Mearsheimer's evidence, or misrepresents it as absence of evidence: "Mearsheimer has triumphantly demonstrated" that any "reader" of Liddell Hart's papers can "reconstruct what appears to be missing." In a late endnote, he repeats the fallacy, within an unsubstantiated claim that Gat had "demolished" Mearsheimer's book, through superior "sleuthing."

Kathleen seemed indecisive about the product, until Danchev copied to her a positive review by the BBC producer John Grist (1925-2017), in response to which she praised Danchev's "gift as a biographer." However, on her death bed in 2001, just short of her 99th birthday, she indicated to Bond "a terrible mistake." Howard admitted the same to Bond, but his memoirs ignore every biography and potential biographer, and his own role in them. Reid describes Danchev's book as "awful" and damaging to both Danchev's and Liddell Hart's reputations. Danchev cannot answer for himself, as he died (from a heart attack) in 2016, aged 60 years (KLH to Danchev, 14 September 1998, and 9 November 1998, University of St. Andrews, ms39008/1/1/41; Bond 2018: 110-111; Reid, emails to author, 2024).

Legacy

Within 28 years of Liddell Hart's death, his disciples released two book-length biographies, at least two books claiming to rebut the only critical biography, and countless article-length reviews, opinions, and rebuttals. The frequency reflects controversy and dissatisfaction. Liddell Hart's official biographies are dissatisfactory for the same reason that his memoirs are dissatisfactory: the subject and his mentees were biased by self-selection, selection, and contracted constraints. By the 2000s, they gave up, dissatisfied and recriminatory, but ascendant.

Liddell Hart's disciples left the subject's reputation divided between two modes. The smaller mode is over-compensatory – in danger of throwing out the water with the dirt. For instance, Correlli Barnett (1999: 62) found that Liddell Hart's influence 30 years after death is "a cause for wonder and regret," having previously reported Liddell Hart as lead inventor of "Blitzkrieg" (1970: 414, 422, 426).

The larger mode is faithful – pretending or genuinely believing that the water is clear. This faith is somewhat self-protective. Criticism of Liddell Hart inevitably casts doubt on the methods and shibboleths that dominate Anglophone studies of military affairs. Increasingly, academics shadow-cancel challenges to the consensus (contrary to the scientific imperative to challenge), even by misrepresenting peer reviews to justify rejections of my articles on Liddell Hart (Newsome 2023b).

Their agenda has not been helped by an incoherent, chaotic pamphlet by Lutz Unterseher (1942-), a German sociologist who shifted into military commentary while advising the Social Democrat Party (of Germany) and the African National Congress. Nominally, Unterseher introduces and entitles his pamphlet as a rebuttal to Mearsheimer, but the rebuttal waits until the third chapter (of four chapters). The book begins with a biography of Lawrence, and ends with recollections of Wallach, which, "to a considerable extent inspired" the book and his own "very personal assessment of LH" (2023: 83). Unterseher relies on secondary sources, especially Danchev's biography, including for most quotes from Liddell Hart's writings. Even where Unterseher cites Liddell Hart directly, the lack of context suggests he had not read directly. The impression is enhanced by his self-declared "rejoinders" to Mearsheimer, where he mostly acknowledges Mearsheimer's findings, and ends with a few uncited myths. He claims that Liddell Hart prescribed "combined-arms warfare, especially the integration of (armour-protected) mechanized infantry," in the 1930s (2023: 70), that "LH was one of the first to think systematically about how to defensively counter a deep tank attack" (74), that "Guderian...gave the Briton credit for his contribution to the development of the *Panzertruppe*" (46), and that the Briton's confidence in defence-dominance was actually confidence in French mechanized reserves and fortifications, neither of which failed in 1940 (64-68). In conclusion, Unterseher (88) admits "Liddell Hart has deceived numerous experts," but was also "a great inspirer and very respectable teacher of experts as well as to a wider public."

My biography is released 55 years after Liddell Hart's death. It is the first full biography not commissioned, authorized, and written by a mentee or a student of a mentee, and the first to cite Fuller's archives in America, the Tank Museum's archives in Britain, and publishers in both countries.

Now we can admit Liddell Hart as spoiled child, frustrated sportsman, fragile psychology, disloyal husband, indifferent father, productive but shallow scholar, inflated genius, fake scientist, over-compensatory claimant of truth, manipulative arguer, awkward lecturer, energetic correspondent, selective tolerator, inspired but unsound theorist, false logician, false inventor of operations research, anti-militarist who briefly became a militarist, lonely soldier, psychological casualty, war hero who nonetheless fabricated heroism, historian who briefly lionized his Generals before blaming professional soldiers for all disappointments of the Great War, historian who fancied himself as an academic but was careless about sourcing and methodology, unaware applicatory historian, infantry platoon trainer who aimed for a pedestrian solution to defence-dominance, doctrinist who repudiated official manuals after rejection, memorable but unstable strategist, influential but polemical journalist, peacetime soldier who fancied himself as a great commander but put historical study before practical experience, Generals' pet who nonetheless railed against professional soldiers, voluntary convalescent posing as involuntary invalid, Army propagandist and leaker, part-time soldier who chose to retire earlier than necessary but blamed the Army, self-reflected Great Captain, fuzzy liberal, anti-democrat, admirer of fascism, apologist for Nazism, progressive socialist, appeaser, rejected wartime official, quitter of war without victory, regime change, criminal justice, or territorial restitution, advocate for a long, indecisive war through economic and moral pressure – behind a defensive posture – until political revolution, philosopher of femininity, frustrated post-war journalist and academic, hero to Americans and Israelis who preferred to credit him for German success in war, influencer of London University's shift from Military to War Studies, rejected but honorary academic at Oxford, dropout professor at California, skilled author and publisher, reinventive memoirist, self-serving historian of the Second World War, and manipulator of memorialists and biographers from beyond the grave.

We cannot ignore the greatest influence on Anglophone military thought in the last 100 years, even though his insight is sometimes flawed or misrepresented. His insights (and misrepresentations) deserve particular attention on tanks (Newsome 2024), infantry doctrine, tank raids, Blitzkrieg, and manoeuvre warfare generally (2025a), indirect approach (2025b), and other issues of continuing import, as future books must show, free of the biases that have corrupted prior studies.

References

Addison, Paul (1971). "Lloyd George and the Compromise Peace in the Second World War," in A.J.P. Taylor, ed., Lloyd George: Twelve Essays, London: Hamilton: 361-384.
Alexander, Bevin (2000). How Hitler Could Have Won World War II: The Fatal Errors that Led to Nazi Defeat, New York: Crown.
Allon, Yigal (1965). "The Making of Israel's Army: The Development of Military Conceptions of Liberation and Defence," in Howard 1965: 337-371.
Allport, Alan (2020). Britain at Bay: The Epic Story of the Second World War, 1938-1941, New York: Alfred Knopf.
Andrew, Christopher (2009). Defend the Realm: The Authorized History of MI5, New York: Alfred A. Knopf.
Aron, Raymond (1970). "The Evolution of Modern Strategic Throught," in Alastair Buchan, ed., Problems of Modern Strategy, New York: Praeger and Institute for Strategic Studies: 13-46.
Ashley, Maurice (1968). Churchill as Historian, New York: Charles Scribner's Sons.
Aster, Sidney (1971). "Ivan Maisky and Parliamentary Anti-Appeasement, 1938-39," in A.J.P. Taylor, ed., Lloyd George: Twelve Essays, London: Hamish Hamilton: 317-357.
Barnett, Corelli (1970). Britain and Her Army, 1509-1970: A Military, Political and Social Survey, London: Allan Lane.
- (1999). "Basil Faulty?" Journal of the Royal United Service Institution, 144/2: 62-63.
Baynes, John (1995). Far From a Donkey: The Life of General Sir Ivor Maxse, London: Brassey's.
Beadon, R. H. (1933). "A Vindication of Force." The Army Quarterly, 25/2, January 1933, pp. 281-288.
- (1936). "Some Strategical Theories of Captain Liddell Hart." RUSI Journal, 81/524: 747-760.
- (1938). "Defence or Defeat," RUSI Journal, 83: 58-68.
Beadon, R.H., and J.R. Kennedy (1935). "A Reply," Army, Navy & Air Force Gazette: 36.
Beaufre, André (1965). "Liddell Hart and the French Army, 1919-1939," in Howard 1965: 131-141.
Beaverbrook, Lord (Max Aitken) (1956). Men and Power: 1917-1918, London: Hutchinson.
Ben-Moshe, Tuvia (1981). "Liddell Hart and the Israel Defence Forces: A Reappraisal," Journal of Contemporary History, 16/1: 369-391.
Bidwell, Reginald George Shelford (1970). Gunners at War: A Tactical Study of the Royal Artillery in the Twentieth Century, London: Arms & Armour.
- (1973). Modern Warfare: A Study of Men, Weapons and Theories. London: Allen Lane.
Blumenson, Martin (1996). The Patton Papers: 1940-1945, New York: Da Capo Press.
Bond, Brian (1972). The Victorian Army and the Staff College, 1854-1914, London: Eyre Methuen.
- (1973). ed., Chief of Staff: The Diaries of Lieutenant-General Sir Henry Pownall, Volume 1, 1933-1940, London: Archon Books.
- (1974). ed., Chief of Staff: The Diaries of Lieutenant-General Sir Henry Pownall, Volume 2, 1940-1944, London: Archon Books.
- (1977). Liddell Hart: A Study of his Military Thought, London: Cassell.
- (1978). "From Prophecy to Prediction: Liddell Hart and the War in Europe, 1939-1940," Futures, 10/5: 421-427.
- (1979). "The Fuller-Liddell Hart Lecture," RUSI Journal, 124/1 (March 1979), 21-31.
- (1980). British Military Policy Between the Two World Wars, Oxford University Press.
- (1991), ed., The First World War and British Military History, Oxford: Clarendon.
- (2002). The Unquiet Western Front: Britain's Role in Literature and History, Cambridge University.
- (2014). Britain's Two World Wars against Germany: Myth, Memory and the Distortions of Hindsight. Cambridge University Press.
- (2015). From Liddell Hart to Joan Littlewood: Studies in British Military History, Solihull: Helion.
- (2018). Military Historian: My Part in the Birth and Development of War Studies, 1966-2016, Solihull: Helion.
Bond, Lionel Vivian (1922). "Tactical Theories of Captain Liddell Hart (A Criticism)," The Royal Engineers Journal, 36/3: 153-163.
Brooke, Alan (2002). War Diaries, 1939-1945, Alex Danchex and Daniel Todman, eds., London: Phoenix.
Brogan, Hugh, ed. (1997). Signalling from Mars: The Letters of Arthur Ransome, London: Cape.
Buchanan, Patrick J. (2008). Churchill, Hitler, and 'The Unnecessary War': How Britain Lost its Empire and the West Lost the World, New York: Three Rivers.
Bury, John Bagnell (1930). Selected Essays, Cambridge University Press.
Bury, John Patrick Tuer (1952).The College of Corpus Christi and of the Blessed Virgin Mary: A History from 1822 to 1952, Cambridge University Press.
Campbell, John P. (2000). Review of "Alchemist of War," International History Review, 22/2: 457-458.

Carey, B. (1935). "Whither the Tank Brigade?" RUSI Journal, 80/520: 745-748.
Castel, Albert (2003). "Liddell Hart's Sherman: Propaganda as History," Journal of Military History, 67/2: 405-426.
Cato [Michael Foot, Peter Howard, and Frank Owen] (1940). Guilty Men, London: Victor Gollancz.
Central Intelligence Agency, Chief of Europe Division (1972). "Intel Call: Unique Published Reference to Molotov-Ribbentrop Meeting in 1943." https://www.cia.gov/readingroom/docs/GEHLEN%2C%20REINHARD%20%20%20VOL.%206_0136.pdf
Chadwick, Kenneth (1970). The Royal Tank Regiment, London: Leo Cooper.
Chisholm, Anne, and Michael Davie (1993). Lord Beaverbrook: A Life, New York: Alfred A. Knopf.
Citino, Robert M. (2002). Quest for Decisive Victory: From Stalemate to Blitzkrieg in Europe, 1899-1940, Lawrence: University of Kansas.
Clark, Alan (1961). The Donkeys, London: Hutchinson.
Clark, Robert M. (2020). Intelligence Analysis: A Target-Centric Approach, Los Angeles: SAGE.
Clausewitz, Carl von (1942), Principles of War, Hans W. Gatzke, tr. and ed., Harrisburg, PA: Stackpole.
- (1873). On War, translated by J.J. Graham, London: N. Trübner.
- (1943). On War, translated by O.J. Matthijs Jolles, New York: Modern Library and Random House.
- (1984). On War, edited and translated by Michael Howard and Peter Paret, revised edition, Princeton, N.J: Princeton University Press.
Cohen, Eliot A., and John Gooch (1990). Military Misfortunes: The Anatomy of Failure in War, New York: Free Press.
Colville, John R. (1972). Man of Valour: The Life of Field-Marshal the Viscount Gort, London: Collins.
- (1985). The Fringes of Power: 10 Downing Street Diaries, 1939-1955, London: W.W. Norton.
Colvin, Ian Goodhope (1971). The Chamberlain Cabinet, London: Victor Gollancz.
Corrigan, Gordon (2003). Mud, Blood and Poppycock: Britain and World War I, London : Cassell.
Crawford, Fred D. (1998). Richard Aldington and Lawrence of Arabia: A Cautionary Tale. Carbondale: Southern Illinois University Press.
Crossman, R.H.S. (1958). The Charm of Politics and Other Essays in Political Criticism, London: Hamish Hamilton.
Danchev, Alex (1991). "Bunking and Debunking: The Controversies of the 1960s," in Bond 1991: 263-288.
- (1997). To Hell, or, Basil Hart Goes to War," Journal of Strategic Studies, 20/4: 66-93.
- (1998a). Alchemist of War: The Life of Basil Liddell Hart, London: Weidenfeld & Nicolson, 1998a.
- (1998b). "Liddell Hart and Manoeuvre," RUSI Journal, 143/6: 33-35.
- (1999a). "Liddell Hart's Big Idea," Review of International Studies, 25/1: 29-48.
- (1999b). "Liddell Hart and the Indirect Approach," Journal of Military History, 63/2: 313-337.
Davison, Peter (ed.) (2012). George Orwell Diaries, New York: Liveright/Norton.
Deighton, Len (1977). Fighter: The True Story of the Battle of Britain, London: Jonathan Cape.
- (1980). Blitzkrieg: From the Rise of Hitler to the Fall of Dunkirk, New York: Knopf.
Dupuy, R. Ernest, and George Fielding Eliot (1937). If War Comes, New York: Macmillan.
Edmonds, James E., & G.C. Wynne (1927). History of the Great War: Military Operations: France & Belgium, 1915, Volume I, Winter 1914-15: Battle of Neuve Chapelle: Battles of Ypres, London: Macmillan.
- (1935). Military Operations: France and Belgium, 1918, Volume I: The German March Offensive and its Preliminaries: London: Macmillan.
- (1937). "The 5th Army in March 1918," Journal of the Royal United Services Institute, 82/525: 17-31.
Emmerson. James T. (1977). The Rhineland Crisis, London: Maurice Temple Smith.
Falls, Cyril (1959). The Great War, New York: Capricorn.
Feiling, Keith (1946). The Life of Neville Chamberlain, London: Macmillan.
Ferguson Niall (1998). The Pity of War: Explaining World War I, New York: Basic Books.
Forbes, Neil (1987). "London Banks, the German Standstill Agreements, and 'Economic Appeasement' in the 1930s," Economic History Review, 40/4: 571-587.
Freedman, Lawrence (2013). Strategy: A History, Oxford University Press.
- (2017). The Future of War: A History, New York: PublicAffairs.
French, David (1991). "Sir James Edmonds and the Official History: France and Belgium," in Bond 1991: 69-86.
Fuller, J.F.C. (1919) "Strategical Paralysis as the Object of the Decisive Attack," in Weekly Tank Notes, 31 May and 7 June 1919, in Fuller 1928: 83-105.
- (1920). Tanks in the Great War, 1914-1918, London: John Murray.
- (1923a). The Reformation of War, London: Hutchinson.
- (1923b;). "Capt. Liddell Hart and Lieut.-Colonel Bond: A Summary and a Judgment," The Royal Engineers Journal, 37/1: 57-65.
- (1926). The Foundations of the Science of War, London: Hutchinson.

- (1928). On Future Warfare, London: Sifton Praed & Company.
- (1929). The Generalship of Ulysses S. Grant, New York: Dodd, Mead & Company.
- (1932). Lectures on F.S.R. III (Operations Between Mechanized Forces), London: Sifton, Praed.
- (1936). Memoirs of an Unconventional Soldier, London: Ivor Nicholson & Watson.
- (1943). Armored Warfare: An Annotated Edition of Lectures on FSR III, Harrisburg, Pennsylvania: Military Service Publishing Company.

Gardner, Brian (1970). Churchill in Power: As Seen by His Contemporaries, Boston: Houghton Mifflin.
Gat, Azar (1989). The Origins of Military Thought: From the Enlightenment to Clausewitz, Oxford University Press.
- (1992). The Development of Military Thought: The Nineteenth Century, Oxford University Press.
- (1996a). "Liddell Hart's Theory of Armoured Warfare: Revising the Revisionists," Journal of Strategic Studies, 19/1: 1-30.
- (1996b). "The Hidden Sources of Liddell Hart's Strategic Ideas," War in History, 3(3): 293-308.
- (1997a). "British Influence and the Evolution of the Panzer Arm—Myth or Reality?" Part One, War in History, 4/2: 150-173.
- (1997b). "British Influence and the Evolution of the Panzer Arm—Myth or Reality?" Part Two, War in History, 4/3: 316-338.
- (1998). Fascist and Liberal Visions of War: Fuller, Liddell Hart, Douhet, and Other Modernists, Oxford: Clarendon Press.
- (2000) British Armour Theory and the Rise of the Panzer Arm: Revising the Revisionists, Houndmills, England: Macmillan Press, 2000.
- (2001). A History of Military Thought: From the Enlightenment to the Cold War, Oxford University.
- (2018). War and Strategy in the Modern World: From Blitzkrieg to Unconventional Terror, Cass.

Germains, Victor Wallace (1927). The "Mechanization" of War, London: Sifton, Praed.
Gibbs, Norman H., Grand Strategy, Vol. I., London: H.M.S.O, 1956.
- (1965). "British Strategic Doctrine, 1918-1939," in Howard 1965: 187-212.
Gibbs, Philip (1920). Realities of War, London: William Heinemann.
Gibson, Irving M. [Arpad V. Kovacs] (1943). "Maginot and Liddell Hart: The Doctrine of Defense," in: Edward Mead Earle, with Gordon A. Craig and Felix Gilbert, eds., Makers of Modern Strategy: Military Thought from Machiavelli to Hitler. Princeton: Princeton University Press: 365-387.
Gilbert, Martin (1983). Winston S. Churchill, Volume VI, Finest Hour 1939–1941, London: Heinemann.
Graves, Richard Perceval (1990). Robert Graves: The Years with Laura, 1926-1940, New York: Viking.
Graves, Robert (1938). T.E. Lawrence to His Biographer Robert Graves, London: Faber & Faber.
Green, Andrew (2003). Writing the Great War: Sir James Edmonds and the Official Histories, 1915-1948, London: Taylor & Francis.
Griffith, Paddy G., (1994). Battle Tactics of the Western Front: The British Army`s Art of Attack, 1916-18, Yale University Press.
Halewood, Louis, and David Morgan-Owen (2021). "Captains of War: History in Professional Military Education," RUSI Journal, 165/7: 46-54.
Harris, J. Paul (1995). Men, Ideas and Tanks: British Military Thought and Armoured Forces, 1903-1939, Manchester University Press.
Hattendorf, John B. (1990). "The Study of War History at Oxford, 1862–1990." in John B. Hattendorf and Malcolm H. Murfett, eds., The Limitations of Military Power, London: Palgrave Macmillan: 3-61.
Higham, Robin (1966). The Military Intellectuals in Britain, 1918-1939, Rutgers University Press.
Hinsley, F.H., Edward Eastaway Thomas, C.F.G. Ransom, and R.C. Knight (1979). British Intelligence in the Second World War: Its Influence on Strategy and Operations, Volume 2, London: HMSO.
Howard, Michael (1958). Disengagement in Europe, London: Penguin.
- (1961). The Franco-Prussian War: The German Invasion of France, 1870–1871, London: Macmillan.
- (1965). ed., The Theory and Practice of War: Essays Presented to Captain B.H. Liddell Hart on his Seventieth Birthday, London: Cassell.
- (1966). "The Liddell Hart Memoirs," Journal of the Royal United Services Institute, 111/641: 58-61.
- (1969). Problems of Modern Strategy, Adelphi Paper 54, London: Institute for Strategic Studies.
- (1970a). "BHLH 1895-1970," Survival, 12/3: 105.
- (1970b). "Liddell Hart," Encounter, 34/6: 37-42.
- (1970c). Studies in War and Peace, London: Temple Smith.
- (1972a). The Continental Commitment: The Dilemma of British Defence Policy in the Era of the Two World Wars, London: Temple Smith.
- (1972b). History of the Second World War, United Kingdom, Military Series, J.R.M. Butler, ed., Grand Strategy, Volume 4, August 1942 – September 1943, London: HMSO.
- (1975). The British Way in Warfare: A Reappraisal, London: J. Cape, 1975.

- (1976). War in European History, Oxford University Press.
- (1979). "The Fuller-Liddell Hart Lecture," RUSI Journal, 124/1: 21-31.
- (1983). The Causes of Wars and Other Essays, London: Temple Smith.
- (1984). The Causes of Wars and Other Essays, 2nd edition, enlarged, Harvard University Press.
- (1989). The Continental Commitment: The Dilemma of British Defence Policy in the Era of the Two World Wars, paperback edition, London: Ashfield Press.
- (1991). "British Grand Strategy in World War I," in Paul Kennedy, ed., Grand Strategies in War and Peace, New Haven: Yale University Press: 31-41.
- (1999). "An Introduction" to Basil Liddell Hart, Thoughts on War, Staplehurst, Kent: Spellmount: v-ix.
- (2006). Captain Professor: The Memoirs of Sir Michael Howard, London and New York: Continuum.
Icks, Robert J. (1952). "Liddell Hart: One View," Armor, 61: 25-27.
James, Robert Rhodes (1970). "Total War and the Military Historian," RUSI Journal, 115/660: 54-56.
Jameson, [Margaret] Storm (1949). The Moment of Truth, London: Macmillan.
- (1969). Journey from the North, 2 volumes, London: Collins.
Jeffery, Keith (2010). The Secret History of MI6, New York, NY: Penguin Press.
Keegan, John (1976). The Face of Battle, New York: Viking Press.
Kendall, Paul (1957). The Story of Land Warfare, London: Hamish Hamilton.
Kennedy, John F. (1940). Why England Slept, New York: Wilfred Funk.
- (1960). "Book in the News," Saturday Review: 17.
Kennedy, John N. (1957). The Business of War, edited by Bernard Fergusson, London: Hutchinson.
Kennedy, Paul (1991). "Grand Strategy in War and Peace: Toward a Broader Definition," in Paul Kennedy, ed., Grand Strategies in War and Peace, New Haven: Yale University Press: 1-10.
- (2014). "The War at Sea," in The Cambridge History of the First World War, Volume 1, Global War, Cambridge University Press: 321-348.
Kitchen, James E., and Stuart Mitchell (2022). "Michael Howard and the Historian's Craft," British Journal for Military History, 8/2: 2-26.
Kitchen, Martin (1988). "The Political History of Clausewitz," Journal of Strategic Studies, 11/1: 27-50.
Larson, Robert H. (1980). "B.H. Liddell Hart: Apostle of Limited War," Military Affairs, 44/4: 70-74.
- (1984). The British Army and the Theory of Armored Warfare, 1918-40, Newark, N.J.: University of Delaware Press.
Lawrence, T.E. (1919). "Demolitions Under Fire," Royal Engineers Journal, 29/1: 6-10.
- (1920). "Evolution of a Revolt," Army Quarterly, 1/1: 55-69.
- (1938). Seven Pillars of Wisdom: A Triumph, De Luxe Edition, Garden City, NY: Doubleday.
Lehmann, John (1960). Autobiography, II, I Am My Brother, London: Longmans.
Lewin, Ronald (1971). "Sir Basil Liddell Hart: The Captain Who Taught Generals," International Affairs, 47(1): 79-86.
Liddell Hart, Adrian (1953). Strange Company, London: George Weidenfeld & Nicolson.
Liddell Hart, Basil H. (1918a). Outline of the New Infantry Training, Adapted to the Use of the Volunteer Force, Cambridge University Press.
- (1918b). New Methods in Infantry Training, Cambridge University Press.
- (1918c). Battle Drill, or Attack Formations Simplified, Cambridge University Press.
- (1919a). "The 'Ten Commandments' of the Combat Unit: Suggestions on its Theory and Training," RUSI Journal, 64/454: 288-293.
- (1919b). "Suggestions on the Future Development of the Combat Unit: The Tank as a Weapon of Infantry," RUSI Journal, 64/456: 666-669.
- (1920a). "The Essential Principles of War and Their Application to the Offensive Infantry Tactics of Today," United Service Magazine, 61/1097: 30-44.
- (1920b). "The 'Man-in-the-Dark' Theory of War: The Essential Principles of Fighting Simplified and Crystallized into a Definite Formula," National Review, 75/448: 473-484.
- (1920c). "A New Theory of Infantry Tactics Based on a Direct Application of the 'Man-in-the-Dark' Theory of War," National Review, 75/449: 693-702.
- (1921a). "The 'Man-in-the-Dark' Theory of Infantry Tactics and the 'Expanding Torrent' System of Attack," RUSI Journal, 66/461: 1-23.
- (1921b). "A Science of Infantry Tactics," The Royal Engineers Journal, 33/4: 169-182.
- (1921c). "A Science of Infantry Tactics: A Lecture Delivered at the SME on 6th Jan., 1921," The Royal Engineers Journal, 33/5: 215-223.
- (1921d). "The Soldier's Pillar of Fire by Night: The Need for a Framework of Tactics," Journal of the Royal United Service Institution, 66/464: 618-626.
- (1922a). "A Study of the New French Infantry Regulations," The Royal Engineers Journal, 35/5: 233-256.
- (1922b). "Are Infantry Doomed?" The National Review, 79/471: 455-463.

- (1922c). "Infantry – 'The New Model'," The National Review, 79/473: 712-722.
- (1922d). "The Future Development of Infantry," The National Review, 80/476: 286-294.
- (1922e). "Colonel Bond's Criticisms (A Reply)," The Royal Engineers Journal, 36/5: 297-309.
- (1922f). "A Study of the French 'FSR' – Instruction Provisoire Sur L'Emploi Tactique Des Grandes Unités," RUSI Journal, 67/468: 666-677.
- (1923a). "Study and Reflection v. Practical Experience: A Critical Examination of the Claims of Age, the Professional, and the 'Practical' Soldier to Unique Authority on War," Army Quarterly, 6/2: 318-331.
- (1923b). A Science of Infantry Tactics Simplified, London: William Clowes & Sons.
- (1924a). "The Next Great War," Royal Engineers Journal, 38/1: 90-107.
- (1924b). "Two Great Captains: Jenghiz Khan and Subutai," Blackwood's Magazine, 215/1303: 644-659.
- (1924c). "The Development of the 'New Model' Army," Army Quarterly, 9/1: 37-50.
- (1925). Paris or the Future of War, London: Kegan Paul.
- (1926a). A Greater Than Napoleon: Scipio Africanus, London: Blackwood.
- (1926b). "World War," in Encyclopedia Britannica, 13th edition, London: 1072-1094.
- (1926c). A Science of Infantry Tactics Simplified, London: William Clowes & Sons.
- (1926d). The Lawn Tennis Masters Unveiled, London: J.W. Arrowsmith.
- (1927a). "The Army of a Nightmare," The Fighting Forces, in 1941a: 69-81.
- (1927b). The Remaking of Modern Armies, London: John Murray.
- (1927c). Great Captains Unveiled, W. Blackwood and Sons, London.
- (1927d). "Back to Armour: Sir George Milne and Future Warfare – The Power of Petrol," Royal Tank Corps Journal: 191-192.
- (1927e). "Army Training, 1927," RUSI Journal, 72/488: 746-754.
- (1928a). Reputations: Ten Years After, London: John Murray.
- (1928b)."Some Impressions of Fascist Italy," Daily Telegraph, 10, 12, 14, 16 January, LH 10/1928/1 to 4.
- (1929c) "The New Romulus and the New Rome," The Atlantic Monthly, 142/1, July 1928c: 108-119.
- (1928d). "Armoured Forces in 1928," RUSI Journal, 73/492: 720-729.
- (1928e). "The Army and the Future – Lessons of 1928: Brakes on Mechanised Efficiency," Royal Tank Corps Journal: 242-244.
- (1929a). The Decisive Wars of History: A Study in Strategy, Boston: Little, Brown, & Company.
- (1929b). Sherman: Soldier, Realist, American, Boston: Dodd, Mead & Company.
- (1929c). "The New British Doctrine of Mechanized War," The English Review, in 1941a: 92-107.
- (1930a). Sherman: The Genius of the Civil War, London: Benn.
- (1930b). The Real War, 1914-1918, London: Faber & Faber.
- (1930c). "The Army Exercises of 1930," RUSI Journal, 75/500: 681-690.
- (1931a). Foch: The Man of Orleans, London: Eyre & Spottiswoode, 1931a.
- (1931b). "Economic Pressure or Continental Victories," RUSI Journal, 76/503: 486-510.
- (1932a). "War and Peace," English Review, 54: 438-440.
- (1932b). "Aggression and the Problem of Weapons," English Review, 55: 71-78.
- (1932c). The British Way in Warfare, London: Faber & Faber.
- (1932d). "The Tale of the Tank," The Nineteenth Century and After, 112: 595.
- (1933a). "The Grave Deficiencies of the Army," The English Review, 56: 147-151.
- (1933b). The Future of Infantry, London: Faber & Faber.
- (1933c). The Ghost of Napoleon, London: Faber & Faber.
- (1934a). A History of The World War, 1914-1918, London: Faber & Faber.
- (1934b). T.E. Lawrence in Arabia and After, London: Cape.
- (1934c). "Looking ahead – And Back," Army Quarterly, 28: 255-259.
- (1934d). "Are the Generals Ready? The True State of the Armed Forces of Europe," Scribner's Magazine: 129-137.
- (1934e). "Speed! – and More Speed! – in War," New York Times Magazine, 2 December 1934: 3-18.
- (1935a). When Britain Goes to War: Adaptability and Mobility, London: Faber & Faber.
- (1935b). "Would Another War End Civilization?" Harpers Magazine, 170/4: 312-322.
- (1936a). The War in Outline, 1914-1918, London: Faber & Faber.
- (1936b). "Future Warfare," The Atlantic Monthly, 158: 687-695.
- (1937). Europe in Arms, London: Faber & Faber.
- (1938a). "The Defence of the Empire," Fortnightly Review, 143/848: 20-31.
- (1938b). "Does the Organization of the Army Fit its Functions?" Fighting Forces: 32-33.
- (1938c). "Strategy and Commitments," Fortnightly Review, 143/858: 645-648.
- (1938d). "Military and Strategic Advantages of Collective Security in Europe," New Commonwealth Quarterly, 9/4: 144-155.

- (1938e). Through the Fog of War, New York: Random House.
- (1938f). "Britain's Military Situation," Yale Review, 28: 230-244.
- (1938g). T.E. Lawrence to His Biographer Liddell Hart, London: Faber & Faber
- (1939a). "Britain is in Danger," Evening Standard, in 1941: 126-133.
- (1939b). The Defence of Britain, London: Faber & Faber.
- (1940a). "Hore-Belisha's Resignation," Sunday Chronicle, 7 January, in 1941a: 171-173.
- (1940b). "The Background to Hore-Belisha's Removal," Sunday Express, 14 January, in 1941a: 173-179.
- (1940c). "The Way to Win the War," Evening Standard, 3 February, in 1941a: 180-186.
- (1940d). "Should We Go to the Assistance of the Finns?" Evening Standard, 10 February,in 1941a: 222-6.
- (1940e). "Will the Cities Be Bombed?" Sunday Express, 11 February, in 1941a: 195-201.
- (1940f). "Is It Stalemate in the West?" Sunday Express, 18 February, in 1941a: 202-208.
- (1940g). "The Best Guarantee Against Aggression," 27 February, in 1941a: 164-168.
- (1940h). "Tortoise to Tank," World Review, 9/1: 15-21.
- (1940i). Dynamic Defence, London: Faber & Faber.
- (1941a). The Current of War, London: Hutchinson.
- (1941b). The Strategy of Indirect Approach, London: Faber & Faber.
- (1942a). This Expanding War, London: Faber & Faber.
- (1942b) The British Way in Warfare, London: Penguin.
- (1944a). Thoughts on War, London: Faber & Faber.
- (1944b). Why Don't We Learn from History? London: George Allen & Unwin.
- (1946a). The Revolution in Warfare, London: Faber & Faber.
- (1946b). The Strategy of Indirect Approach, London: Faber & Faber.
- (1948). The Other Side of the Hill: Germany's Generals, Their Rise and Fall, with their own Account of Military Events, London: Cassell.
- (1949). "The German Generals Talk," Infantry Journal, 64/1: 31-34.
- (1950). Defence of the West, London: Cassell.
- (1951). The Other Side of the Hill, revised edition, London: Cassell.
- (1952). "The Objective in War: National Object and Military Aim," Naval War College Review, 5/4: 1-30.
- (1953). The Rommel Papers, London: Collins.
- (1954a). Strategy: The Indirect Approach, London: Faber & Faber.
- (1954b). "Night Action – and Its Development," Army Quarterly, 66/1: 4-6.
- (1956a). ed., The Soviet Army, London: Weidenfeld & Nicolson.
- (1956b). ed., A Battle Report: Alam Halfa, Quantico, VA: Marine Corps Association.
- (1957). "The Great Illusions of 1939," Military Review, 36/10: 3-11.
- (1959a). The Tanks: The History of the Royal Tank Regiment and its Predecessors Heavy Branch Machine-Gun Corps Tank Corps and Royal Tank Corps, 1914-1945, London: Cassell.
- (1959b). "What is Military Genius?" Marine Corps Gazette, June 1959: 20-21.
- (1959c). "The Basic Truths of Passchendaele," RUSI Journal, 104/616: 433-439.
- (1960a). Deterrent or Defence: A Fresh Look at the West's Military Position, London: Stevens & Sons.
- (1960b). "Armed Forces and the Art of War: Armies," in by J.P.T. Bury, ed., New Cambridge Modern-History, Volume X, The Zenith of European Power, 1830-70, Cambridge University Press: 302-330.
- (1965). The Memoirs of Captain Liddell Hart, 2 volumes, London: Cassell.
- (1967). Strategy: The Indirect Approach, second revised edition, London: Faber & Faber.
- (1968). "The Second World War," in Mowat 1968: 735-797.
- (1969). "The Military Strategist," in A.J.P. Taylor, ed., Churchill: Four Faces and the Man, London: Allen Lane, Penguin: 153-202.
- (1970). History of the Second World War, London: Cassell.
- (1972). Why Don't We Learn from History? Revised edition, Herman Ould, ed., London: George Allen.
- (1976), edited by Adrian Liddell Hart, The Sword and the Pen: Selections from the World's Greatest Military Writings, New York: Thomas Y. Crowell.
- (1992). Scipio Africanus: Greater Than Napoleon, London: Greenhill.
- (1993). Sherman: Soldier, Realist, American, Boston, Mass.: De Capo Press.

Lloyd George, David (1938). War Memoirs of David Lloyd George, 2 Volumes, London: Odhams Press.
Lord, David (1997). "Liddell Hart and the Napoleonic Fallacy," RUSI Journal, 142/2: 57-63.
Luvaas, Jay (1964). The Education of an Army: British Military Thought, 1815-1940, Chicago University.
- (1965). "European Military Thought and Doctrine, 1870-1914," in Howard 1965: 69-94.
- (1970). "Basil Liddell Hart," American Historical Review, 75/3: 1573.
- (1986). "Clausewitz, Fuller, and Liddell Hart," Journal of Strategic Studies, 9/2: 197-212.
- (1990). "Liddell Hart and the Mearsheimer Critique: A 'Pupil's' Perspective," Parameters, 20/1: 9-19.

Macready, Gordon N. (1935). "The Trend of Organization in the Army," RUSI Journal, 80/517: 1-20.
- (1965). In the Wake of the Great, London: William Clowes & Sons.
Macksey, Kenneth (1965). To the Green Fields Beyond: A Short History of the Royal Tank Regiment, Bovington: Royal Tank Regiment.
- (1967). Armoured Crusader: A Biography of Maj Gen Sir Percy Hobart London: Hutchinson.
- (1972). "Liddell Hart: The Captain Who Taught Generals," The Listener: 895.
- (1979). The Tanks: History of the Royal Tank Regiment, 1945-1975, Arms & Armour Press.
- (1981). The Tank Pioneers, London: Jane's.
- (1983). A History of the Royal Armoured Corps and its Predecessors, 1914-1975, Beaminster: Newtown.
- (1988). Tank Versus Tank: The Illustrated Story of Armored Battlefield Conflict in the Twentieth Century, London: Grub Street.
Manchester, William (1988). The Last Lion: Winston Spencer Churchill Alone, 1932-1940, New York: Little, Brown, & Company.
Marshall-Cornwall, James H. (1935). Geographic Disarmament: A Study of Regional Demilitarization, London: Oxford University Press and Royal Institute of International Affairs.
- (1984). Wars and Rumours of Wars: A Memoir, London: Leo Cooper, Secker & Warburg.
Martel, Giffard le Quesne (1927). Report on the Staff Conference held at the Staff College, Camberley, 17th to 20th January, 1927, London: His Majesty's Stationary Office.
- (1931). In the Wake of the Tank: The First Fifteen Years of Mechanization in the British Army, London: Sifton Praed.
- (1945). Our Armoured Forces, London: Faber & Faber.
- (1949). An Outspoken Soldier: His Views and Memoirs, London: Sifton Praed.
Maurice, Frederick Barton (1929). British Strategy: A Study of the Application of the Principles of War, London: Constable.
McDonald, Iverach (1984). The History of the Times, Volume 5, Struggles in War and Peace, 1939-1966, London: Times Books.
McEntee, Girard Lindsley (1937). Military History of the World War, New York: Charles Scribner's Sons.
McLachlan, Donald (1971). In the Chair: Barrington-Ward of The Times, 1927-1948, London: Weidenfeld & Nicolson.
Mearsheimer, John J. (1988). Liddell Hart and the Weight of History, Ithaca: Cornell University Press.
Mick, Christopher (2014). "1918: Endgame," in The Cambridge History of the First World War, Volume 1, Global War, Cambridge University Press: 133-171.
Minney, R.J. (1961). The Private Papers of Hore-Belisha. Garden City, NY: Doubleday.
Montgomery, Bernard Law (1958). Memoirs, Cleveland: World Publishing Company.
- (1968). A History of Warfare, London: Collins.
Morgan-Owen, David, and Michael Finch (2022). "The Unrepentant Historian: Sir Michael Howard and the birth of War Studies," British Journal for Military History, 8/2: 55-76.
Morris, L. Robert, and Lawrence Raskin (1992). Lawrence of Arabia: The 30th Anniversary Pictorial History. New York: Anchor Books.
Mosley, Oswald (1968). My Life, New Rochelle, NY: Arlington House.
Mowat, Charles Loch (1968). ed., The New Cambridge Modern History, Volume XII, second edition, The Shifting Balance of World Forces, 1898-1945, London: Cambridge University Press.
Mumford, Lewis (1934). Technics and Civilization, New York: Harcourt, Brace & Co.
Mungo, Melvin (2022). "Revisiting the Translators and Translations of Clausewitz's On War," British Journal for Military History, 8/2: 77-102.
Narizny, Kevin (2003). "Both Guns and Butter, or Neither: Class Interests in the Political Economy of Rearmament," American Political Science Review, 97/2: 203-220.
Neilson, Keith (2005). Britain, Soviet Russia and the Collapse of the Versailles Order, 1919–1939, Cambridge University Press.
Newman, Bernard Charles (1935). Spy, Victor Gollancz.
Newman, Simon (1976). March 1939, Oxford: Clarendon Press.
Newsome, Bruce Oliver (2003a). "Don't Get Your Mass Kicked: A Management Theory of Military Capability," Defence and Security Analysis, 19/2: 131-148.
- (2003b). "The Myth of Intrinsic Combat Motivation." Journal of Strategic Studies. 26/4: 24-46.
- (2007). Made, Not Born: Why Some Soldiers Are Better than Others. Westport, CT: Praeger.
- (2016). An Introduction to Research, Analysis, and Writing: Practical Skills for Social Science Students, SAGE.
- (2021a). The Rise and Fall of Western Tanks, I, 1855-1939, Coronado, CA: Tank Archives Press.
- (2021b). The Rise and Fall of Western Tanks, II, 1939-1955, Coronado, CA: Tank Archives Press.

- (2023a). A Practical Introduction to Security and Risk Management, Coronado, CA: Perseublishing.
- (2023b). "Peer review as shadow canceling," Quillette.
  https://quillette.com/2023/03/21/peer-review-as-shadow-cancelling/
- (2024). Sir Basil Liddell Hart and Tanks, Coronado, CA: Perseublishing.
- (2025a). Tank Raids and Blitzkrieg: The Development and Misrepresentation of Maneuver Warfare from the Great War to the Second World War, Coronado, CA: Perseublishing.
- (2025b). Indirect Approach: From SunTzu to Liddell Hart, Coronado, CA: Perseublishing.

Noel-Baker, Philip John (1936). The Private Manufacture of Armaments, London: Victor Gollancz.
- (1979). The First World Disarmament Conference, 1932-1933: And Why it Failed, Oxford: Pergamon.

Ogorkiewicz, Richard M. (2021). Observer of Cold War Tank Development, Bovington: Tank Museum.

O'Neill, Robert John (1990). "Liddell Hart Unveiled," Twentieth Century British History, 1/1: 101-113.

Owen, Frank (1955). Tempestuous Journey: Lloyd George: His Life and Times, New York: Macgraw-Hill.

Pearson, Frederic S. (2001). Review of "Fascist and Liberal Visions of War," American Political Science Review, 95/4: 1034-1035.

Pennington, Leon Alfred, Romeyn B. Hough Jr, and H.W. Case (1943). The Psychology of Military Leadership, New York: Prentice Hall.

Pile, Frederick (1949). Ack-Ack: Britain's Defence against Air Attack During the Second World War, London: George G. Harrap.
- (1965). "Liddell Hart and the British Army, 1919-1939" in Howard 1965: 169-183.

Plumb, J.H. (1969). "The Historian," in A.J.P. Taylor, ed., Churchill Revised: A Critical Assessment, New York: The Dial Press: 133-169.

Poore, C.G. (18 November 1934). "Liddell Hart on War," New York Times, Book Reviews: 26.

Portway, Donald (1971). Memoirs of an Academic Old Contemptible, London: Leo Cooper.

Reid, Brian Holden (1987). J.F.C. Fuller: Military Thinker, London: Macmillan Press.
- (1990). "JFC Fuller and BH Liddell Hart: A Comparison," Military Review, 70/3: 64-73.
- (1999). "The Legacy of Liddell Hart: The Contrasting Responses of Michael Howard and Andre Beaufre," British Journal for Military History, 1/1: 66-80.
- (2006). "A Signpost That Was Missed? Reconsidering British Lessons from the American Civil War," Journal of Military History, 70/2: 385-414.
- (2009). "Michael Howard and the Evolution of Modern War Studies," Journal of Military History, 73/3: 869-904.

Repington, Charles à Court (1924). Policy and Arms, London: Hutchinson.

Reynolds, David (2014). The Long Shadow: The legacies of the Great War in the Twentieth Century, New York: Norton.

Ripsman, Norrin M., and Jack S. Levy (2007). "The Preventive War That Never Happened: Britain, France, and the Rise of Germany in the 1930s," Security Studies, 16/1: 32-67.

Ropp, Theodore (1959). War in the Modern World, Durham, North Carolina: Duke University Press.
- (1962), War in the Modern World, revised edition, New York: Macmillan.

Ross, Gordon MacLeod (1976). The Business of Tanks, 1933 to 1945, Ilfracombe: Arthur H. Stockwell.

Sayle, Timothy Andrews (2011). "Defining and Teaching Grand Strategy," The Telegram: Newsletter of the Hertog Program in Grand Strategy, 4: no page numbers.

Schuker, Stephen (1986). "France and the Remilitarization of the Rhineland, 1936," French Historical Studies, 14/3: 299–338.

Searle, Alaric (2001). "Fuller and Liddell Hart: The Continuing Debate," War in History, 8/3: 341-347.

Self, Robert, ed., (1988). The Neville Chamberlain Diary Letters, Volume IV, The Downing Street Years, 1934-1940, Aldershot, Hampshire: Ashgate.

Sheffield, Gary (2001). Forgotten Victory: The First World War: Myths and Realities, London: Headline.

Sheppard, E. W. (1938). Tanks in the Next War, The Next War Series, edited by Liddell Hart, London: Geoffrey Bles.

Skidelsky, Robert (1990). Oswald Mosley, 3rd edition, London: Macmillan.

Stearns, S.J. (1972). "Introduction," Liddell Hart, Paris or the Future of War, New York: Garland: 5-17

Stevenson, Francis (1971). Lloyd George: A Diary, A.J.P. Taylor, ed., New York: Harper & Row.

Strachan, Hew (1983). "The British Way in Warfare Revisited," The Historical Journal, 26/2: 447-461.
- (1991). "The 'Real War': Liddell Hart, Cruttwell, and Falls," in Bond 1991: 41-67.
- (2019). "Michael Howard," Biographical Memoirs of Fellows of the British Academy, 20: 223–244.
  https://www.thebritishacademy.ac.uk/documents/4300/20-Memoirs-11-Howard.pdf
- (2020). "Michael Howard and the dimensions of military history." War in History, 27/4: 536-551.
- (2022). "Michael Howard and Clausewitz," Journal of Strategic Studies, 45/1: 143-160.

Strong, Kenneth (1968). Intelligence at the Top, London: Cassell.

Swain, Richard M. (1990). "B.H. Liddell Hart and the Creation of a Theory of War, 1919-1933," Armed Forces & Society, 17/1: 35-51.
Tanks Victory Club (1946). Twenty-Five Thousand Tanks: A Record of the War Effort of Those Who Provided the "Armour in which We Trusted", London: Tanks Victory Club.
Taylor, A.J.P. (1961). The Origins of the Second World War, London: Hamish Hamilton.
- (1963). The First World War: An Illustrated History, London: Hamish Hamilton.
- (1965a). English History, 1914-1945, Oxford University Press.
- (1965b). "Soldier Out of Step," The Observer Weekend Review, 30 May: 26.
- (1965c). "A Prophet Vindicated," The Observer, 31 October: 27.
- ed., Lloyd George: Twelve Essays,
- (1969). "The Statesman," in A.J.P. Taylor, ed., Churchill Revised: A Critical Assessment, New York: The Dial Press: 15-60.
- (1971). "Rational Wars?" New York Times Review of Books, 4 November: 51-52.
Temperley, Arthur C. (1938). The Whispering Gallery of Europe, London, Collins.
Terraine, John A. (May 1959a). "Passchendaele and Amiens – I," RUSI Journal, 104/614: 173-183.
- (1959b). "Passchendaele and Amiens – II," RUSI Journal, 104/615: 331-340.
- (1978). To Win a War: 1918, The Year of Victory, London: Sidgwick & Jackson.
Thomson, David (1950). England in the Nineteenth Century, 1815-1914, London: Penguin.
- (1960). The New Cambridge Modern History, Vol. 12, The Era of Violence, 1898-1945, Cambridge University Press.
Thorne, Ian D.P. (1985). "Interpretations: Liddell Hart After 15 Years," RUSI Journal, 130/4: 48-51.
Travers, Tim (1987). The Killing Ground: The British Army, the Western Front, and the Emergence of Modern Warfare, 1900-1918, London: Allen & Unwin.
Trythall, Anthony John (1977). "Boney" Fuller: Soldier, Strategist, and Writer, 1878-1966, New Brunswick, NJ: Rutgers University Press.
Unterseher, Lutz (2023). Liddell Hart and the Weight of Criticism: Military Theorist in the Crosshairs, Berlin: LIT Verlag.
Updegraff, L.V. (7 February 1932). "Faith, Not Strategy, as the Keystone of Foch's Strategy," New York Times Review of Books: 3.
Walters, Robert E. (November 1961). "Interview with Capt. B.H. Liddell Hart," Marine Corps Gazette, 45/11: 22-29.
Wavell, Archibald P. (1934). "From T.E. Lawrence to T.E. Shaw," The Listener, 11: 404.
- (1948). The Good Soldier. London: Macmillan.
- (1960). Armed Forces and the Art of War: Armies, in David Thomson, ed., New Cambridge Modern History, Vol. 12, The Era of Violence, 1898-1945, Cambridge University Press: 255-277.
Weidhorn, Manfred (1974). Sword and Pen: A Survey of the Writings of Sir Winston Churchill, Albuquerque: University of New Mexico Press.
Wheldon, John (1968). Machine Age Armies, London: Abelard-Schuman.
Wilkinson, Spenser (1927). "Killing No Murder: An Examination of Some New Theories of War," Army Quarterly, 15/4: 14-27.
Winton, Harold R. (1988). To Change an Army: General Sir John Burnett-Stuart and British Armored Doctrine, 1927-1938, Lawrence, Kansas: University Press of Kansas.
Woodward, Llewellyn (1967). Great Britain and the War of 1914-1918, London: Methuen & Company.
Wolff, Leon (1958). In Flanders Fields: The 1917 Campaign. New York: Viking.
- (1963). In Flanders Fields: The 1917 Campaign. 2nd edition, New York: Time.
Wright, Adrian (1998). John Lehmann: A Pagan Adventure, London: Duckworth.
Wright, Patrick (2000). Tank: The Progress of a Monstrous War Machine, New York: Viking.
Young, Robert J. (1996). France and the Origins of the Second World War, Basingstoke: Macmillan.
Zook, David (1960). "John Frederick Charles Fuller, Military Historian," Military Affairs, 23/4: 185-193.

Index

Abyssinia, 102, 143-144, 154, 207
Acland, Richard, 139
Adam, Ronald, 45, 167
Adjutant General, 118, 119, 167
Admiralty, 46, 160, 178
Adolphus, Gustav, 34, 120n
Aeronautical Research Committee, 46
Africa, 181, 193, 227
Air control, 44, 207
Air Defence Experimental Establishment, 46
Aircraft, 64, 90, 112, 186, 201, 213
Aisne, 61
Aldington, Richard, 104
Alexander the Great, 74, 121
Alexander, Bevin, 214
Algerian, 27, 28
All Souls College, Oxford, 101, 126
Allanson, Cecil, 124n
Allenby, Edmund, 112
Allegheny College, 231
Allied Control Council, Berlin, 27
Allon, Yigal, 121, 208-210
Allport, Alan, 141, 146n
Amateurism, 106-107, 112, 128
Ambleside, 179, 197
American Civil War, 77, 186, 231
American Lawn Tennis (magazine), 98
Amphibious warfare, 28, 205
Analogies, 87, 91-93
Ancre, 51
Angell, Norman, 130n
Anglesey, Marquess of, 232
Anti-Aircraft Command, 46, 162, 168
Anti-aircraft forces, 99, 102, 131-132, 168, 192
Appeasement, 9, 11, 103-104, 129-131, 139, 140, 143-155, 159, 171, 195
Applicatory history, 10, 77-78
Armoured cars, 211, 215
Armoured Divisions (see also Mobile Division), 168, 211, 213
Army, 1st, 82
Army and Navy Club, 117
Army Council, 92, 117, 159
Army Education Corps, 81, 105, 217, 221
Army List, 127
Army, Navy & Air Force Gazette, 111
Army Operational Research Group, 46
Army Quarterly (magazine), 67, 90, 108
Aron, Raymond, 88, 218n
Artificial moonlight, 85
Artillery, 64, 89, 92, 147, 186
Asquith, Herbert, 97, 158
Aston, George, 100
Astor, Lord (John Jacob Astor), 99, 103
Astor, Waldorf, 100
Athenaeum Club, 217
Atkinson, G.R., 32

Atlantic Ocean, 228
The Atlantic (magazine), 30
Attack Formations for Small Units (manual), 80
Attlee, Clement, 138-140, 157
Attrition, 59, 67, 69, 74
Atomic Energy Commission, 26
Auchinleck, Claude, 170
Austin, F. Britten, 32, 107, 137
Austria, 147-149, 154, 188, 217
Ayalon, Zeev, 213
Balaclava, 104
Balbo, Italo, 135, 137
Baldwin, Stanley, 99-101, 128, 143, 155
Balkans, 179, 189, 195
Ballanine, 228
Bardell, 108-109
Barker, Arthur, 99
Barrington-Ward, Robert "Robin," 99-104
Barnett, Correlli, 71, 95, 215, 228, 236
Bartlett, Vernon, 130
Bassford, Christopher, 121, 233
Battle of Britain, 162, 164
Beadon, R.H., 7, 95, 111, 112
Beaufre, André, 215
Beaverbrook, Lord (Max Aitken), 11, 103, 104, 157, 158, 161-165, 169, 174-177, 179, 180, 191, 197
Beck, Ludwig, 184
Belgium, 177, 189, 193
Belisha, Leslie Hore, 11, 19, 45, 96, 112, 124, 127, 132, 139, 149, 152, 155, 157, 159, 167, 169, 170, 184, 196, 203
Bentley, Edmund Clerihew, 64
Berlin, 27
Bernal, John Desmond, 45
Bernard, Henri, 215
Bevan, Aneurin, 163
Bidwell, Shelford, 36, 42, 70, 93, 95, 121
Birkbeck College, London, 45
Bishop of Chichester (George Bell), 180-181
Bishop of Lichfield (Edward Woods), 161
Black Sea, 148
Blackett, Patrick M.S., 46
Blackpool, 26
Blackwood, Douglas, 198
Blitzkrieg, 8, 9, 12, 80, 89, 104, 129, 141, 191, 193-194, 199, 204, 206, 213-214, 226, 230-233, 236-237
Blockade, 63, 67, 144, 178, 183, 185, 186, 187, 192, 194
Blumentritt, Günther, 177, 180
Board of Trade, 160
Bols, Louis, 22
Bombing, strategic, 67, 99, 102, 128, 132, 148, 150, 157, 161-162, 172, 178, 179, 183-187, 193-194
Bond, Brian, 7, 19, 28, 29, 32, 36, 38, 39, 40, 41, 42, 47, 51, 52, 53, 55, 59, 67, 70, 71, 73, 74, 75, 77n, 78, 90, 93, 122, 141, 153, 155, 162n, 169, 183, 194-195, 198-199, 208-215, 219-221, 225, 227, 229-236

Bond, Lionel, 33, 36, 41, 43, 101, 105-106
Bovington Camp, 72
Bowra, Maurice, 73
Boxing, 81
Boy Scouts, 47
Bradley, Peter, 228
Brand, Peter, 27
British Expeditionary Force, 10, 57, 60, 80, 159, 167-168, 216
British Union of Fascists, 136-137, 161, 172
Brooke, Alan, 167, 169, 170
Brophy, John, 32
Brumwell, George Murray, 100
Buchan, John, 107n
Buchanan, Patrick J., 152
Buckingham, 96, 133
Burma, 194, 207, 227
Burnett-Stuart, John "Jock," 110, 120, 205
Burnham, Lord (Fred Lawson), 98, 113
Bury, J.P.T. "Patrick," 226
Bury, John Bagnell, 33, 226
Butler, Geoffrey G., 33
California, 13, 221-222, 237
Cambrai, Battle of, 72
Cambridge, 13, 24, 31, 33, 47, 56, 73, 79, 85, 216, 221
Cambridge Modern History, 217, 225-226
Cambridge University Press, 79-80, 225-226
Cambridgeshire Regiment, 56, 79
Campbell, David, 19
Canada, 30, 164, 175, 196
Canary Islands, 223
Capetanakis, Demetrios, 25
Cardiff, 131
Carr, Laurence, 167-168
Carter, Violet Bonham, 130n
Carthage, 74
Cassell, 13, 198-199, 223-225, 228, 231-232
Castel, Albert, 74, 78
Castlerosse, Lord, 50
Cavallero, Ugo, 135
Cavan, Lord (Rudolph Lambert), 109, 114
Cecil, Lord (Robert), 130n, 139, 157
Central Intelligence Agency, 181
Chamberlain, Austin, 136
Chamberlain, Neville, 99, 101, 127, 132, 139, 143, 146, 152n, 154-155, 158-160, 163, 174, 176, 178n, 185-188, 191, 231
Chess, 16, 92-93
Chichele Professor of Military History (History of War), 13, 90, 101, 115, 197, 215
Chief of the Imperial General Staff, 82, 84, 98-99, 109, 113-117, 124, 159, 167, 168
Chiefs of Staff Committee, 187
China, 147
Chindits, 207
Chorley (neé Hopkinson), Katherine, 32
Churchill, Randolph, 130-132, 212
Churchill, Winston, 11, 66, 124, 128-130, 133, 138-141, 152n, 155, 157-163, 166-167, 170, 172, 176-177, 180, 189, 191, 193, 212, 228, 230-231
Clark, Alan, 69, 215
Clarke, Campbell, 131
Clarke, F.A.S., 68
Clausewitz, Carl von, 36, 44, 59, 66, 74, 87-90, 120, 213, 218, 226, 230-231
Clay, Henry, 197
Cliveden, 99
Cohesion, 49
Cold War, 63, 77, 89, 94, 199, 229-230
Collective security, 143-144, 152, 172
Combined Operations, 26
Commander of the Order of the British Empire, 116
Committee, 1922, 146, 187
Committee for Imperial Defence, 60, 187
Committee for the Scientific Survey of Air Defence
Communism, 135, 137, 139n, 172, 178
Concentration, principle of, 63, 134, 213
Conscription, 11, 48, 131-133, 172
Constantinople, 117n
Continental Commitment, 99, 168, 172, 195, 216
Contracting funnel, 81, 107
Cooper, Alfred Duff, 127, 164
Corps, XV, 82
Corps, XVIII, 80, 82n
Corpus Christi College, Cambridge, 24, 221
Corrigan, Gordon, 59
Corsets, 18, 24, 30
Cripps, Stafford, 157, 180
Criterion magazine, 64
Croquet, 16
Crossman, R.H.S., 184
Cruttwell, C.R.M.F., 62n
Cudlipp, Hugh, 166
Cummings, Arthur John, 177
Curzon, George, 231
Czechoslovakia, 102, 129, 132, 148-152, 154, 188
The Daily Express, 103, 158, 160, 163-164, 197
The Daily Mail, 97, 179, 196
The Daily Telegraph, 7, 11, 67, 97, 98-102, 109, 113, 115, 117, 125, 131, 135
Dalton, Hugh, 130, 153, 157
Danchev, Alex, 7, 19, 32, 36, 38, 39, 41, 51, 52, 53, 55, 70, 76, 141, 155, 162n, 183, 194, 225, 229, 234-236
Dartington, 24, 174
Darwin, Charles, 42
Davies, David, 130
Davin, Dan, 232
Dawson, Geoffrey, 99-101
Dayan, Moshe, 211
Deduction, 43
Deedes, Charles, 127
Defence-dominance, 12, 89, 147-148, 171, 177, 183, 185-186, 190-191, 204
Deighton, Len, 194

Delbrück, Hans, 218n
Denmark, 189, 193, 203
Deputy Chief of the Imperial General Staff, 167-168
Deterrence, 11, 91, 95, 97, 146, 150-157, 172, 188, 191, 193, 195, 203
Deverell, Cyril, 37, 84
Devon, 24, 29, 174-175, 179
Dialectic, 44
Dilks, David N., 231
Dill, John, 167-168
Director of Artillery, 131
Director of Infantry Records, 55
Directorate of Military Intelligence, 44, 45
Directorate of Military Operations, 44
Directorate of Military Operations & Intelligence, 44, 168, 188
Directorate of Military Training, 44, 168
Directorate of Operational Research, 46
Directorate of Staff Duties, 44-45, 84, 167
Division, 4th, 84
Dorchester Hotel, London, 26, 86
Dori, Yaakov, 209-211
Dorman-Smith, Eric, 32
Drills, Battle or Field, 56, 83-85, 107, 116
Dugan, Winston, 81-83
Dunkirk, 177
Eastern Command, 82, 84, 114
Economy of force, 38, 85, 190
Economic sanctions, 143-144, 185-187, 192
Economic warfare, 12
Edgeborough, Surrey, 18
Eden, Anthony, 157, 180
Edmonds, James, 60-62, 68, 69, 84
Egypt, 64, 110, 144, 165, 166, 193, 203, 209-214, 227
Elam, Horace, 18
Elmhirst, Leonard and Dorothy, 174
Encyclopedia Britannica, 107
Eritrea, 144
Estonia, 165
Eton School, 20, 24
The Evening Standard, 103, 131, 163-164
Evetts, John "Jack," 81-82
Exeter University, 221
Expanding torrent, 81-82, 85, 88-92, 94, 107, 185
Experimental forces, 106-107, 109, 115, 117, 119, 129, 204
Faber, Geoffrey, 173, 198, 226
Falkenhayn, Erich von, 60
Falls, Cyril, 69, 103, 197-198, 215, 217
Far East Command, 168, 205
Fascism, 11, 135-137, 172, 178
Festschrift, 13, 204, 210, 216, 222-225
Fiction, 31, 65, 84, 107
Field Force, 153
Field Service Regulations, 84n, 85
Fighter Command, 161n
The Fighting Forces magazine, 59, 119
Finland, 162-163, 165, 175, 181

Fix-and-flank, 92
Flanagan, Wolfe, 100
Fletcher, Raymond, 69
Flower, Desmond, 198-199
Foch, Ferdinand, 66, 69, 92n, 121
Focus (group), 11, 124, 129-131, 150, 160
Fog, 85
Force density, 101
Force structure, 88-89
Foreign Office, 125-127
Forester, C.S., 84n
Fort Wagner, 85
France, 15, 73, 102, 106, 117n, 119, 120, 137, 139, 143-152, 159, 159-160, 164, 168, 173-174, 177, 182, 188-189, 193, 196, 198
Franco, Francisco, 147-148
Franks, Owen, 234
Freedman, Lawrence, 194
French, David, 62n
French, John, 60
French Army, 82-84, 128, 145, 159-160, 202, 205, 212
French Foreign Legion, 25, 27-28
Freud, Sigmund, 42
Friction, 92
Fritsch, Werner von, 184
Fuller, J.F.C., 23, 34, 36, 39, 43, 69, 75, 76, 77, 78, 115-116, 119-121, 137, 141, 161, 166, 185, 189, 192, 214, 223, 226, 232, 234, 236
Fuller, Sonia, 29
Gabriel, Richard, 74
Galet, Émile-Joseph, 66n
Galili, Yisrael, 212
Gallipoli, 63
Gas, toxic, 53-54
Gaster, Vivian, 113
Gat, Azar, 39, 40, 141, 233, 234, 235
Gaza Strip, 209
General Staff, 82, 85, 92n, 107, 128, 136, 167-168, 182, 184, 186
Germains, Victor, 90
Germany, 80, 97, 102, 121, 130, 133, 137, 144-154, 164, 171-183, 186-195, 203, 204
Gibbs, Norman Henry, 215-217
Gibbs, Philip, 62n
Gibraltar, 147, 167, 168
Gillman, Webb, 117
Gloucestershire (Volunteers) Regiment, 21, 55
Goering, Hermann, 137
Gordon, John, 159, 174
Gort, Lord (John Vereker), 84, 157, 159-160, 167-168
Gough, Hubert, 61
Goutard, Adolphe, 215
Goya, Francisco, 17
Grand strategy, 87
Grant, Ulysses S., 77
Graves, Robert, 29, 32, 40, 76, 102, 175
Great Captain, 11, 34, 120-121

249

Greece, 63-64, 109, 117n, 133-134, 194, 223
Green, Andrew, 62n, 71
Greene, Wallace M., 222
Grigg, Edward William Macleay, 161n
Grigg, James, 11, 46, 157, 166-167
Grist, John, 235
Guderian, Heinz, 184, 199-200, 202, 232-233, 235-236
Guilty Men, 161
Gurion, David Ben, 211-212
Haganah, 207-210, 212
The Hague, 149
Haig, Douglas, 10, 57-58, 60-62, 64, 68, 69, 82n, 112, 124, 126, 227
Halifax, Lord (Edward Wood), 99, 102, 132, 149, 157-159, 177, 193n
Hamilton, Hamish, 13, 221, 223-224
Hankey, Maurice, 125, 161n, 197-198
Hannibal, 74, 120
Harris, J.P., 233
Hart, Bramley Henry, 14, 15-16, 159
Hart, Christopher, 228
Hart (neé Liddell), Clara, 14, 15, 17
Hart, Ernest, 14, 15, 159
Hart, Joan, 16
The Herald of Melbourne, 118
Herbert, Sidney, 139
High Wray House, 179
Higham, Robin, 47, 114
Higher strategy, 87-88
Hinterhoff, Eugene, 86
Hit-and-run, 90
Hitler, Adolf, 129, 134, 137, 143, 149, 152, 153, 162, 174, 176-177, 180-184, 192, 194
Hoare, Samuel, 42, 127, 144, 149, 163, 164
Hobart, Percy, 167-168, 197, 199-200, 204, 227
Hodge, Beryl, 175
Hoffmann, Max, 66n
Holmes, Sherlock, 43
Holt, Benjamin, 64n
Home Forces, 168-169
Home Guard, 168
Horne, Alastair, 215
Horne, Henry, 82-83
Howard, Michael Eliot, 13, 19, 32, 36, 39, 67, 70, 88, 122, 155, 195, 214-224, 229-236
Hull, 64
Human tank, 91
The Hundred Thousand (group), 131, 139
Hungary, 148
Hutchinson, Graham Seton, 137
Hutton, Thomas Jacomb, 117
Huxley, Julian, 130n
Huxley, Thomas, 34, 42
Iceland, 26
Icks, Robert, 12, 104, 201-204
In-and-out approaches, 90
Inchon, 205
India, 127, 161n, 165, 166-167, 197, 207

Indian Army, 33
India Bill, 99
Induction, 43
Infantry, 89, 91, 237
Infantry Journal, 201-202
Infantry manual (French), 82-84
Infantry Training (manual), 10, 79, 82
Infantry and Tank Cooperation and Training (manual), 80
Infantry Training (manual), 79, 81, 84, 99, 107
Inskip, Thomas, 45, 127, 188
Inspector of Artillery, 117
Inspectorate-General of Training, 80, 100, 167, 168
Institute of Historical Research, 219
Institute for Strategic Studies, 219
Institution of Royal Engineers, 107
Insurgency, 64, 94, 162, 207-211
Intelligence, 45, 60, 120, 145-153, 185, 207-208
International institutionalism, 123, 138
International law, 125, 130, 138
International relations, 220n
Ironside, Edmund, 50, 84, 159-160, 167-168, 189
Ismay, Hastings "Pug," 169
Isolationism, 11, 132, 144, 148, 165, 172, 174, 176, 191, 216
Israel, 12, 40, 200, 205, 207-214, 223
Italy, 63-64, 109, 130, 135-137, 143-150, 153, 154, 174, 182, 183, 187, 192-193, 216, 223, 228
James, Robert Rhodes, 78, 228
Jameson, Margaret Storm, 17, 19, 22, 39, 40, 41, 120, 134, 151, 175
January Club, 136
Japan, 143, 147, 150, 183, 187, 189, 193-194, 197, 205, 227
Jeeps, 210
Joffre, Joseph, 60, 66n, 93
Joint Intelligence Committee, 153, 185
Jomini, Antoine-Henri, 43
Jutland, Battle of, 63
Kendall, Paul, 223
Kennedy, John F., 121
Kennedy, Paul, 88, 228
Kenya, 144
Khan, Genghis, 120n
King George VI, 159, 164
King's College Cambridge, 24
King's College London, 13, 217-220, 232
King's Own Yorkshire Light Infantry, 48, 52, 56
Kirke, Walter, 84-85
Kitchen, Martin, 88
Kluck, Alexander von, 76
Knock-out blow, 188, 190-191
Knowles, Lees, 47
Kordt, Theodor, 149-150
Korea, 12, 205
Krulak, V.H., 222
Labour Party, 123, 133, 135-140, 164, 202
Larson, Robert, 88, 214
Laskov, Haim, 211-212, 214

Latvia, 165
Lawn Tennis Journalists' Association, 98-99
Lawrence (of Arabia), Thomas Edward, 21-22, 27, 37, 66, 69, 101, 104, 110, 128-129, 133, 157, 208, 210-211, 223
Lawson, Fred, 100-101
Layton, Walter, 158
League of Nations, 130, 143-144, 152
League of Nations Union, 130, 139
Leeper, Reginald "Rex," 99n
Lees-Smith, Hastings Bertrand, 177
Lehmann, John, 24-25
Lenin, Vladimir, 69
Leopold, King of the Belgians, 25
Lewin, Ernest Ord, 84n
Lewis, Michael Arthur, 226
Liberal Party, 123-130, 133, 138-140, 166, 196, 216
Liberalism, 11, 123, 138, 141
Libya, 144, 207, 227
Liddell, Clive, 84, 167
Liddell Hart, Adrian, 10, 20, 23-28, 38, 41, 78, 94, 141, 159, 162n, 179, 198, 216, 221, 229-230
Liddell Hart, Basil Henry
» Abstractions, 87, 93-95
» Ageism, 11, 18, 108-112, 136, 138
» Anglophobia, 12, 41-42, 135, 202, 215
» Anti-conscriptionist, 123, 131-132, 172
» Anti-democrat, 123, 133-135
» Anti-militarist, 48, 122, 135
» Appeaser, 143-154
» Applicatory historian, 77-78
» Arguer, 38-39
» Battle Drill, or Attack Formations Simplified, 80
» Breakdowns, 17, 21, 30, 41, 51-52, 57, 75, 105, 159
» British way in warfare, 37, 39, 63, 68, 70, 75, 76, 77, 89, 110-111, 121, 136, 143, 146, 185, 186-187, 194, 196, 216, 230
» Christianity, 16, 31, 47
» Commander, 105-107
» Correspondent, 40
» Death, 54, 229
» The Decisive Wars of History, 74, 76, 133, 208
» Deep strategic penetration, 199, 217, 231-234
» Defeatist, 9, 162, 178, 180, 184
» The Defence of Britain, 173, 190, 194
» The Defence of the West, 184, 199
» Doctrinist, 79-86
» Education, 16-18, 73
» Elitist, 123, 133
» Europe in Arms, 119n, 146
» This Expanding War, 196
» Fascist admirer, 135-137
» Femininity, 9, 12, 30, 196, 237
» Framework of a Science of Infantry Tactics, 81
» The Future of Infantry, 208
» Generalizer, 42
» Generals' pet, 107-108
» Genius, 32, 77, 108

» The Ghost of Napoleon, 75, 121
» Great Captain, 120-121
» Great Captains Unveiled, 120
» Heart attacks and disease, 54, 113
» Histories of the Great War, 57-58, 62-64, 74-77, 109, 112, 124, 186
» History of the Second World War, 13, 75, 152n, 162, 181, 198, 205, 224, 227-229, 231
» Indirect Approach, 10, 16, 67, 74, 87, 89, 90, 146-148, 184, 208, 210, 212-214, 217, 231, 233, 234, 237
» Invalid, 114
» Journalist, 41, 97-104
» Knighted, 116n, 140, 225
» The Lawn Tennis Masters Unveiled, 98
» Leaker, 117-118
» Lecturer, 39-40
» Liberal, 123-126, 141, 161
» Logician, 34, 43-44, 206
» Memoirs, 13, 75-76, 173, 195, 198, 224-225, 227, 232
» Methodologist, 75-76
» Militarist, 48-49, 122
» Nazi apologist, 137-138, 171, 182-183
» The Other Side of the Hill, 75, 182, 198-199, 201-202, 223, 227
» Operations Researcher, 44-45, 167
» opposition to orthodoxy, 18, 32, 39, 70, 109, 111, 115, 122, 124, 138, 141, 196, 198, 207, 222
» Pacifist, 123
» Paris, or The Future of War, 59, 90, 109, 115
» Peace-monger, 181-182
» The Pen and the Sword, 229
» Philosophy, 38, 42, 76, 102, 112, 130n, 198, 232
» Physiognomy, 18
» Progressive, 123, 136, 138-140
» Propagandist, 114-116
» Psychology, 19, 47, 49-50, 54-55, 73, 206
» Quitter, 171-172
» Rebel, 122
» Reductionism, 42, 77
» Remaking of Modern Armies, 119
» Retirement from Army, 118
» The Revolution in Warfare, 34, 76, 94, 183, 198-199
» Scholar, 31
» Scientist, 33-36, 159, 166-168
» Self-exile, 179
» Socialist, 11, 48, 123, 135-140
» Sourcing, 74-75
» Strategist, 87-96, 224
» The Tanks (official history of the tank arm), 75, 199-200, 205, 211, 230
» Taxation, 219
» Theorist, 34, 36, 42-43
» Thoughts on War, 32, 196
» Tolerator, 40, 123
» Truth-seeker, 34, 36-38, 78, 103, 196
» on women, 21, 40-42, 196

»Why Don't We Learn From History?, 76, 229
Liddell Hart (neé Stone), Jessie, 20-24, 26, 28, 29, 101, 159, 196
Liddell Hart (neé Nelson, neé Sullivan), Kathleen, 10, 28-31, 32, 159, 170, 175, 196, 198-200, 203, 214, 215, 219, 221-222, 230-236
Lithuania, 165
Liverpool University, 221
Livy (Titus Livius), 74
Lloyd George, David, 11, 19, 37, 60-61, 66n, 69, 97, 124-133, 138, 141, 142, 156, 157-163, 166-167, 171-177, 184, 197
Locarno, 145
Locker-Lampson, Oliver, 129
Logic, 43
Logistics, 95, 185, 193, 210-211
London, University of, 45, 215-220
London District HQ, 80, 81, 105
Long war theory, 185-193
Loos, Battle of, 65
Lord, David, 155
Lord Privy Seal, 165
Luvaas, Jay, 12, 32, 36, 43, 47, 53, 55, 67, 70, 74, 78, 82n, 84n, 85, 93, 104, 114, 118, 121, 201, 203n, 204-205, 215, 219, 226, 229-233
Luxemburg, 177, 189, 193
MacArthur, Douglas, 12, 201, 204-205
MacDonald, Ramsay, 100, 126, 138
Macdonell, Archibald Gordon, 177
Machine-guns, 93, 94, 186
Macksey, Kenneth, 232
Macleod, Roderick "Rory," 159
Macmillan, Harold, 231
Macmillan, Lord (Hugh Pattison), 164
Mahan, Alfred Thayer, 120
Maisky, Ivan Mikhailovich, 148-149, 151, 167, 172, 174
Malaya, 194, 227
Malta, 144, 168
Mametz Wood, 54-55
Man-in-the-dark, 81, 85, 91-92
Manchester, William, 105n, 152n
Manchester Guardian, 98, 136
Manchuria, 150
Manners, 95
Mao Tse Tung, 36
March, Peyton C., 66
Markham, Sydney Frank, 96
Marseilles, 27, 28
Martel, Giffard le Quesne, 117
Martin, Kingsley, 132
Master General of Ordnance, 168
Marx, Karl, 42
Massy, Hugh R.S., 168
Maurice, Frederick, 216
Maxim, 82, 95
Maxse, Ivor, 19, 39, 61, 62, 80-82, 100, 105, 116, 124
Maxse, Leo, 97

Mearsheimer, John, 9, 36, 40, 41, 42, 141, 155, 214, 225, 229, 232-235
Medmenham, 219, 231-232, 234
Mendl, Wolfgang, 221
Mesopotamia, 63, 109
Middle East, 111, 170, 188-189, 194, 207-208, 227
Military Assistant, 115-116, 169
Military Commentators Circle, 86, 196, 218
Military Co-ordination Committee, 164
Military operations research: see operations research
Military Secretary, 115, 117, 127
Military Science, 216
Military Studies, 215-220, 237
Milne, George, 45, 65, 98-99, 109, 114-118
Milwaukee, 26
Minister for Co-ordination of Defence, 45, 127, 188
Ministry of Air, 128, 164, 168
Ministry of Aircraft Production, 164, 166, 168
Ministry of Defence, 100
Ministry of Information, 160, 163-164
Ministry of Supply, 165, 169, 234
Ministry of War Production, 165
Missiles, 94-95
Mobile Division, 167
Molotov, Vyacheslav, 181
Mongols, 106, 205
Montgomery, Bernard Law, 84, 86, 224-225
Montgomery-Massingberd, Archibald Amar, 101, 116-120
Moral pressure, 88, 185, 189-190
The Morning Post newspaper, 11, 97-98, 113
Morris Motors, 117
Moshe, Tuvia Ben, 214
Mosley, Oswald, 136, 161, 172
Mountbatten, Louis, 26
Movement for Freedom, 11, 124, 130-132
Mowat, Charles Loch, 226-227
Mumford, Lewis, 141
Munich, 150, 152
Murray, Archie, 22
Murray, Gilbert, 130n, 175, 197
Murray, John, 198
Mussolini, Benito, 129, 134-137, 143
Napoleon Bonaparte, 42, 59, 63n, 65, 66, 74, 75, 90, 92, 97, 120-121, 128, 134, 226
National Government, 100, 138
National Portrait Gallery, 8
The National Review (magazine), 97
Naval & Military Club, 86
Nazi (National Socialist) Party, 136
Negative training, 106
Negev, 209
Nelson, Horatio, 121
Nelson, Jennifer, 30, 175, 196
Nelson, Judith, 30, 175, 196
Nelson, Tim, 30
Netherlands, 177, 189, 193

New Party, 136
New Writing magazine, 25
New Orleans, 26
New Statesman and Nation (magazine), 132
New York, 26
Newall, Cyril, 161
Newman, Bernard, 17, 53, 65, 107n
Newman, Simon K., 152n
News Chronicle, 158, 177
Newton, Isaac, 36
Night fighting, 85
Nobel Peace Prize, 225
Noel-Baker, Philip, 130n
Normandy, 159, 165, 194
Northcliffe, Lord (Alfred Harmsworth), 97, 99
Northern Command, 80-82, 167, 168
Northern Ireland, 168
Norway, 120, 158-162, 176, 189
Nuclear warfare, 94-95, 122, 183, 184
Nuffield College Oxford, 197
Nuremberg, 183
The Observer, 98, 100, 177
Octopus, 93
Officer Training Corps, 31, 47, 48, 56
Ogorkiewicz, Richard, 29, 212, 227-228
O'Neill, Robert, 38, 39, 78, 114, 122, 195, 215, 233
Operations research, 44, 115, 169
Orwell, George, 179, 180
Outward Bound Sea School, 27
Owen, David Kemp, 180
Oxford University, 13, 24, 90, 195n, 196-198, 213, 215-216, 219, 221-222, 230
Pacific Ocean, 205, 228
Pa'il, Me'ir, 213
Pakenham-Walsh, Ridley, 35
Palestine, 12, 168, 207-209
Palmach, 209
Paramount Films, 160
Paret, Peter, 215, 221-222, 230
Paris, 47
Parker, Kenneth, 232
Passchendaele, Battle (Campaign) of, 67-69
Patton, George S., 17, 169, 202
Paulus, Friedrich von, 181
Peace Aims Group, 158
Peck, Richard, 161-162
Penguin Books, 226
Pershing, John J., 66n
Philippines, 205
Picardy, 51
Pile, Frederick "Tim," 45, 161-162, 168-169
Pillar of fire, 81-82
Pitt, Barrie, 215, 227-228
Plan 1919-89-90
Platoon Training (manual), 80
Poland, 149, 151-154, 160, 165, 171-174, 182, 190-191, 193, 195
Political revolution, 12, 88, 192
Portmeirion, 156

Portsmouth, 179
Pound, Dudley, 178
Powell, Enoch, 65
Pownall, Henry, 168, 188, 231
Price, Frederick, 113
Principles of war, 38, 63, 85, 87, 91, 134, 190, 213
Professionalism, 106-108, 112
Progressivism, 123, 138
Pure strategy, 87-88
Purnell, 227-228
Putlitz, Wolfgang zu, 145, 148-149, 151
Queen Elizabeth II, 8
Rabin, Yitzhak, 212-213
Radar, 46
Rafah el Arish, 213
Raids, 10, 12, 88, 92-94, 112, 119, 128-129, 168, 185-193, 199, 204, 207, 209, 213, 233, 237
Railways, 15, 31
Ransome, Arthur, 16
Rathbone, Eleanor, 130n
Rattigan, Terence, 69
Raynsford, Richard M., 59, 119
Read, Herbert Edward, 64
Reformation of War, 89n, 90
Regius Professor of Modern History, 33, 226
Reid, Brian Holden, 36, 40, 42, 73, 74n, 78, 87n, 95, 121, 141, 155, 159n, 218, 229, 230n, 234-235
Reith, John, 164
Repington, Charles, 98, 113
Retiarius, 93
Reynolds, David, 71
Rhineland, 144-145
Ribbentrop, Joachim von, 181
Richmond, Bruce, 100
Riding, Laura, 175
Robbins, Alfred Gordon, 99
Robertson, William Robert, 61, 124, 227
Rome, 136
Rommel, Erwin, 170, 184, 199-200, 202, 208, 223, 230, 235
Rommel, Manfred, 200
Ropp, Theodore, 12, 78, 114, 201, 204, 226
Ross, Gordon Macleod, 131
Rothermere, Lord (Harold Harmsworth), 158, 179n, 196
Rowlands, Archibald, 32, 46, 166-167, 197
Royal Air Force, 46, 99, 114, 145
Royal Artillery, 84n
Royal Engineers, 33, 106, 107, 117
Royal Flying Corps, 55
Royal Historical Society, 73
Royal Military Academy, Woolwich, 95
Royal Military College, Sandhurst, 48, 66
Royal Naval College, 226
Royal Navy, 63, 67, 114, 144-145, 177, 179, 186, 216
Royal Navy Volunteer Reserve, 25
Royal Tank Regiment, 72, 199
Royal United Service Institution (now: Royal United Services Institute for Defence and Security Studies), 39, 68, 80-81, 105, 107

253

Ruhr, 145
Rumania, 63, 109, 148, 181, 188
Rye, 139
Rylands, George "Dadie," 24-25
Saar, 145
Sadeh, Yitzhak, 207-209
Saint Paul's School, 16, 17, 31
Salter, Arthur, 130n, 157
Samuel, Herbert, 126
San Francisco, 26, 222
Sandhurst: see Royal Military College
Sandys, 130
Sankey, John, 130n
Satellites, 94
Saxe, Maurice de, 120n
Scammell, J.M., 90-91
Scherpenberg, Albert-Hilger van, 145, 149
Schlieffen, Alfred von, 213n
School of Military Engineering, 81
Schurman, Don, 215
Schweppenburg, Geyr von, 145-147, 150
Scipio Africanus, 74, 120, 214
Searle, Alaric, 235
Security, principle of, 38
Secutor, 93
Seine River, 194
Serbia, 63, 109
Sharon, Ariel, 211
Sharett, Moshe, 212
Shell shock, 49, 54
Shepherd, Edwin Colston, 100n
Sherman, William T., 27, 59, 74, 76, 77, 92, 93
Shorncliffe Camp, 82
Sidi bei Abbes, 27
Simkins, Peter, 228
Simon, John, 11, 124, 126
Sinai, 211
Sinclair, Archibald, 126
Small Arms Training (manual), 82
Smoke, 85
Social Science, 36, 220, 222
Socialism, 123
Sociology, 219-220, 230
Soldier's heart, 54
Somaliland, 144
Somme, Battle (Campaign) of, 52-55, 62, 67, 84n
South-East Asia, 168, 188
Southampton, 221
Southern Command, 85, 119
Soviet Union, Soviets, 95, 130, 143-153, 165, 172, 177n, 179, 182, 184, 187-191, 194, 202-203, 227
Spanish Civil War, 129, 146-148, 154
Speidel, Hans, 200
Sports, 16-18, 73, 97-98
The Spectator (magazine), 80
Spens, Will, 48
Spicer, Lance, 53
Squires, Ernest, 167
Staff College, British Army, 17, 33, 60, 73, 122, 146, 187, 211

Stalin, Josef, 134, 151, 165
Stalingrad, 12, 181
Stanford University, 221
States House, 219
Stokes, Richard, 176
Stony Stratford, 96
Stornoway House, 164
Strachan, Hew, 64n, 67, 70, 78, 217n, 218, 221n, 230
Strategy, 87-88, 92
Strong, Kenneth, 17
Stroud, Gloucestershire, 17
Sudan, 207
Sudetendeutsches Freikorps, 150
Sudetenland, 131, 148-152, 154, 180, 188-190
Suez Canal, 144, 223
Sullivan, Alan, 28
Sullivan, Barry "Matthew," 196
Sunday Express, 158, 174
Sunday Pictorial, 166
Sun Tzu, 36
Sunday Dispatch, 97
Surprise, 85
Sweden, 12, 171, 176, 180, 189, 203
Swinton, Ernest, 101, 115, 197
Switzerland, 145, 199, 203
Syrian, 64
Tactics, 88, 92, 94, 224
Tal, Israel, 213
Tank Brigade, 204
Tank Corps, 23, 62
Tankettes, 94, 117, 120
Tanks, 9, 64, 80, 88, 91, 94, 102, 126, 128, 168, 185, 193-194, 199-201, 204, 213, 216, 236
Tassigny, Jean de Lattre de, 27
Tavistock, Marquis of, 176
Taylor, A.J.P., 69, 195n, 224, 228
Taylor, Maurice, 168
Technology, 64, 87, 94, 95
Tennis, 16, 97
Terraine, John, 41, 68, 69-70, 232
Territorial Army, 115, 132
Think-pieces, 99
Thompson, Reginald William, 215
Thomson, David, 226
Thursfield, H.G., 100n
Tilford House, 197n, 199n
The Times newspaper, 11, 68, 69, 81n, 97, 99-104, 131, 143-146, 150, 152, 153, 159, 163, 166, 173-174, 198, 204, 208
Thucydides, 230
Tizard, Henry, 46
Trans-Olza, 149
Transjordan, 168, 207
The Training and Employment of Platoons (manual), 79
Trenchard, Hugh, 22, 115
Trident and net, 92, 93
Trinity College Cambridge, 47

Tristan da Cunha, 221
Trotsky, Leon, 121
Turkey, 63-64, 109
Turn-over pieces, 99
Ukraine, 181
Unconditional surrender, policy of, 12, 171, 180-181
Unilateralism, 11-12, 37, 95, 138, 172-177, 189, 191
Unions, trade and labour, 61, 132, 187
United Nations, 26, 204-205, 209
United Service Magazine, 81
United States Army, 35, 66, 202, 204-205, 231
United States Marine Corps, 202-203, 222
United States Navy, 120, 202
United States of America, 40, 52, 113, 165, 171, 173-175, 178, 184, 187, 189, 191, 195, 200-206
University College London, 130n
University of North Wales, 226
Unterseher, Lutz, 235-236
Ustinov, Kopp, 149n
Vansittart, Robert 150
Versailles Treaty, 144, 151
Vice Chief of the Imperial General Staff, 168
Vietnam, 28, 222
Voltaire (François-Marie Arouet), 36
Walcheren, 68
Wales, 27, 156, 226
Wallace, Edgar, 26
Wallach, Jehuda, 213-214
Wallenstein, Albrecht von, 120n
Wargames, 93, 166
War Department, 99, 128, 166, 167
War Office, 45, 53n, 85, 92n, 109-110, 116-118, 122, 124, 161, 166, 169, 184
War Studies, 13, 215-220, 222, 230, 232
Waterloo, 25
Wavell, Archibald, 9, 95, 110-111, 114, 197, 207, 226
Weigley, Russell, 78
Wellington School, 217
Wells, H.G., 94
Westminster Abbey, 139
Westminster City, 197
Westminster Gazette, 98
Westminster Press Newspapers, 27
Westmorland, 168, 179n, 197m
Westphal, Siegfried, 86
Wheldon, John, 115n, 206
Whig, 123-124
Wilkinson, Spenser, 73, 90-91
Williams, C.H., 219-220
Williams, Harold, 100
Williams, Michael, 215
Willington, 17
Wilmot, Chester, 205, 215
Wilson, Harold, 138, 140-140
Wilson, Henry, 66
Wilson, Horace, 149, 154
Wimbledon, 97

Wingate, Orde, 207-209, 212
Wolfe, James, 120n, 121, 205
Wolfson, Leonard, 227
Wolff, Leon, 69
Wolverton, 199n
Yadin, Yigael, 207-212
Yorkshire, 27, 81
Yorkshire Post, 98
Ypres (see also: Passchendaele), 52, 68
Zeppelins, 64

About the author

Bruce Oliver Newsome, Ph.D., is a historian, political scientist, and defence, risk, and security consultant. He held standing faculty positions at University of Texas, University of San Diego, University of California Berkeley, University of Pennsylvania, and the Defence Academy of the United Kingdom. Before teaching, he spent five years at the RAND Corporation, advising national governments on defence and security. He served in the British Army reserves, US Army National Guard, and Texas State Guard.

Other books by this author

Tank Raids and Blitzkrieg: The Development and Misrepresentation of Maneuver Warfare from the Great War to the Second World War, Perseublishing, 2025

Indirect Approach: From Sun Tzu to Liddell Hart, Persublishing, 2025.

Sir Basil Liddell Hart and Tanks, Perseublishing, 2024.

A Practical Introduction to Security and Risk Management, Perseublishing, 2023.

Panzer III vs. Valentine Tank, North Africa, 1941-1943, Osprey, 2023.

The Rise and Fall of Western Tanks, Volume I, 1855-1939, and Volume II, 1939-1955, Tank Archives Press, 2021.

A Practical Introduction to Homeland Security and Emergency Management from Home to Abroad, Rowman & Littlefield, 2020. With Jack Jarmon.

The Tiger Tank and Allied Intelligence, 4 volumes, Tank Archives Press, 2020.

Countering New(est) Terrorism: Assessing, Negotiating, and Ending Hostage Crises, Kidnappings, and Active Shootings, CRC Press, Taylor & Francis, 2018.

M1 Abrams Main Battle Tank: Owners' Workshop Manual. Haynes, 2017.

An Introduction to Research, Analysis, and Writing: Practical Skills for Social Science Students, SAGE, 2015.

Made, Not Born: Why Some Soldiers Are Better than Others. Praeger, 2007.

Getting Inside the Terrorist Mind, RAND, 2007.

Breaching the Fortress Wall: Understanding Terrorist Efforts to Overcome Defensive Technologies, RAND, 2007.

www.ingramcontent.com/pod-product-compliance
Lightning Source LLC
Chambersburg PA
CBHW061754070526